THE OXFORD HISTORY OF
MEDIEVAL EUROPE

T0130597

THE EDITOR

GEORGE HOLMES is a Fellow of St Catherine's College, Oxford. His previous books include *Dante* (Past Masters, OUP, 1980), and *Florence, Rome and the Origins of the Renaissance* (OUP, 1986).

THE CONTRIBUTORS

THOMAS BROWN, University of Edinburgh: *The Transformation of the Roman Mediterranean, 400–900*

EDWARD JAMES, University of York: *The Northern World in the Dark Ages, 400–900*

† DAVID WHITTON, Wolfson College, Oxford: *The Society of Northern Europe in the High Middle Ages, 900–1200*

ROSEMARY MORRIS, University of Manchester: *Northern Europe Invades the Mediterranean, 900–1200*

PETER DENLEY, Queen Mary and Westfield College, University of London: *The Mediterranean in the Age of the Renaissance, 1200–1500*

MALCOLM VALE, St John's College, Oxford: *The Civilization of Courts and Cities in the North, 1200–1500*

THE OXFORD
HISTORY OF
MEDIEVAL
EUROPE

EDITED BY
GEORGE HOLMES

OXFORD
UNIVERSITY PRESS

OXFORD
UNIVERSITY PRESS

Great Clarendon Street, Oxford OX2 6DP

Oxford University Press is a department of the University of Oxford.
It furthers the University's objective of excellence in research, scholarship,
and education by publishing worldwide in

Oxford New York

Auckland Bangkok Buenos Aires Cape Town Chennai
Dar es Salaam Delhi Hong Kong Istanbul Karachi Kolkata
Kuala Lumpur Madrid Melbourne Mexico City Mumbai Nairobi
São Paulo Shanghai Taipei Tokyo Toronto

Oxford is a registered trade mark of Oxford University Press
in the UK and in certain other countries

The test for this edition first published 1988 in
The Oxford Illustrated History of Medieval Europe

This edition first issued as an Oxford University Press paperback 1992
Reissued 2001

British Library Cataloguing in Publication Data

Data available

Library of Congress Cataloging in Publication Data
The Oxford history of medieval Europe / edited by George Holmes.
p. cm.
Abridged ed. of : The Oxford illustrated history of medieval Europe.
Includes bibliographical references.
1. Europe—Etymology—476–1492. I. Holmes, George, 1927–
II. Title : Oxford illustrated history of medieval Europe.
940.1—dc20 D102.093 1992 91–43488

ISBN-13: 978-0-19-280133-3

Printed in Great Britain by
Clays Ltd, Elcograf S.p.A.

EDITOR'S FOREWORD

WESTERN civilization was created in medieval Europe. The forms of thought and action which we take for granted in modern Europe and America, which we have exported to other substantial portions of the globe, and from which indeed we cannot escape, were implanted in the mentalities of our ancestors in the struggles of the medieval centuries. Since 1500 our civilization has not had to endure any upheaval remotely comparable with the shattering and rebirth which accompanied the migrations and new institutions of the Dark Ages between 400 and 900. And, therefore, it has not seen any flowering of new ways of life and attitudes as fundamentally novel as those which grew up around the cathedrals and universities, the royal courts and the commercial cities in the centuries between 900 and 1500.

Most Europeans live in towns and villages which existed in the lifetime of St Thomas Aquinas, many of them in the shadow of churches already built in the thirteenth century. That simple physical identity is the mark of deeper continuities. The modern nation state grew out of the monarchies created by kings such as Philip Augustus of France and John of England. Democratic forms of government are based on the systems of representation and consent evolved in thirteenth-century parliaments. The idea of popular sovereignty emerges first in the writings of a fourteenth-century scholastic, Marsilius of Padua, who knew the communes of contemporary Italy. Our methods of commerce and banking are derived from the practices of the Florentine Peruzzi and Medici. Students work for degrees already awarded in the medieval universities of Paris and Oxford in courses which have gradually evolved out of those followed in the medieval faculties of arts. Our books of history and our novels are lineal descendants of the works of Leonardo Bruni and Giovanni Boccaccio. Our troubled sense of the distinction between the physical world of nature and the spiritual world of religion and morals derives from the dualism of Aquinas's thirteenth century when popes and universities confronted kings and parliaments and the scholastics struggled to reconcile Aristotle and the Bible.

The rebirth of western civilization and continuity since that time are the reasons why the medieval world is supremely important if we want to understand our own origins. But it is the historian's business to describe the differences in the past, which are less easy to grasp than the similarities, and without which the shape and movement of an earlier society are unintelligible. David Whitton begins his chapter in this book with a description of the world of a great twelfth-century magnate, Henry the Lion, in which the importance of kinship relations and the claim to religious sanction mark a political system different from any that we can know today. Earlier in the book Edward James tells us about Rædwald and Dagobert in seventh-century East Anglia and Gaul, whose kingship was still more remote from modern governments. In other chapters we meet Cathars and Hussites whose medieval nonconformity has something in common with the piety we can meet today but in other respects is mysterious to us. To grasp the lineaments of a distant age we have to balance the similarities which arise from common humanity and a constant inheritance of ideas against the acute distinctions caused by differences of social structure and intellectual traditions. Medieval Europe is not as difficult for us to understand as ancient China or India but it presents a very substantial challenge to interpretation. The devotion of the medieval knight to a life of chivalric warfare and courtly intercourse or of a medieval hermit to a life of constant prayer and total seclusion presents us with ideals of conduct which we cannot easily understand.

The picture which we can now construct of the medieval world is based very largely on the researches and rethinking of the last hundred years. It is very different both from Gibbon's grand dismissal of superstition and from Scott's romantic attachment to Gothic glories. Our present vision of that world is based partly on the printing of vast quantities of medieval documents ranging in type from the narrative chronicles, in whose publication the pioneers were the editors of the German *Monumenta*, to the poems published in series such as those of the Early English Text Society and the ordinary records of governments and courts made available to us by institutions such as the Public Record Office. There is now far more medieval writing easily available to us in print than any scholar could absorb in several lifetimes.

But, equally and perhaps more importantly, the medieval world has been opened up to us by changes of taste and in the direction of our researches. Our understanding of the medieval village and its lord, of medieval courts and tenures, has been developed by a semi-anthropological approach springing from the work of scholars such as F. W. Maitland, which makes a heroic attempt to grasp the different assumptions of a primitive society. Our knowledge of the theology and philosophy of medieval universities has been transformed by the prodigious labours of religious enthusiasts in the tradition of Heinrich Denifle and Franz Ehrle. The picture which we can present of the world of the migrations is now based not only on a few scanty annals but also on innumerable archaeological excavations which enable us to map a mass of artefacts and of dwelling-sites. The economic historians have given us, only in quite recent years, a new demographic history of the Middle Ages which brings to light the enormous expansion of population which filled the countryside and stimulated industry and commerce between 1000 and 1300, and the prolonged decline which followed the famine of 1315 and the Black Death of 1348. There have been massive efforts of research which have shed floods of light on many previously obscure aspects of the medieval world, for example the Byzantine Empire, the crusades, the early Franciscans, Italian commerce, the Hussites. It is possible now to present the history of medieval Europe with an understanding and a precision which would have been impossible in the nineteenth century.

The plan which has been followed in this book is to write the history of Europe in chapters which preserve the division between the Mediterranean basin and northern Europe beyond the Alps and the Pyrenees. This is not, of course, an ideal distinction. In 400 Romanization extended more fully into Gaul than into other parts of the north. Charlemagne's empire in 800 incorporated parts of Italy as well as Gaul. The crusades to the Holy Land drew their main impulse from France and Normandy. Western Christendom, which emerged in the twelfth century and after, covered north and south Europe, unified by acceptance of the authority of the papacy, by the inter-connection of universities in France and Italy, by French con-quests in Naples and Outremer, by the networks of Italian international commerce, by the use of Latin as the language of scholarship and diplomacy. Medieval history, from one point of view, is the story of the movement of the centre of gravity of civilization from one side of the Alps to the other. If we looked for possible centres in 400 we might choose Rome or Constantinople, later perhaps Baghdad or Cordoba. By 1300 north-west Europe, northern France, the Low Countries, and the Rhineland had the most advanced civilization the world had ever seen. It was physically wealthy because of its rich agriculture and cloth industries, intellectually and aesthetically complex because of its universities and cathedrals, its lay literature and its many centres of seigneurial and urban power.

But the division between north and south has great ad-vantages. The Mediterranean was always to some extent a separate world. Most strikingly so in the earlier Middle Ages when the empires of Byzantium and the Arabs scarcely ex-tended beyond the Alps and the Pyrenees. The intellectual and aesthetic efflorescence of the Italian cities in the Renaissance, though it greatly influenced the north, was based on essentially Italian roots in the independent cities, which had no real parallel in the north, in Mediterranean trade, and the Italian devotion to the memory of Rome. The distinction between the Mediterranean and the north, though it divides the western Europe which emerged, provides a convenient arrangement of our subject-matter.

Thomas Brown shows in the first chapter how the decline of Rome in the Mediterranean was promoted dramatically by the invasions of Barbarians and Muslims, in spite of the resurgence under Justinian, and more gradually by social and economic change and the development of Christianity. Edward James tells a very different story of many kingdoms emerging to the north of the Alps out of the obscure confusion of the migrations, of the acceptance of Christianity and Charlemagne's attempt to revive a western empire which was again to be disrupted by the Viking invasions. That newly expansive northern world in the period after 900 is the subject of David Whitton's chapter, which describes the new forms of life emerging among the knightly classes and the new religious orders in a world dominated by the kings of Germany and its dukes, the kings of France, and the Norman and Angevin rulers of England. In this chapter we see Europe as we know it beginning to appear. Rosemary Morris has described the decline of the Byzantine and Arab empires in the central medieval period and the southwards expansion of the northerners in the crusades, the Norman conquests in Italy, and the *Reconquista* in Spain. Peter Denley outlines the complex movements of states and peoples in the Mediterranean basin in the last medieval centuries with the splendid flowering of thought and culture which we now call the Renaissance arising in the central position of the north Italian cities. Finally, Malcolm Vale carries us into northern Europe in the age of the Hundred Years War between England and France, the Valois dukes of Burgundy and the Flemish cities. He argues convincingly that, in spite of the temporary decline of population, this was a period in which secular civilization, which we might call a northern Renaissance, was growing stronger. If we want to pick out the most distinct features of European civilization which have now appeared we should look to the courts of Paris and Brussels and to the cities of Flanders and Tuscany.

   The movement of the centres of civilization from south to north and from east to west during the medieval centuries involved a change from the empires of Rome, Byzantium, and the Arabs, empires of vast geographical extent and great military power but which were relatively loosely controlled. We move in western Europe to a system of smaller, more tightly organized, and more differentiated political units. Modern Europeans contemplating the ancient world have naturally tended to look back to the Greek cities of the fifth century BC rather than to larger states, because they seem to represent the ancient societies which most closely resembled the new ones created in medieval Italy and the Low Countries. The 'world empires' of Rome, Byzantium, and Baghdad receded, to be followed by a plethora of authorities in western Europe, so complex that it cannot easily be described. Though the claims and achievements of the emperors and popes, who sought to dominate western Christendom in the high Middle Ages and to re-create a 'world empire' were great, Europe was never effectively subjected to them or indeed to total sovereignty by any power over even a limited area.

The history of the Middle Ages thus leaves us, above all, with a sense of the extraordinary vigour and creativity which derives from the fragmentation of power and wealth into innumerable centres, competing and expanding into different and unexpected directions. The places where political fragmentation was most complete, such as Tuscany, the Low Countries, and the Rhineland, were perhaps the most creative. That division of authority was caused partly by small political units, partly by the overlapping of royal power, independent cities, strong seigneurs, and finally ecclesiastical authority, which competed everywhere with lay authority. Hence the multifarious creativity of medieval Europeans.

The wealth and cultural diversity of medieval Europe fore-shadow the modern world. It can, of course, be dangerous to look for the ideas of the present in the past. The unique individuality of a life or a movement must never be forgotten: the historian's aim is to emphasize them. We hope that the profusion of remote ways of life presented in this book, and often difficult to understand, will prevent the reader from falling into that trap and leave him with an awareness of the remoteness and complexity of the medieval past. At the same time we study the past because it is interesting in the present. Abelard and St Francis would not attract us if we could not to some extent share their hopes and fears. We hope that the modern inhabitants of London or California will recognize their ancestors in this book and find some help in understanding the origins of the world in which they live now.

GEORGE HOLMES

CONTENTS

LIST OF PLATES

LIST OF MAPS

I

The Transformation of the Roman Mediterranean

400–900

THOMAS BROWN

The Twilight of the Ancient Mediterranean

IN the late fourth century there was little sign of imminent upheaval in the Mediterranean heartlands of the Roman Empire. The disorders of the third century had been overcome by soldier-emperors whose reforms had safeguarded the frontiers and created political stability. Following the conversion of Constantine Christianity had established a firm hold and lavish programmes of artistic and architectural patronage testified to the wealth and self-confidence of a revivified empire.

After the death of the Emperor Theodosius I in 395, however, divisions between the Latin and Greek halves of the empire became more evident. The east far outshone the west in intellectual achievement, prosperity, and the number and size of its cities; whereas Gaul and Britain could muster 114 *civitates*, more than 900 cities constituted the thriving centres of political and economic life in the east. Not only the resources but the ideological backing for imperial authority were stronger in the east, where the Hellenistic heritage reinforced acceptance of the imperial cult and the trappings of autocratic power. Papyri from Egypt and excavations of Syrian villages suggest a level of agricultural prosperity in sharp contrast with the slave-run latifundia of Italy or the peasant hovels of Gaul.

Eastern society was relatively meritocratic, with officials drawn from loyal, capable members of local urban élites, whereas in the west even the 'new men' appointed by fourth-century emperors rapidly adopted the powers, traditions, and arrogance of the senatorial aristocracy. In the east the propaganda of scholar-bishops and the proselytizing of holy men reinforced allegiance to the ideal of a God-given Christian empire, while in the west Christianity was less firmly established and undermined attachment to the empire by offering an alternative to imperial service. In Constantinople the east possessed a cosmopolitan and strategically sited capital which came to surpass Rome and the other imperial residences of the west in size and splendour.

The most immediate problem in 395 was renewed barbarian inroads. In 376 a horde of Germans, mostly Visigoths, had crossed the Danube frontier in search of refuge from the Huns, a fearsome tribe of steppe nomads. Tensions between the incomers and their Roman hosts led to a battle at Adrianople in 378, in which a Roman army was annihilated and the Emperor Valens killed. The immediate threat was contained, but the Goths were permitted to settle on Roman territory. Under their king, Alaric, they launched devastating raids into Greece, before moving north into modern Yugoslavia. In 401 Alaric invaded Italy and for ten years the peninsula remained at the mercy of Gothic plundering and extortion. The Romans lacked reliable forces to defeat the invaders, and the funds necessary to buy Alaric off. In exasperation at not receiving the money and land which he demanded, Alaric besieged and sacked Rome in 410. The destruction caused was limited but the psychological blow to Roman morale of the first sack of Rome since the Gaulish attack of 390 BC was immense. St Jerome wept on hearing the news in his cell in Bethlehem and a bitter polemic exploded between Christians and pagans. Christian views of society and history were worked out in such influential works as Augustine's *City of God* in order to counter pagan attacks.

Italy was spared long-term effects from the rampaging of the Visigoths, since they withdrew to Gaul after Alaric's death in 410. More lasting and disruptive were the effects of imperial weakness in Gaul, where a force of Vandals, Sueves, and Alans broke through the Rhine frontier in the winter of 406/7 and Constantius, a usurper from Britain, set up a short-lived empire based on Arles. By 418 the imperial government got the upper hand over the twin dangers of sedition and invasion by the increasingly familiar expedient of setting a thief to catch thieves. The promise of land and subsidies together with the threat of a food blockade enforced by Roman naval power induced the Visigoths into repelling the Alans and Vandals and settling in Aquitaine as Roman *federati* (allies).

The first half of the fifth century saw the settlement of Germanic peoples in most areas of the western Mediterranean, and in the main this process took place smoothly and peacefully. In Gaul the Visigoths and the Burgundians, who were settled first on the Rhine and later in Savoy, served as a bulwark against peasant rebels and other barbarians, took only a proportion of the land for themselves, and allowed the Romans to retain their institutions as nominal subjects of the emperor. Spain lapsed into a period of confusion and obscurity following the invasion of the Vandals and their Sueve and Alan allies. In 429 the Vandals moved on to Africa and Visigothic overlordship was eventually established over most of the country.

Africa is the province of the western Mediterranean whose fate approximates most closely to the popular view of catastrophic invasion. The Vandals, led by their remarkable king, Gaiseric, were quick to throw off the façade of allied status and seized Carthage and the other cities of what was once one of the richest of Rome's provinces. The Roman population was relentlessly taxed, the Catholic hierarchy was persecuted, and naval raids were launched against Roman targets throughout the Mediterranean.

Italy and the imperial court at Ravenna felt little direct effect from what appeared to be a phoney war against the barbarians. This immunity was the achievement of two capable commanders-in-chief, Constantius and Aëtius, 'the last of the Romans', who manipulated the invaders in order to shore up the tottering empire. Aëtius' balancing act failed when his

Hun allies turned against him and invaded northern Italy. The empire became the plaything of autocratic factions and in 476 the boy-emperor, Romulus, ironically nicknamed Augustulus ('the little emperor') was deposed by Odoacer, the commander of the German mercenaries in Italy, who sought land for his troops and direct rule of Italy for himself.

A graphic account survives of the running down of Roman public life in Noricum (western Austria) in the face of German pressure. Once Roman supplies and payments were cut off, the demoralization of a population accustomed to Roman protection could only be staunched by the leadership of a charismatic holy man, and after his death the province had to be evacuated. In Italy, however, a complex civilian society remained intact, and the senatorial aristocracy maintained its privileged position, including its vast landholdings, its monopoly of lucrative governorships, and the cultivated literary life of its salons.

In Gaul the withering away of the empire left the senators as the main symbol of Roman legitimacy while relieving them of the burdens of imperial rule. Gradually, however, they found their political and social position marginalized as their offices and titles became redundant and their Germanic guests began to flex their muscles. The Visigoths set up a kingdom based on Toulouse, while the Burgundians in south-eastern Gaul established a sub-Roman state with twin capitals at Lyons and Geneva. The difficulties faced by senators in adjusting to new realities are displayed in the letters and poems of the scholar-aristocrat Sidonius Apollinaris. His attitude to the Germans ranged from admiration of a cultivated Visigothic king who played backgammon to exasperation at the 'gluttonous' barbarians billeted on his estate, 'who spread rancid butter on their hair'. His evolution from literary escapism in the seclusion of his estates to conscientious activity as bishop of Clermont reflects a widespread process of clericalization; episcopal election became the means for a disorientated aristocracy to maintain its traditional leadership of the community and for preservation of Roman customs and culture.

With time the passive antagonism of the Roman population

undermined the power of the Visigothic kings, despite their frantic attempts to court support by issuing Roman law codes, and facilitated their defeat at the hands of the newly converted king of the Franks, Clovis, at Vouillé near Tours in 507. Thenceforth the Visigothic kingdom was confined to Spain apart from a small salient north of the Pyrenees in Septimania. The smoothness of the Visigoths' withdrawal into Spain was made possible by the intervention of the Ostrogothic king, Theoderic, who became the most powerful barbarian monarch in the western Mediterranean after seizing Italy from Odoacer in 493. He is also the most interesting, since he combined capable war-leadership and an appreciation of the need to retain the identity of his people with a calculated admiration for the benefits of Roman civilization derived from his own experience of Constantinople as a hostage.

This 'dual' approach provided for lavish patronage of public works, the promotion of economic activity and the safeguarding of Roman customs, especially those of the Senate, whose support he cultivated to reinforce the legitimacy of his rule. His own people were kept segregated in settlements in north and central Italy under their own commanders, while the central and local administration was entrusted to Roman collaborators such as Cassiodorus, a senator from a parvenu Calabrian family. However, Theoderic's position as the leader of a small heterodox people was always vulnerable, and towards the end of his reign uncharacteristically severe measures taken against the Roman population can be attributed to fears concerning the succession and the diplomatic noose which the Byzantines were tightening around his kingdom. Reconciliation between the Roman Church and the aggressively orthodox emperors of the east, combined with the nostalgic yearning of conservative senators for Roman rule, gave rise to suspicions of treasonable negotiations with Constantinople, which in turn led to the notorious episode of the arrest and execution of the philosopher Boethius.

For much of the fifth century the eastern empire had seemed destined to fall into a decline similar to that of the west. Its last representatives of the Theodosian house were equally incapable, its Balkan provinces were ravaged by Hun and Ostrogoth invasions and Constantinople itself was at times threatened. The eastern provinces of Syria and Egypt were racked by religious dissension over the nature of Christ, a matter of spiritual life and death to Christians preoccupied with salvation and with achieving a doctrinal orthodoxy that was pleasing to God. Gradually, however, the east's underlying advantages enabled it to emerge from its difficulties as a resilient and cohesive society. The impression that emerges is one of consensus around the ideal of a God-appointed Christian empire, prosperity reflected in lavish building throughout Asia Minor and the dynamic capital of Constantinople, and political stability enshrined in the rise of a new breed of trained, dedicated bureaucrats. One of the latter, an official named Anastasius, became emperor, and further strengthened the empire by cautious and tolerant policies of reducing taxes and trimming expenses. The full benefits of this political and financial stability were reaped by his successors, Justin I and his nephew Justinian.

Justinian, the most remarkable of Byzantium's emperors, was denounced by a vituperative contemporary for 'ruining the Roman Empire' and 'bringing everything into confusion'. In fact his efforts to turn the clock back to the great days of the universal Roman Empire had astonishing initial success. A small expedition was launched against the Vandal kingdom of North Africa, the longest standing thorn in Constantinople's flesh, under the brilliant general Belisarius, and the people who had terrorized the Mediterranean in the fifth century were rapidly conquered. In the view of the historian Procopius the Vandals had become 'of all nations the most lecherous', and their military prowess had been sapped by their wealth. The emperor's whirlwind success was celebrated in the extravagant prologues attached to the massive Code of Roman Law which he issued in 534. Justinian's legislative activity, like his stalwart defence of religious orthodoxy, was based on an elevated view of the universal empire, which he saw as the terrestrial image of God's heavenly kingdom. His autocratic leanings were reinforced by a savage uprising against his reliance on unpopular ministers in 532 and encouraged by his redoubtable empress, the former actress Theodora.

Throughout the 530s Justinian undertook a lavish programme of building, including the Church of Hagia Sofia in Constantinople with its dome of unprecedented size. His military success continued with an invasion of Sicily and Italy, and by 540 the Ostrogoths had lost their main political centres of Rome and Ravenna. Although his propaganda stressed the renewal of Rome's greatness, his actions resulted in the replacement of the cosy bureaucratic system of the east by a 'Stalinist' regime based on his own megalomaniac energy, ruthless political and fiscal oppression of his subjects, reliance on unpopular toadies, and rigorous enforcement of doctrinal orthodoxy.

In the 540s Justinian's luck ran out. Persia launched a devastating invasion of the east, the Slavs infiltrated the Balkans, and under an able new king, Totila, the Ostrogoths reduced the imperial foothold in Italy to a few coastal outposts. In 542 bubonic plague decimated the empire's population, with catastrophic effects on urban and economic life, and in 548 his helpmate Theodora died. The remaining years of Justinian's reign have a relentless, austere quality. In spite of all the vicissitudes the emperor kept his nerve, repelling invasions, sending a force to Italy under Narses which dealt the Ostrogoths the *coup de grâce* in 553, and tirelessly seeking to reconcile his heretical subjects in the east to orthodoxy.

By his death in 565 Justinian appeared to have succeeded in restoring the glories of Rome. The Arian kingdoms of Africa and Italy had been returned to imperial rule, and even the Burgundian kingdom was taken over by Justinian's Frankish allies in the 530s. Only Visigothic Spain held out, and it was threatened by internal dissensions and a Byzantine salient around Cartagena. In other ways Justinian's reign marked a new beginning for the Roman Empire. His ideals of autocracy and Romano-Christian universalism became a programme to which all later Byzantine emperors subscribed. The upheavals of the fifth century had not destroyed the relatively uniform Roman life of the Mediterranean.

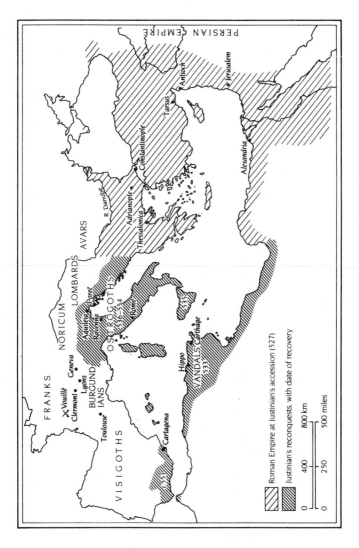

THE MEDITERRANEAN IN THE REIGN OF JUSTINIAN

An Age of Invasions

Justinian's extravagance has been blamed for bankrupting his empire and rendering subsequent set-backs inevitable. In fact the empire remained rich and powerful and, with the exception of Italy, decline seems to have been the result of plague and long-term economic factors rather than war and over-taxation. The Byzantines could still raise revenue efficiently, but the essentially civilian character of the empire made it difficult to raise troops of the quality and quantity required to contain new more numerous and tenacious invaders.

The first of these were the Slavs. The pressure became stronger and more violent with the advent of a nomadic people, the Avars, who organized the Slavs into a loose but effective empire based on tribute and pillage, and launched devastating attacks on the Byzantine Empire from 570 onwards. After the Emperor Maurice was killed in a mutiny on the Danube frontier his ineffectual successor Phocas was unable to prevent the Avars and their Slav allies from occupying most of the Balkans and Greece apart from a few coastal enclaves. An Avar force besieged Constantinople in 626, and Thessalonica, the greatest city in the empire's European provinces, attributed its salvation from repeated attacks only to the intervention of its patron, St Demetrius.

Avar pressure on Pannonia also forced the Lombards, who had hitherto been in the background, to launch the most lasting and destructive of the Germanic invasions in the Mediterranean area. In the sixth century the Lombards had refined their political and military organization through contact with the Romans as mercenaries and some had been converted to Arianism. Under the able leadership of King Alboin the Lombards entered Italy in 568 and within a year had occupied most of the peninsula north of the Po. The Lombard advance benefited from local resentment of imperial taxes and religious policies and the existence of a Germanic fifth column among underpaid mercenaries and the remnants of the defeated Goths. After reorganizing the administration under a military supremo or exarch the Byzantines were able to mount a counter-offensive with Frankish support from the 580s, until the Lombards recovered lost ground under their capable King Agilulf and a truce was agreed in 605 which marked out a lasting division between the new kingdom and the empire. In the north the Lombards controlled most of Piedmont, Lombardy, Emilia, Tuscany, and mainland Veneto, while the south was dominated by the semi-independent duchies of Spoleto and Benevento. All that remained to the empire were the areas of Rome and Ravenna with a fragile corridor in between and coastal enclaves around Venice, Genoa, and the southern ports. This gradual stabilization was not matched by internal peace or prosperity. The writings of Pope Gregory the Great paint a depressing picture of the destruction caused by the 'unspeakable' Lombards: 'the cities have been depopulated . . . churches burned down . . . the land lies empty and solitary.'

The reality was more varied than the outpourings of a Roman churchman would suggest. A distinction has to be drawn between the frontier areas, which became a desolate no man's land, the imperial territories, in which social and administrative adjustment caused more upheaval than direct Lombard attacks, and the Lombard heartland, where the rapid take-over by a new élite of warriors caused little disruption to the lives of ordinary Roman peasants and city-dwellers.

Byzantium's failure to re-establish its authority over Italy and the Balkans can be explained by the threat posed to its most populous and valuable provinces in the east from its revitalized rival Persia. The Emperor Maurice obtained a hard-won peace in 591, but after the usurpation of Phocas in 602 the Persians launched an offensive which resulted in the laying waste of Anatolia and the conquest of Syria, Palestine, and Egypt. The gravity of the crisis was brought home to the Byzantines when the treasured relic of the True Cross was carried off to Ctesiphon in 614 and the Persians reached the Bosphorus in 626. The Persians might have realized the ambitions of Darius and Xerxes but for the resilience of the Byzantines and their emperor, Heraclius, who marshalled the resources of his battered empire to launch a counter-attack from the Caucasus area which brought the Persian Empire to its knees.

The elation produced by Heraclius' stunning success was to prove short-lived. In 630, two years after the True Cross had been restored in triumph to Jerusalem, a former merchant entered the Arabian city of Mecca at the head of an army of Bedouin followers. By the death of the prophet Muhammad in 632 the Arabian peninsula was united behind the new faith which he had preached, and within ten years Persia and the Byzantine provinces of the east had succumbed to Islam.

The phenomenal success of this new movement had its roots in the volatile political, social, and religious climate of Arabia. Tensions had grown between the Bedouin tribesmen and the merchants of the wealthy towns, and the old polytheistic beliefs had been undermined by the monotheistic certainties of Judaism and Christianity. The lid which had been kept on the Arabs' inveterate raiding and political turmoil by Byzantine and Persian diplomacy was removed by the struggle between the superpowers. Muhammad's genius lay in gaining control of this maelstrom by his statesmanship and his powerful yet eclectic vision of an ideal of total submission (Islam) to Allah, and channelling the traditional warlike energies of his people and their new-found fanaticism into an irresistible movement of conquest.

Islam owed its remarkable success both to its own strengths and to its opponents' weaknesses. The prowess and dedication of its warriors, the ability of the early caliphs, the simple appeal of its doctrines, and its proselytizing vigour with its promise of specific rewards all played their part. In contrast with earlier invaders, the Arabs were able to evolve an original and durable synthesis. They took over the more effective and appealing tenets of other faiths and retained viable elements of Graeco-Roman administration and urban culture while maintaining the distinctiveness and vitality of their own culture. Also important was the political and religious alienation of many of Byzantium's subjects. Coptic- and Aramaic-speaking Monophysites in Egypt and Syria saw their Arab fellow Semites as deliverers from Greek tax-gatherers and orthodox persecutors, and both Christians and Jews were treated with toleration in return for the payment of a head-tax. Significantly, however, repeated attacks on Anatolia, the orthodox heartland of the Byzantine Empire, failed to produce permanent conquests.

From 661 until 750 the rapidly expanding Islamic world was governed by the Ummayad caliphs with their capital at Damascus. While emphasizing their desert origins as a segregated warrior élite, the Ummayads showed a practical sense of eclecticism in their adoption of the art and culture of their subjects and their exploitation of local wealth to finance their pleasures and raiding. A vast free-trade zone was established and local populations preserved their culture and their prosperity under a regime which resembled a benign protectorate rather than an empire.

Meanwhile, Byzantium found itself locked in a struggle for survival. The interior of Asia Minor became a no man's land, the scene of a bitter war of attrition. Gradually the empire succeeded in stabilizing its position by a series of drastic measures. The field armies which had retreated in the face of the initial blitzkrieg were stationed in military zones known as themes, and a complete break was made with the traditional division of power between civil and military authority. Local power was devolved into the hands of theme commanders and the state turned a blind eye to the amassing of land by local troops. A scorched-earth policy was adopted, and forces were withdrawn or shut up in fortresses while the enemy's lines of communication grew over-extended, pitched battles were avoided, and guerrilla attacks were launched to harry the Arabs' weak points. General winter also helped: a chronicler reported that in 791 raiders 'met with such cold that their hands and feet dropped off'.

The impact on the Anatolian plateau was catastrophic. Urban life and arable farming became impossible as Arab forays caused repeated devastation and Byzantine 'home guards' shepherded peasants and their flocks into fortresses. Cities in the interior became mere *kastra*, fortified army bases, and even the great cities of the western coast fell into a precipitate decline. Although the tide of Arab raids was gradually stemmed, thanks especially to the military expertise of the Isaurian emperors, the price was the transformation of the Byzantine world into an impoverished, militarized society comparable with that of the early medieval west.

Meanwhile, the Islamic conquests continued for a time. Arab forces penetrated central Asia to the frontiers of India and China, and to the west swept through North Africa. In 695 they seized Carthage, the capital of a Byzantine province which had fallen on hard times as a result of Moorish raids, religious dissensions, and the encroachment of the desert. In 711 they turned their attention to Spain, and after a single battle the Visigothic kingdom lay at their feet.

Ironically the other Germanic kingdoms were strengthened by the Islamic onslaught. Byzantium was forced to turn in on itself, and any hopes it had of reasserting its authority in the west were dashed. The most obvious beneficiary was the Lombard kingdom, and by 643 an aggressively nationalist king, Rothari, rallied his people by issuing a code of Lombard law and overcoming Byzantine outposts in Liguria and the Veneto. By around 680 the empire was forced to make a treaty recognizing the Lombard kingdom, and the subsequent conversion of the Lombards to Catholicism helped to reconcile their Roman subjects to their rule.

The relief afforded by Byzantium's tribulations to Visigothic Spain proved shorter-lived. The Visigoths remained staunchly anti-Byzantine in spite of their imitation of imperial ceremonial and coinage and their conversion to Catholicism in 586. The Church was permitted to hold regular councils which legislated on a wide range of secular and religious matters and which strove to uphold the authority of the king as God-given ruler. One architect of this policy of co-operation was the great scholar-bishop, Isidore of Seville, whose historical works display a patriotic pride in Spain and an antagonism to the deceitful and unmanly *Romani*. The question remains why such a sophisticated monarchy, the only Germanic kingdom able to maintain a land-tax, crumbled so quickly in the face of Arab invasion. Factors such as succession problems and the alienation of the Jewish minority played their part but at the root of the fall of this 'despotism tempered by assassination' lay a weak-

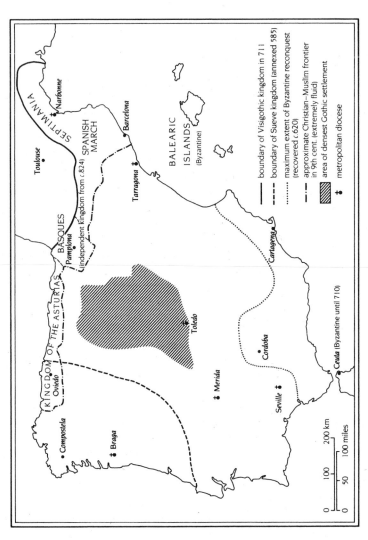

VISIGOTHIC AND ARABIC SPAIN

ness shared by most Germanic successor-states; the military élite of Goths tried to maintain the Roman structures and life-style which so impressed them, while excluding the Romans from real power and wealth.

Despite the sudden collapse of the Visigothic kingdom and the rapid conversion of many Christian nobles to Islam, the legacy which it left to the medieval west was considerable. The Christians of Muslim Spain evolved a lively 'Mozarabic' culture, small but energetic Christian states were set up in the mountainous north to resist the infidel, and a diaspora of Spanish scholars and Spanish texts supplied much of the raw material for the adolescent culture of the west. At first, how-ever, the remorseless advance of Islam continued across the Pyrenees as Arab raiders dealt a death-blow to the Gallo-Roman magnates of Aquitaine and Provence who had escaped from direct Merovingian control in the seventh century and reverted to an impoverished form of the autonomy which the region had enjoyed in the fifth century. The Islamic inroads were checked by the famous victory of Charles Martel, the Frankish mayor of the palace, at Poitiers in 732, and the subsequent Frankish reoccupation of southern France formed a potent barrier to further Arab expansion by land.

More important in relieving the pressure on a beleaguered Christian world was a change in the ruling dynasty of Islam. In 750 the Ummayad caliphs were overthrown by the Abbasids who removed their capital to Baghdad and initiated a shift of emphasis towards the east. Much of the original vigour of the Bedouin was lost, and the cultural and political traditions of the conquered areas reasserted themselves, especially in Persia. As these separatist tendencies came into conflict with the in-creased elaboration and bureaucracy of the court at Baghdad, the immense empire which stretched from the Indus to the Atlantic fragmented into smaller units. Spain was taken over by Ummayad exiles, North Africa came under the vigorous rule of the Aghlabids, and Egypt was taken over by the Tulunids.

More pressing threats to the Byzantines came from the naval power of the emergent Arab states in the west and renewed

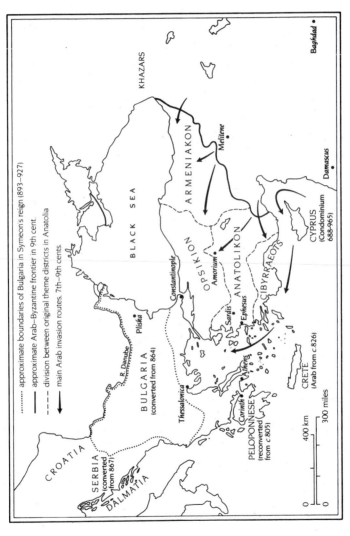

BYZANTIUM AND HER EASTERN AND BALKAN NEIGHBOURS IN THE NINTH CENTURY

.... approximate boundaries of Bulgaria in Symeon's reign (893–927)

⎯⎯ approximate Arab–Byzantine frontier in 9th cent.

- - - - division between original theme districts in Anatolia

↓ main Arab invasion routes, 7th–9th cents.

KHAZARS

BLACK SEA

ARMENIAKON

Melitene

OPSIKION

Constantinople

Amorium

ANATOLIKON

Sardis

Ephesus

CIBYRRAEOTS

CYPRUS
(Condominium
688–965)

Damascus

Baghdad

Pliska

BULGARIA
(converted from 864)

R. Danube

Thessalonica

CROATIA

SERBIA
(converted
from 867)

DALMATIA

Corinth

Athens

PELOPONNESE
(reconverted
from c.805)

CRETE
(Arab from c.826)

0   400 km

0   300 miles

attacks from the north. In 828 Crete fell to Arab pirates from Spain, and throughout the ninth century the western seaboards of the empire were subjected to raids by the Aghlabids. The prosperous island of Sicily was invaded in 827, and after the fall of the capital, Syracuse, in 878, only a few outposts in the eastern part of the island remained in Greek hands. Danger closer to home was posed by the Bulgars, who exploited the collapse of Avar power to build up a strong state in which a Bulgar aristocracy ruled a Slav peasantry. Macabre proof of the Bulgar threat came in 811 when the Khan Krum defeated the Emperor Nicephorus I and had his skull made into a drinking goblet. Ironically, the Bulgar menace proved most serious later in the century after Byzantine missionaries began a programme of conversion to orthodox Christianity; equipped with a more elaborate administration and a hybrid culture stimulated by the introduction of a Slavonic alphabet, the Bulgar state under Tsar Symeon challenged the universality of Byzantium by presenting itself as a legitimate rival empire. Byzantium also faced raids from another northern neighbour, the Rus, Scandinavian adventurers who had established an ascendancy over the Slav population of Russia and who resembled their Viking cousins in the west by combining lucrative trading with destructive raiding.

Gradually, however, Byzantium emerged from its heroic period with its prestige, power, and wealth greatly increased. Byzantine naval power enabled it to reassert its authority over Dalmatia and Venice, and in 876 the first emperor of the Macedonian dynasty, Basil I, exploited the weakness of the Lombard princes of southern Italy in the face of Arab raids to occupy Bari and establish themes in Calabria and Langobardia (modern Apulia). Earlier in the century Byzantine generals had conquered the Slav territories of the Peloponnese and a process of Christianization and Hellenization was undertaken by Greek monks. At home the empire had recovered from the self-inflicted wounds of the iconoclast controversy and enjoyed a period of relative stability under the Macedonians. Equally important was the empire's evolution of a realistic and imaginative policy towards its northern neighbours. The

LOMBARD AND BYZANTINE ITALY

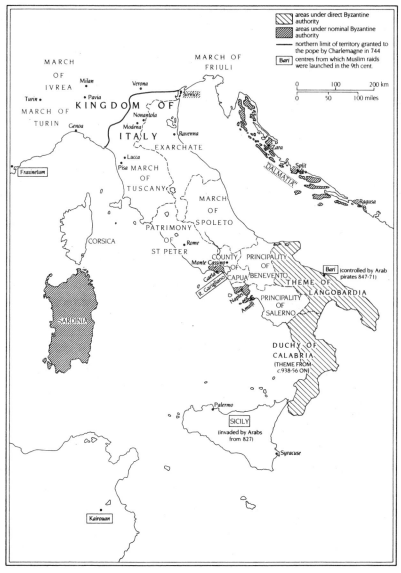

areas under direct Byzantine authority

areas under nominal Byzantine authority

northern limit of territory granted to the pope by Charlemagne in 744

Bari centres from which Muslim raids were launched in the 9th cent.

| 0 | 100 | 200 km |
| 0 | 50 | 100 miles |

MARCH OF IVREA

Milan

Verona

MARCH OF FRIULI

Turin

Pavia

MARCH OF TURIN

KINGDOM OF

Genoa

Nonantola

ITALY

Modena

Ravenna

EXARCHATE

Venice

Zara

Split

"DALMATIA"

Fraxinetum

Lucca

Pisa

MARCH OF TUSCANY

Ragusa

MARCH OF SPOLETO

CORSICA

PATRIMONY OF ST PETER

Rome

Monte Cassino

Gaeta

R. Garigliano

COUNTY OF CAPUA

PRINCIPALITY OF BENEVENTO

Bari (controlled by Arab pirates 847-71)

THEME OF LANGOBARDIA

Naples

Amalfi

PRINCIPALITY OF SALERNO

SARDINIA

DUCHY OF CALABRIA
(THEME FROM *c.*938-56 ON)

Palermo

SICILY
(invaded by Arabs from 827)

Syracuse

Kairouan

THE POLITICAL FRAGMENTATION OF ITALY, *c.*900

Justinianic ideal of universal reconquest receded in favour of a pragmatic extension of Byzantine cultural influence by Slav-speaking missionaries.

In contrast the ninth century proved a period of uncertainty and upheaval in the western Mediterranean. The late eighth century saw the emergence of a new kind of invader from the north who embodied an aggressive commitment to Christianity and self-confident expansionism on the part of a Latin west, which for centuries had lain prostrate in the face of external attacks. The Frankish King Charlemagne, Charles the Great, inherited from his father Pippin III the recently subjugated Mediterranean lands of Aquitaine and Provence and a tradition of intervening in Italian affairs in support of the pope. After their capture of Ravenna in 751 the Lombards had attempted to take over the former Byzantine territories of the exarchate and the duchy of Rome, much to the alarm of the popes, who never ceased to regard the Lombards as barbarian interlopers. The papacy asserted its own claims to these lands by fabricating a remarkably successful forgery, the Donation of Constantine, which purported to record the first Christian emperor's grant to St Peter of 'Italy and the west'. The popes fostered a special relationship with the Franks by playing upon the Carolingians' veneration of St Peter, and finally in response to papal pleas Charles led an expedition to Italy which resulted in the take-over of the Lombard kingdom in 774.

The momentous repercussions of this step included the creation of a papal state which remained a major factor on the Italian scene until 1870. The strengthened alliance between Charles and the pope led to a flow of Roman manuscripts and relics into Francia. The pope crowned Charles emperor on Christmas Day 800, hoping thereby to strengthen his hold over his protector. The Byzantines were outraged, and conceded only limited recognition of the title in 812 after protracted negotiations. For the papacy the restoration of a western empire represented a decisive turning of its back on Byzantium and an opportunity to stress its political as well as ecclesiastical authority in the west. In the long term the creation of a western empire gave a boost to notions of a distinct European identity and helped create a north-south axis which was to dominate the west throughout the Middle Ages.

The Frankish involvement in Italy did nothing to promote the unity of the peninsula. The essential structure of the Lombard kingdom was preserved, although an élite of Frankish officials and ecclesiastics was brought in and vast amounts of land were entrusted to the Church. The position of the former Byzantine territories stretching from Rome north to Bologna remained ambiguous; the pope claimed them as the Patrimony of St Peter, but considerable power remained in the hands of local figures such as the archbishop of Ravenna and the nobles of the Campagna. In practice the Frankish kings exercised extensive influence. To the south the state of Benevento remained a centre of Lombard legitimism under descendants of the old royal house, although later in the century separate princedoms split off, based on Capua and Salerno, and Lombard power was undermined by Arab raids and the Byzantine *reconquista*. Even before 876 the eastern empire possessed a major presence in the form of direct possessions, such as Calabria, the Terra d'Otranto, and Sicily, and the largely autonomous maritime cities of Venice, Gaeta, Naples, and Amalfi. The middle and late ninth century were dominated by the raids of Arab pirates, who went so far as to set up bases on Italian soil and to sack the Vatican suburb of Rome in 846. The resistance, led by the last Carolingian emperor based in Italy, Louis II, and Pope John VIII, was spirited but unsuccessful. Italy's misery was increased by the sudden invasion of the Magyars, steppe nomads who sacked and pillaged their way as far south as Otranto in 899. Political confusion reigned by 900, with the throne of Pavia fought over by rival claimants, the papacy the plaything of noble factions, and the rise throughout the peninsula of magnate families who enforced their control of the countryside by the setting up of fortified villages (*castelli*). On the Christian side the only beneficiary of this disunity was Byzantium, whose prestige was heightened by disenchantment with the weakness and uncouthness of the Franks and by its enduring cultural and artistic influence in Rome and the south.

A broadly similar picture of disorder is presented by Provence, Aquitaine, and northern Spain. The attempts of Charlemagne to push back the Arabs in the area known as the Spanish March had little permanent result, and in the ninth century the Mediterranean coast of France was devastated by the raids of Muslim pirates. Marauding bands set up pirate nests, as at Fraxinetum on the Riviera, in order to prey on pilgrim and merchant traffic crossing the Alps. As elsewhere in the Carolingian Empire external pressure, combined with the disintegration of royal authority, created conditions in which local power accumulated in the hands of squabbling noble families.

Survivals and Disruption: the Case of City Life

The Byzantine and Islamic worlds have often been seen as preserving the political sophistication and urban life of the classical world, while the west suffered a complete break in continuity resulting from the invasions and the settlement of the Germans. The difficulties of such a sweeping approach are obvious. The institutions of the Roman world were undergoing major changes long before the settlement of the barbarians. In certain cases the effects of 'continuity' could be negative and those of 'discontinuity' positive. For example, the increasing domination of military élites evident in most areas of the Mediterranean led to more effective defensive arrangements, and the traditional culture of the civilian aristocracy which such a process undermined was in many respects rigid and sterile. Many factors were outside human control, including plague which remained endemic for at least two centuries after the first great outbreak of 542, and climatic deterioration, which depressed agricultural production between the fourth and the eighth centuries. Contemporaries sought desperately to identify themselves with past ages which they admired; the Ostrogoths sought to create for themselves a classicizing past in which the Amazons were represented as Gothic women, and the historian Agnellus of Ravenna saw no anomaly in writing of the 'Roman Empire' of Charlemagne.

More important than the *degree* of continuity and disruption is the question of the *impact* of surviving institutions and new forces. The complexities involved in assessing survivals can best be seen by examining the fortunes of one key institution which was literally synonymous with ancient civilization, the city.

The popular image of Byzantium as a monument to political and social immobility is in many ways the opposite of reality. The empire of Constantinople did in part owe its survival to its self-confident view of itself as the universal Roman *oikoumenē* (inhabited world), the terrestrial image of God's kingdom, but the institutional and fiscal resources which enabled it to survive crisis after crisis were derived from a capacity for self-regeneration. The most practical elements of its administrative inheritance were retained, while costly traditions such as the free corn dole in Constantinople were abandoned. The empire reinforced its depleted manpower by encouraging the settlement of Slavs and other peoples, and the rigidity of the old civilian aristocracy was replaced by a meritocracy of parvenu soldiers. Subjects' loyalty was fostered by the introduction of new 'populist' symbols and beliefs, and the status of the peasantry increased as free village communities replaced large estates. The simplified society created by invasion, depopulation, and the devolution of power to local commanders represented a caesura with the Roman past, but helped to produce a responsive and efficient military machine.

Nowhere is the transformation of Byzantium more apparent than in urban development. Despite economic weaknesses and the erosion of their municipal autonomy, cities had remained the political and social foundation of the eastern empire in the fifth and sixth centuries and maintained a vigorous civic life, reflected in lavish buildings and the notorious activities of circus factions. In the aftermath of the Persian and Arab invasions, however, the cities of the Anatolian plateau were abandoned or reduced to the level of fortified villages. The relatively more prosperous and secure cities of the coast of western Anatolia also suffered a calamitous decline. In the case of Ephesus the harbour silted up and the baths fell into ruin as the formerly flourishing city was replaced by a small fortified settlement inland. In Sardis the breakdown of traditional municipal life is shown by the building of a seventh-century road through the ruins of civic buildings.

The contraction of urban life was even more dramatic in the Balkans. Many cities disappeared completely during the Avar and Slav invasions, and among those surviving, settlement became confined to the fortified acropolis, as in Athens and Corinth. The evidence of finds of copper coinage points to a drastic decline in local commercial activity.

What is striking is not simply the physical decline but the complete loss of urban consciousness and the change of role. Cities lost their earlier importance as economic and residential centres, and assumed an almost exclusively military and administrative function. Significantly most showed little sign of recovery when a measure of prosperity and stability returned to the empire from the late ninth century.

Large-scale urban life was of course maintained in Constantinople, and to a lesser extent Thessalonica. Even in the capital, however, a drastic fall in population is suggested by the failure to repair the aqueduct of Valens after 626 and Constantine V's efforts to repopulate the city. By the tenth century Constantinople was again an impressive city with a population of several hundred thousand, but it remained an exceptional, parasitic metropolis. Its population catered almost exclusively to the needs of the court and administration for goods and services, and its trade and industry were rigorously controlled by imperial officials and forced to attend primarily to the needs of the state.

It is hardly surprising that an Arab geographer commented that there were only five proper cities in Anatolia in the ninth century. The contrast with the Arab world was very marked. Urban development forged ahead in the areas conquered by the Arabs, with large cities prospering not only in the Levant and Mesopotamia, such as Cairo, Damascus, and Baghdad, but also in the deurbanized west, where Fez, Kairouan, Cordoba, and Palermo rose to prominence. The reasons for this revival include the existence of a vast common market, a renewed influx of gold from Africa and the east, the high status accorded to merchants, and the degree of autonomy enjoyed by urban élites.

In the western half of the Mediterranean urban life changed gear radically because of political upheavals and a sharp drop in trade and monetary circulation, but the decline was much less marked than in northern Gaul or Britain. A large measure of physical continuity was evident in the preservation of Roman walls, aqueducts, and other structures, often through the efforts of local bishops. Temples such as the Pantheon in Rome were converted into churches, Roman street plans were preserved in Lucca, Barcelona, and elsewhere, and on occasion large private buildings became the nucleus of early medieval towns, as in the case of Diocletian's vast palace at Split, which became a refuge from Slav attacks for the population of nearby Salona.

The level of continuity was not, however, uniform. In northern Italy virtually all the Roman *civitates* survived with a few exceptions, but in the south the majority of towns ceased to be recorded as episcopal sees around the time of the Lombard invasions, and urban life was largely confined to the coastal cities which enjoyed the lifeline of Byzantine commerce and naval support. Specific external attacks could be a factor in a city's decline, as perhaps in the case of Aquileia, but in general longer-term factors were more important such as the silting up of harbours, changes in trade networks, and an overall increase in insecurity. Often the need for a settlement in a particular area continued, and the population of exposed Roman towns sought refuge in more defensible sites, either on islands as in the case of Grado and the Venetian lagoon, or on hilltops, as in the Roman Campagna.

The cities which survived presented a sorry sight in the early Middle Ages. In Rome the late Roman population of several hundred thousand had shrunk to perhaps 30,000 by the late sixth century as a result of siege, famine, and plague, important classical buildings lay derelict or were despoiled for building materials, and vast areas of the city were desolate. Although the Roman tradition of lavish municipal patronage had been replaced by a Christian programme of church-building, the edifices erected were small and impoverished, to judge from the fifty-seven churches recorded in Lucca before 900.

Roman patterns of life were steadily eroded in a number of spheres. Among the clergy and the majority Roman population, Roman law persisted, but mainly at the simplest level of notaries transcribing routine formulae to record transactions. Municipal autonomy, already on the wane in the Late Roman period finally disappeared as military aristocrats assumed power in both the Lombard and Byzantine areas of Italy. In Rome the greatest 'town council', the Senate, which had been allotted an important administrative role under the Ostrogoths, found its membership sapped by a drift to the east and its powers taken over by the papal and military authorities. Various activities at the heart of Roman civic life, such as horse-racing, circus games, and public bathing, disappeared in a hostile climate of ecclesiastical disapproval and economic dislocation.

While Roman institutions petered out or were taken over by the Church, a number of Roman traditions remained alive. Cities remained the focus of politics and administration and aristocrats, whether Byzantine, Lombard, or Frankish, maintained the custom of urban living, in sharp contrast with England or most of Gaul. Cities in Italy also retained a sense of identity with their Roman past. This was strongest in the cities which had remained under Roman political control, such as Rome, Ravenna, and Naples, where ecclesiastical writers extolled the past glories and Roman titles such as consul and tribune remained in use. More surprising is the strength of such feelings in Lombard areas: city descriptions survive from eighth-century Milan and Verona which proudly list the walls, temples, forum, and amphitheatres of their cities as well as their churches and relics, and which display a civic consciousness partly founded on Roman legacies.

Particularly significant for the future was the dynamism which Italian cities showed in new spheres. Whereas Roman towns had primarily been residential and administrative centres with little involvement in trade, a number of early medieval towns built their fortunes on commercial activity. Towns had always possessed some role as local markets and royal legislation concerning the protection and taxing of merchants confirms that this continued under the Lombards. By the eighth century salt produced at pans on the northern Adriatic coast became one of the first commodities to be traded over longer distances and promoted the rise of first Comacchio and later Venice. As a subject of Byzantium Venice had privileged access to markets in the east and soon diversified from salt and fish into importing luxuries such as textiles and spices and exporting slaves. The will of a doge shows that by 829 a large part of the aristocracy's wealth lay in investments in overseas trading ventures. In the early tenth century Venetian merchants are recorded at Pavia as paying customary gifts of spices and cosmetics in return for their right to sell oriental luxuries. Venetian commerce acted as a stimulus to Lombard cities, who supplied the coastal city with food and cloth and re-exported its imports to northern Europe. A similar luxury trade also operated to the south in the late ninth century, as is shown by a saint's life in which Venetian merchants praised a Byzantine cloak which the hero had purchased in Rome. Such items constituted catalysts to more general economic activity and were in great demand as status symbols. In the south the chief centres of long-distance commerce were Gaeta, Amalfi, and Naples, subjects of Byzantium which also carried on a flourishing trade with the Arabs.

Inland cities such as Milan and Cremona had their prosperous merchants by the ninth century, but they remained a minor element who tended to use their wealth to buy land or to marry into aristocratic families. The future trading giants of Pisa and Genoa were still little more than villages. Unlike the eastern empire, where such groups saw their interests and ambitions as lying with the metropolitan life of the capital, Italians developed a fierce pride in their local city, which was expressed through the cult of patron saints and even in revolts against royal officials. Cities possessed ill-documented institutions such as the court of 'worthy men' and the 'assembly in front of the church' in which market arrangements and other common concerns were discussed. One example of this civic patriotism is Modena, whose position on the turbulent border between the Byzantines and the Lombards had reduced it to dereliction and which survived through the attachment of the local clergy to the martyr St Gimignano. As in most northern cities the bishop came to exercise everyday administration, and so in the 880s we find its bishop, Leudoin, rebuilding the walls and even inscribing a poem in a chapel which called on the citizens to display vigilance in the best classical traditions of Rome and Troy. Although in the tenth century bishops became unpopular as outsiders and representatives of royal power, in earlier centuries they were the mouthpiece for local interests and feelings and their cathedral chapters were influential as opinion-makers and custodians of their cities' traditions.

This economic and cultural vitality, so missing in the 'cities' of the Byzantine interior, only found its full expression in Italy with the political awakening of the cities in the eleventh century. Most of the other areas of the Christian west lacked the same level of economic activity, occupational diversity, and local pride. Only the cities of Dalmatia, which had economic ties with the Adriatic coast of Italy and benefited from a nominal allegiance to Byzantium, displayed an active commercial and ecclesiastical life and a strong civic consciousness in the face of constant pressure from their Slav neighbours. In the Christian areas of northern Spain economic life was relatively backward and the towns' main importance was as military strongholds. Even in these underdeveloped areas, however, there was a. striking reliance on the written word in legal transactions which contrasts sharply with the northern European position, and an enduring use of Visigothic law codes. In southern France the previously prosperous coastal towns such as Marseilles maintained some commercial role and Roman traditions in such fields as Roman legal practice, but what little evidence survives suggests that their development in the eighth and ninth centuries was retarded by endemic internal disorder and the effects of recurrent Arab raids.

In no area of the Mediterranean, therefore, were urban traditions completely extinguished. In spite of the invasions the modicum of stability necessary for urban life was soon re-established, except in exposed frontier zones, and certain cities developed a novel role as commercial centres. Even in areas where economic life remained depressed, urban values and traditions proved durable and helped to produce a social climate which later proved capable of responding dynamically to new opportunities.

Unity and Fragmentation in the Mediterranean World

'The whole sea shared a common destiny ... with identical problems and general trends.' The historian Fernand Braudel's masterly study of the Mediterranean in the sixteenth century rests on an acceptance of its fundamental unity, which would be shared by students of the classical world. In the early Middle Ages the similarity of certain general trends cannot conceal the fact that the Mediterranean ceased to be a Roman lake, a channel of communication uniting a uniform area, and many historians have attributed the break with ancient culture and society to this development. The classic statement of this view was put forward in the 1920s and 1930s by the Belgian historian Henri Pirenne, who argued that the Arabs destroyed the unity of the Mediterranean in the seventh century and so paved the way for a distinctively western European civilization. Telling criticisms have been made of his approach and data, in particular his exaggeration of the extent of trade, his equation of economic activity with cultural achievement, and his pro-Roman bias. His provocative thesis also involves confusion of cause and effect; the Mediterranean did cease to form the cultural, political, and economic unit it had been earlier, but this fissure was in many respects a symptom of other developments.

Not only the consequences of this momentous change, but also its date and causes are difficult to establish. It has to be remembered that the Mediterranean is in fact a complex of seas, and that the degree of Roman naval control essential for regular trade and communication varied from one to another. In the easternmost basin, the Aegean Sea, Roman sea power and trade continued along traditional lines well into the seventh century: the sea-borne transport of commodities is shown by the state-directed supply of corn from Egypt to Constantinople and by the discovery of a wreck off south-west Turkey which sank around 623 with a cargo of wine in amphorae and other mass-produced utensils. In the western (Tyrrhenian) basin, piracy and the activities of the Vandal fleet in the fifth century dealt long-distance traffic a blow from which it never recovered, even though short coastal voyages continued because they were cheaper and safer than overland communication. Africa's trade in foodstuffs declined into insignificance. Justinian's defeat of the Vandals and Goths only partially restored Roman naval power. Even in the Aegean area the Byzantine naval monopoly was broken when the Ummayads built up a fleet composed largely of Christian renegades, seized Christian bases such as Cyprus and Rhodes, and twice blockaded Constantinople itself.

The Byzantines were quick to appreciate the importance of naval supremacy in defending and provisioning their many coastal provinces, and retrieved the situation by building new 'thematic' fleets supplied from particular areas. This naval recovery was helped by the rise of the Abbasid caliphs based on Baghdad, who were less sea-minded than their Ummayad predecessors. In the ninth century Byzantium's naval hegemony was undermined by a series of revolts in the naval themes and by the emergence of aggressive new Muslim states, especially the Aghlabids of North Africa. As a result of this Sicily was invaded in 827, Crete was lost in 828, and the empire's western provinces suffered devastating raids. Although Byzantine naval dominance was therefore seriously challenged from around 650, the empire retained a strong presence in those waters which were strategic to its survival, thanks to the technical superiority of its ships, the professionalism of its sailors, and the advantage of plentiful timber and naval supplies in comparison with the Arabs. As for communications with the west, the Arabs only seriously threatened Byzantium's control of the middle Mediterranean (Adriatic) basin in the ninth century, when her subject cities of Venice and Amalfi were developing a powerful naval capability.

The vicissitudes of Byzantium's naval strength were only one factor in the weakening of its ties with the west. Equally important was the blocking of the land route by the Avar and Slav invasions, which was only gradually reopened with the conversion of the Balkans in the ninth and tenth centuries. The reasons for the empire turning its back on the west were also psychological. A cultural and linguistic cleavage between east and west already existed in the Late Roman period. In the west knowledge of Greek was confined to a few intellectuals such as Boethius, and in their war with Justinian the Goths did their utmost to exploit the Italians' suspicions of the 'unmanly' Greeks. That the authorities were aware of the political dangers of such antagonisms is shown in a seventh-century show trial in Constantinople when a dissident theologian was accused of 'loving the Romans and hating Greeks'. In the east Latin ceased to be the official language of the administration, and the previously important Latin presence in the capital was thinned out by cultural assimilation and the executions of the Emperor Phocas. While historians of the mid-sixth century could still give exhaustive accounts of campaigns in the west and Germanic customs, their successors offered only occasional asides about the west and by the ninth century the interest of the main chronicler was confined to the hostility displayed by the Roman pontiffs against his *bêtes noires*, the iconoclast emperors. The imperial government displayed a broader view, showing its continued commitment to the west by the dispatch of embassies and gold to the Franks and to renegade Lombards, but it was prevented from deploying adequate resources in men and money by more immediate pressures in the east. A further decline in involvement occurred in the 630s, when the empire's back-to-the-wall conflict with the Arabs led to a decline in the number of oriental troops recorded in Italy and the disappearance of Byzantine tribute from Frankish coin hoards.

A gradual contraction of horizons took place throughout the Mediterranean in response to immediate dangers and economic needs as much as the Arab advance and the disintegration of an increasingly remote and irrelevant empire. An illuminating example is Byzantine Italy where fusion took place between indigenous elements and immigrant soldiers to produce a militarily effective society with a strong sense of local patriotism, whose nominal loyalty to Byzantium rested on little more than inertia. The weakening of ties with the universal empire had its beneficial effects: freed from the domination of a uniform élitist culture and the siren pulling-power of a metropolitan centre, local cultures and communities gradually blossomed. Sometimes this entailed a resurgence of local ethnic traditions, as with the Basques in Spain and Moors in Africa; elsewhere, as in Italy, it found expression in the rebirth of identity and vitality among existing cities.

Long-distance trade was of limited importance in the Roman world, although large quantities of goods and produce were transported through official channels, most notably by state-sponsored shippers. With the breakdown of the state apparatus, especially in the west, such large-scale transport was restricted, and an increasing role was taken by Jewish and Syrian traders who specialized in luxury items from the east. Records of these long-distance peddlars dry up in the seventh century, but eastern goods continued to flow into the west by other means. A great number of items were distributed by the Byzantines as tribute or diplomatic gifts to allies and important churchmen in the west. These objects had a significance out of all proportion to their quantity and price because they were valued as an index of social status and because they served as models for local craftsmen. Even the supply of basic commodities never dried up completely. Although there was a trend towards locally produced parchment, papyrus continued to be used for more important documents in traditionalist centres such as Rome and Ravenna.

The hiatus of the seventh century was therefore confined to the already limited level of *commercial* exchange. This break did not apply to the non-Christian areas of the west; Spain and North Africa developed lucrative trade links with the Levant as a result of their integration into an Islamic free-trade zone. Elsewhere long-distance trade picked up considerably from the eighth century onwards, reflecting increased internal stability and a demographic and climatic recovery. References to wealthy merchants become frequent in documents from Lombard Italy and elsewhere, and in the ninth century a number of cities which were under nominal Byzantine authority such as Amalfi and Venice became active centres of trade with the east. Ironically therefore international commerce took off at the very time when the Arabs were making their naval presence felt in the central and western Mediterranean, and political reality forced cities such as Naples to enter into close relations with the Islamic world, which included the payment of protection money and trading in slaves. By the tenth century the extent of trading links is shown by descriptions of south Italian ports by Arab geographers and by the circulation of an Islamic coin, the tari, in the south of the peninsula.

Other, non-commercial channels remained important for the diffusion of goods. Papal sources abound with references to oriental relics, vestments, and ornaments, many of which must have arrived in Rome as official gifts, and many luxury textiles came to the west by official or unofficial diplomatic means. When the western envoy Liutprand of Cremona was caught smuggling a silken garment out of Constantinople, he was engaging in a widespread practice which the Byzantines sought to prevent to maintain the rarity value of such items.

The question of Mediterranean unity is therefore more complex than a simple following of Pirenne's views would suggest. Ties between east and west changed in nature and extent, but never ceased completely. An awareness of the rich and powerful east survived in the west, kept alive by diplomats and pilgrims rather than traders, while the east had little reason to reciprocate interest in an impoverished west. The flow of artistic objects and luxury goods imported from the east had an important impact in the west, not least in furnishing a *raison d'être* for a number of trading cities, whose steady growth was to have startling repercussions on the economy and culture of Europe, but the effects were confined to a narrow élite. As in the Roman Empire, the economy remained overwhelmingly agrarian, and the peasantry who made up the vast majority of the population lived a harsh life of poverty and self-sufficiency, dominated by the demands of local lords and, in the east, of tax-collectors. The Mediterranean had become transformed into a jigsaw of local communities, and therein lay both its weakness and its strength.

Rulership and Government

One concept which long outlived the reality of a unified Mediterranean world was that of an enduring Roman Empire. Both east and west drew upon a common reservoir of ideological notions of a divinely ordained, universal empire which had been evolved in the days of the great Christian emperors, Constantine and Theodosius. The Byzantines called themselves *Rhōmaioi* (Romans) and had no difficulty in maintaining the claims to universal rule which had been energetically proclaimed by Justinian. The west also drew upon Late Roman traditions as an ideological basis for its kingship, but had to adapt notions of universal empire to transformed political conditions and the predominance of ecclesiastical thought. St Augustine of Hippo recognized the decline of the empire but considered it secondary to God's instruments for salvation, the visible Church and the true community of the just ('the City of God'), while writers in Visigothic Spain saw God's mandate as having passed from the weak and heterodox Romans to the powerful Catholic rulers of the Germanic west. In general, however, the west was content with a vague recognition of the universal authority of the remote emperors of Constantinople, because of the lack of any coherent ideological alternative and the widespread equation of the Roman Empire with the 'Fourth Kingdom' of the Book of Daniel, destined to survive until the coming of Antichrist. The ambivalence of western barbarian kingdoms can be seen in the laws which the Lombard king, Rothari, issued in 643; an unashamedly traditional Germanic code was written up in Latin, almost certainly by a Roman official, and was prefaced by a short history of the Lombard people and a pious statement of the purposes of legislation borrowed from the Novels of Justinian.

A new and more coherent attitude in the west emerged with the coronation of Charlemagne in 800 following the papacy's disenchantment with Byzantium. Thereafter the western emperor became an ideological focus and a *de jure* ruler for the west, even though the unity of the Carolingian Empire soon crumbled and some elements in Rome and southern Italy retained a snobbish attachment to Byzantium for its power and wealth. The rivalries between the two empires were well brought out in a letter of 871 from the Carolingian Emperor Louis II to his eastern opposite number in which Louis justified his claim to the title of Roman emperor on grounds of virtue, inheritance, and divine anointing and condemned the Greeks for their 'cacodoxy'. While the lines were drawn for the suspicion and antagonism which led to the conflicts of the crusading period, awareness of shared Christian belief and common hostility to outside threats could persist. The Byzantine Emperor Theophilus addressed a plea to Louis the Pious for aid in the face of Arab raids and Louis II's polemical letter was written in the context of attempts to forge an alliance against the Arab threat in the central Mediterranean.

Administrative structures in the west had none of the strengths of those of Byzantium. Whereas the latter had inherited a unitary capital, salaried administrators, and a centralized system of justice and finance from Roman times, the power of western rulers rested on the much flimsier basis of military prowess, church support, and an ability to cajole loyalty out of often recalcitrant nobles. Byzantium's strength lay in her ability to control and utilize her resources effectively; most of her provinces were scarcely, if at all, richer than the west's but she had the machinery to extract whatever surpluses existed to finance a glittering court and an all-embracing administration. The bureaucratic and educational capacity remained to keep up tax registers and to employ paid officials to collect imperial dues, and a reliable gold coinage was maintained less for the purpose of stimulating economic activity than in order to facilitate the smooth collection of taxes and their disbursement to troops and officials. Such a sophisticated system gave the administration enormous advantages, but the contrast between a monolithic east and a fragmented west should not be pressed too far.

The capacity of western kingdoms to impose taxes was limited to tolls on trade and imposts on justice; only the Visigothic kingdom of Spain was able to maintain a land-tax on Roman lines. Kings did, however, command substantial resources in land. The Lombards possessed extensive royal estates, and it has been calculated that in the eleventh century, after two centuries of alienations and endowment of the Church, the crown still owned more than 10 per cent of the land in northern Italy. Other valuable sources of royal income included booty, tribute, confiscation of property, the monopoly of minting coinage, and the right to ratify a range of legal transactions and building operations. The main activity to which Roman and Byzantine fiscal resources were devoted was of course the financing of the army. This was a burden which Germanic kingdoms were spared because all free warriors had an obligation to serve their king in the army under their local dukes in return for the land on which they had been settled. The enforcement of this system required constant vigilance on the part of the Lombard kings and their Carolingian successors since there was a relentless tendency for large landowners to reduce peasants to a state of dependence.

Another major prop of the Byzantine state was its control of justice. Not only did centrally appointed judges administer courts at all levels, but the Roman principle of territorial law was maintained with its presupposition that all authority emanated from the emperor; the predominantly Latin Corpus of Justinian was supplemented by the simplified *Ecloga* collection issued by Leo III in 739 and by the authoritative *Basilica* Code promulgated by Leo VI. Law was never as systematic or as uniform in the west; it was personal rather than territorial, with the clergy and the native population 'professing' Roman law as preserved in a simplified local (or 'vulgar') form and their Germanic conquerors 'professing' Gothic, Frankish, or Lombard law. Nevertheless, the kings gained more control over the law than their counterparts in the north. In the case of Italy it was royal officials who administered the courts, and the law codes issued by the kings became increasingly influenced by Roman customs. Royal authority was strengthened with the development of concepts of treason and the king's peace, and new provisions were introduced to allow for the free disposal of property, to discourage feud, and to cater for the role of merchants and other aspects of a more settled urban society.

The features of Constantinople which made most impression on western visitors were the dazzling richness of the court and the elaboration of the central bureaucracy. In the west, a court such as that of the Lombard kings retained certain Germanic features; it was politically imperative for a king to surround himself with a warrior following and traditional servants such as the *marpahis* (groom). Gradually, however, dress and ceremonial came to ape Byzantine models, and many of the officials who appear with bureaucratic duties, such as the chamberlain and notaries, have clear Roman origins. The take-over of Roman traditions was vividly demonstrated when King Agilulf had his son Adaloald presented as king in the circus of Milan. A particularly significant event occurred with the fixing of the royal court in Pavia around 620 and the city's adornment with royal quarters, churches, and even baths followed in the tradition of Constantinople, Ravenna, and the Visigothic capital of Toledo. The Roman character of the court was further emphasized after the Lombards' conversion to Catholicism, and throughout the Lombard and Carolingian periods Pavia remained the cultivated nerve centre of a central administration capable of making its power felt throughout the kingdom.

Local government was the weak spot of all early medieval monarchies, and it was here that the superiority of the Byzantine state was less than might be thought. The eastern empire was compelled by the invasions of the seventh century to replace the largely civilian administration of the Late Roman period with a streamlined system, in which considerable autonomy was granted to theme commanders. The external crisis facing the empire gave rise to a militarized society analogous in many ways to that of the Germanic kingdoms, since the military commanded the lion's share of local power, land, and social status. Byzantine emperors could exercise greater control by virtue of their elaborate system of written instructions and supervision by inspectors, and most forcefully by their power of the purse; Liutprand was astonished to see theme commanders receive bags of gold as salaries in Constantinople. Even so the decentralization inherent in the system could serve as a focus for political and religious tensions and encourage coups and revolts by ambitious warlords. For most of our period, however, the balance between ruler and local strongmen was tipped in favour of the former, and a series of strong dynasties initiated by successful soldier-emperors enabled Byzantium to avoid the fate of Visigothic Spain or Lombard Italy.

Another crucial strength of Byzantium was that local officials at first formed a dutiful meritocracy with no entrenched family position or landed wealth. By the ninth century, however, these figures had put down strong local roots and become a hereditary aristocracy similar to those of the west; as cohesive families emerged with distinctive surnames, their most powerful members amassed vast estates and began to exercise powers of patronage over the thematic soldiers and peasants, the military and fiscal linchpins of the Byzantine state. A Paphlagonian landowner in the late eighth century owned 48 estates and 12,000 sheep, and in the ninth century a Peloponnesian heiress bequeathed 80 properties and 3,000 slaves to the emperor. The conditions were being created for a proto-feudal society comparable to the dominance which western aristocrats exerted in their localities through landholding. In Lombard and Carolingian Italy the monarchy succeeded in keeping their nobles in check by essentially *ad hoc* methods; under the Lombards a king's military prestige could count for more than formal hierarchy, and the Carolingian rulers relied on the appointment of loyal Frankish nobles and their supervision by royal inspectors (*missi*). The death of Louis II in 875 ushered in a period of dynastic uncertainty and administrative weakness as magnates usurped royal rights and lands and built up their local power and wealth. Despite the relative sophistication of royal government in Italy, it lacked the trump card enjoyed by the eastern empire; Byzantine aristocrats had a vested interest in the imperial system, because their ambitions were best served by attachment to a central court which was the source of legitimacy, lucrative offices, and dignities essential to their status.

If central authority in Italy proved a broken reed in the longer term, the materials remained for a vigorous political life at a local level. The measure of decentralization which had existed in the Roman areas since the seventh century came to extend to the Germanic areas as well. In contrast to France, where justice became a private or feudal right, the complexity of Italian life helped to preserve the public nature of courts, written law, and an acceptance of formal legal procedures. The reliance on legal formalities and the written word was in part a reflection of a level of lay literacy which far exceeded other areas of the west: 77 per cent of witnesses who appeared in Lucca charters of the 890s were able to sign their names. Although most Italian towns around 900 had come under the authority of individual lords and bishops, complex nations of community and public ideology survived to form the necessary foundation for the later development of independent communes. The Italian model of devolved political life and public authority was to prove more dynamic than the Byzantine, where autocracy had been maintained at the cost of eliminating local communities and diverting political energies from the provinces to the capital. Oddly the Italian position had closer parallels with the Islamic world, where high levels of wealth and literacy produced a complex society but a superficially autocratic administration in practice limited its role to the collection of taxes and the maintenance of security, leaving local élites control over markets and everyday life in their cities.

Religion and Mentalities

Christianity was already widespread throughout the Mediterranean area in the Late Roman period, although it was stronger in the east than in the west and the countryside was still dominated by the *pagani* (literally 'country-dwellers'). Among the many reasons for its success were its possession of an effective organization centred on bishops ('overseers') based on the cities, and the breadth of its appeal. By taking over the vocabulary and many of the spiritual and ethical preoccupations of Greek philosophical thought, it attracted intellectuals impressed by its moral precepts and its clear-cut monotheism. At the same time it had competed successfully with a host of mystery religions in winning converts among the masses, who sought the solace of eternal salvation and the satisfaction of belonging to a close-knit community. The acceptance of Christianity by the Roman state following the conversion of Constantine came as a bolt from the blue, and also as a mixed blessing. Many of the converts who flocked to the new faith did so for reasons of ambition rather than conviction, and in return for the state's political and financial backing, bishops came to be treated as imperial officials and church councils often had to follow imperial instructions.

The Church's new-found wealth and power aggravated internal tensions among its members. In Africa major conflicts arose between the conservative Romanizing wing, who accepted the Church's new position, and diehard 'Donatist' elements, who favoured a radical rejection of the world and the exclusion of those who had apostatized during earlier persecutions. Disputes also arose concerning the Trinity, the repercussions of which lasted for centuries. For a time the Church bowed to imperial pressure and accepted the heretical view of the Alexandrian priest Arius that Christ the Son was inferior to the Father. Although this doctrine was condemned later in the fourth century it was not before Arian priests had converted Visigoths living in the Balkans to their form of Christianity. During the fifth century Arianism was taken up by most of the German peoples who settled in the empire, in part as a 'national' faith to underline their distinctiveness from the culturally superior Romans.

In the east serious divisions were caused by christological disputes. The orthodox position was upheld at the Council of Chalcedon of 451, but resistance remained strong in Egypt and Syria, particularly among the Monophysites, who believed that Christ's humanity was subsumed into a single divine nature. Although these heresies were not simply political or social movements in disguise, they were undoubtedly fuelled by local resentment of a politically and culturally dominant Greek élite. Such opposition took on a political dimension in a world where orthodoxy was considered essential to individual salvation and to the success of the God-given empire, and emperors desperately sought to restore unity by veering between persecution and the working out of a generally acceptable compromise. The latter policy aroused the staunch opposition of the popes, who, as patriarchs of the west, set their face against tampering with orthodox belief. To make matters worse, tension grew between east and west over the issue of primacy in the Church after the upstart capital of Constantinople was granted patriarchal status in 381.

By the sixth century the ideal of the Church Universal so dear to Justinian persisted but in reality a parting of the ways between east and west was under way. In the west Christians had retained their earlier suspicion of the empire and regarded their faith as a sphere of activity separate from and superior to the secular life, with the Church viewed as a militant group of spiritual shock-troops. These notions were reinforced by the political collapse of the empire, and bishops assumed the secular as well as spiritual leadership of their communities. In the east more of the pluralism and complexity of the ancient world survived and it was unthinkable for the Church to adopt such a 'divisive' attitude. The eastern Church never aimed to isolate itself from or dominate profane society because it regarded the empire as part of God's plan and accorded a greater degree of holiness to the material world. In the west, however, churchmen such as Pope Gregory the Great were forced to adjust to the realities of a changed world. Aware that the barbarian invaders had come to stay, he moved beyond the traditional equation of Christian and Roman and sought to integrate the Lombard and Anglo-Saxon invaders into the Christian world by a deliberate missionary programme.

The increasing differences between eastern and western Christianity should not blind us to the persistence of ties and parallels. Just as Frankish pilgrims could travel to Jerusalem, eastern churchmen and artists settled in the west, such as Theodore, a refugee from St Paul's city of Tarsus, who was a monk in Rome before being sent to Canterbury as archbishop. Throughout the seventh and early eighth centuries Rome's religious and intellectual life was dominated by Greeks and Syrians. The early Middle Ages saw the emergence throughout the Mediterranean of Christian literary forms such as the saint's life and of a popular religious culture centred around processions, icons, and relics; in a simple age men craved tangible tokens of holiness. Patron saints became the revered guardians of cities in east and west, and the liturgy was perfected as an elaborate, dramatic expression of collective devotion.

A move towards greater uniformity is also evident in both parts of the Church. In the east the authority of the patriarch of Constantinople was strengthened by the loss of Antioch, Alexandria, and Jerusalem to the Arabs, and between the fourth and the ninth century a series of ecumenical councils codified the doctrine and discipline of the Church. In the west traditional differences in local customs were gradually eroded by conciliar legislation, papal authority, and the development of canon law, and throughout the Church archbishops and metropolitans were acquiring more fully defined jurisdiction.

A similar trend was also visible in monasticism, originally the most radical and varied sphere of religious activity. The first *monachoi* ('solitaries') were devout laymen who aimed at fulfilling Christ's precepts of poverty and self-denial by removing themselves from the temptations of secular life. The movement started in Egypt, where early desert fathers such as St Anthony attracted thousands of followers. A wide range of monastic communities soon emerged, some loyal to the original hermit life-style, others organized on a coenobitic (communal) basis under an abbot. In the fourth and fifth centuries monasticism rapidly spread northwards to Palestine, Syria, and Anatolia and westwards to Gaul, Italy, and Spain. Amid a ferment of monastic experimentation numerous kinds of holy men appeared. Some of these exerted considerable influence through the simplicity of their lives and the earthy good sense of their counsel, such as St Symeon the Stylite, who remained for thirty-seven years on a pillar near Damascus. In general the emphasis shifted towards the moderate, disciplined regime advocated by the scholar St Basil of Cappadocia, whose precepts came to provide the standard pattern for eastern monasticism.

Although monasticism was rapidly adopted in the west, it underwent a number of changes in the process. It became a fashionable aristocratic movement as senators set up monasteries in their city palaces and on their estates. Some bishops established monasteries for their cathedral clergy, and the movement came to be promoted by the episcopate as an ideal to counter worldliness in the Church. Although a few figures such as the former soldier, St Martin of Tours, broadened its impact through missionary work, many of the Gallic monastic centres in the Jura mountains and on the Riviera left little lasting mark once their original charismatic founders died, although the austere Gallic ideal bore remarkable fruit when it became the basis of ecclesiastical organization in Ireland and Celtic Britain. The search for a formula which would combine order and stability with spiritual fervour continued, and the writings and examples of figures such as John Cassian were utilized in the constructive and imaginative Rule devised by St Benedict of Nursia. In the long term Benedict's blueprint for a tightly knit community following an orderly routine of prayer, work, and study became the norm throughout the Latin west, but in the short term its impact was limited. Benedict's foundation of Monte Cassino was sacked by the Lombards around 577, and although the saint's renown was spread by a life written by Pope Gregory the Great, there is no evidence that his Rule was followed in Rome. Gregory, himself a monk, greatly extended the role of monks by appointing them to key posts in the papal administration and assigning them important tasks such as the mission to England led by Augustine, a monk from his own monastery.

Throughout western Europe the Church came to rely increasingly on monks, since the collapse of Roman urban society left the secular clergy morally and materially ill-equipped for the immense tasks of conversion and reform which confronted it. The same developments weakened the traditional aristocratic monasticism, of which Cassiodorus' scholarly house at Vivarium is a late but distinguished example, and the main momentum was furnished by the simple, aggressive monasticism of the Irish. In Lombard Italy monastic development was at first held back by the Lombards' view of the Catholic Church as a politically suspect 'fifth column', but it took off in the eighth century with the endowment of great Benedictine monasteries such as Farfa, Monte Amiata, Nonantola, and Monte Cassino by kings and dukes, all of which became important cultural and economic centres.

In the east monasticism remained closer to the original Egyptian prototype, as a movement of lay devotion whose holy men attracted popular support in the countryside. Certain developments analogous to those in the west did, however, take place by the sixth century: urban monasteries were established, imperial and conciliar legislation sought to impose greater order and uniformity, and lavish patronage produced rich foundations such as the massive monastery of St Catherine's founded by Justinian on Mount Sinai. The simplicity and grass-roots popularity of Byzantine monasticism enabled it to survive the Arab invasions with its position strengthened, especially since episcopal organization was weakened by the decline of the cities. As spokesmen for popular piety, the monks soon found themselves in the forefront of resistance to the Isaurians' policy of iconoclasm. Their staunch defence of icons led to savage persecution, but the movement emerged from the final condemnation of iconoclasm in 843 with its prestige greater than ever. A dramatic increase took place in the endowment of monasteries, particularly the newly popular *lavra* communities of hermit cells, and in the tenth century the state imposed restrictions out of alarm at the abuses caused by wealth and the loss of manpower and tax revenue to the empire. Two significant developments by around 900 were a new emphasis on learning and copying, best exemplified by the monastery of Studium in Constantinople, and an increase in monastic influence in the 'official' Church; from the ninth century monastic patriarchs became increasingly common and monks provided the backbone of the 'Zealot' party in the Church which resolutely opposed imperial interference in matters of doctrine and discipline.

By the late ninth century the Church's role was essentially the one which it was to play in east and west for centuries. In the west the Church's wealth had grown to the extent that it has been estimated that a third of the land in Italy was in ecclesiastical hands. Lay patronage also posed dangers, as aristocrats usurped church lands and established family control over bishoprics and monasteries. Nevertheless, the Church had scored notable successes in establishing a Christian view of kingship, in setting up enduring centres of education and learning, in moving towards standardization of usages and, most important of all, in promoting itself as a distinct élite corporation whose institutional and sacramental structure was intended to lead man to salvation.

In the east the Church greatly increased its prestige by its victory over iconoclasm and its missions to the Balkans, but its influence on political, economic, and cultural life remained limited. Although the average Byzantine was devoutly religious, the division between laity and clergy was weaker and the emperor's God-given role remained unchallenged. Individual redemption was seen as possible through man's direct communication with God, expressed for example in mysticism, and not as the exclusive concern of an ecclesiastical monopoly.

Such differences in outlook contributed to the increased tension which developed between east and west from the ninth century. Among the more immediate factors which sparked off periods of schism were Roman claims to universal primacy, rival claims to jurisdiction over the newly converted areas of eastern Europe, disagreements over ritual practices and the westerners' addition of the *filioque* clause to the creed, and misunderstandings between individuals. At times the conflicts were patched up, often because of the papacy's need for Byzantine political support, but the bringing under the spotlight of differences in doctrine and discipline created an atmosphere of polemical intolerance which was to lead to the final schism of 1054.

Christianity also played its part in one of the most fundamental changes of the early Middle Ages, the replacement of the classical ideal of rationalist self-sufficiency and self-confidence by a conceptual world which emphasized the individual's helplessness in the face of supernatural forces outside his control. In his *Confessions* St Augustine portrayed his friend Alypius as a personification of the ancient ideal and then described how he succumbed to base feelings of bloodlust after visiting a gladiatorial contest; this 'reverse conversion' was presented as a lesson in the need for humility and divine grace. In part the change reflected a movement already under way in the Late Roman period as relatively scientific notions gave way to a more popular preoccupation with the other-worldly and the superstitious; a historian with such a thoroughly classical style as Procopius could seriously believe that Justinian and Theodora were demons. Classical ideas of the physical universe such as those of Ptolemy continued to be known, but lacked the wide appeal of Christian theories which were at once literal and allegorical. In the sixth century an Alexandrian merchant called Cosmas Indicopleustes ('sailor to India') wrote his *Christian Topography* in which he described the world as modelled on the Tabernacle of Moses with the earth forming its base and the heavenly kingdom enclosed in the vaulted top.

According to the early medieval world-picture mankind was an instrument of divine providence, with the nations of the world divided among the sons of Ham, Shem, and Japheth. The successes of 'gentiles', whether Muslims or German barbarians, were explained away as punishment for the sinfulness of Christians. History was seen as the universal unfolding of God's purpose with human actions of minor importance in comparison with the watershed of Christ's incarnation and the ultimate goal of the Last Judgement.

Around 250 St Cyprian had written, 'The Day of Judgement is at hand'. Early medieval man remained preoccupied with the impending end of the world. Views of the imminence of the Second Coming were based on biblical prophecies, and could not fail to be strengthened by the deepening crises of the sixth and seventh centuries. Gregory the Great saw the Lombards as presaging the end of the world and when the Caliph 'Umar entered Jerusalem in 638 the patriarch claimed that the abomination of desolation had come to the holy place, as predicted by the prophet Daniel. Although such threats came and went, eschatological notions persisted. Even when Byzantium was at its apogee in the tenth century the end of the world was widely anticipated. Such deep-seated pessimism regarding the prospects for the earthly world could only act as a brake on development, and it is significant that this negative apocalypticism did not extend to millenarianism, with its prediction of a thousand years of peace and plenty, as happened later in the Middle Ages. A hierarchical system of social relations, with each man allotted his place, was the God-given norm, and obedience to authority was a duty imposed by the Bible.

The ecclesiastical writers, who were the main opinion-formers and our only source for contemporary values, regarded the material world with repugnance and upheld an ideal of monastic self-denial. Biblical and patristic texts were employed to justify a view of women as a source of temptation and conflict, thus reinforcing the anti-feminism deeply entrenched in both Roman and Germanic society. The ninth-century historian Agnellus denounced clerical marriage on the grounds that wives became quarrelsome and domineering and resembled 'Jezebel in their falseness and Delilah in their disloyalty'. In practice it was only a few strong-minded noblewomen, queens, and abbesses, who could exert real power, although women enjoyed greater personal and property rights in Roman societies than among the Germans, who regarded them as legally subject to their menfolk from birth to the grave. More beneficial was the Church's impact on family law, as concubinage and divorce were discouraged and marriage elevated into a more formal institution.

Like all traditional societies, the early medieval world placed great emphasis on family solidarity. In societies which had undergone Germanic influence such as Lombard Italy, kin ties extended to quite remote relatives because of practical need for support in war, judicial cases (including feud), and economic activity. As society became more stable and complex new ties such as lordship emerged and the emphasis shifted to the nuclear family and the household, which were always the basic cell of life in the highly individualistic society of Byzantium.

Materialistic and hedonistic behaviour was completely at odds with prevailing Christian values, but does emerge in our sources. Kings and emperors such as Leo VI kept mistresses in spite of ecclesiastical strictures, monks such as the historian Paul the Deacon could delight in traditional tales of the prowess of their lay ancestors, and many Christian writers displayed a prurient interest in cases of debauchery and prostitution. Most striking of all is a ubiquitous fascination with treasure and riches, a preoccupation understandable in a world still dominated by poverty and famine.

Learning, Literature, and Art

Throughout the early Middle Ages in both east and west scholars and writers set themselves the aim of emulating the literary canons and educational norms inherited from antiquity. To see the cultural history of this period in terms of the fragile survival of a classical tradition is in some ways misleading as it overlooks its limited but significant original achievements, not to mention an immense oral tradition now virtually lost to us, but does reflect the priorities of early medieval intellectuals.

The start of our period was marked by an astonishing breadth and vitality in cultural life. Most parts of the Mediterranean retained a degree of stability and prosperity and the senatorial aristocracy continued to cultivate the ideal of *otium* (leisure) involving the composition and copying of traditional secular literature. At the same time the Christianization of the empire produced new genres such as theology, hagiography, and ecclesiastical history. The longest-lasting achievement was the moving dialogue of the liturgy, which was gradually assuming its rich medieval form in both east and west. In the fourth century controversy had raged over the Church's policy towards classical learning, but with time the moderate view proposed by St Augustine prevailed that 'pagan' learning should be tolerated as long as it was kept subordinate to scripture and put to good Christian use. The issue was less important in the east, which had undergone a more thorough Christianization earlier. When Justinian closed down the Platonic Academy of Athens in 529 he did so not to eliminate a threat but to advance his ideal of a uniform Christian community in which a handful of pagan intellectuals had no place. The Neoplatonic notions which dominated Late Roman philosophy had already been absorbed into Christian thought; for example, sixth-century writings which go under the name of the Pseudo-Dionysius depicted the universe as consisting of a hierarchy of beings emanating from God and exerted extensive influence in both east and west. In education the standard curriculum of antiquity was systematized in a treatise by Martianus Capella and then transmitted to the medieval west as the doctrine of the seven liberal arts by Cassiodorus.

The west experienced set-backs as well as advances in the fifth century. The letters and poetry of Sidonius Apollinaris convey an impression of ostrich-like rejection of an unconvivial world through absorption in the traditional pleasures of his class and cultivation of an over-elaborate literary style. Sidonius ended his days as a bishop, and by the sixth century literary and educational activity in Gaul was confined to a few senatorial prelates and a handful of monasteries. In Italy civilian society remained more durable for a time, but cultural activity became increasingly narrowly based and derivative. The important philosophical and scientific treatises of Boethius were less typical of the age than the priest Arator's metrical version of the Acts of the Apostles or the pompous letters of the bureaucrat Cassiodorus. The fragility of literary culture in Italy was shown by its almost complete disappearance after the Gothic War.

In the east the break came later. The middle and late sixth century saw the continued production of histories and other works along classical lines and the existence of a large body of imperial mandarins whose position depended on their educational accomplishments. Literary production also extended down the social scale through a proliferation of more popular historical and devotional works such as the chronicle of

Malalas, with its emphasis on earthquakes and other portents, and the moving Akathistos Hymn dedicated to the Virgin. The range and quality of literary production tailed off sharply with the invasions of the late sixth and seventh centuries. In Italy the system of secular education and literary patronage collapsed, and few works survive apart from the varied output of Gregory the Great. As a former urban prefect Gregory was capable of writing in a classical rhetorical style, but more suited to the times were his theological and exegetical works, which helped to popularize Augustinian doctrines, and his hagiographical *Dialogues*, in which the saints and martyrs of Italy were presented as simple men of God in a direct 'rustic' style intended to appeal to uncultivated audiences. Benedictine monasticism, which did so much to maintain and revive cultural activity in northern Europe, had curiously little impact on Italy until the eighth century. At least as important was the role of Italo-Greek monks who promoted a knowledge of Greek in Rome and southern Italy. In general cultural life seems to have been maintained in more mundane, and unfortunately obscure, circles. The persistence of some schools is suggested by the high level of functional literacy among laymen and by the numbers of notaries and other legal experts. Clearly important were the cathedral chapters committed to the traditions of their cities and sees. It was there that most surviving works were produced and a number of prominent scholars arose. By the ninth century Italy conveys an impression of a gradual recovery, with active cultural centres in northern episcopal cities such as Milan and Verona and a flourishing intellectual atmosphere in the south.

The brightest spot on the cultural map of the Christian west was Spain. Its Church had earlier benefited from an influx of monks and scholars from Africa, and following the kings' conversion to Catholicism their policy of close co-operation with the Church led to an expanded role for bishops as conciliar legislators and ideological guardians of the kingdom. The most active and prolific of these was Isidore of Seville. Foremost in his great corpus of historical, theological, and other writings was the encyclopaedia known as the *Etymologies* whose simple summations of classical learning made it immensely popular throughout the Middle Ages. The work of Isidore and other scholars created a lively and distinctive intellectual tradition which was able to survive centuries of Arab domination and exert a considerable influence throughout Europe.

The most dynamic cultural life was to be found in the areas conquered by the Arabs in the Levant and Spain. The study of Greek science, philosophy, and medicine were maintained at a high level, particularly through the medium of Syriac. Islamic civilization owed its richness and cosmopolitanism to its take-over of Hellenistic and Persian traditions as well as the prosperity and order of Muslim society, and dazzling heights were attained in art and literature at the court of the Abbasids in Baghdad. Islamic culture was not solely derivative, as the period also produced extensive poetry in Arabic, which held a revered status as the language of the Koran.

The beleaguered empire of Byzantium had a much rougher ride. Even so secular education continued on a scale unknown in the west, since it remained the key to employment in the bureaucracy, and classical Greek texts continued to be studied and copied. On the other hand, there was a drastic decline in the literary public in the seventh and eighth centuries and also in literary production, particularly in many of the secular genres favoured in the ancient world. Despite the gradual introduction of a cheaper writing material (paper instead of parchment) and of a more compact 'miniscule' script, books remained scarce and beyond the reach of all but the richest readers; a manuscript of 400 leaves could cost half the annual salary of a high-ranking civil servant. Two developments in particular transformed the intellectual life of Byzantium. One was the collapse of cultural life in the provinces and its concentration on Constantinople which became a magnet for all aspiring intellectuals. The other development was the greater involvement of the Church in education, reflected for example in the role of the Studite monastery in Constantinople, although the hypothesis of a 'patriarchal academy' is now rejected. Representative of the new integration of secular and ecclesiastical cultural concerns were the two most eminent figures of the intellectual recovery of the ninth century: Leo the Philosopher, who wrote extensively on science and mathematics and constructed an optical telegraph linking the capital with the eastern frontier, was archbishop of Thessalonica before becoming head of the philosophy school in Constantinople, and the great classical scholar Photius was a civil servant before becoming patriarch of Constantinople.

Intellectual developments therefore followed a parallel course in the Latin west and the Greek east. In both areas the audience for scholarship contracted sharply, and literary production suffered a crisis between the late sixth and early eighth centuries. An essential framework of schools and texts survived, however, and a secular element remained much more prominent than in the monastic world of northern Europe.

Art, like literature, attempted to cling to classical models, but in practice suffered a decline in quality and quantity. Nevertheless, its apparent naïvety frequently conceals a complexity of symbolical meaning, and the retreat from naturalism exerts a familiar appeal to us today. Changes were already under way in the Late Roman period both in purpose and style. Because of economic difficulties old buildings were despoiled for their capitals and other materials and an increase in state munificence at the expense of individual and personal patronage produced a monumental art which sought to impress subjects with the greatness of the ruler. The spread of Christianity encouraged the production of elaborate vestments and vessels for liturgical use and the building of lavish churches. In an increasingly hierarchical society, the individual realism of classical antiquity gave way to stereotyped full-face depictions with an idealized emphasis on the figure's dignity and rank, as in the ivory diptychs commissioned as high-class calling-cards by senators. At the same time other types of art appealed to a wider audience: frescos, mosaics, and icons proliferated as a means of conveying the Christian message to all levels of believer, and an elaborate Christian iconography was worked out by around 500.

Art also reached new heights in the circles of the rich new Germanic masters of the west. Graves and treasure hoards have revealed sumptuous examples of the jewellery, weapons, and ornaments essential to the life-style of a warrior aristocracy. In southern Europe stylized human and animal representations derived from the classical repertory figure more prominently than the abstract and geometric designs characteristic of the barbarian north, and many lavish objects were the work of Roman craftsmen.

The relatively prosperous and secure east saw a profusion of styles in the fifth and sixth centuries. In the most common 'provincial' form degraded classicism went hand in hand with an emphasis on ornamentation and ostentation. More distinctive and original was the metropolitan art of Justinian's time, reflected for example in the elaborate capitals of St Polyeuctus and the domed prestige buildings of St Sophia and Sts Sergius and Bacchus. At the same time naturalistic traditions of a high standard persisted as exemplified by the pavement mosaics of the imperial palace of Constantinople and the classicizing scenes of the David plates.

In the west artistic production was plunged into crisis by the economic and political dislocation of the sixth century. In a great centre such as Ravenna the building of lavish and cosmopolitan churches ceases after Justinian's reign and the jewellery and sculpture production which continued became poor and provincial. The churches that were built were mostly small and crude. Even in Rome, where creative influences from the east were strongest and the popes strove to maintain a programme of patronage befitting a centre of pilgrimage and ecclesiastical administration, most churches of the period were converted secular buildings such as Sant' Adriano (the old senate chamber), Santa Maria Antiqua (formerly a guard house), and Santa Maria Rotonda (the pagan temple of the Pantheon).

In the east the disruption came later but was even more severe, since the devastating effects of invasions were followed by the hostility of the iconoclasts to depictions of Christ and the saints. The effects of iconoclast persecution were felt much more strongly in Constantinople and Anatolia than in the western provinces of the empire, and even in the capital some art of an anodyne secular character has survived. Only after the final defeat of iconoclasm in 843 was the large-scale production of religious art resumed. In the second half of the ninth century a lavish programme of redecorating churches such as St Sophia with mosaics was undertaken, which was soon followed by an upsurge in the production of manuscripts and such objects as ivories along classical lines. With the onset of this Macedonian Renaissance Byzantine art had finally developed a set of decorative schemes, artistic formulae, and iconographic theories which had their roots in Late Roman art and which were to remain the corner-stone of an increasingly static Byzantine art.

Signs of recovery also appeared in the western Mediterranean. Eastern influences served as a catalyst in such areas as Rome, where the work of Greek craftsmen was visible in the art commissioned by Pope John VII (705–7). A particularly impressive example of oriental influence occurs in the frescos of Santa Maria 'Outside the Walls' at Castelseprio north of Milan; their dating is uncertain, but in the view of many scholars the iconography of certain scenes suggests that they were painted by eastern artists perhaps sent to the Lombard kingdom after its conversion to Catholicism.

More often the dominant influences were home-grown, stemming from enduring local traditions visible, for example, in the continued production of subantique sarcophagi in northern Italy and southern Gaul and the survival of commonplace Roman building techniques. In the Lombard kingdoms the close artistic links with the Byzantine territories found expression in the considerable activity under kings from Liutprand onwards. Masterpieces of this period include the monumental church of San Salvatore in Brescia and the 'tempietto' of Santa Maria in Valle in Cividale with its exquisite stucco figures. The foundation of great monasteries such as Monte Cassino and Nonantola served as a further stimulus to the patronage of art, and especially manuscripts. The persistence of Roman traditions and the number of rich monastic and episcopal patrons restricted the impact of the impulses associated with the Carolingian Renaissance in Italy, although attractive frescos survive in remote Carolingian churches of the Tyrol, such as St Proculus in Naturns. In the case of Rome Carolingian economic and political support helped give rise to an extensive programme of patronage undertaken by the popes in the early ninth century, which found its finest expression in the chapel of San Zeno in the basilica of San Prassede. The native element in the artistic revival in Italy is evident in the first examples of 'proto-Romanesque' building, but Byzantine influences remained strong; the first church of St Mark's, built in Venice around 830, was modelled on the Holy Apostles in Constantinople.

In other areas of the western Mediterranean artistic development suffered greater vicissitudes. In Spain very little art survives from the Visigothic period apart from personal jewellery and such items as the magnificent votive crown of King Recceswinth found in a treasure hoard at Guarrazar near Toledo in 1859. More evidence of the persistence of Roman traditions comes from the kingdom of León, where a number of fine proto-Romanesque churches were built in the ninth century such as San Julián de los Prados near Oviedo and Santa Maria at Naranco. Elsewhere in northern Spain churches were built in the 'mozarabic' style with some use of oriental elements by refugees from Islamic persecution.

For all these glimmerings of promise the art of Christian Spain remained crude and provincial in comparison with the brilliant art and crafts produced in the Ummayad emirate to the south. Its greatest achievement, the Great Mosque at Cordoba, was begun in 785 and could accommodate 5,500 worshippers. In the early medieval Mediterranean the most sumptuous art was that produced in the prosperous lands of the Islamic world. Ironically it was also in the lands first conquered by the Arabs that late antique traditions survived most fully, as is shown by buildings such as the Great Mosque in Damascus, but art soon took a new non-naturalistic direction in conformity with the Koran's prohibition of images.

The Mediterranean on the Eve of a New Age

In some respects the Mediterranean area had by 900 reached the nadir of a decline under way since the Late Roman period. The sea had ceased to be the unifying channel of a vast centralized empire and had become a barrier dividing three largely hostile worlds of Byzantium, Islam, and the west. In the west, the political, economic, and cultural centre of gravity had shifted to the north, as the latter developed new lands and markets while the south suffered ecological and climatic decline.

There is also a more positive side to the picture. By 900 a new political map had emerged which was to remain unchanged in its essentials until 1453, consisting of an increasingly fragmented commonwealth of Islam, the new Rome which we call Byzantium, and the kingdoms of the west. The Islamic world had lost its early wave of expansionist zeal and was fragmenting into smaller states, many of which continued to provide a fertile environment for economic and cultural life. In the Byzantine Empire of the Macedonian emperors renewed stability led to economic prosperity, a *Reconquista* was under way in the Balkans and the east, and an artistic and cultural renaissance reflected a self-confident reassertion of Byzantium's Roman and Hellenistic traditions. As the empire stood on the threshold of its greatest period, however, forces were at work which were to undermine its centralized structure and lead to the 'feudal' dominance of great landowners.

For all its underdevelopment the west was evincing the first signs of a vitality which was later to re-establish the Mediterranean south as the most dynamic area of Europe and a clearing-house for fruitful contacts with the east and south. The ideal of a Christian empire established by the Carolingians maintained its hold on men's minds and had as its corner-stone an increasingly distinctive western Christianity subject to the increasingly powerful authority of the Pope. The south shared in the general economic and demographic recovery, and drew some benefits from its closer links with the resurgent north. It was cushioned from the barbarian attacks which had been its lot earlier, it developed a valuable role as a trading intermediary, and it attracted pilgrims to its shrines, such as Rome and Compostela.

While southern France remained in a state of disorder and underdevelopment, in Christian Spain favourable conditions for growth and social mobility were being produced by an influx of refugees and adventurers and by a flow of cash and booty from raids of Muslim territory. It was Italy, however, that stood poised for the most dramatic take-off. Demographic recovery was accompanied by the more efficient division and administration of estates, the leasing out of church patrimonies to entrepreneurs and the investment in land of capital accumulated by churches and townspeople. As a land market developed and rents were paid increasingly in cash, increased demand and monetary circulation stimulated commerce and urban development. Milan had already grown to the full extent of its walls, and the vitality and collective awareness of townspeople can be glimpsed in episodes such as an uprising of Cremona merchants against their bishop in 924.

Much of the history of the Mediterranean area in the early Middle Ages is perforce 'subterranean' history. The most visible developments are the negative ones of political disintegration and physical upheaval. A great deal of the classical inheritance was preserved, such as Roman law and administrative traditions in Byzantium, ancient science and medicine in the Muslim world, and an enduring attachment to urban life in Italy. The early Middle Ages were a period of creative achievement as well as fragile survival and agonizing transformation; in the three spheres of the Mediterranean religious structures and beliefs acquired their developed form and the decentralization brought about by weak central authority helped to promote local trade and political and cultural activity, especially in Italy and the Islamic world. With the rigidities of ancient society broken down, new durable institutions, more adaptable social groups, and new dynamic communities had emerged to meet the challenges of better times.

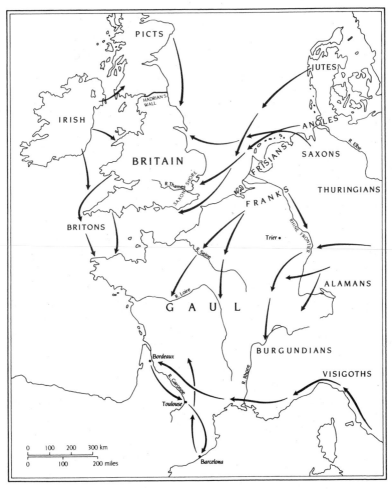

PICTS

IUTES

ANGLES

IRISH

SAXONS

HADRIAN'S
WALL

R. Elbe

BRITAIN

THURINGIANS

R. Thames
SAXON SHORE

FRISIANS

FRANKS

RHINE FRONTIER

Trier •

BRITONS

R. Seine

R. Loire

ALAMANS

G A U L

BURGUNDIANS

Bordeaux

R. Garonne

R. Rhone

VISIGOTHS

Toulouse

0   100   200   300 km

0   100   200 miles

Barcelona

MOVEMENTS OF PEOPLES IN THE FIFTH CENTURY

2

The Northern World in the Dark Ages

400–900

EDWARD JAMES

FOR Romans, or at least for their rulers and the aristocratic élite who provide us with the bulk of our written sources, northern Europe was at the fringes of civilization or beyond it, and barely worth attention. Those parts of it in the Roman Empire—central and southern Britain, and northern Gaul— were much less heavily Romanized than the provinces around the western Mediterranean. It is significant that the earliest surviving Latin writings from those provinces are from the very end of the Roman Empire, and from writers who may have learnt their Latin in Christian rather than secular schools. The only time that Britain and northern Gaul impressed themselves upon the consciousness of Roman authorities was when they produced usurpers or were attacked by still less civilized peoples from beyond the frontiers: the Franks, the Alamans, the Saxons, the Picts, or the cannibal Atecotti. The northern provinces were merely buffer states to help protect the empire from the barbarians beyond.

The five hundred years with which this chapter is concerned saw a tremendous change in the role of the north in the history of Europe as a whole. By the eighth and ninth centuries the north was the political centre of Europe, and could claim to be its intellectual leader as well. The Channel and North Sea ports were giving the area an economic vigour it had never had in Roman times. The coronation in 800 of a Frank, Charlemagne, as the first northern emperor, has often been seen, and rightly, as symbolic of this shift of balance from south to north which is one of the most important developments of the early Middle Ages. Another, still more important for the historian, is that in this period the north finds its own voice. In the Roman period we know about it only through the writings of Romans and Greeks; now, thanks to the spread of Christianity, some northerners themselves begin to write, in Latin, Germanic, or Celtic languages. The north (except for Scandinavia and the lands east of the Elbe) emerges into the light of history for the first time.

The Migrations

The end of the western Roman Empire was marked by movements of peoples. Whether these movements caused the end of the Roman Empire, or merely took advantage of it, is still a matter for debate among historians, as is the terminology; are these movements to be called 'the migrations' (the *Völkerwanderungen*) or 'the invasions'? As far as northern Europe is concerned the former term is probably more appropriate. Germanic-speaking and Celtic-speaking peoples moved into areas from which, in most cases, Roman armies had already withdrawn, and sometimes they did so with Roman encouragement. And it is likely that some of these migrations were on a much larger scale and had much greater cultural impact than the Germanic invasions of southern Europe. Large areas of the north-western Roman Empire became Germanic in language and culture: most notably England, but also a swathe of territory to the west of the Rhine and the south of the Danube, in modern Belgium, Germany, Switzerland, and Austria. The modern map of Europe owes some of its most obvious names to the incoming peoples of the fifth and sixth centuries: England (with county names such as Sussex or Essex), Scotland, France, Brittany, Alsace, Bavaria. And, of course, the political vacuum left by movements of peoples into the Roman Empire also allowed for migration and invasion of peoples in territories further to the east, in Germany, Scandinavia, and the Slav lands. It was not until the tenth century that the linguistic and ethnic map of northern Europe settled down and began to take its modern shape.

By its very nature, migration in a largely pre-literate age is very difficult for the historian to follow. The sources of the time tend to mention leaders, but give no reliable information about followers, and at a time when communications were difficult and rumour rife even the role played by leaders may be inaccurately reported. Men of whom we know reliably no more than the name—Arthur is the best example—may have been highly important political figures having influence over large areas, or else ephemeral leaders of purely local significance. Archaeologists have tried to map the movement of ordinary people, by looking at the thousands of cemeteries which have survived from this period. But it is an uncertain task. Skeletons of immigrants cannot be distinguished from those among whom they settled, and the jewellery and other objects buried with the dead which might be categorized as 'Saxon' or 'Frankish' are as much a response to fashion or product availability as evidence of the ethnic identity of the corpse. Archaeology confirms, however, that migration took place. Those who came from north Germany to East Anglia, for instance, buried the ashes of their dead in pots made and decorated precisely as they had been in their homeland. And archaeology may suggest reasons for migration too. It seems that the land level in the coastal areas of north Germany was sinking in the fifth and sixth centuries, causing frequent or permanent flooding. Some inhabitants responded by building their settlements on mounds, or *terpen*; others, quite clearly, by making the crossing to Britain.

In 400 the Rhine, patrolled by ships such as those found recently at Mainz, was still a major dividing line between Roman and barbarian. Certainly some Franks had been ceded land to the west of the mouths of the Rhine, while other Germans captured in the fighting, including Franks, were settled in small groups throughout northern Gaul to serve as recruiting pools for the Roman army. The Franks in particular were just as often allies as enemies: in the late fourth century a number of them rose to be commanders-in-chief of the Roman army and even consuls. But the defensive system in Gaul, set up after the serious inroads made by the Germans in the third century, still functioned well and most of Gaul, governed still from Trier, remained secure from attack. Even in Britain the Roman army and navy successfully repelled a number of attacks by Scotti (as Romans called the Irish), by Britons and Picts from north of Hadrian's Wall, and by sea-borne Germans. Each attack brought fresh refortification in its wake; in 399, Stilicho, the German general who commanded the Roman armies in the west, himself came to Britain to supervise operations.

The picture changed dramatically in a very few years. Various Germanic peoples, notably the Vandals, Burgundians, and Sueves, crossed the Rhine into Gaul in the winter of 406–7, possibly fleeing the Huns, Asiatic nomads who were extending their domination over much of the area north of the Danube at this time. A general called Constantine, appointed emperor by the Roman troops in Britain (just as Constantine the Great had been a century earlier), brought most of his army across the Channel to deal with the barbarians in Gaul. When Saxons attacked Britain in 408 there were hardly any Roman soldiers left to defend it. The Emperor Honorius was forced to concede British civilians the right to take up arms for self-defence, no doubt thinking that Roman authority could be reasserted once the crisis had passed, as such crises always had done before. This crisis, however, was different; continuing political problems on the Continent made it impossible for the empire to concern itself again with Britain. There begins a period of nearly two centuries when historians can know very little about what was happening north of the Channel. The few sources are all ambiguous, difficult to interpret, and infuriatingly allusive. And the archaeological evidence, which exists in relative abundance, can only with great difficulty and caution be used to illustrate historical events. But certain facts, and many speculations, emerge. Roman Britain, before and after

410, was attacked from three sides: by the Picts from the north, by the Irish from the west, and by various Germanic peoples from the east and south. The attacks of the Picts seem to have ceased in the fifth century; they do not seem to have made any settlements south of Hadrian's Wall. The Irish founded settlements in western Wales, and the kingdom which they founded in south-west Scotland, Dalriada, remained an important political force for several centuries. And the Germanic peoples, the Angles and Saxons from north-west Germany, the Jutes from Denmark, the Frisians from the Low Countries, gained political control over south-eastern Britain, and gradually moved their sphere of political, cultural and linguistic influence further westwards, until, by the tenth century, they had gained the whole of modern England.

The Saxons, a term which for Roman writers meant all the north Germans who were involved in the settlement of Britain, played a similar role to that played by the Vikings four centuries later. They raided the coasts of Gaul and Britain, and founded settlements, perhaps initially no more than pirate bases, by the mouths of the Garonne and the Loire, and near Bayeux, as well as in Britain. The tradition in Britain was that the first Saxons—Hengist and Horsa—had been invited in as mercenaries by a British leader, and had then rebelled and set up their own kingdom in eastern Britain. This is a simplified version of what happened in the case of several German peoples on the Continent, and it is not impossible that it happened in Britain. But the very fact of the sea barrier made the effects of the migration to Britain different from other migrations. Any organized crossing was out of the question. Migration must have been in small groups, spread out over several generations. In most areas there was no smooth transition of political power and institutions from Romans to Germans as so often happened on the Continent. Excavations at the Bernician palace of Yeavering in Northumberland suggest that the incoming Angles took over a pre-existing British political centre and used it as their own. The Anglian kings in Bernicia (Northumberland and Durham) and Deira (Yorkshire)—both words of Celtic origin—must have ruled kingdoms whose populations were largely British, and some British or Roman traditions may have survived. But further south, where the bulk of the Anglo-Saxon settlement took place, it is unlikely that much remained of the Roman way of life. Towns disappeared (if they had not already done so earlier, in the third or fourth centuries), and so did the new religion of the Roman Empire, Christianity.

The fate of the descendants of the Roman civilians of Britain was varied. Many were enslaved or at least ruled by the barbarian newcomers. Others lived in various independent kingdoms in the west; these the Anglo-Saxons called 'Welsh', their word for 'foreigners'. But other Britons took part in a migration of their own, to what subsequently became known as Brittany. Whether the Britons were invited by the Roman authorities to keep order in that area, which had revolted against the Romans at least twice in the fifth century, whether they were invited by the rebels, or whether they simply came as refugees, it cannot now be said. But the establishment of Brittany (or Lesser Britain, as it came to be known in the Middle Ages, distinguishing it from Great Britain) ensured that throughout most of the Middle Ages this Celtic-speaking province pursued a fiercely independent policy. Even in those periods of nominal Frankish rule, the Bretons kept their own rulers, whom the Franks called counts but whom the Bretons themselves no doubt regarded as their kings.

The first two decades of the fifth century were just as chaotic on the Continent as in Britain. After the 'Great Invasion' of 406–7, the Rhine frontier collapsed, and the capital of the Gallic provinces moved to the safety of Arles. The Vandals and Sueves were deflected into Spain, with the help of the usurper Constantine and his British troops. But the Burgundians remained, setting up a kingdom on the middle Rhine, while the lower Rhine seems to have been largely abandoned to the various peoples known collectively as the Franks. The political instability at this time seems to have caused many Roman aristocrats to desert northern Gaul for more secure homes in the south. The Roman army was no longer able to protect the north; indeed, the Roman army in Gaul was, by the 430s or

440s, a very motley collection of Roman soldiers, German mercenaries, and Germanic federate troops. The Roman general Aëtius, who dominated military affairs in Gaul in those years, himself depended heavily on Hunnic troops; he used those Huns to destroy the Burgundian kingdom of the Rhine, and to re-establish the Burgundians in the area between Lyons and Geneva ('Burgundy') under a treaty which pledged Burgundian support for the Roman Empire. When Aëtius put together an alliance to defeat the invasion of Attila's Huns in 451 it was Visigothic, Burgundian, and Frankish troops who made up the bulk of the 'Roman' army. With the assassination of Aëtius by Valentinian III in 454 (and the subsequent assassination of Valentinian by Aëtius's loyal followers in 455) there was to be no clear Roman leadership in northern Gaul again.

A new direction in northern Gaul came with the emergence of Childeric as king of one group of Franks. Although our information about him is scanty, it seems that he collaborated with the Romans—or with one group of Romans—against the Visigoths and the Saxons of the Loire, that (although a pagan) he co-operated with the Gallic Church, and that he laid the foundations of the kingdom which his descendants were to rule for the following three centuries. In the confused years which followed the death of the last generally accepted western emperor in 455, and still more after the deposition of the last resident western emperor in 476, Childeric must have seemed a natural ruler to many in northern Gaul. He died in 481/2 and was buried at Tournai, in a grave which reveals some aspects of his power: several hundred gold coins minted in Constantinople, sent perhaps as a subsidy, and a gold brooch like those worn by Roman generals.

Childeric was succeeded by his son Clovis, usually seen as the real founder of Frankish power in Gaul. The details of his reign, recorded for us by Bishop Gregory of Tours some seventy years after Clovis's death, are in some dispute, but his achievements are plain. He united the Romans of north Gaul under his rule, by force of arms and by the expedient of converting to their own religion, Catholic Christianity. He united

THE MEROVINGIANS

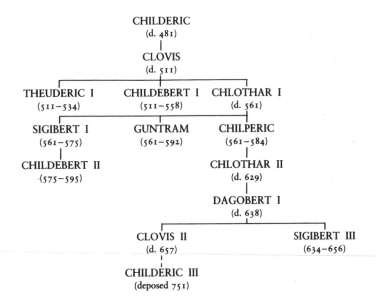

the Franks under his own rule, partly at least by having all rival kings assassinated. And both Romans and Franks must have been impressed by the success with which he led his armies against other Germans: he conquered the Thuringians to the east, and the Alamans, who were moving from their homes in south-west Germany into what is now Alsace and northern Switzerland; and in 507 Clovis led his followers south across the Loire to destroy the Visigothic kingdom of Alaric II. When he died in 511 the kingdom was ruled jointly by his four sons, and it was they who destroyed the Burgundian kingdom and who, by offering military aid to the Ostrogoths in exchange, annexed Provence to their kingdom. By the middle of the sixth century the Frankish kings descended from Childeric and Clovis, known as the Merovingians, had become by far the most powerful of the barbarian heirs to the Roman Empire. Almost all Gaul was under their direct rule; they had a foothold in Italy and overlordship over the Thuringians, Alamans, and Bavarians in Germany; and the suzerainty they claimed over south-east England may have been more of a reality than most English historians have thought. The dying words of Chlothar I, by 561 the last surviving son of Clovis, were quite understandable: 'Wa! What kind of king is it in heaven, who kills off kings as great as me?'

The Franks succeeded in bringing a new kind of political stability in the sixth century, as heirs to the Romans. But the age of the migrations was not over. The collapse of Hunnic hegemony after the death of Attila in 453, and the movement of peoples into western Europe, allowed other peoples to move south or west. The Bavarians moved into the upper Danube area in the early sixth century. The Avars, a nomadic people from central Asia, came into the middle Danube region (Hungary) in the mid-sixth century (persuading the Lombards to move into Italy); there they set up a powerful kingdom, which raided as far west as Thuringia and as far east as Constantinople, and survived until the campaigns of Charlemagne in the late eighth century. The Bulgars established themselves further east, in the seventh century. And finally, there were the movements of the Slavs themselves, the indigenous peoples of north-east Europe, which are only now being disentangled by the archaeologists. In the sixth century the Slavs were moving south across the Danube frontier into the Balkan provinces of the Roman Empire, and west into Bohemia and Moravia, and into the area between the Vistula and the Elbe which had previously been inhabited by Germans, and threatening the Germanic territories of Thuringia, Saxony, and Denmark.

The Spread of Christianity

In the year 400 most north Europeans worshipped one or more non-Christian gods; by 900 Christianity had reached most of the north-west, and had even begun to spread into Scandinavia and eastern Europe. In 400 the attack on non-Christian worship by means of legislation had only just begun, bishops such as St Martin of Tours had only recently started going into the countryside on the offensive, and Christian institutions such as monasticism were almost unknown. By 900, in Gaul, Germany, Britain, and Ireland, Christianity was enforced by the state, baptism was, in theory, universal, the Church had become important politically and in the economy, and monasticism was the most important spiritual and cultural force in Europe. The slow process of Christianization, which began normally with the conversion of kings and aristocrats, is clearly one of the most important developments of the period. With Christianity other elements of Roman civilization reached the barbarians inside and outside the former Roman Empire: ideas of law and government, the art of writing, and the wealth of Latin and Christian learning and literature. It is possible that it was only with Christianity that Latin, and subsequently French, became the language of the rural population of northern Gaul. We have the paradox that the process of Romanization reached its climax in the west only after the collapse of the Roman Empire.

The barbarians who settled in southern Europe were almost all Christians by the time of their settlement, though they were all Arian heretics. Clovis, king of the Franks, owed some of his political success to the fact that he brought his people to Catholic Christianity, thus making the Franks acceptable to the Gallo-Romans he wished to rule. The Church in Gaul, which continued to be run largely by Gallo-Romans rather than by Franks, was duly grateful, and offered its support to Clovis's dynasty. Gallic churchmen continued their work of conversion of the peasants of northern Gaul, including those Franks who had come into the area, but they seldom concerned themselves with the pagans beyond their own diocese. The Catholic establishment in the Roman Empire had no missionary policy for the pagan barbarians of the north. It was generally believed that God had brought the Roman Empire into being as a receptacle for Christianity, and that those outside it remained outside by the will of God. The more optimistic could believe that the barbarian invasions were part of God's plan for spreading Christianity. Thus, if bishops were sent outside the empire, as

Pope Celestine sent Palladius to Ireland in 431, it was not primarily to convert pagans but rather to act as bishop to Christians already living outside the empire. Indeed, we know the name of one of the Christians in Ireland for whom Palladius might have acted as bishop: a Romano-British boy captured in a slaving raid on the western coasts of Britain, called Patrick. This remarkable person—the first British writer resident in these islands whose writings have survived—was the first to quote the Gospels in support of the mission to all men, and the first to see it as his moral duty to go outside the empire to convert the heathen.

The conversion of the Irish, in which Patrick was one of the first to be involved, was an experiment without any real precedents. No one had tried to introduce a religion organized around towns and dependent upon proclamation of the Word of God, in its original Greek or in Latin translation, into a tribal society which had no towns and which knew neither Greek nor Latin. Where would bishops be based? How would priests be trained? How would the Church fit into a society with strong kinship bonds and different property-owning customs from those of the Roman Empire? These were questions faced by all missionaries in northern Europe in the early Middle Ages, but a number of the solutions were first worked out in Ireland, and some of those solutions were exported by the Irish themselves to Britain and the Continent.

These solutions in the main relate to a new role assigned to monasteries within the missionary church. In the Roman Empire monasteries had been places of retreat from the world; the Church itself was run by the secular clergy, quite separate from the monasteries. In Ireland and in the rest of the barbarian north, monasteries were central institutions: bases for missionary activity, centres for basic education in Latin, for book production, for the training of clergy, and, as Christian lay men and women gave them more and more land, major economic and political centres as well. Bishops frequently resided in monasteries and, in Ireland in particular, were quite overshadowed by the abbots, who were, in earthly rather than spiritual terms, much more important than they.

There were other repercussions of the arrival of the Church into a wholly rural and tribal society. Those who donated land to monasteries were unwilling, and perhaps, according to barbarian land law, often unable, to regard these donations as absolute. In barbarian societies the kin had certain rights in the land which was controlled by the head of the family. Inheritance was according to fairly rigid rules, which differed from people to people, but all of which insisted on family property going to particular relatives, sons, daughters, brothers, uncles, of the deceased. A will, as in Roman law, which left land to the Church or to some individual, by its very nature disinherited the rightful heirs. The Church, which depended for its survival and expansion upon gifts of property, was familiar with Roman legal ideas of property and fought hard to introduce changes in barbarian custom, with the help of kings. In the Frankish kingdom we find Frankish nobles disregarding Frankish law in the sixth century, and making wills in favour of the Church (although, Gregory of Tours lamented, King Chilperic used to tear such wills up). Kings seem to have been able to intervene to change the status of land, or nobles could get round the law by donating the land which the king had given them as a reward for their services, rather than alienating their ancestral land. The charters which recorded the donation of land to monasteries always threatened those who violated such donations with dire penalties; it was probably the legitimate heirs of the donor that the monastery was most worried about, and occasionally they did indeed try to take the land by force. But in Ireland a compromise came into being, which was to be followed elsewhere in northern Europe, whereby the donor's kin were agreed to have certain rights in the monastery. Thus many monasteries became 'family monasteries', where the abbot was drawn from the founder's kin, monastic estates would be leased at good terms to them, hospitality given them, and other favours granted. The kinship system which pervaded society thus invaded the monasteries too, which was obviously a worry for those enthusiasts who saw monasticism as a way of escaping all the ties and temptations of this world. One of these enthusiasts, Columbanus, a nobleman from Leinster, was advised to go on 'minor pilgrimage', to avoid family ties by leaving his province and becoming a monk at Bangor, in Ulster. But even this was not enough for his ascetic spirit: as a greater penance he decided to go on 'major pilgrimage'. In 590, with twelve companions, he left Ireland altogether, to become a perpetual pilgrim.

Columbanus, or Columba the Younger, was one of many Irish clerics who left Ireland for the sake of their souls in the early Middle Ages. He came to Gaul, founded several monasteries in Burgundy, notably Luxeuil, and after some disagreement with the royal family (he persisted in having no more awe for kings than he had at home), he left Gaul, to found another monastery at Bobbio in north Italy. The Church in Gaul was in a well-established position when he arrived, with hundreds of monasteries, particularly in the south, and a well-educated and powerful Gallo-Roman episcopate which kept those monasteries as firmly under control as possible. But Columbanus's asceticism, his determination to keep his own monasteries free from episcopal interference, and the model he presented of large rural monasteries, all seem to have appealed to the Frankish aristocracy. In the half-century after Columbanus' death large numbers of monasteries for both men and women were founded in northern Gaul, many of which drew their inspiration from Luxeuil.

Twenty-five years before Columbanus left northern Ireland, Columba, from a royal family of Ulster, had left in the opposite direction. With his followers he came to the island of Iona, off Mull, and there founded one of the most influential of Irish monasteries. The Anglo-Saxon historian Bede tells us that he even converted the Picts to Christianity. But Bede's contemporary Adomnán, successor of Columba as abbot of Iona, did not go so far. Columba did preach to Bridei, king of the Picts, but apparently not successfully, nor was this the main aim of his arduous journey to the north: he went to Bridei's court in order to plead for the safety of Irish monks who wanted to settle in the Orkneys. There were numerous monastic settlements made in Scotland during Columba's life, many under his patronage, but most of these monks were more interested in their own souls than those of others—as were undoubtedly the Irish monks who settled in the otherwise uninhabited Iceland! But inevitably these monasteries became means by which Christianity could be introduced to those in the vicinity. The conversion of the Picts which Columba began was certainly achieved within a century of Columba's death, but thanks to men such as Donnán of Eigg or Maelrubai of Applecross.

The involvement of Iona was more direct in the history of English Christianity. The first two Christian Anglo-Saxons we know of were monks at Iona during Columba's lifetime. The Anglian Oswald stayed at Iona during his exile, and when he became king of Northumbria in 635 he asked Iona to send him clerics to help him convert his kingdom. Aidan was chosen, and he founded the island monastery of Lindisfarne as the centre for his bishopric of Northumbria. For Bede, writing his history of the English Church less than a century later, and only a few kilometres from Lindisfarne, Aidan was the ideal bishop, pious, humble, forever travelling the diocese and preaching to his flock, and impressing his saintly example upon the kings he had to deal with. Lindisfarne became a training centre for missionaries, and in the mid-seventh century, when Northumbria was the most powerful kingdom in England, these men spread the word to those kingdoms under North-umbrian domination. Even Wilfrid of York, the great champion of Roman rather than Irish customs, began his monastic career at Lindisfarne and shared in its missionary tradition, bringing Christianity to Sussex and starting the mission to the Frisians in the Low Countries.

The conversion of the Anglo-Saxons began in the south of England, not the north. Pope Gregory the Great sent the monk Augustine to Britain to re-establish the Church, clearly thinking that the Roman province of Britain had survived in some re-cognizable form. Augustine was charged to set up metropolitan sees at London and York, with the intention that there should be twenty-four other bishops established in appropriate towns. When Augustine arrived in Kent in 597, with his Frankish interpreters, he found the situation very different from what Gregory had expected. But he carried out his task as best he could, converting King Æthelberht of Kent (who, through his Christian wife Bertha, a Frankish princess, must have known a great deal about Christianity already), and setting up his see in a town in Æthelberht's kingdom, Canterbury: a town, that is, in the sense of being enclosed by Roman walls, though in 597 it was, like other Roman towns in Britain, no more than a collection of ruins inhabited, perhaps, by a few Anglo-Saxon farmers. The final achievement of the Gregorian mission was the founding of an episcopal see in York in 627, and the baptism of Edwin of Northumbria by Paulinus, the last of the missionaries sent by Gregory. But Edwin's successors apostatized, and Paulinus had to flee back to Kent. Iona and Lindisfarne took over from Rome and Canterbury as the driving forces behind the conversion of the English. This caused some problems, notably in the area of church customs. In the mid-seventh century northern Irish clerics (but no longer those from southern Ireland) calculated Easter according to an outmoded system, and wore tonsures which possibly owed more to druidic practice than to Roman precedent. The settlement of the dispute which arose, in Rome's favour, at Whitby in 664 did not end the influence of the Irish Church. English clerics went to Ireland for their education, and brought back books from Irish monasteries. The new connections with Rome, however, made it possible for the English Church to have the best of both worlds. The Northumbrian nobleman Benedict Biscop made four expeditions to Rome, collecting books there and in Gaul for his twin monastic foundation of Jarrow and Monkwearmouth. This monastery had probably the best stocked library in northern Europe; it is not surprising that in the early eighth century it produced northern Europe's greatest teacher and scholar, the Venerable Bede.

By the 680s all the English kingdoms had been nominally converted, and Anglo-Saxon kings were beginning to enforce Christianity by law. The Church had been reorganized under the vigorous rule of the elderly imported Syrian, Theodore of Canterbury, and seemed now secure. The energies of its more idealistic clergy began to turn outwards, and to think of the souls of their Germanic cousins on the Continent. Wihtberht spent two years trying to convert King Radbod and the Frisians; Willibrord followed him, with rather more success, and with the backing of the Frankish ruler Pippin II and the pope he became first bishop of Utrecht. Swithberht went as missionary to the Bructeri, and the two brothers called Hewald, who had been living in Ireland, went to Saxony, there to meet savage deaths as martyrs.

The most successful of the Anglo-Saxon missionaries was Boniface, from Wessex, whose main sphere of activity was in central Germany, in an area where, in the seventh century, the Irishman Killian had met his martyrdom. He went to Rome to receive papal permission for missionary work, worked under Willibrord in Frisia, and, after initial successes in central Germany, was created bishop in 722, and given the title archbishop ten years later. He founded the monastery of Fulda as his base for the conversion of central Germany, and was killed in 754, while still trying to convert the Frisians. He was a reformer and organizer as well as a missionary. He organized the Bavarian and central German churches into sees, presided over a number of reforming councils in the Frankish kingdom, and, as archbishop of Mainz, was able to preside over the unification of the Church in Germany. In all this he was supported by the rulers of the Franks, Charles Martel and his son Pippin III, and Boniface's legacy of a reformed and reorganized Church under the headship of the pope was an essential foundation to the rise to royal power of this Carolingian dynasty.

The conversion of Germany in the early eighth century went hand in hand with the reimposition of Frankish power in those areas. The advantage of the Anglo-Saxon missionaries, apart from the closeness of their language to that of the Frisians or Saxons, was that they could distance themselves from Frankish politics to some extent. But the Franks made no pretence that the conversion of Saxony was not part and parcel of their savage wars of conquest. In the first campaign, in 772, the first blow in the conversion took place: Irminsul, the sacred oak tree of the pagan Saxons, was felled. Baptism came to be regarded as an affirmation of loyalty to the Franks; in 785 Charlemagne decreed that if any of the conquered Saxons refused to be baptized, or insulted Christianity by, for instance, eating meat during Lent, he should suffer the death penalty. A church structure was set up in Saxony, and Christianity was enforced with the help of the Frankish army. The protests of Charlemagne's own close associate, the scholar Alcuin of York, were to no avail; indeed, it is possible that it was another Anglo-Saxon, Boniface's disciple Lull, who urged Charlemagne on.

The horrific 'conversion' of the Saxons marked the last great conquest of Christianity in the period before 900. But beginnings were made elsewhere, both north and east. Anskar, a Frankish monk, was made archbishop of Hamburg to supervise the mission to the north, and founded churches in Denmark and even in Sweden, at Birka, but his mission did not lead to any lasting Christian communities, largely because of the ensuing Viking raids. The attempts at the conversion of Slavs by missionaries from Bavaria likewise came to little, though for different reasons: the German missionaries came up against the rather more successful Greek mission of Cyril and Methodius, sent from Constantinople in 863. These two brothers worked in the first organized Slavic state, Great Moravia, and with some success, as the excavated churches in fortified centres such as Mikulčice show. But the collapse of the Moravian state, and the invasions of the Magyars, brought their mission too to ultimate failure.

What I have described above is the slow process by which kings and aristocrats were introduced to Christianity and brought to adopt it in their countries. This is the most visible, but not necessarily the most important, element of conversion. The real process of Christianization, the training of priests, preaching to people in the countryside, the elimination or Christianization of pagan customs, the teaching of Christian doctrines, was a process which lasted centuries.

The Barbarians

To Romans all those who lived outside the Roman Empire were barbarians: it was a legal or political category, rather than a racial one. Nowadays historians categorize these barbarians in various ways, either following linguists and speaking of Germans, Celts, and Slavs, or else using the political terms used at the time, and writing of Franks, Picts, West Saxons, Obodrites, or whatever. It is important to remember that these are not racial terms either. Many subjects of the Anglo-Saxon kings in the eighth century were descendants of Welsh-speaking citizens of the Roman Empire, yet by then those 'Celts' (or Romans) spoke Old English and thought of themselves as Anglian or Saxon. Many or most of those calling themselves 'Franks' by the seventh century were descendants of Gallo-Romans who had been ruled by the Franks since the fifth or sixth century. Thus we have a great variety of so-called 'barbarian' kingdoms, ranging from those in which a small minority of barbarians ruled a largely Roman populace, as in Gaul, to those in which not even Roman ideas like Christianity had penetrated, such as the kingdoms in Norway or Russia. And the historian could categorize them in other ways. There were those barbarians who had taken part in the migrations of the fourth to sixth centuries, and those who had not. And there were those barbarians who in the early Middle Ages learnt the art of writing, and who left some record of themselves, and those who still existed in a prehistoric or protohistoric state, like the Picts or the Scandinavian and Slavic peoples, about whom we can only know in this period from the garbled accounts of foreign contemporaries or from the speculative researches of modern archaeologists.

The tendency of historians until recent times to think in racial terms, of German, Celt, Slav, or Roman, has concealed very real similarities between the various barbarian kingdoms of northern Europe. There is no reliable evidence from this period about Slav society, but later evidence suggests that even the Slavs shared in these general patterns. Barbarian society was strictly stratified, with slaves and semi-free at the bottom, and some kind of aristocrats and royalty at the top. Aristocratic birth normally determined membership of this group, but entry might be gained by sufficient landed wealth, acquired often as a result of service to the king. A man's legal status was rigidly defined by the law codes; each man had his 'man price' (*wergild*, for Anglo-Saxons and Franks) or 'honour-price' (*galanas* in Welsh, *lóg n-enech* in Irish). A free Frank was worth 200 solidi, a free Anglo-Saxon 200 shillings, a free Irishman 6 séts, and aristocrats perhaps three times those sums or more. In the event of murder these were the sums paid to the man's kin by the murderer and his kin. The value of a man's oath in court among the Irish, Welsh, and English might be measured in terms of his 'man price'; an oath sworn by an aristocrat or a king would be worth more than that of an ordinary man and, depending on the seriousness of the crime, might serve to clear himself or another of the charge.

In all these societies the kin-group was an important social and legal institution. We have seen in the previous section that the kin possessed rights in land held by individual heads of family, unless the king had granted that land, or transformed its legal status. The kin also had certain duties in law, notably that of bringing anyone who had wronged the kin to justice. In extreme cases the kin could kill someone who murdered one of their number. This so-called 'blood feud' was accepted, if occasionally deplored, by churchmen, because without its threat the guilty person would seldom be induced to come to court. All court cases were private affairs, the injured party or kin bringing the case and making the accusation; whoever presided over the court, a king, his representative, or a local dignitary, merely acted as arbitrator. Among each people there were men recognized as legal experts: Frankish *rachinburgii* or English 'doomsmen'. In Ireland lawmen formed a well-defined learned class; whereas our primary legal sources in other barbarian kingdoms consist of law codes issued in the name of the king, from Ireland we have law tracts written by individual jurists, who themselves played a major role in the administration of the law. But we must not assume that there is a great contrast between Ireland, in which jurists were supreme in the law, and the rest of barbarian Europe, in which kings were supreme. For most of the time the truth, that is, legal practice, lay somewhere in between. The example of the Roman emperor—'the word of the prince is law'—was always there to inspire western kings. Roman example persuaded barbarian kings to have the customary laws of their peoples written down, and the very act of issuing written law codes gave the king more of a role in the law than he had had before.

The man at the head of each group of barbarian people was the king: *rex* in Latin, the related word *rí* in Irish, but *cyning* ('man from the kin') in Old English (although his kingdom was the *rice*). In Ireland there were several grades of king: the ordinary king of the tribe (*rí túaithe*), the tribal king who was overlord over other tribal kings (*ruiri*), the provincial king (*rí ruirech*, or 'king of kings'); some ambitious kings even claimed to be high king of all Ireland, or king of Tara (*ardrí, rí Temra*). There are signs that this hierarchy of kingship was shared by some Germanic peoples, even after the political turmoil caused by the invasions had altered the traditional patterns. The Franks seem to have been ruled by a number of tribal kings before the emergence of the Merovingian dynasty, which eliminated other royal families, and mysterious personages called *subreguli, principes,* or *duces regii* in early Latin documents from England may be the equivalent of tribal kings. There is even an English equivalent to the *ardrí*, the *bretwealda*, or 'ruler of Britain': this too probably represents ambition as much as reality. Some peoples may have only elected 'over-kings' in times of emergency: Bede says that the Saxons on the Continent did not have a king, but were ruled by 'satraps' (tribal kings?) and only when war threatened the whole people did they elect a war-leader. Where political circumstances did not create a need for permanent war-leaders, as among the Irish, Saxons, or Scandinavians, powerful kings with large kingdoms did not emerge. The Frankish and Anglo-Saxon kings were primarily war-leaders, which is not true of their Irish or continental Saxon equivalents.

This is one of the most important distinctions between those barbarian peoples who migrated and those who stayed put. The process of migration broke up old tribal groupings, and the often stormy circumstances brought war-leaders to the fore. Those war-leaders gathered warriors around them, who were rewarded with the spoils of war: gold, precious objects, but above all land. Small, relatively unstratified rural communities, for whom war was the amusement of summer months and seldom led to the conquest of territory, were transformed into stratified societies with a powerful monarchy and a landed aristocracy accustomed to a military way of life. This militarization of society even affected the one part of the former Roman Empire which did not succumb to barbarian rule, but was forced to defend itself from barbarians under its own kings: Wales. The Welsh poem the *Gododdin*, which portrays an aristocratic life of fighting and feasting, where the young warrior sought glory and, if he was lucky, worldly renown, does not show us a society differing very much from that of the better-known Old English poem *Beowulf*. The male graves from the new Germanic kingdoms in the north show, from the late fifth century onwards, the new status that warriors had in society: weapons, spears, one-sided swords (the sax or scramasax) or, in the case of aristocrats, long-swords with gold-foil hilts and golden jewelled pommels, were laid with the man in his grave. Those royal graves which survive show that royal families paraded their dominance (or attempted to buttress it) by spectacular displays of conspicuous expenditure.

To survive politically, the king had to reward these warriors. He might give them gold, in the form of coin or jewellery; and he might, particularly in the case of those retiring from his household service, give land, or the use of land for the lifetime of his follower. Gifts in barbarian society imposed duties on the recipient—to such an extent that Lombard law recognized the right of someone to use force to recover a gift if he had never received a gift in return. They could be used therefore as a political tool; by the giving of gifts a king could ensure loyal service. And from all sides he was told that generosity was the most desirable quality in kings. The problem was, to find the wherewithal. The Frankish kings had fewer problems than any others. Not only did they acquire vast estates in the course of their take-over, including most or all of those which had been imperial estates, but they had also taken over the Roman taxation system, which may have been somewhat ramshackle by that time but was still capable of supplying them with considerable quantities of gold and goods in kind. They also had the inestimable advantage of enemies from whom they and their warriors could win booty with relative ease. Sometimes Frankish warriors were so eager for booty that they went ahead without royal permission and against royal advice, with disastrous results. But on the whole Frankish armies in the sixth century were remarkably successful. Their kings led them to victory over most of their neighbours, and after the Byzantine invasion of Italy in 536 they found themselves frequently involved in Italy, winning booty and subsidies alike from both Ostrogoths and Byzantines.

The importance of continual warfare as a means of bringing in land and booty for political survival can be seen also in England, where probably no shadow of the Roman taxation system survived. There it is the kingdoms which could continually push forward their borders which prospered. In the sixth century, before political boundaries had become firm, it was possible for kingdoms in the east, such as Sussex or Kent, to become militarily powerful and hence politically important. By the seventh century this was almost impossible: the kingdoms in the east stagnated, and it was those with frontiers to the west and north which did well. Northumbria's expansion was brought to an end only in 685, when King Ecgfrith and most of his army were killed at Nechtansmere, north of Dundee, while attacking the kingdom of the Picts. Ecgfrith's own subject Bede interestingly saw this defeat as God's judgement for the unjustified attack that Ecgfrith had made the previous year on the Irish, 'a harmless people always very friendly to the Angles', despite the warnings of the holy Egbert. Indeed, to the Irish the all-out wars of conquest of the Franks or the Angles must have seemed strangely perverse and wicked. The warfare of the Irish kings was usually no more than cattle-raiding or the attempt to win tribute from neighbouring kingdoms; territorial expansion was not their aim.

Three Barbarian Kingdoms

To write a political history of the northern barbarian kingdoms from the fifth to the eighth centuries would result in a confus-

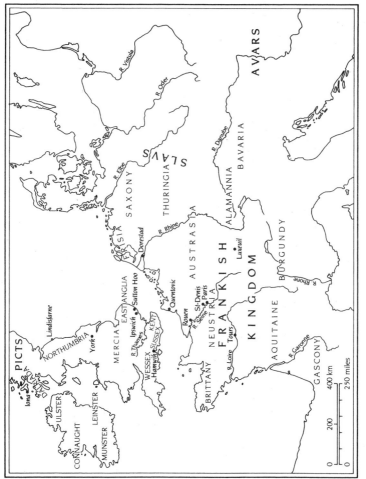

NORTHERN EUROPE, c.600

ing list of names of kings and battles, and a bewildering lack of any information about motives or personalities. At any one time in this period there were probably over two hundred kings in northern Europe. To understand the workings of different barbarian kingdoms and of the problems faced by kings in northern Europe it may be best therefore to look at just three kings from three very different barbarian societies, each from the first half of the seventh century: Dagobert of the Franks, Rædwald of the East Angles, and Congal Cáech of the Cruthin in Ulaid (East Ulster).

Congal Cáech or Cláen (the Squinting or Half-Blind) was king of Dál nAraidi, whose inhabitants were called the Cruthin (Old Irish for 'Picts'). The kings of the dynasty of Dál nAraidi ruled over the central part of modern County Antrim, with the Dál Fiatach to the south and the Dál Riata to the north. This latter dynasty had established a colony in south-west Scotland in the fifth century, and from the sixth century their kings usually ruled their Irish kingdom from Scotland. In 627 Congal became over-king of the whole of Ulaid, receiving tribute from the other kings. In 628 he went to battle against the powerful Uí Néill dynasty to the east, killing their over-king, Suibne Menn. In 629 he fought in Dál Riata, killing not only their king, but also a number of Bernician princes who had gone into exile in Dál Riata when Edwin, with Rædwald's help, had conquered Northumbria. In that same year, however, Congal invaded the Uí Néill, and was defeated by their new over-king Domnall mac Aedo. He survived the battle, and by 637 had managed to persuade the Dál Riata to abandon their old alliance with the Uí Néill and to join with him. Together with Domnall Brecc of Dál Riata he fought Domnall mac Aedo in the great battle of Moira, in County Down. On the same day the Dál Riata, together with one group of Uí Néill, clashed with Domnall mac Aedo's fleet off the Mull of Kintyre: it looks as if Congal had been successful in playing one Uí Néill group off against another. But Congal was killed on the battlefield, and the Uí Néill's dominance over the north was henceforth unchallenged. The *Annals of Ulster* give the title of 'king of Ireland' to Domnal mac Aedo when he died peacefully in 642, the first king credited with that no doubt largely honorary title.

An early Irish law tract on the law of bees, *Bechbretha*, says that damages caused by bee stings are the responsibility of the owner, a decision established after 'the crime of bees against Congal Cáech whom bees blinded; and he was king of Tara until it put him out of his sovereignty'. The Uí Néill who later dominate the honorary but prestigious 'high-kingship of Tara', seem otherwise to have effectively expunged the memory of anyone holding this position who was not of their family. It is another hint of the important position which Congal held in north-east Ireland, and of his political ambitions. And the reference to the incapacitating effect of blinding is not implausible. Irish kings inhabited a very different world from that of the Germanic kings further south. They were set apart from their subjects by ancient rituals, such as that of marriage with their kingdom, and by an elaborate web of taboos (*gessa*) and prerogatives (*buada*). Some of these ideas about kingship are paralleled very closely in the Sanskrit literature of ancient India, and go back to the prehistoric roots of European civilization. It is with the Irish that we can get closest to understanding the nature of pre-Roman European society.

At this time the kingdom of the East Angles was ruled by Rædwald. Rædwald was, at the start of his reign, under the overlordship of King Æthelberht of Kent, then the most powerful king in southern England; at this time, willingly or not, Rædwald accepted Christianity and was baptized in Kent. But the Northumbrian monk Bede says Rædwald 'was seduced by his wife and by certain evil teachers and perverted from the sincerity of his faith', and thereafter used to have a Christian altar and a pagan altar in the same building. This fine compromise may have made good political sense when people must have been bitterly divided by their religious opinions. Rædwald managed, even before Æthelberht's death in 616, to make his kingdom the dominant power in southern England. When he died, probably in the late 620s, his son Eorpwald was persuaded to convert to Christianity by Edwin of Northumbria. But he was killed and succeeded by a pagan, who reigned for three years. Then Eorpwald's brother Sigbert returned to become king and to establish Christianity on a much firmer footing. He had been in exile in Gaul, possibly at Dagobert's court: it is interesting that he bears the same name as Dagobert's son, a traditionally Merovingian name. With him from Gaul came Bishop Felix, who, 'as his name signified', said Bede, brought the kingdom to great felicity by his preaching.

The only other fact we know about Rædwald is that he was once bribed by Æthelfrith, the Anglian king of Bernicia who had united both Bernicia and Deira into one kingdom of Northumbria, to kill the exiled Deiran prince Edwin, then living at Rædwald's court. Instead Rædwald took his army up north, defeated Æthelfrith, and installed Edwin as king. Archaeology and place-name studies are still adding to the few facts we can glean from Bede. Ever since the discovery of the ship burial at Sutton Hoo in 1938, with its gold jewellery and its enigmatic objects, such as the great whetstone interpreted by some as a royal sceptre, there has been speculation that it may be Rædwald's tomb. The grave in any case provides a fascinating glimpse into the interconnections of the northern world. The custom of ship burial is a Scandinavian one, and the Scandinavian, or specifically Swedish, manufacture of the helmet and shield found in the tomb underline that connection, which may suggest a Scandinavian origin for Rædwald's Wuffinga dynasty. The hanging bowls in the grave are of British manufacture; the silver bowls and the two silver spoons inscribed Paulos and Saulos (perhaps a baptismal gift) were made in Byzantium. The sword may be of Frankish manufacture, and the garnets which decorate much of the gold jewellery were probably imported via Francia. Inside the purse with its gold and garnet decorated fittings were thirty-seven gold coins, each minted in a different place in the Frankish kingdom. Altogether the Sutton Hoo find is a remarkable illustration of the far-reaching links which royal courts could have with the rest of Europe.

The nature of those links has been the subject of some controversy in recent years. It has become obvious that in the seventh century trade across the Channel and North Sea was beginning to be important, and there are signs that it was becoming organized. The steady and orderly replacement of gold by silver in the Merovingian coinage, culminating in a completely silver coinage by the 660s, has been seen by some as an attempt to provide a coinage more suited to commercial transactions. The Frankish king, Dagobert, was clearly trying to encourage trade when he granted Saint-Denis the right to hold an annual fair. And there are trading-places in the mid-seventh century which are clearly becoming important. Many are characterized by a place-name suffix meaning 'trading-place': *-wic* or its local equivalent. There was Quentovic on the north French coast, Wijk bij Duurstede (or Dorestad) in the Netherlands, Schleswig in Jutland, Hamwic (Southampton), Eoforwic (York), and, some twelve kilometres from Sutton Hoo, Ipswich. Early medieval pottery has been found on many sites in modern Ipswich, which may indicate a sizeable settlement area; from the evidence of the pottery one might imagine peaks of activity in the early seventh century (in the time of Rædwald and Sigbert) and again around 800. Much of this pottery is imported from the Rhineland, and there are fragments of Rhenish glass also, and numerous boat rivets. Some archaeologists believe that Ipswich, and other *wics* in the seventh century, may have been seasonal ports of trade, established by kings to control the flow of prestige goods, such as wine or luxury cloths, into their kingdom. Kings did this for a twofold purpose, presumably: to benefit from tolls and to obtain a monopoly of items with which to reward followers and subjects, thus in both ways increasing their power.

As we move from Ireland to East Anglia to Francia there is a dramatic increase in scale. There were over a hundred Irish kings reigning in any one year during the time of Rædwald, each of them with a kingdom the size of a half or third of a modern county. And as we move south again across the Channel we witness another great leap in scale. Although Rædwald's armies could take him hundreds of miles from East Anglia, to force other kings to submit to him and offer him tribute, his own kingdom was very small in comparison with Dagobert's, confined as far as we can see largely to the coastal regions of East Anglia. Dagobert's power stretched over the whole of modern France and the Low Countries, and much of modern West Germany, and to any other barbarian monarch his wealth must have seemed quite enormous.

Dagobert was the son of Chlothar II, who had reunited the Frankish kingdom in 613 after torturing to death the dominant figure in Frankish politics for twenty years, his aged aunt Brunhild. In 622 Chlothar II made Dagobert king in Austrasia, the north-eastern portion of the Frankish kingdom, while he himself kept the rest of Gaul under his direct rule, residing in Neustria, the region centred on Paris. Dagobert's chief advisers were two Austrasian aristocrats, Arnulf, bishop of Metz, and Pippin, who was made mayor of Dagobert's palace. (It was a marriage arranged between Arnulf's son and Pippin's daughter that was to form the powerful dynasty known later as the Carolingians.) Chlothar II died in 629, and Dagobert became sole king. According to the chronicler Fredegar, a contemporary, the first years of his reign over Gaul were very auspicious. Fredegar clearly approved of the way in which Dagobert tried to put local aristocrats, the real powers in the provinces, in their place. He tells us of a royal visit to Burgundy, for instance, which caused great alarm to bishops and aristocrats, and joy to the oppressed; 'such was his great good-will and eagerness that he neither ate nor slept, lest anyone should leave his presence without having obtained justice'. For Fredegar things went sour when Arnulf retired and Dagobert left Pippin's side to take up residence in Neustria. 'He forgot the justice he had once loved.' One of his foreign campaigns illustrates his internal problems. He sent an expedition of Austrasian Franks to Bohemia, against the Wends, a Slavic people. The Wends were led by Samo, an enterprising Frankish merchant, who had so impressed the Wends that they ruled them, and his twelve Wendish wives, for thirty-five years. Dagobert's Austrasians were defeated, not, according to Fredegar, because of the strength of the Slavs but rather through the demoralization of the Austrasians, who apparently felt that Dagobert had deserted them by going to live in Neustria. Samo's Wends were encouraged by this victory, and by an alliance with the Sorbs, another Slavic people, and began raiding in Frankish territories further west. In 631 the Saxons offered to help Dagobert against the Wends if he remitted the 500 cows they had paid yearly—to the Austrasians—since the time of Chlothar I; Dagobert agreed, but to little effect, said Fredegar, for in the following year, the Wends were attacking again.

Dagobert was rather more successful within Gaul. He mollified the Austrasians by giving them as king his infant son Sigibert, with two of their number as regents; later he persuaded his magnates to accept that his other son Clovis would be heir to Neustria and Burgundy. In 635 his army defeated the Basques who were invading Gascony from their Pyrenean homes, and he forced King Judicael of Brittany to come to terms. According to Fredegar, Judicael came to Dagobert's palace at Clichy, near Paris, but refused to eat with Dagobert because of the king's sins; he dined instead with the head of the royal bureaucracy, Audoen, later the saintly bishop of Rouen. Dagobert died in 638, and was the first French king to be buried in the church of Saint-Denis, which he had enlarged and 'magnificently embellished with gold, gems and precious things'. There was no succession dispute, even though Dagobert's sons were both minors. Sigibert continued to rule in Austrasia, and Clovis took over in Neustria and Burgundy, both under regents.

Dagobert has been claimed as the last Merovingian king to be effective ruler over the whole Frankish kingdom, but the nature of his rule shows up some of the problems of the Merovingians. Neustria was the centre of royal power, and the favourite royal villas were none of them far from Paris. Dagobert made one trip to Burgundy, and clearly impressed Burgundians (such as Fredegar himself) with his power and his goodwill. But for most of the time the local aristocracy in Burgundy and the rest of southern Gaul were able to carry on their lives and their administration undisturbed by the king. Dagobert may never have visited Aquitaine, although he no doubt kept in touch with developments there through such men as Desiderius, a court official who succeeded his brother as bishop of Cahors (and whose correspondence survives). Despite Dagobert's military successes, the south-west of Aquitaine was being slowly overrun by the Basques (turning its name from Novempopulana to Vasconia or Gascony). But the most serious symptoms of local independence were much nearer home, in Austrasia. In Dagobert's reign the antagonism between Austrasia and Neustria, which was to colour Merovingian politics for the rest of the seventh century, was already apparent. The difference between the two provinces was in part cultural: the language of the Neustrians was very largely Latin or proto-French, while that of the Austrasians was largely Frankish or German. The Rhineland Franks had been conquered by the Salian Franks at the time of Clovis, but their separate identity was acknowledged and even fostered under Clovis's descendants. They successfully persuaded Dagobert to give them their own king, and it was under Dagobert that their own law code, *Lex Ribvaria*, was first written down.

Although it is possible to see in this regional fragmentation a foretaste of the break-up of the Merovingian kingdom later in the seventh century, there were positive aspects to Dagobert's rule. The right of the Merovingians to rule the kingdom was never questioned. Indeed, the record of the Merovingian dynasty in monopolizing royal power among the Franks for two and a half centuries is unparalleled anywhere else in early medieval Europe. As the dynasty grew older it survived partly because it was old, and hence endowed with immense prestige and mystique, and eventually because it was so powerless it was harmless. But it was also the only dynasty in north Europe which could justly claim to be the heirs to Roman power. The Byzantine emperor remained, in the eyes of the kings, their nominal sovereign. And Merovingian methods of government, even in the time of Dagobert, were recognizably Roman. Government and administration were still by the written word (the earliest surviving governmental documents are from the reigns of Chlothar and Dagobert), frequently still written on imported papyrus, following Roman bureaucratic norms, and the documents themselves, all in Latin, still used many of the old legal formulae. Administrators were still largely educated laymen, although from Chlothar II onwards there is an increasing clerical presence. Frankish pride in their own achievement bore fruit in Dagobert's reign in the emergence of the tradition that the Franks were descended from the Trojan royal family, and were thus equal to the Romans. By the eighth century Franks would boast that they were superior to the Romans; Romans had persecuted Christians, while the Franks were powerful protectors of the Church.

Dagobert's own achievements and ambitions were quite the equal of his sixth-century ancestors. He chose a Frankish duke for Thuringia; he organized the Church in Alamannia, and he had law codes drawn up for the Alamans and the Bavarians. Even those Germanic peoples adjacent to Slav and Avar territory were prepared to acknowledge his rule. The monarchy still had considerable amounts of land at its disposal, and Dagobert and his aristocracy were able to bestow large quantities of it upon the Church. This was a period of monastic renewal in northern Gaul, inspired by the Irish holy man Columbanus. Several of the court officials of Chlothar and Dagobert were involved in this movement, including Audoen and Desiderius. The best known was an Aquitanian called Eligius (immortalized in a French nursery rhyme about St Eloi and Dagobert's trousers). He was a goldsmith and jeweller, brought to Paris to embellish some of the great churches of Neustria, including Saint-Denis, but also to act as a senior financial official at court. He acted also as a moneyer; coins bearing his name are well known to numismatists. He entered the church not long after Dagobert's death, became bishop of Noyon, and won a reputation as a holy man concerned with evangelizing his diocese. There were in northern Gaul at this time a number of clerics originating in the Gallo-Roman aristocracy of Aquitaine, who still preserved the learning and traditions of the Roman world. Their influence was strong in the revival of book production and learning in the Merovingian monasteries of the north, which in turn laid foundations for the revival of learning in the eighth century known nowadays as 'the Carolingian Renaissance'.

The Carolingians

The family which was to produce the most powerful rulers in Europe in the eighth century came from Austrasia, where they, the descendants of Dagobert's one-time advisers Pippin and Arnulf, had maintained an almost uninterrupted ascendancy throughout the seventh century. Pippin I's son Grimoald and grandson Pippin II were both mayors of the palace in Austrasia. Pippin II managed by the battle of Tertry in 687 to unite both Neustria and Austrasia under his own puppet Merovingian king. But the power struggles in northern Gaul seriously weakened the power of the Merovingians and their mayors. In the south regional identities were being forged. The Aquitanians had their own duke; the *patricius* of Provence was virtually an independent ruler; the aristocrats of Burgundy paid little attention to the Franks in the north. The various Germanic peoples beyond the Rhine who had still been under Frankish overlordship in Dagobert's day were asserting their independence. And even in northern Gaul the Merovingians and their mayors were often powerless to stop the activities of local aristocratic families, resting as they did on their own land and on the control of church land through their family monasteries and, occasionally, dynastic bishoprics.

It was Pippin II's illegitimate son Charles Martel who began the reunification of Gaul, and who gave his name to the dynasty, the Carolingians. With his own puppet Merovingian king he reunited northern Gaul and began the reconquest of other former possessions of the Merovingian kings. He is best known for his victory in 732–3 over the Arabs of ʿAbd ar-Rahman, who were approaching Tours, intending to loot the wealthy shrine of St Martin. Some have seen this battle, almost certainly wrongly, as a great turning-point in history, in which Charles thwarted the Arab conquest of western Europe. But it is perhaps a major turning-point in Gallic history, for it demonstrated Charles's superiority over Duke Eudo of the Aquitanians, and began the series of campaigns which not only drove the Arabs back beyond the Pyrenees but, more importantly, established the Franks once more as rulers of southern Gaul. The campaigns lasted decades. Charles Martel led several campaigns into Burgundy and Aquitaine. His son Pippin III campaigned in Burgundy and Provence, and restored those provinces to his rule. It took ten years of warfare in the

750s to drive the Arabs out of Septimania, and to persuade the Goths of Septimania that Frankish rule was preferable to that of the Arabs. But Aquitaine was the severest test of Frankish power. Charles Martel campaigned against Eudo, Pippin fought against Eudo's son Hunald, and, throughout the 760s, with Hunald's son. It was only in the first years of the reign of Pippin's son Charlemagne that the Aquitanians were finally subdued. In 781 Charlemagne recognized their persistence, and their sense of identity, by granting them his own son Louis as king of Aquitaine.

The early Carolingians were fighting on other fronts as well, in Brittany, Saxony, Alamannia. Some of the funds they needed for this constant warfare could come from booty or conquered lands, but clearly that could not pay, for instance, for the often fruitless skirmishes on the borders of Aquitaine. No doubt the Carolingians rewarded their close followers with land from the extensive estates of the Carolingians themselves. And, as later generations would recall with distaste, Charles Martel often rewarded his followers with church land. Later generations had probably forgotten that much church land and, indeed, bishoprics and abbacies, had been held by lay aristocrats before Charles Martel came along. The confiscation of church land by Charles Martel and his successors was an unavoidable part of the elimination of local aristocratic opposition, and an equally unavoidable aspect of church reform.

The first agent of Carolingian reform was St Boniface, as we have seen. He supported Pippin III in his attempts to get rid of worldly bishops and to restore proper monastic rule to houses which had become mere pawns in secular politics. The church councils held in the early 740s at the instigation of Pippin's brother Carloman called for the restoration of correct rules of clerical life, regular synods, and the elimination of pagan practices from every diocese. Boniface's work was continued by Franks, notably by Chrodegang, who was made bishop of Metz in 742 and succeeded to the title of archbishop on Boniface's death in 754. Chrodegang began the drive for uniformity in liturgy and religious practice, with Rome as its model, which was to characterize the Carolingian Church. He

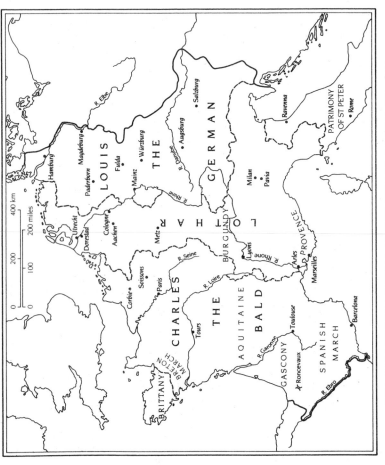

THE CAROLINGIAN EMPIRE AT THE TREATY OF VERDUN, 843

established a school for teaching Roman, so-called Gregorian, plainchant, and under his influence the 'Roman' monastic rule, that of St Benedict, began to be recommended as a model for monastic living.

The close rapport with Rome which Boniface and Chrodegang worked to establish was achieved also on the political front. When Pippin's brother Carloman retired from political life, he went to live in a monastery in Rome. Three years later Pippin III, who still called himself 'duke' or 'prince', sent an embassy to Pope Zacharias to ask if it was just that he who held power should not have the title of 'king'. Zacharias sent back the correct answer, and in 751 Pippin III packed Childeric III, the last Merovingian king, into a monastery and had himself inaugurated king at Soissons. This ceremony was the first in Francia to incorporate anointing with holy oil, and perhaps the first in Europe to emphasize the act of crowning by a bishop. Pippin, now King Pippin I, wanted to take no chances that anyone would object to the legitimacy of his revolutionary move. The role which the Church was thus given in royal inauguration was to have important consequences later in European history: Pippin's grandson was to be deposed by bishops, who felt that if they could make kings, they could unmake them as well. Equally crucial was the visit which Pope Stephen II made to Francia in 753. He came to appeal for Frankish help in Italy to restore those territories taken from the Roman Church by the Lombards. Stephen reanointed Pippin and his sons, and the Carolingians were established as the new protectors of the papacy, replacing the increasingly ineffective Byzantine emperor. Pippin set off for Italy, and forced the Lombards to sue for peace and to restore territory to Rome.

Pippin is much less well known than his son Karolus, called 'Magnus' (the Elder) to distinguish him from his own son Charles; Charles has become known as Charles the Great or Charlemagne for very good reasons. His long reign changed the face of Europe politically and culturally, and he himself would remain fixed in the minds of people in the Middle Ages as the ideal king. In more recent times, many historians have taken his reign to be the beginning of the Middle Ages 'proper'. Yet in terms of territorial expansion and consolidation, church reform, and entanglement with Rome, Charlemagne's reign was merely bringing the policies of his father Pippin to their logical conclusions.

Charlemagne became the subject of the first medieval biography of a layman, written by Einhard, one of his learned courtiers. Following his literary model, Suetonius' word portrait of the Emperor Augustus, Einhard described Charlemagne's appearance, his dress, his eating and drinking habits, his religious practices, and intellectual interests, giving us a vivid, if not perhaps entirely reliable, picture of this Frankish monarch. He was strong, tall, and healthy, and ate moderately. He loved exercise: riding and hunting and, perhaps more surprising, swimming. Einhard tells us that he chose Aachen as the site for his palace because of its hot springs, and that he used to bathe there with his family, friends, and courtiers. He spoke and read Latin as well as his native Frankish, and could understand Greek, and even speak it a little. He learnt grammar, rhetoric, and mathematics from the learned clerics he gathered around him, but although he kept writing-tablets under his pillows for practice (he used to wake up four or five times in the night) he never mastered the art of writing.

Einhard's biography starts, very appropriately, with Charlemagne's wars. It was because he was a tireless and remarkably successful general that he was able to make such a mark upon European history. As we have seen, he concluded Pippin's wars with Aquitaine, and proclaimed his son Louis as king in 781; the one serious defeat he suffered was in these wars, at Roncevaux in the Pyrenees, a defeat one day immortalized in *The Song of Roland* and later *chansons de geste*. He added Saxony to his realm, after years of vicious campaigning, and towards the end of his reign moved against the Danes; he destroyed the kingdom of the Avars in Hungary; he subdued the Bretons, the Bavarians, and various Slav peoples. In the south he began the reconquest of Spain from the Arabs, and established the Spanish March in the north-east of the peninsula. But perhaps his most significant campaigns were south of the Alps, in Italy. Pope Hadrian appealed to

Charlemagne for help against Desiderius of the Lombards. The campaign in the winter of 773-4 was short and decisive. Desiderius was exiled, and Charlemagne, 'king of the Franks', added 'and of the Lombards' to his title; later he appointed his son Pippin as king of Italy. But popes were still not free of all their enemies. In 799 Leo III was ambushed by a rival party of Roman aristocrats, who tried to gouge out his eyes and cut off his tongue. Leo fled to Charlemagne, who was at Paderborn preparing for another war against the Saxons. Charlemagne ordered Leo III to be restored, and later in the year 800 came to Rome himself. On Christmas Day, in St Peter's, Pope Leo III crowned Charlemagne emperor of the Romans.

Probably no event in medieval history has occasioned more scholarly comment, to less effect. Contemporary accounts of the event differ. We do not know if the coronation had been planned beforehand by Charlemagne, or whether it was a plot of Leo's to bind the king of the Franks closer to the Roman cause. Who were the 'Romans' of whom Charlemagne was to be the emperor, the inhabitants of Rome, or those of the papal states (Romagna)? Was it only afterwards that Charlemagne and his clerics began to think of it as a 'restoration of the Roman Empire', or was that inherent in his acclamation as *Augustus* in St Peter's? Is it relevant that even before the coronation the former head of the palace school at Aachen, Alcuin of York, had been talking in terms of Charlemagne's *imperium* or that Alcuin had written to Charlemagne reminding him that the Empress Irene's deposition in 797 of the legitimate emperor in Constantinople had upset the world order? The usefulness of the imperial coronation from Charlemagne's viewpoint may have been that it gave him, who ruled as king and duke over a wide variety of realms, a simple and awe-inspiring title, and one that all were free to interpret as they chose. It would be interesting to know more about how contemporaries regarded it, like Irish kings, who, according to Einhard, 'never addressed him as anything but their lord, and called themselves his slaves and subjects', or the Northumbrians, whose rightful king Charlemagne and the papal envoy were somehow able to restore to power. The emperor himself may have regarded the new title as a personal one; certainly when he drew up his will in 806 he divided his empire among his sons and made no provision at all for the survival of the imperial title. It was the subsequent death of two of his three sons which convinced him, and his son Louis the Pious, that God intended the empire to survive as a unity.

From early in his reign Charlemagne and his clerical advisers were concerned to order the Frankish lands in accordance with God's will. A whole series of decisions, 'capitularies', made at the annual councils witness to their determination to restore strict canon law to the Church, conformity to a rule in the monasteries, and correct Christian living throughout the kingdom. The most urgent necessity was education, above all for the clergy. It was not only the clergy for whom German was the first language who needed to learn Latin; the spoken language of those living in Gaul had diverged so far from written Latin, along the path to French, that accurate comprehension of the Bible or the liturgy had become difficult. Charlemagne's *Admonitio generalis* of 789 stressed the importance of education for clergy and people, and urged the establishment of schools for both. The Anglo-Saxon and Irish clergy whom Charlemagne gathered around him, Alcuin at their head, were to be of great importance in this process. They had developed textbooks for teaching Latin to non-Latin speakers, and had also great familiarity with some of the basic books of Christian learning, some of which were unknown in northern Gaul. It has been suggested that one of the contributions made by the Anglo-Saxons and Irish was the introduction of a new method of Latin pronunciation, as recommended in Alcuin's own textbook on correct Latin. It treated Latin as a dead language (which it was not, in Gaul), giving each syllable equal weight, and pronouncing all the consonants clearly, as written. Thus the proper word-endings, giving the grammatical function of the word, could be heard; thus could be avoided such problems as the Bavarian priest encountered by St Boniface, who, by being unclear about his word-endings, baptized in the name of the Fatherland, the Daughter, and the Holy Spirit. But in the process Latin *did* become a dead language, comprehensible only to the clerical élite. The liturgy could no longer be understood by most of the lay congregation. Sermons had to be, however. Capitularies not only demanded that sermons should be delivered in every church, but also that they should be in the language of the ordinary people, 'in rustic Roman' (Old French, or Romance) or in German. Manuals of preaching were produced for use in the parish churches which had, by the ninth century, been established over most of the Carolingian lands, and episcopal statutes were issued by bishops in an attempt to ensure that parish priests knew their duty and had the basic library needed to accomplish it. For the first time in the west, Church and State united to try to bring Christianity to all under their control.

The movement for the basic education of the clergy had a number of useful by-products. Charlemagne was provided with an ever-growing number of literate clerics who could be used in his administration and, in the newly reformed Latin and the new more legible script, had a precise and international written language that could be used throughout his multilingual empire. And the long study of late Latin grammars and classical Latin literature which was needed to produce that reformed classical Latin produced a generation of scholars—poets, historians, textual critics, theologians, philosophers—whose achievements really did begin to rival those of late antiquity. This classical revival, the central part of what has earned the blanket term 'the Carolingian Renaissance', began at the royal court itself. Most of the scholars there were foreigners: Peter of Pisa and Paul the Deacon from Italy, Theodulf of Orléans from Spain, Alcuin from Northumbria, Joseph from Ireland. There were some Franks, however, including Angilbert (whose liaison with one of Charlemagne's unmarried daughters gave the world the historian Nithard) and Einhard (whose main criticism of Charlemagne concerned the emperor's tolerant attitude to the behaviour of his unmarried daughters). The Renaissance came to its climax in the reign of Charles's grandson Charles the Bald, by which time there were a number of major centres of book production and scholarship in the kingdom. It is an ironic fact of history that the Carolingian intellectual achievement was at its height when the Carolingian Empire was itself falling apart. Book production and education require wealth and some sort of political stability; by the later ninth century both were in increasingly short supply.

When the aged Charlemagne finally died, in 814, prospects still looked bright. There was only one heir, Louis the Pious, so the empire would remain united; Louis's nephew Bernard had taken the kingship of Italy after his father Pippin's death, but would remain under imperial overlordship. Louis's clerical advisers, notably Benedict of Aniane, saw the opportunity to continue church reforms; in 816 the Rule of St Benedict was proclaimed the sole rule for monks in the empire. But seeds of future trouble were already present. When Louis had come to Aachen he had exiled some of Charlemagne's closest advisers, including two cousins. When in 817 it was decided that Louis's eldest son Lothar would become emperor on his father's death, and that the two other sons, Louis 'the German' and Pippin 'of Aquitaine', would be kings within his empire, there was a revolt, led by Bernard of Italy, who had not been mentioned in the succession document: this was put down by Louis, who had Bernard blinded. Any discontent that arose could now centre around Lothar, who had already been crowned emperor; it came to a head in 822, when Louis was forced to undergo penance and to recall his cousins to court. But the crucial event was the birth in 823 of a son to Louis's second wife. Louis was determined that this son, Charles ('the Bald'), would share in his inheritance; the three other sons naturally considered any change in the 817 arrangements as an attack on their own position. From the late 820s until the end of his life in 840 Louis was in continual struggle with one or more of his sons, being deposed by a council of bishops at one point. The conflicts of loyalty which arose inevitably weakened the prestige of the crown, and encouraged the aristocracy to place their own survival above the health of the kingdom. Bitter civil war followed Louis's death as well, until, by the treaty of Verdun in 843, Charlemagne's empire was split by Lothar I, Louis the German, and Charles the Bald into three kingdoms.

Lothar retained the title of emperor and a kingdom which included the two imperial towns of Rome and Aachen, but he had no authority over Louis's kingdom in Germany or Charles's kingdom in West Francia. On Lothar's death his 'Middle Kingdom' was itself split, and Louis and Charles began fighting for predominance. A new element was now added to this situation of dissolution and civil war: the Vikings.

The Vikings

The inhabitants of Scandinavia appear for the first time in our written sources when, suddenly, in the reign of Charlemagne, pirates crossed the North Sea to raid monasteries and settlements in north-west Europe. Scandinavians were not unknown in the west before this, as merchants. Indeed, the word 'Viking' may originally have meant traders, 'men who go to *wics* (trading places)'. Such men had brought furs, walrus ivory, amber, and slaves: all valuable items greatly in demand. Glass, pottery, metalwork, including swords, and coins all found their way in return back to the north, and have been discovered by archaeologists. In the eighth century the demand seems to have been greater than ever, and there is evidence that Scandinavian merchants were active in the eastern Baltic, collecting furs for the western market. This flourishing trade must have stimulated improvements in ship design: long ships fitted with a mast and capable of sailing right across the North Sea and far into the Atlantic were part of what made the whole Viking episode possible. It has been suggested that Scandinavian merchants went to Russia and brought vast quantities of silver from the Abbasid Empire in the east to Charlemagne's kingdom. This silver did much to finance Carolingian church-building, and to stimulate both the Carolingian and Scandinavian economies. The drying up of supplies of silver in the 820s and 830s caused by political troubles in the Abbasid Empire precipitated a crisis in the Carolingian Empire, and forced Scandinavians whose position had depended on the silver trade to turn to piracy. This hypothesis cannot as yet be proved, but it reminds us that the growth of the Carolingian Empire, the most power-

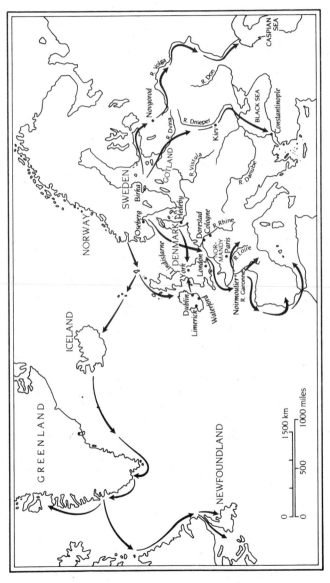

VIKING ROUTES

CASPIAN SEA

R. Volga

Novgorod

R. Don

R. Dvina

R. Dnieper

BLACK SEA

Constantinople

Kiev

SWEDEN

R. Vistula

GOTLAND

Birka

R. Danube

Oseberg

Hedeby

NORWAY

DENMARK

Dorestad

Cologne

Lindisfarne

R. Rhine

York

London

NOR-MANDY

Paris

R. Loire

Dublin

Limerick

Waterford

Noirmoutier

R. Garonne

ICELAND

GREENLAND

NEWFOUNDLAND

0   500   1500 km

0   1000 miles

ful political organization in Europe since the Roman Empire, may in some sense have initiated the Viking expansion, if only by stimulating trade and thus giving the opportunity for piracy.

In the 790s both Charlemagne and King Offa of Mercia were organizing coastal defences against the Vikings. But the first recorded attacks were further north, on three of the most famous northern monasteries: Lindisfarne (793), Jarrow (794), and Iona (795). Recorded attacks are not the same thing as attacks, of course; to be recorded means a nearby monastery to mention the attack in its annals, and a monastery which subsequently survived, thus preserving the record. Few records of attacks survive from Northumbria: the attacks were so sustained that, in the course of the early ninth century, monasticism became virtually extinct and monastic libraries almost totally destroyed. On the other hand, large numbers of attacks are recorded on Irish monasteries: Irish monastic annals provide us with very detailed records, and the monasteries mostly survived the attacks.

The earliest raids were carried out by small numbers of ships, and never penetrated far inland. It was not until the 830s that more large-scale raids were organized, taking advantage of knowledge gained earlier and, in Francia, taking advantage of the political troubles of Louis the Pious. Dorestad was raided three times between 834 and 836. Raids reached right into central Ireland, and forced the monks of the island monasteries of Lindisfarne and Noirmoutier (by the mouth of the Loire) to move themselves and their relics further inland. Viking fleets wintered for the first time in Ireland in 840/1, and founded permanent settlements, including Dublin. The first wintering in France was at Noirmoutier in 843; in 851 the Vikings wintered in southern England, on Thanet.

The raiding Vikings seem to have been sensitive to changing circumstances, moving to the area of northern Europe which could offer the most profit, in booty or in tribute. Louis the Pious built coastal forts and reorganized his fleet in the late 830s, and the Vikings began attacking the southern English coast. On the death of Louis the Pious in 840 there was civil war in Francia, and the Vikings sailed up the Seine in 841 and made numerous attacks on the north coast, culminating in a threatening move against Paris in 845, when they were bought off by 7,000 pounds of silver. From then on, for twenty years, it was western France which suffered most from the Vikings, who used great rivers such as the Seine, Loire, and Garonne to reach right into the interior. The Middle Kingdom, reached by the Rhine and its tributaries, was largely spared, because Lothar I allowed Harald and his nephew Roric, two Danish Vikings, to settle by the mouths of the Rhine in the neighbourhood of Dorestad, thus defending Lothar's kingdom from further attack. But in western Francia Charles the Bald was too busy establishing himself and eliminating the threat from his nephew Pippin II of Aquitaine to devote all his attention to defence. In the 860s, however, he devised what seem to have been very effective measures, building forts and fortified bridges. The lower Loire and Seine were abandoned to the Vikings, but the wealthy cities and monasteries inland were protected. Thus in 865 'the Great Army', under several royal Scandinavian generals, moved from Francia and landed in East Anglia. In 866 they seized York from the warring Northumbrian kings and set up a kingdom based on that town; they then conquered eastern Mercia and East Anglia. The attacks on King Alfred's Wessex failed, although in 878 Wessex was attacked from both east and west and the Vikings narrowly missed capturing the king himself. Alfred rallied his subjects, and forced the invaders to make peace, agreeing on a frontier between West Saxon territory and what became known as the Danelaw. Perhaps the Vikings had just heard the good news from Francia: in 877 Charles the Bald had died. His son Louis the Stammerer died two years later, and a period of civil confusion followed. An army gathered at Fulham, and crossed the Channel in 879. This time they attacked not only the northern part of Charles's kingdom, but the northern part of the Middle Kingdom as well; Roric had died as well, and no longer protected this region. Flanders was devastated, and in 882 there was a great raid up the Rhine to Cologne and Trier. A large-scale attack on Paris in 885/6 failed, however, thanks to the defence of Count Odo, and fortifications elsewhere lessened the impact of the raids. In 888 the energetic Odo became the first king of Francia who was neither Merovingian not Carolingian, and the Vikings suffered a number of defeats. They moved back to England, but discovered that in the mean time King Alfred had learnt much from his Frankish neighbours. He too had built up a series of forts, or *burhs*, and had equipped himself with an effective navy. In 896 the Scandinavian army split up, part going to Northumbria and East Anglia, and part south again to the lower Seine. It was not until 911 that the Frankish king, Charles the Simple, legitimized the authority of these Vikings by granting the area around Rouen to the Northman Rollo, thus creating what became the duchy of Normandy. The period of Viking expansion had ended and, in some areas, the 'reconquest' began: in Flanders, in central England under Alfred's son Athelstan, and even in Ireland, where in 902 an alliance of Irish kings temporarily expelled the Dublin Vikings.

The effects of these Viking raids on northern Europe are very difficult for the historian to assess. For a long time the negative aspects were paramount; historians influenced by the image of bloodthirsty pirates found in contemporary sources stressed the destruction of monasteries and the political confusion, and blamed the Vikings for the destruction of the Carolingian Empire and of the traditional and relatively peaceful ways of Old Ireland. More recently other historians, following Professor P. H. Sawyer in particular, noted the small-scale nature of Viking raiding and settlement. They pointed out that monasticism was on the wane in England before the Vikings; that the Carolingian Empire collapsed for internal structural reasons; that the Vikings did not bring an end to the immunity of the Irish Church from secular violence, for Irish monasteries had for decades been the victims of attacks by Irish kings, and indeed by the abbots of other Irish monasteries. Archaeologists, impressed by Scandinavian artistic and seafaring achievements, began emphasizing the positive contribution of the Vikings as craftsmen, sailors, merchants, and farmers. The Jorvik Viking Centre, which displays the results of the important excavation at Coppergate in York, exemplifies this approach. The similarities between the societies of raiders and victims have been pointed out, which made it relatively easy for the Vikings to be assimilated or at least accepted as allies. But now, perhaps, historians are swinging in the other direction. If Coppergate (a Scandinavian name meaning 'street of wood-turners') shows the Vikings at work, so do the excavations at Repton (Derbyshire), which have revealed the careful way in which the Vikings plundered a monastery and stripped it of all its precious objects. Viking poetry, it has been argued, reveals a taste for violence 'verging on the psychopathic', while the Vikings may have been fanatical in their paganism, sacking monasteries as much for ideology as for opportunism, and sacrificing their opponents in a peculiarly bloody way.

Raiders or traders? The Vikings, of course, even individual Vikings, were both at the same time, for booty can easily be brought to a trading-place and exchanged for other goods, while, for a trader, theft was one easy way of obtaining goods. Other Viking leaders, like those in the Great Army, may have had political ambitions, while in the wake of successful armies came farmers and artisans. As far as the ninth century is concerned, however, the primary legacy of the Vikings was that of destruction; the more peaceful phase came later, as small-scale piratical raids were replaced by well-led expeditions with political aims, and as settlement and peaceful commerce followed stabilization. It is in 910 or thereabouts that Vikings in York laid out streets and tenements in the Coppergate area.

The first area of north-west Europe affected by the Vikings was probably Scotland and the Isles. In Orkney and Shetland the native language disappeared, and so, probably, did the natives: these islands remained Norwegian throughout the Middle Ages. The Outer Hebrides became Norse-speaking also: Gaelic did not take over until the sixteenth century. Viking settlement appears to have been less concentrated in the Inner Hebrides and mainland, although pagan inscriptions and graves show that the Isle of Man had become an important Viking base in the ninth century. Many of the Vikings who settled in south-west Scotland or in north-west England may have come via Man or the Isles, or perhaps from Ireland.

The Vikings first attacked Ireland in the 790s, and the earliest raids and settlements were in the north and east of Ireland. The raids seem to have been most severe in the 830s and early 840s, when the Vikings established a number of permanent coastal settlements (Dublin, Waterford, Limerick, and others). Thereafter the number of recorded raids diminishes, and Irish kings are accredited with a number of victories against the foreigners. The Norwegian Vikings in Ireland were further weakened by the arrival of a large Danish fleet in the late 840s, which initiated a period of civil war, which included a great sea-battle in Strangford Lough in which several hundred ships were involved. A Norwegian fleet came to restore control of the Scottish Isles and Ireland. The ambitions of the Dublin kings were thereafter directed more towards Scotland or, in the tenth century, to the Viking kingdom of York, than towards the interior of Ireland. From the 850s on the Viking coastal settlements were no real threat to the Irish kingdoms, save that they were used by various Irish kings as allies in their own internal wars. The short period of intensive raids disrupted monastic life and monastic workshops, destroyed countless irreplaceable libraries, and sent scholars and books overseas to the Carolingian court; in the long term the Viking presence may have moved the cultural and political strength of Ireland from the coastal regions to the interior, and, by the introduction of trading towns and, later, coinage, may have had a vitalizing effect on economic life.

Similar problems occur when trying to assess the impact of the Vikings in Francia. Were they anything more than an irritant, a complication in an already complex political picture, a potential ally for a discontented count, or an occasion for him to build up a local reputation as a defender of his county? They were all those things. But it is also clear that the numbers involved in raiding in Francia were far larger than in Ireland, partly because the potential profits were so much larger, and the periods of raiding were prolonged and intensive. Attacks on towns and insecurity in the countryside put a premature end to the commercial boom of Charlemagne's reign. There must have been considerable depopulation in coastal districts, from Flanders right round the coast to the Bordelais. The broader political results are less clear. The Carolingian Empire would no doubt have fallen apart, and the power of Carolingian kings waned, above all in West Francia, even if the Vikings had not appeared. But the inability of successive kings to deal with the problem quickly enough must have weakened their credibility, and the successes that some of their counts did have against the Vikings must have strengthened their local power. Eastern Francia, made up of ethnic duchies such as Saxony, Franconia, Swabia, Bavaria, was hardly affected by the Vikings and continued at least until 911, and the arrival of a non-Carolingian on the throne, to preserve its Carolingian political structure. But western Francia began effectively to fragment into several dozen separate political entities, and some of those entities were ruled by men who rivalled the king in power. Some owed their origins very directly to the Vikings. One of the great political powers of the tenth century, the count of Flanders, succeeded because he could move into an area whose traditional structure had been shattered by the Vikings. And the two ancestors of the dynasty that was to replace the Carolingians in France, the Capetians, both Robert and his son Odo, made their names in the wars against the Vikings.

In England the effects were different again. Scandinavian settlement was probably more extensive than anywhere else in Europe. There are hundreds of place-names of Scandinavian origin, and standard English even today has a large Scandinavian element, while local dialects have an even heavier input. But it is very difficult to date these linguistic elements, and impossible to know the scale of immigration required to produce them. Does one place-name ending in -*by* indicate that the place was acquired by one Viking landowner, or settled by a whole Viking community? Does a wholly Scandinavian place-name element mean that the people living in the vicinity, who gave that place its name, were largely Scandinavian-speaking? On the whole linguists favour the idea of large-scale settlement; historians are more sceptical. There is no doubt about the political impact of the Viking period, however. In 800 England was split into a number of separate kingdoms, dominated by

Mercia. Devon and Cornwall were still independent British kingdoms. By 900 there was only one English kingdom left, that of the West Saxons, whose kings were already calling themselves 'kings of the English' and starting to 'liberate' the rest of Britain. Liberation was not welcomed by all; some enemies of the West Saxons, such as the Northumbrians, or the Britons of Devon and Cornwall, could see the Vikings as useful allies. But it is difficult to imagine how England could have emerged by the late tenth century as a wealthy, powerful, and united kingdom had not the Vikings destroyed all native dynasties except that of the West Saxons. The English nation was, in a sense, created by the Vikings, with the help of the West Saxon propagandists.

Our contemporary written sources deal almost exclusively with the literate world of western Europe. But thanks to later traditions, to reports by Arab travellers, and to archaeology we can see how much larger the Viking world was. Vikings travelled from the Scottish Isles north-west to Iceland. They first landed there, by accident, in around 870, and colonization of this empty and inhospitable land began almost immediately, with settlers coming from Ireland (not just Vikings, but Irish too, as slaves or as wives), from Scotland, and from Norway. Further expansion westwards, to Greenland and Newfoundland, took place in the following century and a half. More significant in the long run was the movement east, primarily from Sweden, to found trading-places all round the Baltic and deep within Russia. Thanks to the writings of the Emperor Constantine Porphyrogenites we know about one of the trade routes; he describes how the Rus traders from Novgorod and elsewhere gathered at Kiev, and then travelled down the Dnieper to the Black Sea and thence to Constantinople. In 860 and on other occasions these fleets decided to attack Constantinople rather than trade with it, but to little effect. Arab traders met these Rus also, and leave us in little doubt that they were Scandinavians. Sometime in the late ninth century Rurik led some of these Rus to take Kiev and found a princedom which, a century later, was the most powerful in Russia. Rune-stones in Sweden record the deaths of men in far-flung places, and remind us that the effects of the Viking experience were just as profound in Scandinavia itself as in the parts of northern Europe touched by the Viking raids. The raids brought Scandinavia into much closer contact with other parts of Europe, paving the way for conversion to Christianity, and bringing economic and social changes which were to lead to the political unification of Sweden, Norway, and Denmark. For a while at least, around 900, Scandinavia was at the centre of a whole network of connections and exchanges which gave northern Europe a kind of unity which it never had before or since.

3

The Society of Northern Europe in the High Middle Ages

900—1200

DAVID WHITTON

An Abortive Kingdom

IN about 1175 a magnificent set of the Gospels was copied at the Saxon monastery of Helmarshausen. It was destined for another church, St Blasius, which had quite recently been founded at Brunswick by Henry the Lion, greatest of German nobles, who was duke of Saxony and Bavaria. Brunswick was his principal residence in Saxony—there he built a palace which outshone even those of his sovereign, the Emperor Frederick Barbarossa—and the new Gospels for his church were sumptuously illustrated. One of its illustrations featured the duke himself, with his English wife, Matilda. Each knelt in humility before Christ, who was in the act of placing crowns upon their heads. The crowns formally signified their dedication to Christ's service, but the picture implied other statements as well. The very character of the portrait carried exalted connotations; dukes and their consorts were not normally so portrayed, though kings were. Those who missed this point could not but have observed that the picture placed an unusually great emphasis upon Henry and Matilda by presenting them on almost the same scale as Christ himself. Other elements reinforced this emphasis. Each held a cross, which recalled the duke's acquisition of a fragment of the True Cross. Above them there stood, on Henry's side the saints to whom he had dedicated cathedrals and other major churches in Saxony, on Matilda's two saints closely associated with England, Gregory the Great and Thomas Becket, thus stressing her English parentage. Behind the couple could be seen a number of their ancestors, carefully selected to emphasize the illustriousness of the pair. Henry's included a grandfather who had been crowned emperor as Lothar III, and his own father, Henry the Proud, for whom Lothar had, vainly, sought the succession. Behind Matilda were her father, King Henry II of England, and his mother, Matilda, who had once been empress. In this context the spiritual crowns could readily be taken in a more earthly sense, and they were probably intended to be, for the duke was almost certainly in pursuit of a crown.

Within five years his dream lay in ruins; in 1180 Barbarossa declared both his duchies confiscate and the duke was driven into exile. The portrait thus stands as a poignant memorial. But it is far more than that, for it illustrates matters central to the course of history at this time. All the relatives and ancestors who stood at either side of the couple came from families which had been obscure in Carolingian times, and all had risen through marriage; Lothar to the heiress of Saxony, Henry the Proud to Lothar's daughter, Matilda to the Emperor Henry V, Henry II by Matilda's subsequent marriage to his father, the count of Anjou, and by the death without male heir of King Henry I of England. Henry the Proud and Henry the Lion came from the most eminent of all these families, the Welfs, who had provided wives for Louis the Pious and Louis the German and had occupied the throne of Burgundy; but they came from a junior branch of it, and Henry the Proud's grandfather had been an Italian nobleman who had married into the family. Each of these figures was heir to their Carolingian forebears only in the most tenuous sense.

Good marriages were an essential element in their elevation, but those marriages had themselves mostly taken place with the approval of kings, whether to win allies, reward service, or provide for the succession. The relations between a king and his magnates could not be stable for they rested upon the accidents of birth and death, anticipations fulfilled or frustrated, the

GENEALOGY OF HENRY THE LION

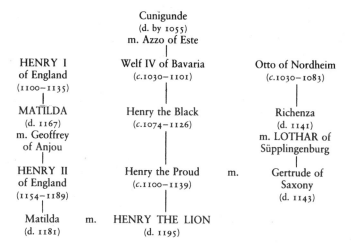

Cunigunde
(d. by 1055)
m. Azzo of Este

| HENRY I of England (1100–1135) | Welf IV of Bavaria (c.1030–1101) | Otto of Nordheim (c.1030–1083) |

| MATILDA (d. 1167) m. Geoffrey of Anjou | Henry the Black (c.1074–1126) | Richenza (d. 1141) m. LOTHAR of Süpplingenburg |

| HENRY II of England (1154–1189) | Henry the Proud (c.1100–1139)   m. | Gertrude of Saxony (d. 1143) |

| Matilda (d. 1181)   m. | HENRY THE LION (d. 1195) |

passing of generations. Kings had to bind men to them through providing them with some form of reward, and the process was continual since the bond so created was unlikely to survive the death of either partner, and might well come to an acrimonious end before. Henry the Lion himself provides a good illustration of this. The marriage to Matilda pictured in his Gospels had been contracted as part of an alliance between Frederick Barbarossa and Henry II of England; but later it provided for a safe refuge with the English king when Henry the Lion and his family broke with Frederick and were driven from Germany. A great noble's position depended, as did a king's, upon his relations with other men, his neighbours and vassals, and these too were volatile. The great estates at Henry's disposal had been secured and extended by a ruthless trespass upon the rights of others, and had been maintained largely because Frederick had turned a deaf ear to complaints. When it suited him to do so, he listened to those complaints, deprived Henry of his duchies, and thereby gave his enemies full licence to recover their own by force.

One further point may be noted in the portrait. The saints on Henry's side of the picture were ones with whom he had a special relationship. To them he had dedicated great churches, and those churches he had endowed with grants of land. In the Gospels these saints whom he had honoured now returned the favour, as sponsors of his spiritual and secular claims. Henry thought his ambitions pleasing to God and his saints, and had been careful to solicit their favour. The spiritual and secular were not distinct spheres but were part of the same picture and of the same world.

The Lineaments of Power

Henry's story is unusual only in its scale. Its essential feature— the volatility of fortune and of power—is common to the entire political life of northern Europe during the tenth, eleventh, and twelfth centuries. Henry's aspirations and fall remind us that although it is possible to talk of a kingdom of France and a kingdom of Germany throughout this period, the development of those kingdoms and their internal coherence continued to depend upon a complex network of relations between kings and magnates, among the magnates themselves, and between the magnates and their own men. It was a period which saw great changes in almost every aspect of life, but these changes did not yet alter the nature of politics.

Before turning to consider what changed we should consider what endured. The Welfs traced their descent back to Charlemagne; their claim was not entirely valid, though it was true that they had provided a bride for Charlemagne's successor, but it was a natural claim to make. Charlemagne stood as the archetype of a Christian ruler. He had created a great empire, bestowed lands and offices, been a patron of Christian learning, extended the bounds of Christendom. In legend he had made a pilgrimage to Jerusalem and brought back priceless relics, and he had waged war upon the Saracen in Spain. He stood as an exemplar to kings; in 1000 Otto III of Germany had his tomb opened, in 1165 Frederick Barbarossa had him canonized, while later Philip II of France stressed his descent from Charlemagne even though it had been his own forebears who had seized the throne from Charlemagne's descendants. The strength of his memory and legend made him the natural originator of lordship, the best legitimization. If the links were tenuous that was all the more reason to stress them, and where they did not exist that was all the greater reason to invent them.

The first family tree to come down to us from any of the great noble families is that of the counts of Flanders, compiled about 950. It does not much stress their male ancestry; rather the whole emphasis is placed upon the (actual) marriage of an ancestor to the daughter of Charles the Bald. Such marriages were the landmarks of a family's arrival, but they were also a recognition of the status and power which it had already gained, of close ties and loyal service to a king's predecessors. To remember them and celebrate them in a family tree was discreetly to remind kings that their own greatness had come from the valour, loyalty, and skill of those who served them, and so not to grudge what had been given for their service.

Great men justified their own status and identified themselves in other ways as well. They named their children to remind themselves and others of their own descent and kin, often taking a name from a bride's family if it had particularly illustrious connotations. The bonds of kinship could stretch very wide. In 1148 a member of a relatively minor Roman family boasted of his kinship to King Stephen of England by virtue of the king's Lombard grandmother. Such ties could also nurture strong bonds within the kin. On one occasion the same Stephen was on the point of taking a castle and wished to execute its garrison. Kinsmen of those inside implored his clemency, and in recognition of their service he had to grant it. Kinship could also be a handicap, however. In Flanders it became the custom that both parents must be of noble origin if a child were to be regarded as noble. Marriage into a family of servile origin, however great it might have become, could lose a man his own nobility.

Nobility could mean different things at different times. In essence it referred not to a man's valour or his power or his virtue but to his birth. Not all children could succeed to their father's eminence and so from the outset the term was not synonymous with greatness because lands might be partitioned or descend to only one child, whereas the qualification of nobility passed to all the children. This view of nobility continued to have force in the twelfth century, even though it was evident that ignoble men had sometimes gained great wealth and power. One such family was that of the Erlembaldi in Flanders, who acquired the hereditary castellanship of Bruges and a network of marriage relations with many Flemish nobles. When Count Charles of Flanders wished to break them, he threatened to investigate their servile origins, thus at once challenging their own position and demeaning the noble families into which they had married; it was an unwise move for it provoked them successfully to plot his assassination in 1127. Later in the twelfth century it became more acceptable to claim humble origins. As one family history put it, 'At the time of Charles the Bald many new men, better capable of good and honour than the nobles, became great and famous.' Sometimes humble origins were even invented. The counts of Anjou vaunted their own ability by claiming descent from a forester and overlooking their close marriage ties with leading figures in the Carolingian nobility; perhaps it helped them feel easier when they were at war with the king of France.

As nobility became less rigidly defined by birth alone, so it extended to a much wider group of men than it had previously. On occasion the word might be used to describe all freemen, though so wide a usage was unusual. Its use for those who held castles was common, even from the tenth century, and it might also be employed, though less frequently and less exclusively, for knights. Thus one of those who had married into the Erlembaldi and who faced dishonour when their social origins became known was a knight. Uncertainty about the proper application of the term noble was not simply a reflection of social mobility; it also reflected widespread change in society, occurring with differing forces and to differing degrees in different parts of Europe, and often recognized only after it had already taken place.

These developments mainly concerned the relations between greater and lesser men, and they came about partly as a response to military developments, partly as a reflection of economic recovery, but perhaps also because they favoured interests which could not indefinitely be gainsaid. Kings and great lords were essentially military leaders; they were held in esteem, or not, according to their ability to fight, whether in defence of their rights and lands or in conquest. A retinue of trained fighters was an indispensable consequence of this function. Such a retinue could be gathered and maintained in various ways. It might consist of paid men, such as the Polish dukes were able to gather about them in the tenth century. It might consist of men attracted to a particular leader by the prospect of conquest and plunder, as was the case among the Vikings in the tenth and eleventh centuries and as was much of Duke William of Normandy's army when he successfully invaded England in 1066. It might consist of landless nobles who looked for their keep while hoping to achieve something better, as was the case with the forces employed by King Henry I of England during his continental campaigns in the first quarter of the twelfth century. It might also consist of men who had contracted particular bonds to a lord or king, generally as free men but in Germany often as unfree soldiers, or *ministeriales*. Despite the great variety of arrangements which might be made and aspirations which might be shared, there was a general pressure for service to be rewarded by grants of land. Possession of land freed a man from the accidents of life such as a quarrel with his lord or years of sickness and old age and it was an essential for those who sought wives.

Land could be owned or held upon many different terms. If owned it was termed an allod; as such it passed within a family according to the dictates of local, customary law, though a lord or king might be asked to intervene if this provoked disagreement. Those who owned allods did not necessarily do so unconditionally. Public obligations to provide military service and attend local courts had been an essential feature of Carolingian government, and in due course these might be supplemented by an obligation to pay some form of taxation.

With the collapse of Carolingian government these obligations might be directed to a lord rather than a king—to some extent they always had been—and allods might come to be regarded as fiefs, lands held upon condition of performing certain services. Hence there was great variety of tenures.

This very variety accounts for the wide range of senses in which the social and political structure of this period has or has not been defined as 'feudal'. Even within a broad definition of the term which views feudalism as the association of the obligations owed by a vassal to his lord with the lord's grant of a fief to him it is impossible to accept that relations between lords and vassals were wholly feudal. Men could take lords by an act of homage without accepting that their lands thus became fiefs, and men could receive fiefs without accepting that this placed them under an enduring obligation to their lords. Relations between lords and vassals were feudal in the sense that lords came to assert that their vassals held their land as fiefs, and that they must therefore render military service, attend their courts, pay them dues, and accept their judgement over the succession to their lands. These assertions were not invariably accepted by the vassals themselves; instead they often gave rise to bitter and violent dispute. This was a direct consequence of ambiguities in the nature of lordship itself. Rights delegated to the magnates by the Carolingians were not greatly different from those which lords now demanded from their vassals. It was thus unclear how far the rights of magnates and the obligations due to them derived from the public authority which had been delegated or usurped or from the act of homage. The result was a fusion of obligations and a highly varied, frequently turbulent, pattern of relations between lords and vassals.

The dynastic disputes between the descendants of Charlemagne and the Viking and Saracen attacks of the ninth century had been an essential catalyst for the development of systems of vassalage and tenure, and Magyar attacks ranging across much of Germany and France during the first half of the tenth century provided a similar stimulus. Even so the development of lordship continued well into the eleventh century when these pressures had been removed. It did so with differing intensity in different regions and occurred here earlier and there later because the dynamic was essentially local; the lord who consolidated and developed his powers obliged his neighbours to do likewise if they preferred not to be drawn into his lordship, but equally the lord who was less active in these respects gave much smaller reason to his neighbours to construct and intensify their own lordships. Local pressures were also accentuated by technological developments in war, and by the varying degree to which different lords or entire regions might adapt to the greatly increased costs which these developments brought in their train.

Wars might be fought for plunder or for conquest. In the former case the essential elements for the attacker were surprise and mobility, while the effective response for the defender was to keep wealth in well-fortified and well-garrisoned places. In the latter case the attacker needed an army strong enough to deal with the forces which would be led against it or to make its escape if those forces proved too great, but his principal aim was to waste the countryside. Campaigns were generally limited to the months immediately before harvest, though southern regions, dependant upon viticulture, fruit, or olives were vulnerable throughout the year. The requirements for this means of waging war were sufficient speed to launch an attack, intercept one, or evade an interception, and sufficient protection and training to destroy an inferior force or hold off a superior one. These requirements were best met in the mounted knight; protective mail armour and shield, a horse bred to bear the weight of a man so equipped, a high saddle and stirrups which enabled the rider to put his horse's momentum behind his spearpoint, and the lengthy training which gave him the skill to control these elements and to act in concert with his fellows made the knight the dominant force in battle. Knights were never the most numerous element in any army—they were too expensive for that—but they did represent the element which could force a battle by its mobility and win it by its strength. Describing the French knights who passed through Constantinople in 1097, the Greek historian Anna Comnena observed, 'A mounted knight is irresistible; he would bore his way through the walls of Babylon.'

Their importance can be seen in the fact that the Normans brought trained war horses with them when they invaded England in 1066; by contrast their Viking predecessors in the ninth century had counted on capturing horses in East Anglia so that they could move more quickly. In Germany trained knights proved an effective response to Magyar attacks in the tenth century and Slav ones thereafter; so much so that the political structures which the Slavs had built around war bands had to be redeveloped on the western model. At the same time the ship-borne raids of the Vikings became increasingly ineffective as their potential victims evolved forces of knights to counter them. The Viking threat, still major during the tenth century, thus became less serious during the eleventh, being directed against societies which had not developed armies of knights (England, Ireland, the Northern Isles, southern shores of the Baltic) or within Scandinavia.

Knights represented one answer to the threat of attack, and equally offered better prospects to the aggressor, but the period saw still more expensive developments in the construction of fortifications. A war-leader who held men to him by prospect of plunder still needed to provide safe places in which shrines could be built and cattle driven in the event of a crisis. In tenth-century Poland these were provided by a score of massive log and earthenwork forts which the Polish duke garrisoned with paid soldiers. Further west fortifications tended to be a good deal more modest, though the Polish forts had some counterpart in the castles which Henry I of Germany and his successors constructed against Magyar, Danish, and Slav raids. The normal form was a wooden building and stockade, perhaps on a natural or artificial mound; but such structures were vulnerable to fire and we know that one of them was torn down by a priest and his parishioners, enraged at its lord's exactions from them. For those who could afford it the alternative was to build in stone, and there are examples of such castles in Anjou from the late tenth century. In Germany their construction came about a century later.

A lord thus found himself in an arms race with his neighbours; if they collected a force of knights or constructed castles, so must he. The impetus to this development came not from the invasions by Vikings and Magyars which were contained and then defeated in the course of the tenth century, nor from economic decline and the dictates of a natural economy; on the contrary the process reached its height during the eleventh century at a time of economic recovery and happened earliest and most intensively in those regions which were most advanced economically, Flanders in particular. The thrust came from the anxiety of lords to maintain, consolidate, and extend their lordships.

As primogeniture became the norm, in northern France during the tenth century, then in Germany and southern France during the eleventh, there was a dual pressure on lords to find fresh lands both for members of their own families and for those of their vassals. Emigration might reduce this pressure. Nobles from many northern French lands found their way to England in the wake of the Norman Conquest or joined in the Norman settlement of southern Italy and Sicily. Others, mainly during the twelfth century, took service with the king of Scotland. Many went to fight the heathen in the Holy Land or Spain, as much to redeem their souls as to secure fresh lands (indeed, one early twelfth-century chronicler took it as proven that the First Crusade had been shaped by God because for him it went against all nature for there to be 'such a contempt for material things in the hearts of savage and greedy men'). Even so formidable pressures remained. They could be met in several ways: by the acquisition of fresh territories which could then be distributed, by the regulation of vassals' tenures as closely as possible, permitting inheritance at will rather than as a matter of course, or by granting greater rights to vassals and by moderating or waiving demands for service from them. But such rights were not unlimited and the bonds so created were not likely to be any more enduring than those established by cruder acts of patronage. Kings and lords made use of all three of these techniques of control and conciliation, often simultaneously, but each left immense probability of friction and dispute, and at worst of civil war.

Underlying stability is a less obvious feature of the period, but it was there and should not be disregarded. The high costs of fortification and the strong forces which successful kings or lords could bring to bear upon their rebel vassals both tended by the mid-eleventh century to prevent the disintegration of lordships and kingdoms. Overlordship might pass from one king or lord to another, but it did so only when the nobility of a region were prepared to transfer their allegiance because a new lord was an essential element in throwing off the old. Since it was rare for a regional nobility to act with any great unanimity in such matters, and since it was seldom obvious that the new lord would be more acceptable than the old, such transfers of territory were rare. Where they occurred they were prone to be a response to a manifest imbalance of power, and such imbalances were normally enduring. As a result the boundaries of kingdoms and of many great lordships showed a remarkable continuity and the divisions of the ninth and tenth centuries largely proved permanent. When Henry the Lion dreamed of his crown, he is likely to have been thinking of exclusive rights within his territories and not of a division of Germany between himself and its actual king.

A Reviving Economy

The social and political evolution described above was not the hallmark of a weak subsistence economy, but rather of one that was strongly reviving during this period. The costs of lordship, of its military expenditure, of service from vassals and of generosity from lords, were all incentives to encourage fresh forms of wealth as well as attempting to take a larger share of what there was already.

At the beginning of this period the main source of wealth was agriculture, and it remained so throughout. Lords had established their control over it in much the same way that they had established their rights over men, amalgamating rights which had been theirs on their own estates with public rights and then extending them over as many people as possible within their lordships. The control of local justice and of obligations to forced labour, the offer of 'protection' and levying of taxation, were the essential means by which free peasants were reduced to servitude, hereditarily bound to their tenements and liable to arbitrary levies and labour services. Poor harvests and flight from marauders were both factors which could lead a freeman to surrender his liberty, but it is likely that the pressure came from above and was not willingly conceded from below, because the most rapid subjection of the peasantry came not in the tenth century, at the time of greatest instability, but rather in the eleventh when harvests were improving and lords looking for the means to build in stone rather than wood. The process was still in train well into the twelfth century. Between 940 and 980, 80 per cent of the donations made to Chartres cathedral were by peasant freeholders; between 1090 and 1130 the equivalent figure had fallen to 8 per cent, but during the thirty years before that the figure was still as high as 38 per cent. Further south in Burgundy the abbot of Cluny still hoped during the 1130s that he could attract freeholders to surrender their plots to his abbey in return for a milder lordship than they might find elsewhere. Further east on the borders of Saxony the peasantry was also able to retain its freedom longer; slaves taken from its pagan neighbours offered an alternative source of labour and the vulnerability of these lands to raiding meant that lords had to treat their peasants more generously if they were to hold them at all.

From the eleventh century lands began to be cultivated which had previously lain fallow. This is evident in southern France from the 1020s, northern France and Spain from the 1060s, and in Germany from the 1130s. Forest clearance, improved drainage, and in Flanders a laborious reclamation of land from the sea, all brought fresh land under cultivation. The process was partly a response to a growth in population, but was also, and perhaps more significantly, a means by which lords aimed to increase their revenues. When Abbot Suger of Saint-Denis (near Paris) founded new villages on his abbey's estates in the 1130s, he was quite consciously attempting to increase the monastery's revenue rather than reacting to any overpopulation in his existing villages. At the same time cereal production was improved by an increasing use of horses rather than oxen for ploughing, by a shift in some areas to a three-field rather than two-field system of ploughing, so that land was less often fallow (though in the long run also less fertile), and by a general improvement in climate from the 1160s. Even so the margin of survival remained thin and a succession of severe winters in northern Europe at the end of the twelfth century brought widespread famine.

These developments were accompanied by a sharp rise in population. In some regions this could be contained within the available food resources, in others considerable emigration could reduce the pressure, but in some there came a point when the demand for food began to rise above what was available. When this happened the result might be a sharp inflation which could have profound political effects. Despite the increasing acreage brought under cultivation by land reclamation, and despite the development of alternative means of making a living in the woollen industry, Flanders was clearly suffering from overpopulation by the early twelfth century. As early as c.1113, Archbishop Frederick of Bremen looked there for settlers to farm the eastern lands of his see, and other Saxon prelates and nobles followed his lead throughout the twelfth century. They did so to such effect that the population of Saxony is thought to have risen tenfold in the period 1000 to 1300, as opposed to a threefold increase for Germany as a whole. Such measures helped to relieve the pressure in Flanders but could not entirely curb its less welcome effects. The resultant inflation undermined the position of the Flemish nobility and brought what had been one of the best consolidated principalities into political uncertainty by the later twelfth century. Such developments operated with varying intensity and at different times in different parts of Europe and the respective strengths and weaknesses which they brought in their train could very greatly affect the relative strength of kingdoms and principalities.

With the growth of population came the growth of towns. They were supported largely by manufactures for the local market such as utensils or cloths but income also came from offerings at their shrines and the expenditure of their lords, who for their part looked to raise revenue from market tolls, or from the profits of their mints. The areas of dense population saw the most rapid development of towns and of the political importance of their inhabitants; when Count Charles of Flanders was murdered in 1127 the townsmen of Ghent and Bruges played a major part in the civil war which resulted, and in the resolution of the succession to Thierry of Alsace. Some twenty years before the inhabitants of Laon had themselves dramatically illustrated the emergence of townsfolk as a political force when they murdered their bishop after he had refused to grant them a commune, or rights of self-government, and about the same time the bishop of Compostella was experiencing revolt from the citizens of his much less-developed city. Faced with such pressures other lords compounded their rights into fixed dues and granted defined customs to their citizens, which could be an important factor in encouraging immigration to their towns. Once made grants were difficult to renegotiate, however, and this could put lords at a disadvantage in times of inflation.

During the twelfth century towns assumed further functions. Some, such as Paris, drew income from the students attracted to their schools. Others drew income from banking and mortgaging land, which could raise considerable sums when nobles were running into financial difficulties, or churches were caught midway in expensive building programmes. Jews, unencumbered by the Christian prohibition of usury, played a prominent part in these activities, and paid a heavy cost for it. They were liable to pogroms, such as those which swept the Rhineland cities in 1096, and to arbitrary levies by their lords; when the king of France arrested the Jews in the crown lands in 1180, he was able to ransom them for the considerable sum of 15,000 marks. Alongside banking there were larger-scale manufacture and long-distance trade. Here there were three principal exports: slaves, taken by the Germans on their eastern border or by the Vikings, and particularly in demand by the Muslim caliphate of Cordoba before its collapse in the early eleventh century; Flemish cloths and woollens, increasingly manufactured from English wool; silver, of which major deposits were discovered in Saxony during the eleventh century. Through Italy and the inland waterways of Russia these goods were traded for luxuries from the east, particularly silks and spices, which were at once valuable and relatively easy to transport.

The development of such trade gave lords fresh sources of income. In the first instance it offered easy targets for robbery or for the extraction of tolls. The construction of many northern French castles in relatively weak sites close to roads was one manifestation of this trend. Great lords and kings reacted sharply against these acts, partly under injunction that it was their Christian duty to do so, but also because they could thereby establish a monopoly on tolls themselves. In the late eleventh century a count of Flanders was renowned for having boiled alive a knight who had taken vengeance at a fair, while Louis VI of France (1108—37) spent much of his reign campaigning against lords who preyed on traders; this did not prevent either of them from requesting such dues themselves. Other lords took more positive action to encourage trade within their territories, and of this there is no better example than the way in which the counts of Champagne in the twelfth century encouraged a great annual cycle of fairs in which Flemings and Italians dealt with each other. The volume of trade was so considerable that the coin of the district became the model for the standard currency in much of Italy in the second half of the twelfth century. Behind this there may also have been another more baleful trend; it is possible that the cost of the north's imports was not yet covered by the value of its exports, and could only be met by the export of bullion.

Lords at Prayer

When Henry the Lion associated his own dedication to Christ with dreams of a more secular nature, he made a connection fundamental to his time. Kings identified their duties to their subjects with their obligations to God, and defined them as the punishment of oppressors, protection of the helpless (particularly widows, orphans, and churches), and extension of the word of God to pagan neighbours. That kings might sometimes neglect or contravene these principles made them more rather than less significant, for without them there could be no justification for a permanent secular authority. It is thus no accident that the sacral character of kingship was most fervently and explicitly asserted during the worst periods of disorder. By virtue of the old Carolingian traditions, the kings of Germany, particularly as emperors, developed a very strong sacral tradition, justified by their efforts in the conversion of their eastern and northern neighbours, in their protection of the papacy and their rescue of it from the unworthy creatures of Roman faction, and, sometimes, in their claim to superiority over the other kings of Europe. Other kings were also assiduous in stressing the holy nature of their office; Philip I and Louis VI of France both made a practice of touching for scrofula, while Alfonso VII of Castile claimed an imperial title in 1135 by virtue of his role in recovering souls from the Muslims.

Sacral claims could sometimes be in conflict with more worldly considerations. Under Otto I of Germany the archbishops of Hamburg–Bremen were active in the Christianization of Denmark and Sweden, and Otto himself founded a great archbishopric at Magdeburg for the conversion of the Slavs. The conversion of these peoples was closely linked with the extension of ecclesiastical jurisdiction, and sometimes of outright lordship, and this provoked opposition. Fourteen years after Magdeburg's foundation the great Slav revolt of 982–3 undid almost all that had been achieved; the see was never again to be a missionary centre of any significance. Eastern rulers had been quick to see the threat that was posed and the opportunities which conversion offered. Mieszko I of Poland and Stephen I of Hungary both forestalled German attack by accepting missionaries from Germany, but each also accepted missions from Bohemia and in Stephen's case from Byzantium too and thus prevented the Germans from gaining control over their churches. Their independence was formalized in 1000–1 when Otto III conceded Mieszko's successor, Boleslav Chobry, a new archbishopric at Gniezno, to be directly subject to Rome, and when Stephen submitted his kingdom directly to the papacy. Poland and Hungary thus avoided German control. At the same time Mieszko and Boleslav were able to use their recent Christianization in the conquest and conversion of pagan Pomerania and Stephen to do likewise in the subjection of the other Magyar dukes. Elsewhere paganism was harder to eradicate because it provided the main political focus against foreign domination. Saints Adalbert and Bruno of Querfurt were among the missionaries who lost their lives in Pomerania around the turn of the tenth and eleventh centuries, and in the 1120s Otto of Bamberg found that force was essential since the pagan temples had to be taken and destroyed. Even where such considerations did not apply, the progress of conversion was slow and often superficial. Norway had been Christianized from the end of the tenth century and had its own bishops from the 1050s, but the pagan practices of libations and of exposing infants were still common a century later.

The role of kings thus came to seem ambivalent, valued for the essential force which they might bring to a conversion, but criticized for prejudicing that conversion by attempting to associate it with political domination. Some kings themselves undermined the ideal, as Henry II of Germany did through his alliances with pagan Slavs against Christian Poland, though he later atoned by the foundation of a missionary bishopric at Bamberg. The sacral role of kings was being undermined in other ways too. They were not, and never had been, the only founders and patrons of great churches and monasteries, but from the tenth century the nobility took an ever larger part in these activities, and to a still greater extent in the building of parish churches on their lands. Secular interests sometimes lay behind such acts. Parish churches could bring income to their lord while monasteries might serve as advanced bastions in the extension of a lordship, as did the Angevin house of Holy Trinity, Vendôme, in the counts' contest for Tours with the counts of Blois during the first half of the eleventh century. Great lords no longer occupied lay abbacies after the early tenth century, but by granting disputed lands to a monastery under their control, and then protecting them as its advocate, they had a barely less potent means of domination.

This is not to say that spiritual considerations were necessarily far from their minds. Great churches were dedicated to saints and richly endowed with their relics. Something of the importance which these had can be seen from the eagerness with which relics were purchased or stolen. Otto I of Germany's Italian expedition of 962 was marked by a very considerable transfer of relics, while in the twelfth century Barbarossa rewarded an archbishop of Cologne for his service by granting the relics of the Three Kings to his see. One of the tactics adopted by a bishop of Compostella against a rival see was the theft of its relics in 1102. Saints could make a marriage fertile or cure illness, and their friendship had to be won by gift at their shrine or the foundation of a church in their honour, which was probably the main reason for the proliferation of churches in the eleventh century. Churchmen liked to point out that saints could be less friendly, bringing a sudden end to those who mocked them. The victims might include the founder or his kin if they disregarded a church's rights; but they were more likely to include their secular rivals and enemies. Secular and religious ends could march in perfect harmony because saints and lords were linked in competition with their rivals.

In this sphere kings thus lost some of the importance which they had once had. It was more common in Germany than in France for great churches to look to them for protection from their oppressors, but they were likely to look closer to home as well, and to judge a king by his willingness to vindicate their rights. When Otto II of Germany suffered a shattering defeat in Italy in 982, a chronicler interpreted the disaster as divine punishment for the incorporation of the see of Merseburg within Magdeburg. A century later successive archbishops of Magdeburg, whose interests had not been well served by the intervening kings, were in the forefront of the opposition to the monarchy.

Within the Church a series of developments took place which were to deal still heavier blows to the position of kings as representatives of God. In the disorder of tenth-century France, churchmen began to express new views on the relations between clergy and laity, evolving the famous theory of the Three

Orders, which divided society between those who worked, those who prayed, and those who fought. The duty of the fighters to use their weapons only in defence of the helpless and of the Church was the theme of Abbot Odo of Cluny's biography of the noble St Gerard of Aurillac, and from the end of the century similar ideas were implicit in a series of councils, first in southern France, but by 1030 in northern France too, in which laymen were enjoined under pain of excommunication and heavy penances to observe the Truce of God and not to fight within specified periods. Bishops thus took over the maintenance of order for themselves, though they were less ready to do so, save by the sporadic sentence of individual offenders, in Germany where the monarchy retained much of its authority until the late eleventh century. Besides attempting to limit wars, churchmen bagan to claim the authority to launch them. That war could be meritorious and benefit the souls of those who undertook it was a view first enunciated among Cluniac monks, but it found enthusiastic support from the papacy. In 1064 Pope Alexander II granted an indulgence to those joining the expedition against Muslim Barbastro, and in 1074 Pope Gregory VII attempted by similar means to raise an army for the defence of eastern Christians from Muslim persecution. His preaching fell on stony ground, but in 1095 Pope Urban II renewed the appeal at the Council of Clermont and found an enthusiastic response. Effectively he had set a precedent which made the promulgation of crusades a papal prerogative, one which it would in time abuse. Though kings themselves took part in several of the ensuing expeditions, the authority to license war against the pagan had passed from them to the pope. Their role as war-leaders was thus diminished, particularly when popes began by the end of the twelfth century to claim that all wars fell within their jurisdiction.

The second of the developments within the Church which affected the position of kings consisted of a general change in the character of monasticism. Though broadly following the Rule of Benedict, practice from one monastery to another varied considerably according to local custom but also according to their ability to preserve the essentials of the monastic life against what could be very heavy odds. When kings, nobles, or bishops wished to found or reform a monastery they generally turned to another one, attracted by the renown of the institution or particularly of its abbot. In northern Germany John of Gorze was especially active, but his influence was personal and after his death was increasingly taken over by the Burgundian monastery of Cluny, founded in 909 and favoured by an extremely impressive succession of abbots. During the eleventh century under Abbots Odilo (994–1049) and Hugh (1049–1109) the relationship between Cluny and the houses it reformed became increasingly one of affiliation, though the closeness of the bond still varied considerably; the result was a dramatic increase in the number of houses affiliated to Cluny, from thirty-eight in 998 to several hundred on Hugh's death. The importance of these affiliations lay not so much in the subjection of so many houses to Cluny—despite extensive rights over them the abbots of Cluny generally kept them on a loose reign—as in their exemption through that affiliation from the authority of their local bishops. This could be very much to the advantage of those nobles entrusted with the estates of a church, its advocates, because it substituted a distant authority for the local one with which they might be at loggerheads. At the same time it gave the monasteries a source of appeal beyond local pressures and intimidations if either advocate or bishop proved too troublesome. So far as kings were concerned Cluny was less immediately threatening. The abbots of Cluny were respectful of them, did not challenge their rights over churches within their kingdoms, and on occasion mediated between antagonistic popes and kings. Even so kings were cautious because the subordination of monasteries to a centre outside their own sphere of influence struck at the roots of their control over them.

Towards the end of the eleventh century a new and more austere form of monasticism began to exercise strong attractions. Older monasteries were closely bound to society since much of their activity had come to centre on the liturgy, and in particular on prayer for their founders, benefactors, and those who had been admitted into confraternity with them.

In this context it did not greatly matter that many of their recruits were admitted by their parents as children, which was a boon to parents who could not otherwise provide for them without a risky diminution of their estate; nor that only a short noviciate was required, which was a boon to those who wished to become monks shortly before death in order to benefit from the prayers of the community. The wealth of an abbey's estates was justified by the size of community which it could support, the splendour of its buildings by the honour which they did to God and his saints, and by the manner in which they provided a proper context for reverence. When the monks of Cluny first celebrated the office in the third and greatest of their churches there, one of them described it as being 'like Easter every day'. In the twelfth century all these things came into question: the admission of children and the short noviciate because many unsuitable men thereby became monks, monastic wealth because it embroiled monks in unseemly disputes over property, great churches because they embodied the snares of this world rather than the flight from it. Such thoughts were not new, but in the twelfth century they came to attract and justify not small bands of hermits as hitherto but a monastic order which soon came to rival Cluny in size and eclipse it in influence. The Cistercian Order had its origins at Cîteaux, founded in 1098; by 1153 it comprised some 350 houses, spread throughout Europe. For the most part they were sited in relatively remote places; this at once suited the interests of benefactors, who could give land not as yet profitable, and those of the monks themselves, who sought to distance themselves from the world and its cares but at the same time wanted to reintroduce manual labour into the monastic life. The high ideals of the order, sometimes fairly described by its detractors as insanely conceived, necessitated a much tighter system of administration than Cluny had evolved; this took the form of a regular chapter-general for the order as a whole.

If Cluny had represented interests and ideals implicitly dangerous to the sacral position of kings, the Cistercians now developed them and combined them with fresh ideals of their own. The incorporation of their houses into an order represented a greater threat than that of Cluny because their organization was so much tighter. When Barbarossa insisted upon the recognition of an antipope, the German Cistercians followed the lead of their order as a whole and refused to acknowledge him; German and Burgundian Cluniacs did, and split their order in consequence. More serious than this, however, was the way in which the ideals of Cîteaux insisted upon the prior obligation of men to God, rejected the comfortable compromise with the demands of the world which Cluniacs had been ready to make, and scorned the things which were the touchstones of the secular power. Individual churchmen had always stood for such claims, but it was something new for a whole range of new orders to be doing so.

The third development, and the one most obviously opposed to the sacral power of kings, came in the growth of papal authority. The competing claims of churches and saints, and the vulnerability of churches to lay depredations, particularly in regions where political authority had broken down, greatly increased the need for an institution which might subject one church to another, free it from such subjection, or take it and its property under its own protection, thus adding St Peter's anathema to their own in the event of an infringement. Papal co-operation was essential to Otto I of Germany in the creation of the archbishopric of Magdeburg against the opposition of other German bishops, just as the papal protection of Poland was essential to its rulers when they sought to avoid political and ecclesiastical domination by Germany. At the same time the pope might quash an election if there were clear evidence of irregularity; thus Hugh Capet of France was in the 990s unable to install his preferred candidate as archbishop of Rheims. During the eleventh century popes exercised their rights more energetically; following the reform of the papacy by Henry III of Germany in 1046, popes began to travel outside Italy (albeit sometimes as refugees from the turbulent Italian politics of the time) and to intervene decisively when they did so. To investigate abuses and encourage appeals they also sent out cardinals and legates, and sometimes gave that authority to local bishops, much to the chagrin of their colleagues.

These practices they undertook because they and those around them became increasingly convinced that all was very far from being well with the Church. It seemed to them to have been tainted by worldly values, so much so that its divine message had been obscured. From the beginning two abuses particularly drew their fire; the propensity of the clergy to marry and the obtaining of holy orders or of a benefice by the gift or promise of money and land (termed simony). There were strong material considerations here; married priests were prone to use church goods to provide for their wives and children, and might bequeath their churches too, while the simoniac was likely to commit his offence at the expense of his church. Reforming propaganda did not stress this, however; instead it emphasized the sacramental role of the priest. Hands dedicated to the re-creation of Christ in the Eucharist should not be tainted by impure activities. It proved difficult to enforce these ideals. In some regions the clergy claimed the privilege of marriage and threatened to murder bishops such as Siegfried of Mainz who attempted to enforce the papal prohibition. Almost everywhere it proved impossible to bar the sons of priests from becoming priests themselves. The co-operation of bishops was essential for the prosecution of reform, but when the charge of simony was allowed against bishops as well as their inferiors that support was often lost. Bishops complained, often with justice, that malign rivalries between the canons of their churches, and between the noble families from which they came, were all too liable to lie behind such charges, and that their authority was undermined if such appeals were heard.

This discontent reached a head during the pontificate of Gregory VII (1073–85), particularly among German bishops, whose appointments during the troubled minority of Henry IV had often incurred suspicion of simony. Henry himself came under suspicion of assenting to these practices and shielding the offenders, and rashly offended the pope by appointing bishops to three sees in Italy which the pope claimed as his own, or where there was already a papal appointee. At this point Henry made common cause with the majority of his bishops and withdrew his obedience from Gregory at the Diet of Worms in January 1076. The ensuing conflict was a landmark in the history of the papacy. Gregory excommunicated Henry and urged his subjects to force him to subjection, and eventually he recognized a German prince, Rudolf of Rheinfelden, as king. For his part Henry, after a brief period of reconciliation achieved under pressure at the famous meeting at Canossa in 1077, campaigned successfully to replace Gregory by a more pliable pope and refused to recognize Gregory's reforming successors. When he died in 1106 he was still excommunicate.

The conflict generated an immense pamphlet literature from the advocates of both sides. In the course of this, issues which had been peripheral became central, and at the heart of these was the question of the rights which kings might exercise within their churches. From the early eleventh century kings had begun to invest prelates with a ring and staff, symbolizing both the office which was being given and the estates of the Church. In the event of a chapter presenting an unwelcome candidate, the final word lay with the king, who could block the appointment by withholding investiture. Gregory himself had attempted to prevent Henry from following this custom, and his successors, Popes Urban II (1088–99) and Paschal II (1099–1118) had a series of decrees passed which were intended to ban the practice everywhere. They did so on theological rather than political grounds. Hands which consecrated the Eucharist risked contamination when joined with those of men who handled swords, and on the same grounds they prohibited the clergy from doing homage to laymen. The principle that kings could dispense ecclesiastical office was thus effectively rejected. At the same time it came to be accepted that a king, though able to provide an essential support to the Church in resisting the encroachment of the local nobility, was as liable as they to excommunication if he turned his authority to more oppressive uses. Eventually, in agreements reached with the English and French monarchies in 1106–7, and with the German monarchy in the Concordat of Worms in 1122, none of them explicitly permanent, it was agreed that kings might be present at episcopal elections and invest the successful candidate with the estates of his see. The conflict thus ended with an agreement on investitures, and from this it rather misleadingly takes its name.

The practical results of the controversy were smaller than the theoretical ones, but were not negligible. Kings no longer had a decisive voice in episcopal elections though their words could still be very influential. Attempts to override a determined opposition generally provoked an appeal to the papacy, though the extent to which that appeal was heeded could vary considerably according to political considerations. The possibility of a strong papal intervention thus became another of the numerous considerations which kings had to bear in mind, sometimes at the expense of otherwise preferable factors. At the same time, it became much harder for kings to shield their bishops from the appeals of their inferiors and the judgements of popes and their legates, and this at once fixed some bounds to their conduct and lessened the extent to which bishops looked in the first instance to the king.

The Twelfth-century Renaissance

Developments within Christendom and within the Church thus came to change the nature of kingship. Other intellectual currents had a more ambivalent effect. During the twelfth century the example of Ancient Rome and a wave of fresh intellectual and artistic initiatives combined with an exceptional fertility; the term Renaissance is not misapplied. Perhaps the first area to be affected was that of law. Roman law had been replaced by tribal customs in most of northern Europe, and these customs were seldom collected and seldom consciously altered. It is rare before the eleventh century to find any king following the example of his Carolingian predecessors and issuing fresh law. Two influences helped to change this situation. One was the survival of Roman Law in much of Italy, where German kings were often active. The other influence was also Italian; from the time of Gregory VII's pontificate a number of collections of canon law had been produced, and about 1140 they were distilled in the collection compiled by Gratian. His attempt to reconcile contradictory precedents by identifying the underlying principles and then extending them to analogous cases indicated in the clearest possible way that precedent did not make law though it might help to justify it. The making of ecclesiastical law was reserved to the papacy, and the legislation it issued began to encourage kings to do likewise.

The re-creation and transformation of Roman example was something which touched almost all spheres of thought and art, though the achievement was more superficial in some spheres than others. The literature of antiquity had been preserved almost entirely through the work of monks, and monks were the principal compilers of history. In many cases they took the events of the present and recent past and then put them into the context of events since the Creation. The divine framework thus enclosed the Roman. At the same time, however, Roman historians began to influence their successors more independently. Their histories had been written in terms of the deeds of great men, and their deeds had been evaluated in terms of their benefit to the state; the supernatural was largely absent. Both of these strands can be seen in the works of northern historians from the eleventh century. The result was the emergence of a style of historical writing which at once provided a fresh basis of authority, conceived largely in secular terms, and a series of criteria by which its representatives might be tried and found wanting.

Theology was also the preserve of monasteries, and then of cathedral schools, during the tenth and eleventh centuries. During the twelfth century some of these schools began to attract celebrated teachers, not in their employ, who lived off the fees which they could draw from their pupils; such were the origins of the University of Paris. Verbal acumen, a readiness to challenge older doctrine and that of his colleagues, and a responsiveness to new trends became the hallmarks of the successful teacher. Nobody exemplified these characteristics more clearly than Peter Abelard; he taught that acts were good or sinful according to the intention which lay behind them, and delighted in indicating the contradictions between different statements in the Bible. This went too far for some of his contemporaries, and he was twice condemned, in 1121 and 1140, ending his days as a monk of Cluny. Despite this his teaching influenced many of his less provocative colleagues and successors. The works of Aristotle were becoming better known through the work of translators in Toledo and Sicily, and the possibility that there might be a natural order of things in which God did not intervene directly was already being taken seriously. How this might be without limiting the omnipotence of God was yet to be resolved but was already being debated.

An equivalent development can be seen in the art and architecture of the period, again more noticeably in France than elsewhere. Its characteristics were a trend towards more realistic depiction on the one hand, attempting to indicate character through features rather than allegory, and on the other the adoption of a style of church architecture intended to give maximum play to light, symbolizing the influence of God himself. The technical means adopted here broke away from Roman precedent, above all in the use of rib-vaulting, but the process of evolution was gradual rather than sudden. Two of its most pronounced features were to be seen in a church which was traditional in everything save its vast size, that built at Cluny from the end of the eleventh century. One was the circuit of chapels around the apse, each dedicated to a particular saint and offering fresh sources of light to the east end of the church; the other, introduced when the roof proved to be inadequately supported, was the flying buttress, equalizing lateral and vertical structures and so making the provision of larger windows possible. The possibilities inherent in these innovations were consciously employed in the rebuilding of the abbey church of Saint-Denis (Paris) in the 1140s, and then in a whole sequence of French Gothic cathedrals during the next generation. Laon and Notre Dame were the first-fruit of this movement, followed by Chartres at the end of the twelfth century; after this lead the style became so dominant and its monuments so impressive that they have come for many to symbolize the Middle Ages. Elsewhere these innovations were slow to take root; in Germany the prevalent trend followed Roman and Italian example, though greater size forced some technical change. In art, as in other respects, Germans looked back to an increasingly irrecoverable world.

Germany and its Neighbours

For most of these three centuries the kingdom of Germany stood supreme in western Europe. It would have been hard to foresee this in 919 when Henry I came to the throne. Designated by Conrad I, his succession was initially recognized only within his own duchy, Saxony, and Conrad's, Franconia. Force having failed, he was obliged to gain recognition from the dukes of Swabia and Bavaria by allowing them to appoint bishops within their territories and by allowing them to take over the crown lands. With these grants he appeared to have conceded the essentials of kingship; estates upon which the ruler and his entourage might stay when travelling through the kingdom to hear pleas, offices which could be filled with trusted servants. By the time of Henry's death the losses had been recovered, but the example of Henry the Lion reminds us that dukes long after were seeking the same rights as their distant forebears. The course of German history is not one of smooth development within which the monarchy could establish its own authority and traditions; nor was it one of an inevitable degeneration into princely particularism. Rather it lay in the violent oscillation between the two.

Henry I's success lay upon two foundations. As a vigorous war-leader he was able to contain the threat from Denmark to the north of his duchy, and in 933 to inflict a major defeat upon the Magyars, who had menaced the whole of eastern Germany and many points further west since their destruction of the Moravian kingdom in 906. The scale of the threat made the dukes his far from unwilling partners, and it brought other rulers, Wenceslaus of Bohemia chief among them, under his overlordship. Henry's other asset lay in the comparatively recent rise of his family, the Liudolfings: he had succeeded his father, Otto, as Duke of Saxony in 912. The law of consanguinity was not yet fully defined, and churchmen were as yet hesitant in invoking it, but it was already the case that marriage could for several generations prevent the marriage of descendants; in time the number of generations was defined as seven, but this was not strictly enforced. A new dynasty thus had the advantage of an old one, for it still had a reasonably free choice of the politically most advantageous marriages before it. The asset was naturally a wasting one, but it helped Henry draw Lotharingia back into the kingdom under his brother-in-law, Duke Giselbert, and was to be a major element in the success of his son and successor, Otto I (936—73).

Upon Henry's foundations Otto was able to raise the German monarchy to one of its greatest peaks. In this he was aided by a happy combination of circumstances. To the east he unleashed a series of campaigns against the pagan Slavs between the Elbe and the Oder, who were also being menaced from the nascent duchy of Poland under Mieszko I; that helped to provide territory and manpower with which he might bind men to him. To the west he was favoured by the intermittent conflicts between the Carolingians and Robertians which made it unappealing for the dukes of Lotharingia to throw off his rule for they could expect little help from France if they did so. Within Germany marriages of his relatives into the ducal families secured their accession to Swabia and Bavaria, while Lotharingia was bestowed on a son-in-law. To the south the turbulent politics of Italy provided a fruitful sphere in which to intervene, bringing Otto the crown of Italy in 951, the imperial crown in 962, and a rich harvest of relics with which he could endow the great eastern bishoprics and monasteries. By appointing bishops to sees well distant from their native parts he helped to create alternative sources of support should their neighbours prove restive and was at the same time able to impose military obligations on the Church to defend the eastern frontier and provide troops for more distant expe-

THE OTTONIAN RULERS OF GERMANY

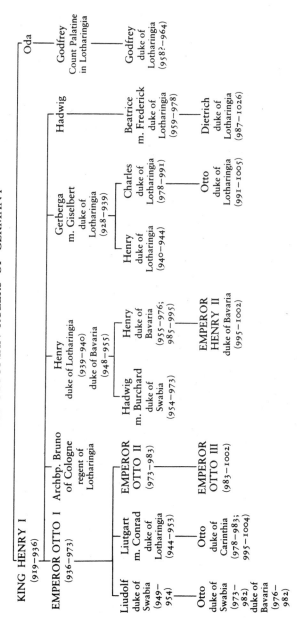

OTTO I ESTABLISHED HIS CONTROL OVER MOST OF THE GERMAN DUCHIES through the marriages of his children, nephews, and nieces. In time these links became too distant to be of much political advantage yet still too close to permit their being cemented by further marriage. Lotharingia was frequently divided between dukes hence the large number of incumbents.

NORTH SEA

NORTH MARCH

MARCH OF THE BILLUNGS

MARCH OF LAUSITZ

MARCH OF MEISSEN

FRIESLAND

SAXONY

WESTPHALIA

THURINGIA

LOWER LOTHARINGIA

FRANCONIA

UPPER LOTHARINGIA

ALSACE

SWABIA

BAVARIA

BOHEMIA

MORAVIA

MARCH OF AUSTRIA

MARCH OF STYRIA

KINGDOM OF HUNGARY

CARINTHIA

VERONA

KINGDOM OF FRANCE

COUNTY OF BURGUNDY

KINGDOM OF BURGUNDY

KINGDOM OF ITALY

ADRIATIC SEA

Hamburg · Bremen · Osnabrück · Minden · Hildesheim · Münster · Halberstadt · Utrecht · Liège · Cologne · Cambrai · Merseburg · Naumburg · Meissen · Trier · Mainz · Worms · Bamberg · Würzburg · Verdun · Metz · Speyer · Eichstadt · Toul · Strasbourg · Augsburg · Freising · Passau · Salzburg · Constance · Chur · Brixen

R. Elbe · R. Danube · R. Neckar · R. Main

boundary of German kingdom c. 962

regional boundary

lands of German duchies

main concentrations of the Ottonian lands

archdiocese

diocese

0 50 100 150 km
0 50 100 miles

THE GERMAN KINGDOM IN THE TENTH CENTURY. The lands of the Ottonians were largely concentrated in Saxony, but as each duchy fell vacant it also proved possible to recover some of the crown lands, particularly those in Swabia. Otto III and Henry II spent more time in southern Germany than their predecessors.

ditions. Despite these opportunities and achievements he also faced periods of very great danger. His stepbrother and younger brother regarded themselves as alternative candidates for the throne and in turn revolted; so too did other dukes, including his son, Duke Liudolf of Swabia, when he feared that Otto's marriage to Adelaide of Italy would preclude him from the succession. What set the seal upon Otto's achievements was fortune; at the time of the most serious of the revolts, Liudolf's, fresh Magyar hosts burst upon the scene. King and rebels united against this threat and at the Lechfeld, near Augsburg, gained one of the most decisive battles in the course of history (955).

Otto's victory established him as the leading monarch of the day; immediately afterwards he was hailed as emperor, though his actual coronation had to await the convenience of the papacy. For the time being there was no question of the disintegration of the kingdom he had forged. For the next two centuries such disputes as arose over the succession concerned the kingdom as a whole and did not envisage its partibility, and the disputes which arose between kings and princes were largely over questions of inheritance and of the respective royal and princely rights within their lands, not over the principle of royal overlordship. Outside Germany its greatest effect was probably in the east. It encouraged Otto to press for the creation of his great missionary archbishopric at Magdeburg and to send missions as far afield as Kiev, and it helped to accelerate the pace of conquest from the Slavs. At the same time, however, it removed a major threat from the emergent duchies of Poland and Bohemia, and encouraged the Magyars to settle and eventually create a formidable state in what became the kingdom of Hungary. Disputes between and within the three countries enabled the German kings to secure an almost permanent overlordship of Bohemia and a sporadic one over Hungary, and it also brought tribute from Poland for territories conquered from the Slavs, but the bonds were loose, continually had to be restored by force, and brought only Bohemia into the ambit of the German kingdom. The long-term significance of these developments was immense; if

German kings were to bind men to them by rewarding them at the expense of Germany's neighbours, they now had to do so to the south in Italy where there was no consolidated power to bar the way.

The first German king to recognize this was Otto's grandson, Otto III (983−1002). His father, Otto II (973−83) had followed in Otto I's footsteps, intervening as he had done in the troubled affairs of the French kingdom and to the east extending German domination as far as the Oder. A disastrous defeat in southern Italy sparked off a great Slav revolt in 982−3, however, and German rule was again marked by the Elbe. A series of fruitless campaigns to recover the lost lands during the 990s may have made Otto III pause to consider; so too may the martyrdom of the revered Adalbert, exiled bishop of Prague, at the hands of the Pomeranians. A pilgrimage to his tomb at Gniezno in 1000 led to the foundation of an archbishopric there, directly subject to Rome, and an equivalent foundation was made for the Hungarians at Esztergom the next year. At the same time relics were transferred there and Boleslav Chobry was recognized as semi-independent ruler of Poland, though he did not take a crown for himself until 1024. Otto III himself spent much of the latter part of his reign in Italy, having settled eastern affairs to his satisfaction and facing little danger in Lotharingia from the French king or magnates. How far he dreamed of a renewed empire as head of a federation of Christian kingdoms, and how realistic such a project was, are questions which have exercised historians ever since, not least since they are unanswerable, Otto dying prematurely at the age of 21.

Unlike his predecessors Otto III left no heir. Events on his death were an unwelcome portent of things to come, for the succession of his cousin, Henry of Bavaria, was opposed by two other magnates, Ekkehard of Meissen and Hermann of Swabia. Each had powerful adherents, Boleslav Chobry and the archbishop of Magdeburg respectively, and their opposition illustrates the fragility of the state which the Liudolfings had created. Ekkehard was related to Boleslav by marriage; time and again the ties which magnates might contract within and outside the kingdom gave them support and bonds which might make them unmanageable, and when Ekkehard was murdered the result was a war between Henry and Boleslav which lasted much of his reign. As for the archbishop, he was faced with demotion from his see, which had absorbed his previous bishopric; kings could appoint trusted and capable men to bishoprics but the competing claims of rival churches might still bring them out against the crown. Henry spent much of his reign (1002–24) in Germany, but it is unlikely that this represented a conscious reaction against the policies of his predecessor rather than a simple and very necessary attempt to close up the fissures which had opened when Otto had died. Extensive grants of comital rights which he made to the Church, particularly in Saxony, show his desire to secure a reliable basis of support.

The accession of Conrad II (1024–39) marked the first of the major dynastic changes in the history of the German monarchy, for Henry II died without heir. Such changes could weaken the monarchy; in time princes would learn to give or withhold their support in return for lands and rights, and crown lands and rights were readily lost when the king's power basis shifted to the regions in which he already held lands. At the same time the changes could also provide strength; Conrad was not pre-empted by any earlier marriages in seeking a Danish bride for his son and heir, Henry III (1039–56), though Henry himself later came under criticism for his subsequent marriage to Agnes of Poitou, an important match which helped to secure his hold over the kingdom of Burgundy, taken into the German kingdom on the childless death of King Rudolf in 1032. Conrad II and Henry III followed their predecessors' examples in taking advantage of succession disputes in all three of the eastern states to insist upon their overlordship, and in attempting to make their rule in northern Italy, at least, a reality. In order to safeguard their position in Germany they resorted to two dangerous expedients; the first, successfully employed by Conrad against a rebellion by Duke Ernst of Swabia, was to detach his vassals from him by offering them secure tenure and inheritance of their lands, the second, adopted by Henry in Lotharingia, was to intervene in the succession to the duchy and insist upon its division. Each of these measures had something to be said for it, the first through its success in quelling a dangerous revolt, the second from the danger which an undivided Lotharingia might represent if its duke made common cause with the French king or other magnates who were now in a stronger position than before to interest themselves in the region. Against these short-term gains there were longer-term losses. Manipulation of their vassals' inheritances was one of the essential means by which lords maintained their hold over those whom they had enfeoffed, so too was the right to confiscate the lands of those who had defaulted from their service; when these powers were restricted great lords came to find difficulty in holding their vassals to their obligations without making further concessions to them, and by extension could come to question and resent the demands for service which the crown continued to impose on them. At the same time the king's own tendency to intervene in questions of inheritance infringed precisely those rights of the magnates in which they were now barred from intervening where their own men were concerned. The result was a heady sense of grievance which brought Germany close to major revolt. When Henry III died in 1056 leaving the infant Henry IV as heir, there were those who wished to deny him his throne 'lest he turn out like his father'. As so often, the strongest kings left the most difficult legacies.

Henry IV's minority gave the opportunity for the discontent to emerge and allowed others to develop. His predecessors had built up a carefully structured polarization of influence, lands, and wealth but in doing so they had infringed rights which their victims regarded as inalienable. A succession of regents, archbishops Anno of Cologne and Adalbert of Bremen in particular, took the chance to reinforce their own position, and at the same time provided the means by which others could regain or acquire their due. Duchies held directly by the crown were granted to great nobles, Swabia to Rudolf of Rheinfelden, Bavaria to the Saxon Otto of Nordheim, Saxony to Ordulf Billung, who proceeded to take over many of the crown lands, and on Adalbert's fall many of those of the see of Bremen as well. When Henry came of age he faced an insuperable problem; any attempt to recover what had been lost could only succeed with the support of men who had themselves made great gains at his expense, men who might well fear that the treatment handed out to others would next be applied to themselves. His attempt to recover royal lands in Saxony and to garrison them provoked revolt, and when that revolt was crushed in 1075 the harsh penalties which the king imposed on the leaders may well have made his own supporters think again. Pope Gregory VII's excommunication of the king in 1076 gave them their opportunity, but did not cause the civil war which ensued; Rudolf of Rheinfelden's election as king in Henry's place came directly after the news of Henry's reconciliation with Gregory at Canossa.

The war which resulted went initially in Henry's favour; by 1080 Rudolf had died of wounds and Henry was free to launch a series of campaigns in Italy against Gregory VII. His success was transitory, however, partly because grants made to his supporters such as that of Swabia to Frederick of Staufen hardened the resistance of alternative claimants and progressively created an almost insoluble complex of rivalries. Each success thus paved the way for further revolts, skilfully encouraged by Popes Urban II and Paschal II who for a time held Duke Welf of Bavaria in the opposition by marrying his son to Matilda of Tuscany, then encouraged the revolts of Henry's sons Conrad (from 1092) and Henry (from 1104). As Henry IV aged it became increasingly obvious to his supporters that they would need to reach some accommodation with his successor, and his unhappy reign ended with the defection of the dukes of Austria and Bohemia, both previously loyal, capture by his son Henry, the confiscation of the royal insignia, and an unconsecrated grave at Liège where he died still excommunicate in 1106.

The accession of Henry V (1106–25) did not mark an end to Germany's problems for these lay largely outside his control. In the circumstances it was impolitic to provoke the opposition of Paschal II by going so far as to kidnap him during the imperial coronation in 1111 in order to secure his recognition of the royal right to invest bishops. The resultant excommunication gave ample cloak to those who meditated revolt on other grounds, notably Lothar of Süpplingenburg whom Henry had appointed Duke of Saxony and the Rhenish archbishops whom Henry had alienated by the grant of some of their lands to his supporters. Resistance thus continued after the princes had forced Henry to reach a settlement with the papacy in the Concordat of Worms in 1122 and for most of the reigns of his successors, Lothar of Süpplingenburg (1125–37) and the Staufen Conrad III (1138–52). Conrad and his brother, Frederick of Swabia, were thus in opposition to Lothar for much of his reign, while Lothar in turn built up links with the duke of Bavaria, Henry the Proud, his son-in-law and prospective heir to both Saxony and the crown. When Lothar died these hopes were thwarted since the magnates had little to gain from assenting to the election of the immensely powerful Henry and very much more to gain, largely at Henry's expense, from supporting Conrad instead. On this basis Leopold of Austria and then his half-brother Henry Jasomirgott were granted Bavaria while Saxony was granted to Albert the Bear. An attempted compromise by marriage failed with the death of the essential partner (Henry the Proud's widow) in 1143, and matters were made worse by the subventions with which Roger II of Sicily and Geza II of Hungary provided the opposition in order to forestall Conrad's intervention against themselves. When Conrad was succeeded by his nephew, Frederick Barbarossa, duke of Swabia, it was an open question whether the polarization of interests and rivalries within the German magnates could ever be resolved.

Barbarossa (1152–90) was the greatest of German kings since the days of Henry III, but like him he mortgaged Germany's future to achieve that greatness. His first task was to settle the rivalries and territorial disputes which had developed over the past century. Henry the Proud's son, Henry the Lion, was restored to the duchy of Saxony at the expense of Albert the Bear, and in due course built up a highly formidable lordship there. Before long he was also appointed to

Bavaria, Henry Jasomirgott being compensated with the grant of Austria on terms which gave him effective autonomy within his lands, and exemption from military service, save on its frontiers. For his part Frederick had to build up his power in Burgundy, Swabia, and southern Saxony, though this eventually brought him into conflict with Henry the Lion since it blocked his own claims there. At the same time he sought to recover the imperial rights in Italy. The time was reasonably propitious; in the treaty of Constance (1153), Pope Eugenius III had engaged his assistance against the Commune of Rome, while in the south it remained to be seen whether the kingdom of Sicily would survive the anticipated death of Roger II. At the same time the imperial rights in Italy promised substantial revenues, could they be secured, and there were also lands, mostly assigned to Henry the Lion's uncle, Welf VI, until he sold them to Barbarossa. Prospects were thus favourable in Italy; at the same time intervention there represented almost the only sphere in which Barbarossa could build up his power and gain alternative sources of wealth and patronage without disturbing the fragile settlement which he had established between his magnates.

In the event, Barbarossa faced years of hard and very expensive campaigning before the Peace of Constance assured him most of what he had sought. The effects of the campaign in Germany had been somewhat ambivalent. The archbishops of Mainz and Cologne, his leading generals in Italy, had largely dissipated the resources of their sees in the endeavour, others had used his need for troops to make ever more pressing demands upon the crown. Chief among these was Henry the Lion, who at last began to aspire towards a royal position and sought the vestigial royal estates in Saxony to round off his territories. When Frederick refused to agree, Henry in turn denied him troops which were very much needed at the height of the Lombard campaign (1176). Four years later Barbarossa took advantage of the hostility which Henry had aroused in Saxony to deprive him of his duchies, and Henry was indeed driven from his lands, which passed to a number of magnates, the archbishop of Cologne, Albert the Bear's son, and the

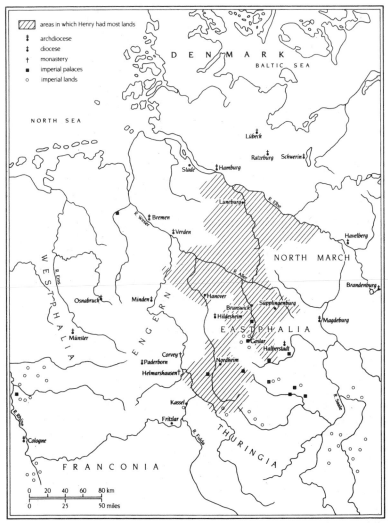

THE DUCHY OF SAXONY UNDER HENRY THE LION. Henry's lands were
concentrated in eastern Saxony. Frederick had estates to the east and south,
but only the lands around Goslar could serve as a focus for imperial authority
within the region dominated by Henry. The breach came when Henry demanded these lands and was refused.

Wittelsbachs chief among them. It was a dangerous step for it revived the territorial animosities and rivalries which had for so long set the magnates against each other. For the time being the partial restitution to Henry and his sons of some of the Saxon estates helped to maintain the peace when Barbarossa left Germany to die on crusade, but it was unlikely that Henry's sons, now coming into their prime, would accept the loss even if their ageing father were disposed to do so.

Some rapprochement with their interests was reached by Barbarossa's son and successor, Henry VI (1190–7). His energies were largely devoted to the conquest of the kingdom of Sicily, then to grander projects still, though these proved abortive. To achieve these he had to do all he could to smooth affairs in Germany. Lübeck was restored to Henry the Lion, but ominously this did not prevent Henry's eldest son from deserting the emperor's army, obtaining from Pope Celestine III a bull which made the family liable only to his own sentence of excommunication and not that of bishops, and rebelling. The revolt was suppressed and Henry was able to go on to conquer Sicily, but even with this great success behind him he was unable, at the Diet of Würzburg in 1196, to persuade all of the German princes to agree to the hereditability of his kingdoms. On his death in 1197 the claims of his infant son Frederick were discounted and groups of princes proceeded to the elections of Henry VI's brother, Duke Philip of Swabia, and of a son of Henry the Lion, Otto of Brunswick. Civil war descended upon Germany again. Only time would tell whether it would prove any more damaging to the monarchy than those which had preceded it.

It was Germany's tragedy that its monarchy asserted itself most vigorously and thereby awoke the deepest resentments at a time when the purposes, prerogatives, and duties of kingship were largely undefined and at a time when the development of lordship was still following its cumulative ramification in that country. It thus happened that the crown simultaneously suffered a challenge to its traditional, theocratic basis, while its secular opponents lacked the inclination, perhaps even the notion, of attempting to define the areas within which

kings could and could not move. Instead the princes kaleido-
scopically grouped and regrouped around rival candidates
for the throne, and saw their best prospects in the gratitude
of those whom they supported. The result, not primarily
intended, was to deny the crown the continuity of lands,
rights, personnel, law, customs which could alone make a
monarchy secure when its roles as theocratic ruler and war-
leader had passed.

The Kingdom of France

France also saw the rise and fall of a great dominion during
this period, but that dominion was not that of the French king.
It had been formed largely to his prejudice and when it began
to crumble the French crown enjoyed the advantage of coming
to the fore at a time altogether more propitious for the development of a stable and enduring state. The dominion which
was to fall had its roots during the reign of Charles the Simple,
when that king granted Rouen and its environs to a Viking
leader, Rollo, in order to buy off his attacks. By the end of
the tenth century Rollo's descendants had secured extensive
territories from this base and forged the duchy of Normandy.
Its duke, William, became king of England in 1066 by conquest, and in so doing created a dominion which far outshone
in resources and power any of the northern French lordships,
including that of the French crown in the area around Paris.
On his death in 1087 his territories were divided between his
sons, but this proved temporary. The interests of their vassals
were not suited by the dual allegiance which resulted, and with
greater resources the kings of England were in a better position
to take the whole than the dukes of Normandy. Already there
were signs that these developments might enhance the very
standing of the Norman duke in France. Norman dukes
claimed that they need travel only to their own borders to do
homage to the French king, and when King Henry I of England
conquered Normandy from his brother in 1106 he began to
assert that he could give no homage for Normandy since kings
could not give homage, only receive it. The next generation

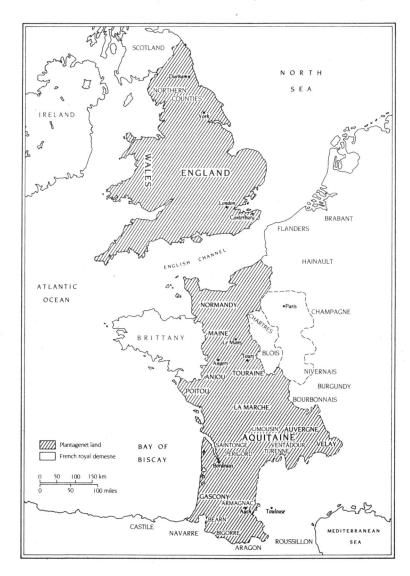

SCOTLAND

NORTH

SEA

Durham

NORTHERN
COUNTIES

IRELAND

York

WALES

ENGLAND

London

Canterbury

BRABANT

FLANDERS

ENGLISH CHANNEL

HAINAULT

ATLANTIC

OCEAN

NORMANDY

•Paris

CHAMPAGNE

CHARTRES

BRITTANY

MAINE

Le Mans

Tours

BLOIS

Angers

TOURAINE

NIVERNAIS

ANJOU

BURGUNDY

POITOU

BOURBONNAIS

LA MARCHE

LIMOUSIN

AUVERGNE

AQUITAINE

VELAY

Plantagenet land

French royal demesne

BAY OF

SAINTONGE

PÉRIGORD

VENTADOUR

TURENNE

0   50   100   150 km

BISCAY

Bordeaux

0   50   100 miles

GASCONY

ARMAGNAC

Auch

•Toulouse

CASTILE

BÉARN

NAVARRE

BIGORRE

ROUSSILLON

MEDITERRANEAN

SEA

ARAGON

THE ANGEVIN LANDS IN 1154

saw the extension of the Anglo-Norman lands to a still greater degree with the marriage of Henry's daughter to Count Geoffrey of Anjou, the eventual succession of their son to the English throne as Henry II and also to Normandy, Maine, and Anjou, and the acquisition of Poitou and Aquitaine as well by marriage to its heiress, Eleanor, who had just been divorced by King Louis VII of France. In the course of these developments Louis had been able to receive homage for all of the continental lands but it was an open question whether he and his successors would continue to be able to do so.

In some ways the history of France is that of Germany in reverse. Its period of greatest turmoil came first, and it was not forged into a unity until the thirteenth century when the circumstances were more propitious and the conflicts of earlier days played out. It was not tempted by the opportunities on its borders or forced by the threats beyond them into a premature unity. When that unity was achieved it was willingly accepted and consciously manufactured and therefore endured. Little of this could be seen at the time; the fall of the Angevin lands was to come swiftly and unexpectedly, the sudden and vast extension of the French crown coming as a great windfall rather than something long and consciously striven for. Yet arguably it would never have happened at all had the French monarchy not decayed almost to vanishing point for much of this period.

That decay came first from the struggle between the Carolingians and Robertians for the crown through much of the tenth century, and then from the exceptional stability which the Capetian dynasty enjoyed after its accession in 987 to what became an uninterrupted and unchallenged possession of the crown. The conflict was the more obvious factor. The election of Count Odo of Paris to the crown after Charles the Fat's abdication in 887 had not resulted in a permanent change of dynasty. Before Odo died he had been obliged to recognize the succession of Charles the Simple. His election, nevertheless, served as a potent example to his descendants who took advantage of Charles the Simple's incapacity to secure the succession first of Odo's son Robert in 922 and then after Robert's death the following year of his son-in-law Raoul of Burgundy. At this stage France was in a condition not greatly dissimilar from that in which Germany was so often to find itself after the reign of Henry III. Great lordships, some very temporary, were in the process of creation and consolidation; emerging as they did from a fusion of royal grant, usurpation, and coercion, each stimulated by fear of the equivalent process on the lands of a neighbouring lord, it was natural for their lords to exploit the struggles between Capetian and Robertian and even to foment them, for a prospective monarch was likely to be more generous than an incumbent one. Once such polarization of interests was created only two things were likely to bring it to an end; the extinction of one or other of the contestant families, or the development of the great lordships to a point at which they need no longer fear or encourage royal action.

Although Count Odo's descendants and relatives did not again occupy the throne between 936 and 987, there was always the possibility that they would. The reigns of the Carolingian Louis IV (936–54), Lothar (954–86), and Louis V (986–7) were dominated by the threat which Robert's son, Hugh the Great, and then his grandson, Hugh Capet, could offer only too readily. In this climate the kings could do little but look on as the great magnates usurped offices, rights, and lands, attempted to gain control of the great churches as Herbert of Vermandois did at Rheims on behalf of his son, and murdered their rivals without fear of retribution. External circumstances provided little cheer; Magyar and Saracen attacks came and went too rapidly for the kings to present themselves as great war-leaders in the way that the Ottonian kings did. At the same time the very strength of the German monarchy made uninviting the prospect of binding men to the crown through the attempted recovery of Lotharingia which had been drawn into the German ambit. When this was tried during one of the few periods of German weakness it provoked the interests of great families to such a degree as to move them to the direct support of the Robertian alternative; the interests of Archbishop Adalbero of Rheims' relatives in

Verdun were decisive when he crowned Hugh Capet as king of France in 987.

When Hugh came to the throne both conditions for a cessation of hostilities had effectively been met. The surviving Carolingian candidate, Louis V's uncle Charles of Lorraine, was disqualified by marriage into a knightly family, and perhaps still more by his treachery during hostilities between Lothar and Otto II. At the same time the lordships of northern France, though not yet fully defined and consolidated, had for the most part reached the point at which a further prolongation of the struggle offered fewer rewards than risks, so that Charles's bid for the throne found little support. In short Hugh Capet came to the throne at a time when much of its power had already been lost, and this was a major factor in the survival for more than three centuries of the dynasty which he founded. The conflicts of the tenth century affected the monarchy in another way as well. During their course Carolingians and Robertians had looked for great allies through marriage; each had, for example, taken wives from Otto I's sisters. For much of the eleventh century the consequence was that the politically most beneficial marriages were either barred to the Capetians by consanguinity, or liable to be challenged on that ground if they nevertheless contracted them. Something of the implications of this can be seen in the family trees produced for the house of Roucy, which had been closely bound to Hugh at the time of his bid for the throne. In the eleventh century they made nothing of their link with the monarchy, and only began to vaunt their relationship with the royal family during the last half of the twelfth century when Louis VII was enjoying a resurgence in the powers of the crown.

As a result of these developments the reigns of Hugh's son Robert (996–1031), grandson Henry (1031–60), and great-grandson Philip (1060–1108) marked the lowest point in the history of the monarchy. Great lords such as William V of Aquitaine and Odo of Blois struggled for prospective inheritances in Italy, Burgundy, and Lotharingia without let or hindrance from the crown; others such as Fulk of Anjou carved

THE CAPETIANS

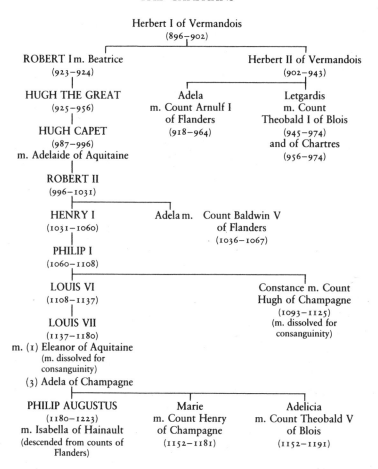

Herbert I of Vermandois
(896–902)

ROBERT I m. Beatrice
(923–924)

HUGH THE GREAT
(925–956)

HUGH CAPET
(987–996)
m. Adelaide of Aquitaine

ROBERT II
(996–1031)

Adela
m. Count Arnulf I
of Flanders
(918–964)

Herbert II of Vermandois
(902–943)

Letgardis
m. Count
Theobald I of Blois
(945–974)
and of Chartres
(956–974)

HENRY I
(1031–1060)

PHILIP I
(1060–1108)

Adela m.   Count Baldwin V
of Flanders
(1036–1067)

LOUIS VI
(1108–1137)

LOUIS VII
(1137–1180)
m. (1) Eleanor of Aquitaine
(m. dissolved for
consanguinity)
(3) Adela of Champagne

Constance m. Count
Hugh of Champagne
(1093–1125)
(m. dissolved for
consanguinity)

PHILIP AUGUSTUS
(1180–1223)
m. Isabella of Hainault
(descended from counts of
Flanders)

Marie
m. Count Henry
of Champagne
(1152–1181)

Adelicia
m. Count Theobald V
of Blois
(1152–1191)

HERBERT II OF VERMANDOIS WAS A CRUCIAL ALLY of Robert I and Hugh the Great in their struggles against the Carolingians. His progeny included the counts of Flanders and of Blois-Chartres-Champagne and as these lines endured it was difficult for the Capetians to contract durable marriages with these families until the reign of Louis VII; otherwise they were liable to dissolution for consanguinity. Hugh Capet's marriage to Adelaide of Aquitaine had a similar effect.

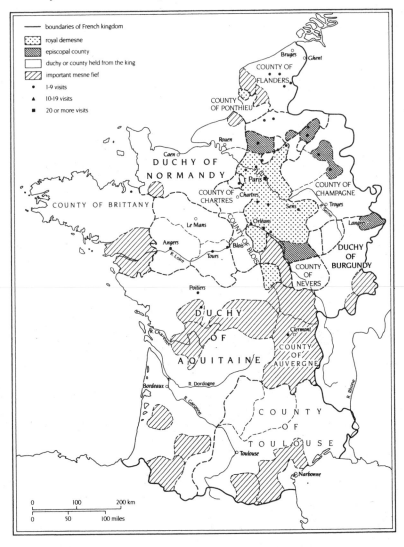

boundaries of French kingdom
royal demesne
episcopal county
duchy or county held from the king
important mesne fief
• 1-9 visits
▲ 10-19 visits
■ 20 or more visits

Bruges
Ghent
COUNTY OF
FLANDERS
COUNTY
OF PONTHIEU
Rouen
Caen
DUCHY OF
NORMANDY
Paris
COUNTY OF
CHAMPAGNE
COUNTY OF
CHARTRES
Chartres
Sens
Troyes
COUNTY OF BRITTANY
Le Mans
Orleans
Langres
Angers
R. Loire
Blois
Tours
COUNTY OF BLOIS
DUCHY
OF
BURGUNDY
COUNTY
OF
NEVERS
Poitiers
DUCHY
OF
AQUITAINE
R. Charente
Clermont
COUNTY
OF
AUVERGNE
Bordeaux
R. Dordogne
R. Garonne
R. Rhone
COUNTY
OF
TOULOUSE
Toulouse
Narbonne

0   100   200 km
0   50   100 miles

PHILIP I OF FRANCE'S ROYAL DEMESNE. The weakness of the French crown under Philip I can be seen from the smallness of the royal demesne and the infrequency of his journeys outside it.

out formidable lordships for themselves in northern France, barely impeded by the intermittent opposition of kings; one, William of Normandy, by his conquest of England created the great Anglo-Norman dominion which overshadowed each of the northern French lordships, that of the king included. During this period the Capetians were able to add very little land to that under their control. Their greatest acquisition, the duchy of Burgundy, had to be ceded to Henry I's brother to buy off his bid for the crown; against loss on this scale the additions of the Gâtinais and Bourges to the crown lands in the reign of Philip was small compensation, though they did represent territories which could be held securely, which may not have been the case with Burgundy. Intermittent crises in each of the principalities allowed the kings to make sporadic interventions in their affairs, as when Henry I helped Duke William defeat Norman rebels in 1047, and from time to time Philip sought to balance Blois-Chartres or Anjou against Normandy, but although these interventions helped to preserve the royal right to intervene, and the subordinate status of the princes, they had little further effect. Philip was at least spared one indignity. The crown had preserved its right to invest over approximately a third of the French bishoprics, but he did not follow Henry IV's example in risking a full-scale conflict with the papacy to retain the right or to protect bishops from the investigations and castigations of Hugh of Lyons, Gregory VII's formidably principled legate in France. The choice was sensible for the lands and political power of many bishops had passed to the counts and viscounts of their cathedral cities. In the event the French crown gained more than it lost from the Gregorian Reform because the new insistence upon the right of cathedral chapters to elect their bishops made it more difficult, and perhaps less attractive, for the greatest families to provide for their relatives in this way. As a result an increasing proportion of French bishops after 1100 came not from the grandest families but from smaller noble families, more likely by reason of their relative smallness to be rivals of other local families, also with their relatives or associates in the chapter, and therefore in need of a figure to which they might look if their count or duke proved unsympathetic to their interests or promoted those of their rivals. How much scope this left for crown intervention depended upon the intensity and durability of these rivalries, and upon the varying extent to which the great lords could regulate them, but in general that scope enlarged quite considerably from the beginning of the twelfth century. Similar opportunities came with the growth of towns during the same period and the request of some of them for the grant of a commune. By granting the request kings could limit the power of an unco-operative bishop or lord, by refusing it gain his support.

By the beginning of the twelfth century trends were thus again beginning to run in favour of the monarchy, and they were assisted by the opportunity which the Capetians had to make politically advantageous marriages now that they would no longer be too evidently consanguinous. The turning-point came in the reign of Louis VI (1108–37). Louis's great contribution to the history of the French monarchy was to bring the royal lands, or demesne, firmly under his control, destroying castles whose lords illicitly levied tolls upon travellers and merchants and building his own from which these dues could be raised by the crown. In this he was doing no more than other lords, but his biographer, Abbot Suger of Saint-Denis, was able to depict him as the archetypal Christian monarch, protecting his churches and the poor against the ravages of the wicked, and simultaneously champion and standard-bearer of St Denis, apostle of the French. Together these provided an ideological foundation which came less readily to other lords. Something of the same trend can be seen in his practice of touching the poor for scrofula. Nor was Louis inactive outside the demesne. Skilful diplomacy and an occasional campaign secured him the homage, if not of the reluctant Henry I of England then of his prospective heir and later that of the contestants in the civil war which followed Henry's death in 1135. In Flanders his intervention helped to block the succession of a count too closely aligned with Henry when Charles the Good was murdered in 1127. Such interventions helped to revive the ties between the crown and the princes; they did not differ in kind from those of his predecessors, but they were more consistently effective because Henry's great strength upset the political balance of northern France and so drove his opponents into alliance with the monarchy. Two episodes particularly indicate the revival in the fortunes of the monarchy. The first came in 1124 when almost all of the French magnates sent contingents to help the king against an invasion by Henry's son-in-law, Henry V of Germany. The other came at the end of the reign when the duke of Aquitaine, a region in which royal authority had been conspicuously absent, looked to Louis's son and heir when seeking a husband to protect the rights of his daughter and heiress, Eleanor.

In the event the marriage proved impermanent. In 1152 she divorced Louis VII (1137–80) and married Duke Henry of Normandy, who was shortly to become king of England and count of Anjou and Maine as well. Arguably this vast accumulation of territory and power was less dangerous than that of Henry I had been, because its still greater size and power helped intensify the ties which the crown was able to establish with the other great families of France. Louis VII's third marriage was to Adela of Champagne, with whose counts his relations were consistently friendly for the rest of his reign, while the first marriage of his son, Philip Augustus (1180–1223), was to Isabella of Hainault, politically beneficial until her death and disputes over her dowry. At the same time the huge scale of the possessions over which Henry II of England and his successor Richard (1189–99) ruled provided considerably more scope for appeal to and intervention by the crown. Despite being almost consistently on the move Henry and Richard were absent from many of their lands for too long to be able to anticipate revolts by the discontented, and these problems worsened in the second half of Henry's reign when his sons began to anticipate and fight for their share of his inheritance, in which Louis and Philip were not slow to give their support. Each of Henry's sons in turn was encouraged to press for an effective grant of territory, each made apprehensive of his father's intentions for him, each encouraged to revolt. This process began as soon as they were reaching adulthood when Louis made the grant of lands to Henry's eldest son an essential feature of the Peace of Montmirail in 1169, and it continued in Richard's reign when his brother John was similarly encouraged to revolt. Equivalent steps were taken in respect of Henry's other subjects; in the settlement following the great revolt of 1173–4 against Henry, Louis made it an article of peace that the rebels should not be deprived of their lands.

In a number of ways the tide was running in favour of the Capetians. Their position as Henry's overlord and their upholding of the rights of his vassals meant that hostilities generally occurred on their initiative and not his, on his territories and not theirs. The Angevins had to be strong everywhere and for much of the time, whereas the Capetians could use their resources more sparingly, deciding the time and place of attack, sapping the will to resist by wasting lands. The Angevins depended heavily on their English resources to finance their campaigns and Richard I drew heavily upon them after Philip had taken advantage of his absence on crusade and his captivity in Germany to secure some key Norman fortresses. But the crusade and Richard's ransom had already strained those resources, and heavy inflation in England, coupled with difficulty in adjusting revenues accordingly, was beginning to put the English king at a disadvantage. This was accentuated by Philip's acquisition of Artois, Amiens, and Vermandois as a result of his marriage to Isabella of Hainault and the more efficient exploitation of his demesne. The famine of 1194–7 hit his war effort as it did Richard's, but the economic revival in the demesne had not reached the point, as it had in England, at which overpopulation produced inflation and brought heavy pressure to bear on the nexus of relations between kings, lords, and their vassals. Here too fortune favoured the late developer.

The twelfth century saw the emergence of a more secular, utilitarian, concept of rule which evaluated the deeds of a ruler in terms of the benefits they brought to his people, and classified them as tyrannical when harm resulted instead. In part this came from the study of history, in part it was a result of the blows which had been dealt to the older theocratic view in the Investiture Contest, but it was also a reflection of the way in which princes had regularized their rule, defining the obligations due to them but also recognizing the rights of their subjects. The crown had persistently if sporadically involved itself in this process through its readiness to hear the complaints of men against their lords. Here was another process which worked in favour of the Capetians, for it limited the freedom of the Angevins to deal as they might with their vassals, and at the same time encouraged those vassals to believe that there could be no wrong in supporting the king against their lord if that lord abused his position.

Little of this was evident when Richard died in 1199. Nobody could have foreseen that the bulk of the Angevin lands would have been forfeited to the French crown within five years, least of all Philip Augustus who fortified Paris and set scholars to work to counter a prophecy that the Capetians would rule France for only seven generations, his own being the seventh. This, perhaps, was the final advantage which fate dealt him; since the true nature of his strength was not fully apparent his enemies played all the more readily into his hands.

Scandinavia and Eastern Europe

Finally, some mention should be made of political developments in Scandinavia and in the three eastern European states, Poland, Bohemia, and Hungary. In each case the principal factor which determined their history came from outside these societies rather than internally, the eastern states through the development of a powerful neighbour to their west in Germany, the Scandinavian through the reduction of opportunities for freebooting in either east or west, and through the cessation of the supply of plunder and Islamic silver which had fuelled its most formidable expeditions during the ninth and tenth centuries.

Of the eastern kingdoms, it was Hungary which least suffered from the attentions of its western neighbour, and which had sufficient opportunities elsewhere to provide a focus and justification for its monarchy. The transition from the loose federation of Magyar bands of the tenth century into the kingdom of the Hungarians was thus eased because unity provided sufficient force to resist the interventions of Germany and of Byzantium, and at the same time gave sufficient strength to establish an effective domination over Croatia for most of the twelfth century. Gold and silver mines and a considerable demesne made the monarchy relatively strong despite a number of succession disputes. Poland was less fortunate; it had less opportunity to develop into a powerful and unified state because Pomerania and the other Slav lands to which it aspired were also being sought by the German king and magnates, from Henry II's time only too ready to ally with the pagan tribes to prevent the development of too formidable a Poland. To its south was the Bohemian duchy, most closely bound to Germany of all the eastern states and thus able to establish its own dominion of Moravia to the exclusion of Polish claims there. By 1138 Poland's once formidable Piast dynasty of monarchs had fragmented into mutually opposed branches, each willing to call in German help as it suited them. Bohemia had meanwhile enjoyed comparative stability, but at the expense of effective incorporation into the German kingdom, albeit under its own line of Přemyslid dukes; the crowns granted to Wratislaw II for his assistance against Henry IV's Saxon opponents or to Wladislaw II for the large troop contingents he led to Italy on Barbarossa's behalf were small compensation for this subjection, though the interregnum in Germany on Henry VI's death was shortly to provide the opportunity for its mitigation.

Where the Scandinavian countries are concerned the irony is that the powerful states which barred the way to their expansion were largely of their own creation. The Norman settlement on the Seine attracted immigrants, not war parties. The possibility of raiding and then launching a full-scale invasion of England was a powerful spur to Viking unity, but once it had been achieved that function ceased. Settlers and lords in the conquered territories had no interest in harnessing their endeavours and risking their lives in the acquisition of less attractive lands elsewhere. When the Normans were able to gain possession of England this chapter in Viking history came to a close. Continued raids and conquests in the Northern Isles, Ireland, and in Iceland kept the Viking ethic flickering, but could not provide much stimulus for the achievement of a now superfluous political unity.

Of the three Scandinavian kingdoms, only Denmark was able to remain relatively stable and undivided; Norway and Sweden both spent much of this period in political confusion. In each case external pressure represented the main spur to unity, more or less consistently from Germany in the case of Denmark, very sporadically from Denmark in the case of the other two countries. Like Poland and Hungary these countries adopted Christianity in the first instance for political reasons to forestall conquest by their Christian neighbours; but only in Denmark did the Church become much of a support to the crown, since the basic facts of Nordic geography led to a fragmented regional society with few towns, mostly scattered along the seaboard, which could not function as centres of government. The familiar features of government are thus only fully recognizable in Denmark during this period; when a disputed succession occurred one or both parties might look to the German king or magnates in the manner of the competing Piasts, sometimes acknowledging German overlordship. At the same time there developed a feudal aristocracy not greatly different from that of Saxony. For their neighbours it was fortunate that the Danes no longer sent forth the warrior hosts which had ravaged most of the northern coasts of Europe, twice conquered much of England, and burnt Hamburg among many other cities; for the Danes it amounted to a relegation into a very marginal role in European history.

Casting an eye back over the ground surveyed, the most striking feature of the history of northern Europe during these three centuries is how little the political map of Europe had yet changed. The development of great lordships had been almost universal, so too had the arrival of a relative peace and prosperity. One view of kingship had been decisively challenged, but the materials with which another might be constructed were already to hand. Despite these immense changes France did not seem closer to political unity nor Germany to political disintegration at the close of the twelfth century. The ground was prepared for a series of huge upheavals, but when they came they took men by surprise. Neither Henry the Lion nor Frederick Barbarossa were anachronisms; each acted with the confidence of many precedents and parallels, reaching back for centuries. In the end it was this very confidence, even blindness to change, which was to give it the shattering, unexpected, impact which was to burst upon Europe in the thirteenth century.

4

Northern Europe Invades the Mediterranean

900–1200

ROSEMARY MORRIS

Old Empires and New Challenges

There are two lordships, that of the Saracens and that of the Romans,
which stand above all lordship on earth, and shine out like two mighty
beacons in the firmament.

IN the world of the Patriarch Nicholas I, writing in about
914, there were two powers which commanded honour and
respect. One was the Abbasid Caliphate based on Baghdad,
the ruler of the lands of the Near East; the other the Roman
Empire, based since the fourth century on its new, Christian
capital, Constantinople. Both powers were conscious of a
long tradition of rule; the people of the eastern empire always
referred to themselves as *Rhōmaioi* ('Romans') and the rulers
of the lands to the east of the Mediterranean were similarly
conscious of a Muslim tradition which stretched back to the
days of the Prophet. But how far did these grandiose concepts
of imperial might correspond with reality in the period after
900? There was no place in the patriarch's world-view for the
lands and rulers of the western Mediterranean and not the
slightest indication that Byzantine power closer to home might
often be challenged. It was a description of the world as it
should have been, rather than as it was. By 1200 the new
realities were there for all to see. Whilst the old ideal of the

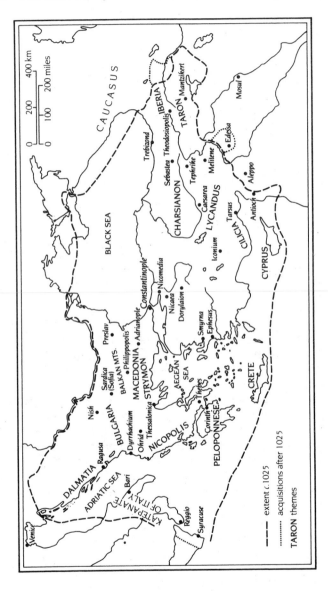

THE BYZANTINE EMPIRE, c.1025

- — extent c.1025
- ⋯⋯⋯ acquisitions after 1025
- TARON themes

Roman Empire still remained potent, it was redefined and in many parts of the Mediterranean the power of the old empires—Byzantine, Carolingian, and Muslim—had been replaced by smaller, localized states, some of them only the size of cities. Centralized authority had become eroded and the bonds which held distant territories together were more often those of religion and cultural tradition than of a single political authority.

Nowhere was this more true than in what has aptly been termed the 'Byzantine Commonwealth': territories either under the authority of Constantinople or within its powerful cultural orbit. In the three hundred years after 900 the armies of the empire expanded its frontiers to their widest extent since the sixth century but then proved unable to maintain their supremacy against new and unexpected outside threats. The tenth century was the great age of expansion and reconquest. There were three main areas where this was most noticeable: the eastern frontier, Italy, and parts of the Balkans. In the east, *stratēgoi* (military governors) are found in Charsianon in 873, in Sebastea in 911, in Lycandus (east of Caesarea/Kayseri) by 916, and Tephrike (to the west of the upper reaches of the Euphrates) between 934 and 944. By the end of the century they are mentioned in such areas as Tarsus, Theodosiopolis (modern Erzerum), and the Taron region of Armenia to the north-east of Lake Van. In Italy, the existence of the *stratēgoi* of Langobardia (by 911) and Calabria (c.948–52) testifies to a re-establishment of Byzantine power in southern Italy, which culminated in the reign of the Emperor Nicephorus II Phocas (963–9), who created a new post of katepan of Italy to oversee the administration of all Byzantine territories there. In the Balkans, the establishment of such themes (administrative districts) as Strymon and Nicopolis (northern Greece) and Dalmatia at the end of the ninth century marked the revival of Byzantine authority in lands which had previously fallen to Slav and Avar attack. More were added after the successful conquest of Bulgaria by Basil II at the beginning of the eleventh century.

The means by which these successes were achieved themselves posed a threat to the unity of the empire. Byzantium had defended herself in the 'dark ages' by withdrawing her populations within the walls of her cities or by resorting to defensive guerrilla warfare. Now that she turned to the offensive, new tactics and a new style of leadership were called for. The soldier-farmers (*stratiōtai*) settled on the land in the seventh century were now required to equip themselves as heavy cavalry—an expensive business. Their leaders now needed to be professional soldiers of high calibre and it is in the tenth century that we first hear of the great families such as those of Phocas, Argyrus, Doucas, and Comnenus (all of which provided emperors before 1100) whose members both held great estates in the provinces and followed careers as professional soldiers. Military success could lead to higher ambition; the celebrated general Nicephorus Phocas crowned his triumphs on the eastern frontier and on Crete with a *coup d'état* in 963 by which he gained the imperial power. It was a process frequently repeated in the eleventh century and a major source of instability in Byzantium, for where one provincial magnate could succeed, what could prevent another? When a strong, militaristic emperor such as Basil II (976–1025) ruled, the centrifugal tendencies of the 'powerful' of the provinces could be kept in check by firm political action such as the confiscation of the estates of 'overmighty subjects'. But as the families jockeyed for the imperial power in the eleventh century, central authority was increasingly challenged by provincial factions. By the time strong dynastic rule was again re-established in the reign of the Emperor Alexius Comnenus (1081–1118), political disunity in the empire had already had serious consequences.

The most serious of these was an inability to curb the growing incursions of Turkish nomads into Asia Minor—the heartland of the empire in terms of both manpower and food production. The first appearance of Turkish raiders in Armenia in 1016–17 was later described in apocalyptic terms by the historian Matthew of Edessa, writing at the end of the eleventh century. But the presence of the 'ferocious beasts covered in blood' went largely unnoticed by Byzantine commentators until the 1040s when their raiding bands began to lay waste the easternmost themes of the empire and the nomadic tribes who followed in their wake began to encroach upon the pasture lands of the Anatolian plateau. The Armenian and Georgian client princes of the empire held them back as long as they could, but were forced to flee into the Caucasus or southwards towards Cilicia. The armed forces, so successful in the previous century, were now involved in the power politics of Constantinople or in attempting to stem attacks on the western lands of the empire. It is of some significance that the Byzantine defeat at Mantzikert (1071) at which the Emperor Romanus IV Diogenes fell into the hands of the Turks took place in the same year that Norman forces captured Bari, the capital of Byzantine Italy. Not for the first time in imperial history, the challenge of maintaining the defence of long frontiers from a distant capital was to prove almost too great. By the time the forces of the First Crusade arrived in Constantinople in 1097, the Byzantines had issued a series of appeals to the west for help against the infidel and many 'Franks' had responded by joining the increasingly polyglot mercenary forces of the emperor: Germans, Varangians (Scandinavians), Russians, and even English amongst them.

The costs of the warfare of the later eleventh century took their toll of the imperial revenues. Whilst the debasements of the coinage which took place in the first half of the century can now be seen as attempts to increase the amount of coin in circulation to take account of buoyant production of both agrarian and manufactured goods, by the reign of Alexius Comnenus the most serious drain on imperial resources was the payment and equipping of the troops levied to fight the Turks in the east, the nomadic incursions across the Danube, and Norman intervention in Italy and the Balkans. It is no wonder that Theophylact, archbishop of Ohrid at the turn of the eleventh and twelfth centuries, could complain of the 'locust-like' presence of the imperial armies and tax-collectors in the Balkans and the apparent lack of concern in Constantinople for the plight of the provinces. Alexius Comnenus' reform of the currency and the system of gathering taxes went some way to redressing the losses to the imperial treasury, but his officials' zeal in uncovering blatant tax frauds, especially by monastic houses, did nothing to endear the government at Constantinople to the 'powerful' of the provinces.

The twelfth century saw a partial recovery in Byzantine fortunes, both territorial and monetary. The Comnene emperors, Alexius I, John II (1118–43) and, particularly, Manuel I (1143–80) all built upon the success of the crusades in reconquering areas of Asia Minor and whilst they never re-established the frontiers of the tenth century, their treaties with the Seljuk rulers at least ensured that the western regions of Anatolia were relatively free from attack. Manuel also launched an attempt to regain the old Byzantine lands in Italy. The expedition's failure was mainly due to the untrustworthiness of potential allies (including the papacy), disease, and the old problem of supplying troop reinforcements over long distances. But there was another, more fundamental reason for the failure of the central government in Constantinople to reassert its authority over one of its more distant provinces—just as true in the Balkans as it was in Italy.

The Byzantine practice of using religious, diplomatic, and cultural weapons rather than military force to establish hegemony in the Balkans worked well in the eleventh century after the threat of Bulgarian expansion had been removed. Local dynasties in Serbia, Croatia, and Dalmatia ruled with judicious support from Constantinople and, further afield, the kingdom of Hungary, Christian by the year 1000, seemed grateful enough to accept the political patronage of Byzantium. But the late twelfth century saw the development of local territorial ambitions which drew Constantinople into a series of wars. The expansion of the kingdom of Hungary towards the Adriatic caused a fundamental realignment in the western Balkans. Byzantium's unsuccessful interference in the dynastic rivalries of the Hungarian ruling house culminated in her acceptance of Hungarian rule in Croatia and Dalmatia—a development which seriously alarmed Byzantium's old ally, Venice, on the opposite shore of the Adriatic. In 1166 the Serbians revolted under Stephen Nemanja and in 1185 two

BYZANTINE EMPERORS OF THE TWELFTH TO THIRTEENTH CENTURIES

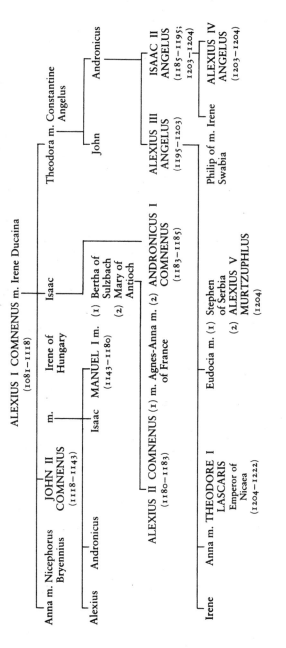

Bulgarian nobles, Peter and Asen, led a rising which was to lead to the establishment of a virtually independent Bulgarian state with the tacit acceptance if not approval of Constantinople.

Why did the tried and tested methods of Byzantine diplomacy fail in the twelfth century? Perhaps primarily because they *were* traditional. Alliances with newcomers concerned not merely to bask in the political glow of Byzantine hegemony, but to claim power for themselves—such as the usurping Normans or the land-hungry Turks—were impossible. In any case, the newcomers were of a faith which made their incorporation into an orthodox 'commonwealth' inconceivable. They had, therefore, to be fought, and military victory against these 'barbarians' became the main measure of imperial success. After the crushing Byzantine defeat by the Turks at Myriocephalon (1176) this became ever more difficult and became a pretext for the dynastic rivalries between the members of the houses of Comnenus and Angelus which bedevilled Byzantium in the last thirty years of the twelfth century. Disunity in Constantinople was fed by growing military insecurity and the growing isolation of the empire from its old allies on the periphery. When, under Manuel I (1143–80), the empire turned to the west for friends, new dangers accompanied the treaties and marriage alliances. For the rivalries of the western Mediterranean cities—Genoa, Pisa, and Venice—and the ambitions of the German emperors were imported into Byzantium and Constantinople, once the nerve-centre of a confident and expansionist empire, became in 1204, the target of western territorial ambitions.

The tenth century also inaugurated a period of great change in the Islamic world. It saw the final disintegration of the Abbasid caliphate based on Baghdad and the evolution of a number of independent Muslim states whose unity was most strongly expressed not by loyalty to the caliph in Baghdad (since the Fatimids had set up a rival caliphate in Egypt) but by the common use of the Arabic language for governmental purposes and by such important rituals as the annual *hajj* or pilgrimage to Mecca. More distant Muslim provinces, such as Ifriqiya, had paid only a token tribute to Baghdad and by about

926 little finance was reaching the city from the outlying regions of Egypt, Syria, Mosul, Iran, and much of Iraq itself. It has been aptly remarked that it was bankruptcy not military defeat which brought the Abbasid caliphate to an end and the disorders of the tenth century were caused to a great extent by the inability of the caliphs to finance the great armies which were the basis of their rule. The *kharaj*, the land-tax collected annually by the officials of the central government, was being progressively replaced either by the appointment of tax-farmers whose reliability could not be assured, or by the increased grant of *iqtas*—the assigning of the revenues from a given area to an individual who, whilst often providing a certain number of troops or money, also became the accepted local leader. These centrifugal tendencies were aggravated by the factionalism which pervaded the capital. This had two distinct though connected strands: political and religious.

Since the caliphs were the only form of legitimate power in Islam, many forces attempted to control them. The Abbasid court was a byword for intrigue. In order to secure their own positions, the powerful men in the Abbasid state recruited military followings, often made up of mercenary chiefs and their paid warriors (*ghilman*) from Turkish or mountain peoples and these chiefs began to play an important part in the government of the state. In the early tenth century, three Persian soldier brothers, the founders of the Buyid dynasty, gained power in Iran and Baghdad. Whilst in theory they governed on behalf of the Abbasids, in reality they ruled the caliphate until it fell under Turkish control in 1055. The caliph, a virtual prisoner in his great palace, could be controlled by those with the military strength to back their demands and it was within the ranks of the army that some of the most important changes of the period were taking place. From the ninth century onwards, Turks provided the basis of the army and their nomadic culture brought to the fore the skills of cavalry manœuvre and mounted archery. But where they were employed, their tribes had to be rewarded with grazing lands previously held by other longer-established groups. The changes in the structures of the armies, which in any case did not include members of the main, sedentary body of the Muslim population, led to increasing instability as rival groups fought to control the organs of the state and regional commanders became *de facto* rulers in their own right.

The other major cause of instability in Islam, was the Shiʿi—Sunni split. Under the Buyid rulers in Baghdad, 'Twelver' Shiʿism—the belief in the twelve imams (teachers) of Islam beginning with the cousin and son-in-law of Muhammad, ʿAli—began to take on the form of a political movement as well as a religious faction. Its adherents denigrated the memory of the first two caliphs, developed their own festivals on the days commemorating the murders of early Shiʿa leaders, and began to venerate the tombs of members of ʿAli's family. They were particularly strong amongst the merchant groups in Baghdad. The caliphs, however, continued to follow the Sunni form of Islam and to emphasize their devotion to the memory of the early followers of the Prophet and the first four caliphs. The early years of the eleventh century saw a revival of Sunni influence in the city, with the caliph's refusal in 1003 to recognize a prominent Shiʿa as chief judge and the employment of the strongly Sunnite Turks in positions of military influence. Such were the tensions caused by the growing hardening of attitudes, that when, in 972, an army was raised to march against the Byzantines, it was diverted by its Turkish commander to attack the Buyids and their supporters even before it had left Baghdad.

Thus even before the Turkish invasions of the eleventh century, the world of Islam was a divided one. Two caliphs with their own administrative structures lay at the centre and a host of lesser states, such as those of the Hamdanids of Aleppo and Mosul, the minor families controlling the coastal cities of Palestine, the Kurds of the regions south of the Caspian, and the Bedouin dynasties of the Syrian desert lay at the periphery. It was against these furthest outposts of Islam that the Christians of Byzantium and the west first came into conflict, and the inability of the caliphate to provide military assistance to them was one reason for the successes of the Byzantine state in the tenth century and the First Crusade in the eleventh. The only positive benefit that seems to have emerged from this fragmentation of power was the increased opportunities it provided for Muslim administrators and scholars to find both posts and patronage at the courts of those who had set themselves up as regional rulers. The tenth century has been described as the 'Islamic Renaissance', during which the literary treasures of the past were preserved and in which arts and sciences flourished.

The reunification of Islam in the twelfth century can be seen as a direct consequence of Christian involvement in the Near East. Those who were able to lead successful campaigns against the Latin Kingdom and to rally troops from the entire Islamic world to the cause of *jihad*, seized the political initiative. Whilst the great Emir Saladin is most famous for his exploits against the crusaders in the late twelfth century, he and his family were also chiefly responsible for the downfall of the Fatimid caliphate in Egypt. After his defeat of the Sudanese troops who provided the caliph's main support, Saladin was able, on his death in 1171, to have the Abbasid caliph publicly recognized in the mosques of Cairo as the one leader of Islam.

In the west, Charlemagne's ideal of a single empire, coterminous with the Christian world but independent of the empire centred on Constantinople, was revived in a potent form after 900. Since the city of Rome itself had a major part to play in this scheme, it was inevitable that much of the political activity associated with the imperial ambitions of the German emperors should be played out in Italy. The extensive German conquests of the Ottonian emperors encouraged them to consider themselves as more than mere kings and to plan to reassert control over the lands of the old Middle Kingdom inherited from the Carolingians. The pretext for Otto I's interference in Lombardy in 951 was an appeal from Adelaide, the widow of Lothar II, king of Italy, for help against her rival, Berengar, count of Ivrea who had had himself proclaimed king. Many of the ruling houses to the south of the Alps were involved in complex political manœuvres in northern Italy at this time and Otto was particularly concerned to maintain control over the routes and passes to the south of his realm.

A further crucial figure entered the picture when Pope John XII appealed to Otto for protection against Berengar's attacks near Rome. It was a recognition of his role as protector of the papacy that Otto I was crowned emperor in February 962. Thus began the process of what was to become known as the *renovatio imperii Romanorum*—the 'renewal of the Roman Empire'. The relationship between pope and emperor was to be one of mutual dependency; the *Ottonianum*, the agreement drawn up between Otto I and John XII, had clauses inserted in it which demanded that a newly elected pope should take an oath to fulfil his obligations to the emperor, though these were, dangerously, not spelled out. The emperor in his turn would undertake to protect the interests of the Church and the see of St Peter. By the end of the tenth century, imperial activity in Italy was established in two, often interlinked, areas: the attempt to establish political hegemony over the old imperial territories in Italy and the protection of the position of the papacy.

The next hundred years saw frequent imperial interventions in northern Italy. Conrad II, in the first year of his reign, was promised the loyalty of the city of Milan by its bishop, Aribert, and went on to punish the citizens of Pavia for rioting and destroying the royal palace in the city, which, he reminded them, was a symbol of the state, not merely a private building. In 1026, he put down a revolt in Ravenna against the imperial officials and received the submission of Lucca as he moved southwards to Rome for his coronation. The 1030s saw a series of expeditions to impose obedience against the towns, which, as we shall later see, were, in the words of the contemporary historian Wipo, 'making a great turmoil . . . and covenanting together against their lords', moves which marked the beginning of the communal movement.

The assistance given to the papacy often consisted in disciplining the unruly nobles of the city of Rome itself. The position of pope, for so long a perquisite of the predominant urban faction, became one in which the western emperor took a personal interest and men of a much higher calibre began to hold the office. Many, such as the distinguished scholar

1. THEODOSIUS THE GREAT was the first emperor to enforce orthodox Christianity on his subjects, and the last to rule a united empire. This silver plate represents him enthroned in majesty and flanked by bodyguards and co-emperors while granting an official his letter of appointment. Below, a female personification of the earth looks up to the emperor in a submissive pose.

2. A VANDAL NOBLE LEAVING HIS VILLA, from a mosaic (*c.* 500). According to a Byzantine historian, 'The Vandals used to indulge in baths every day, enjoyed a table rich in all things . . . and passed their time . . . above all in hunting . . . all kinds of sexual pleasures were practised among them.' Their decadence played a part in their rapid conquest by the Byzantines in 533.

3. THE FINAL DEFEAT OF ICONOCLASM and the resumption of lavish artistic patronage came about in the late ninth century under the Macedonian dynasty. In a mosaic in the Church of St Sophia in Constantinople the Emperor Leo VI is shown prostrated before Christ. The humility of the Emperor reflects his role as an intermediary between God and the empire.

4. THE FRANK AGILBERT illustrates the close connections between the various northern churches. He was trained in Ireland, became bishop in Wessex, was present at the Synod of Whitby, and ended his days as bishop of Paris. His tomb is now at Jouarre, east of Paris. The closest sculptural parallels to this vivid portrayal of human souls at the Last Judgement are to be found in Northumbria.

5. THE PALACE CHAPEL AT AACHEN was begun in the early 790s, near the warm-water baths which Charlemagne loved. The building is probably modelled on San Vitale in Ravenna, newly conquered by Charlemagne, and would provide a suitable setting for imperial ceremonial in following decades. Charlemagne's throne is on the first floor, overlooking the main altar.

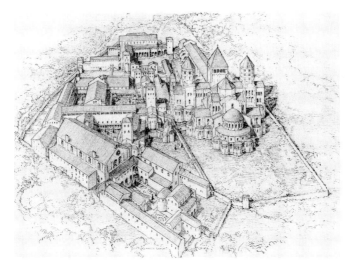

6. A RECONSTRUCTION OF CLUNY as it was about 1157. The rapid growth of the monastery can be seen in the contrast between the second of the abbey's churches, built under Abbot Maieul (948–94) in the centre of the drawing and the huge church to its right, begun in 1088.

7. GERMAN CHRONICLERS often spoke of their empire as a continuation of that of Rome. Something of that attitude can be seen in this bronze column of around 1015–22, commissioned by Bishop Bernward of Hildesheim. It depicts scenes from the life of Christ and is modelled on Trajan's column.

8. MOUNTED ARCHERS played an important part in the Seljuk successes of the eleventh century. This thirteenth-century *sgraffito* ('incised') ceramic dish shows the expert horsemanship characteristic of the Turks, who could control their mounts even whilst drawing their bows.

9. CASTLES provided a vital form of defence in the Holy Land where relatively few strong points could control vast tracts of land. Krak des Chevaliers, first captured in 1099, was later refortified by the Hospitallers. It did not fall to Muslim forces until 1268.

10. VENETIAN MERCHANTS exchanging cloth for oriental produce (early to mid-fourteenth century). The Venetian empire grew through a system of depots and colonies to which local merchants would bring their wares.

11. THE FLORENTINE PAINTER SANDRO BOTTICELLI (1445–1510) was in close contact with the Neoplatonic circle around Lorenzo de' Medici, and later with the Dominican Savonarola. His *Calumny of Apelles* (1485–95) is typical of his interest in classical allegorical themes, while also revealing some of the drama and intensity that was to characterize his later religious works.

12. THE TEMPTATION OF CHRIST ON THE MOUNTAIN, from Duccio's *Maestà*, a vast altar-piece of over fifty separate panels painted between 1308 and 1311 for the altar of the cathedral in Siena. The stylized landscape and figures are compositionally balanced with the walled urban scenes which, to the modern eye, convey something of the tightly packed proximity of medieval town life.

13. THE *ANNALES* OF GILLES LE MUISIT vividly describe the outbreak of the Black Death at Tournai in 1349. This miniature is one of a series which depicts the burning of Jews, a procession of flagellants, and, in this instance, the burial of plague victims.

14. JAN VAN EYCK'S ALTAR-PIECE (dated 1436) for George Van der Paele, canon of St Donatian's church in Bruges, is an example of the highly realistic religious painting of this period. The elderly donor is presented to the Virgin and Child by his name saint, St George. The patron saint of his church—St Donatian—stands to the left.

Gerbert of Aurillac (Pope Sylvester II), the tutor to the young Otto III, moved in imperial circles and brought with them able clergy from the north to act as papal administrators. Though the danger of the Roman mob was never absent from papal considerations—there were numerous occasions when the pontiffs were forced to flee from the city—its pernicious influence could, for a time, be lessened by the assistance which the emperors were prepared to provide. But the principles upon which this association was based were not to remain unchallenged. Though the 'Reform Movement' in the papacy, with its two main tenets of clerical purity and the redefinition of the bases of power and authority in the Church was to have considerable repercussions in all areas of the Christian life, its effects on the relationship between pope and emperor were particularly profound. Eleventh-century German emperors, such as Henry II and Henry III, were much in favour of reformed monasticism and the abolition of clerical abuses, but it was, ironically, the support that they gave to these parts of the reformist programme which was to encourage men such as Nicholas II and Gregory VII to go further. The Election Decree of 1059 declared that only a small group of high clergy (later to become the College of Cardinals) should elect the pope; the assent of the Roman clergy and people should be sought *after* the election and only vague references were made to the need to render to the emperor the honour that was due to him. This was not a view that the young Emperor Henry IV, brought up to believe in his duty to assure the right governance of the Church, could be expected to adhere to and it was, indeed, an argument which deeply offended many of the most pious laymen in the west. But the development of the idea that the Church was independent of lay control and, more fundamentally, the assertion that the spiritual power vested in the pope by St Peter was superior to that of any lay ruler, led to a conflict that was played out on both the theoretical and the political level.

At their root lay the reassessment of the respective roles of emperor and pope. If it were true, as the theoreticians that the popes increasingly gathered around them maintained, that the spiritual sword wielded by the heir to St Peter was superior to the temporal weapons at the disposal of the emperor, then the whole basis of imperial power, especially imperial claims to the secular leadership of Europe, came into question. Both sides turned to the 'new men' of the twelfth-century schools to provide them with manpower and ammunition for a debate which was to continue throughout the Middle Ages. At the same time that courts throughout western Europe were developing improved systems of administration, so too the papal curia attracted to its service able clerics to process the increasing amount of business—judicial appeals, complaints, questions of morality, and, increasingly, the organization of crusades—which poured into Rome in the twelfth century. Tradition, always one of the strongest weapons at the disposal of a papacy which increasingly emphasized the Petrine claim and used the talents of men such as Gratian, the celebrated canon lawyer, to delve back into the papal archives to rediscover the forgotten rights of the pope, was also called upon by the defenders of imperial rights. For them, the justification for imperial intervention in Italy rested on the rock of Roman Law, for it was precisely in the Justinianic *corpus* that the unchallenged rights of the emperor to superiority in secular matters in the empire and guardianship of the Church were most clearly stated. The schools of Bologna, famous in the twelfth century for their training in law, produced men who could argue the case both for papal supremacy and for the theoretical strength of the imperial position.

It was, therefore, with renewed confidence that the Emperor Frederick I Barbarossa invaded Italy for the first time in 1154. In the next thirty years, until peace was made at Constance in 1183, he led numerous expeditions against both the pope and the towns of Italy and amidst the complexities of this period of alarmingly confused alliances, the principles behind his intervention do emerge. One could be seen in his response to the appeals made to him by smaller towns in Lombardy (such as Lodi) which resented the growing power of Milan. It was in the old guise of imperial overlord that he promised to restore justice and the old peace of the empire. In return, the *regalia*, the imperial rights, should be recognized by the towns which sought the help of the emperor. The Roncaglia Decrees of 1158, drawn up, interestingly, by a team of four lawyers from Bologna, spoke of the right to extract the *fodrum*, the tax to support imperial armies on the march; to extract tolls and taxes from the cities and, most fundamental of all, the imperial *bannus*—the emperor's personal suzerainty over property and justice. Imperial officials were to be appointed to oversee these rights.

If the Roncaglia Decrees had been carried out, imperial power in Italy would have been restored to an extensive degree. But the fact that they soon became a dead letter is evidence of the political realities which undermined any attempt to re-establish strong imperial authority. The communes of the north resented attempts to dictate their form of government even more than they hated the territorial encroachments of their powerful neighbours. The popes, having provided themselves with the theoretical justification that they needed for taking political action, tried to guard against a potential growth in imperial territory by alliances with the emperor's enemies: the communes in the north and the Norman kingdom in the south. It was a dangerous game and one in which the state of play was dramatically altered by the accession of the young Emperor Henry VI to the throne of Sicily in 1194. But it was one in which the claims of the *imperium* came to have real political significance. Unlike the Byzantine state, which retained the theory whilst losing much of the substance of empire, the re-establishment of German claims over Italy, the old heart of the Roman Empire, provided, for a time, a real territorial basis for empire which was lacking elsewhere. It was certainly not to be found in the western lands of the successors of Charlemagne.

After the disintegration of the Carolingian Empire, the kings of the Franks had little influence over the lands of the Midi and the Spanish March. Though charters were often still dated by the reigns of the distant kings north of the Loire, they were seldom seen in the Mediterranean provinces. The Rhône valley was the territory of the kings of Burgundy and to the south, the collapse of the old Carolingian administrative system led to the emergence of local noble dynasties. In the Midi, the most powerful came to be the house of Toulouse. During the course of the eleventh century, it came to control the land from the Rhône to Angoulême and from the Pyrenees northwards to the mountains of Auvergne. Its main rivals in the region were the counts of Barcelona. Under Count Raymond-Berengar I (1035–76), the lands of Barcelona were extended north of the Pyrenees to include the town of Carcassonne. A distinctively Catalan entity began to emerge. The power of the Catalans increased when Raymond-Berengar IV became heir to the king of Aragon by virtue of his marriage to the king's daughter. This new state clashed periodically with Toulouse in the course of the twelfth century and the expansion of Aragonese power in the Midi was only brought to a halt at the death of King Alfonso II in 1196, when the lands of the kingdom were divided between his two sons: Peter gained Aragon and Barcelona and Alfonso the lands north of the Pyrenees.

The methods used by the great houses of the south to extend both their territory and their influence were remarkably similar; not surprising in a region where Roman traditions both of public law and of landholding were still preserved. The *allod*, or freeholding, was prevalent in the south and this meant that a lord's power was not implicit in his followers' land tenure as it was in the feudal lands to the north of the Loire. Homage was rarely extracted as a prerequisite of landholding; and lands were often granted out in return for rents rather than services. Many were for a period measured in lifetimes rather than in hereditary tenure. Thus feudal relationships could not be used as a basis for the extension of seigneurial power. Instead, the great landowners of the region concentrated on extending their own demesnes (especially by judicious marriages) and by extracting oaths of loyalty (*fidelitas*) from their followers. Such men were often rewarded by appointment as castellans in charge of the proliferation of strongholds which had been constructed in the tenth century as defensive centres against Muslim attack. Whilst these castellanies themselves became the centres of power for new knightly houses, their ambitions were generally kept in check by the greater houses of the region. Two main factors were responsible for this. The first, the prevalence of the idea of a public law administered by the noble houses of each region rather than law private to each locality (as in parts of the north) contributed to the emergence of a sense of regional rather than local identity. The codification of laws, on the Roman model, such as the promulgation of the *Usatches* of Catalonia by the count of Barcelona in *c.*1150, stood as a practical application of such theoretical claims. In addition, both the houses of Toulouse and Barcelona developed their own administrative structures particularly concerned with the collection of tax—another means of emphasizing the authority of the count. A second sphere of activity, which did more to enhance the reputation of the counts of both Barcelona and Toulouse than any improvement in the efficiency of their territorial administration could, was their involvement in both ecclesiastical reform and in the prosecution of the holy wars and crusades associated with it. Raymond IV of St Gilles, count of Toulouse, was one of the leaders of the First Crusade, having previously fought against the infidel in Spain, and his successors in the twelfth century took a similar interest in the affairs of the Holy Land. The counts of Barcelona and the Spanish kings took an active role in the Christian reconquest of Spain. They were not the only ones to benefit; lesser nobles joined eagerly in these enterprises, accepting not only the rewards in lands and booty which accrued to the victors, but by implication the claims to leadership of the great noble houses whose representatives led the expeditions. Coupled with their reputations as generous patrons of reformed churches and monasteries, the great lords of the south stood as the champions of an increasingly aggressive Latin Christianity.

Spiritual Reform and the Ascetic Challenge

The redistribution of political power affected only a small section of the powerful élites of the Mediterranean world, but throughout the Christian community as in the Muslim world, new questions began to be asked about how believers could best serve God and ensure their own salvation. Although it is traditional to see the period as one of growing conflict between the Greek and Latin Churches, it is remarkable how similar spiritual developments in the Mediterranean seem to be and there are strong grounds for suggesting a considerable flow of spiritual currents between east and west.

There was, for example, a growing enthusiasm for all forms of the monastic life. Monasticism was, of course, of eastern provenance and the orthodox Church of the tenth and eleventh centuries harboured a variety of monastic styles seeing no need to regiment monks into monastic orders but merely to allow adherence to the general precepts earlier laid down by St Basil. But two main styles prevailed—the coenobitic or communal and the lavriote, where monks lived alone in cells, sometimes quite widely scattered, but met together for the liturgy each week. The coenobitic style emphasized the virtues of the sublimation of the individual will to that of the community and emphasized the necessity of obedience to the abbot; the lavriote style concentrated rather on the individual's spiritual development and lonely fight against the temptations of the Devil. It continued the eremitic tradition of the Desert Fathers. In tenth-century Byzantium, monasteries which combined the two styles began to emerge and this change is epitomized by the new monastic foundations on Mount Athos. Although the mountain had been famous for its hermits in the ninth century, it was not until the foundation of the Great Lavra by St Athanasius in 963 that the new 'hybrid' monasticism, first developed in the monastic communities of western Asia Minor, began to gain influence there. Most of the monks lived a communal life in new buildings built with the aid of patrons who included the Byzantine emperors, but a few, advanced in the spiritual life, were allowed to leave the house and live solitary lives in the vicinity. Whilst traditional, communal urban monasteries continued to be founded, the attraction of this kind of life, which theoretically allowed every monk the possibility of being permitted to live the 'higher' spiritual life, is demonstrated by the vast expansion in the numbers of monks on Athos in particular (the Great Lavra may have had as many as 1,000 monks by 1100).

A similar enthusiasm for the ascetic life coupled with a certain discontent with existing forms of monasticism is evident in the west and there has been much debate about possible influences from the Byzantine world. The possible area of contact must surely have been southern Italy, where great Greek monastic leaders such as St Nil (d. 1005), the founder of the Monastery of Grottaferrata, were also widely known in Latin circles and where monasteries such as the Benedictine house of Monte Cassino were patronized by both German and Byzantine emperors. A number of Latin houses in Italy— St Romuald's foundation at Camaldoli (early eleventh century); John Gualberto's house at Vallombrosa (*c.*1036) and the monastery of Fonte Avellana which was joined by the celebrated theologian Peter Damian—all emphasized the concentration on the ascetic life. Vallombrosa was coenobitic, but the monks' concentration on spiritual matters was assured by the use of lay brothers to perform the manual work of the monastery. In Camaldoli and Fonte Avellana, groups of hermits were attached to the houses in what seems a remarkably 'Byzantine' manner.

In other parts of Italy, southern France, and Spain, monastic reform was led by the Cluniacs. In Rome, particularly, the reforming zeal of Abbot Odo of Cluny (926–44), who made six journeys to the city, was supported by the Senator Alberic, who allowed the new house of St Mary on the Aventine to be founded in one of his palaces. In the eleventh century, great houses like those of Subiaco and Farfa accepted the observances of Cluny, though not without considerable opposition from many of their monks. Cluniac success depended on the support of local lay rulers—particularly evident in northern Spain where Alfonso VI of León-Castile (married to Constance of Burgundy a niece of Abbot Hugh of Cluny)—placed a number of houses under Cluniac control. Other reforming houses with influence in the south, such as that of the Benedictine abbey of Saint-Victor at Marseilles, similarly relied upon both the patronage and more practical assistance of the local nobility.

There was never any doubt about aristocratic concern for the Church; in both Byzantium and the west this took the form of donations of land, money, and privileges, but the problem arose when the forms of involvement conflicted with new theological initiatives. The purchase of the archbishopric of Narbonne for his son by Count Guifred of Cerdaña with the sum of 100,000 solidi was just the kind of simoniac behaviour condemned by the Reform papacy, but it did mark a concern on the count's part that his family should take their rightful place in the church hierarchy of their region. When, at the end of the eleventh century, the patriarch of Constantinople condemned the *charistikarioi* (lay protectors of monastic houses who often contributed to their maintenance and the improvement of their estates) he may have been asserting the principle of the inviolability of church property, but he was also challenging a traditional expression of lay piety. Why, then, did such initiatives also gain widespread support amongst powerful lay interests?

A persuasive explanation is that the Reform Movement of the eleventh century encompassed support at the highest levels in the Church for activities which seized the imagination of contemporaries. In a southern context, where political authority was fragmented, the Peace of God movement found many supporters and a series of councils at which oaths were sworn to keep the peace was held in the Rhône valley in the 1030s. Many nobles, including the counts of both Toulouse and Barcelona, sought to increase their local prestige (and to deny the claims of others) by becoming vassals of the see of St Peter. On a more popular level, pilgrimages were encouraged as an expression of repentance and the most popular sites of the period, Rome, Compostella, and even Jerusalem itself, lay within the reach of the people of the Mediterranean lands. Travellers discovered new and powerful cult sites: the shrine of the Archangel Michael on Monte Gargano in southern Italy; the new Church of St Nicholas at Bari (1087), complete with the bones of the saint stolen by merchants from Myra in Asia Minor, and even the relic-charged city of Constantinople itself. Rome was not immune from this new enthusiasm for the outward expression of spirituality, for the eleventh and twelfth centuries saw a spate of church-building which helped to enhance the reputation as well as the appearance of the Holy See.

There was much, then, to attract those who did not find themselves in direct political conflict with the papacy and, as we shall see, the aggressive assertion of the Christian faith against non-believers was to have considerable political consequences. But there were dangers. Growing suspicion between Greek and Latin resulted from papal claims to supremacy in the Church and an increased suspicion of differences in theology and ritual which, paradoxically, sprang from greater mutual contacts. There was also a much more dangerous problem, that of those who followed paths to spiritual improvement of which the Church hierarchies could not approve.

Those whom the Church dubbed heretics always believed that they were practising what Christ had taught, even when this conflicted with what the representatives of the Church were declaring as truth. From the Church's point of view, however, heretics were those who embraced *any* belief explicitly or implicitly condemned by the papacy, or who, when confronted with the evidence of their error, refused to obey the teaching of the Church and retract their own beliefs. Heretics, however genuinely their beliefs might be held, were seen as those through whom the Devil worked to undermine the faith. They constituted a major source of infection and disease within the body of the faithful.

Heresy was not solely a Mediterranean phenomenon, but there is no doubt that some of the strongest influences on western heresy came from its contacts with the east. The change in the nature of heresy in the twelfth century is a testimony to these contacts. In the eleventh century, heresy had often taken the form of a flight from the world and a concern to live the life of poverty taught by Christ. An Italian group, led by one Gundulf, may serve as an example of this type of behaviour. Gundulf and his followers rejected the validity of church possessions and all the outward symbolism of the services—bells, incense, and altars. They denied the sacraments, especially baptism, for they declared that if a life of *iustitia*, 'righteousness', were observed, then baptism was superfluous, as it also was, in a somewhat different sense, for those who did not amend their lives after they had received it. They lived a life of simple manual labour. Another group, centred on the castle of Monforte in Piedmont and which had as adherents members of the local nobility as well as more simple people, demonstrated a similar disillusionment with the official structures of the Church and tenets of the faith. Absolution for sin, they maintained, should not be the prerogative only of the priesthood. They denied the authority of 'the Roman pontiff' in favour of that of their leader, Gerard. In the cities, this new 'puritanism' was to have more disruptive effects. The Patarenes, or 'rag-pickers' of Milan, under their leader Erlembald, a member of a family of lesser knights, posed a serious threat to the peace of the city in the years 1056–75. Not only did they attack the clergy of the Church of St Ambrose as corrupt and immoral, but they set up their own churches in which celibate clergy provided for the spiritual needs of the group. The Patarenes were initially supported by such major figures in the Reform Movement as Gregory VII and Peter Damian and indeed their concerns, though perhaps over-enthusiastically proclaimed, were very much those of the Reform papacy. But their increasingly violent behaviour turned public opinion against the Patarenes. Erlembald was murdered by his enemies and many Patarenes fled from the city. The papacy, intent on gaining influence amongst the Milanese clergy, abandoned them in favour of the new reformist clerics who had begun to emerge. Whilst the Patarenes in Milan and other cities such as Brescia, Cremona, and Piacenza to which their movement spread, never, in the strict sense, went beyond the declarations of the reforming councils of the Church, the zeal of their activity led them to be considered as heretics for it questioned the sole authority of the Church to discipline its clergy and claimed a right of action for the laity against errant ecclesiastics which could not be conceded. The aggression of the Patarenes, however, set the tone for heretical developments in the twelfth century. Instead of small groups content to live out the teachings of the Gospel in relative seclusion, widespread and open preaching challenged the fundamental tenets of the Church. The centres of these movements were in northern Italy and Languedoc. Some of them, such as the Waldensians in Lyons, or the Humiliati of northern Italy were groups in the old tradition. The Humiliati earned their simple living as weavers, whilst many of the followers of Peter Valdès were merchants who had given away their wealth to follow a life of poverty.

But two somewhat different figures, Peter of Bruis and Henry the Monk, were active in the mid-twelfth century and, in their teaching, revealed much more extreme views than those voiced by the advocates of apostolic simplicity. Henry the Monk, active for a time in northern France, appeared in the lands of the count of Toulouse about the year 1145, preaching the validity of wandering clergy with no sacramental functions and the need to eliminate the mass. His teaching had much in common with that of Peter of Bruis, but the Petrobusian condemnation of church buildings, the externals of worship, masses, and prayers for the dead shows even more clearly the indications of contact with the heretical tradition of the eastern Mediterranean, in particular the influence of the Bogomils.

For Byzantine theologians, the adherents of the priest Bogomil were merely 'filthy Manichaeans', later followers of the fourth-century heretic Mani who had taught that there were two creative urges, good and evil, and that all earthly creation was the work of the Devil. Man's spirit, imprisoned within the prison of the flesh, would only be released by death and the only purpose of his existence was a struggle to escape from the evil of the material world. Bogomilism certainly belonged to this dualist tradition, but its adherents in Bulgaria and the northern Balkans also resented the authoritarian influence of the Church in Constantinople and the increasing use of Greek-speaking clergy in the regions which came under Byzantine control after the campaigns of Basil II. Whilst Bogomilism was far from the 'nationalist opposition' postulated by some modern Balkan historians, the account of Bogomil practices composed by the tenth-century orthodox priest, Cosmas, indicates that it did present a challenge to the institutions of the orthodox Church and to its most fundamental doctrines. The Incarnation could not but be a mistaken belief, for how could Christ have taken upon Himself a nature which was essentially evil? It followed, therefore, that the doctrine of Redemption was similarly void as were the sacraments since matter—wine, bread, and water, by definition polluted—was made use of in them. Churches and their holy vessels—icons, images, and the cross itself—were irrelevant to the dualists, who practised a simple faith with the Lord's Prayer as their only invocation and a form of confession made to each other.

It is the spread of dualist cosmology *coupled* with criticism of the institutions of the Church which points the connection between movements such as the Petrobusians, the supporters of Henry the Monk, and, most widespread of all, the Cathars, with the eastern heretical tradition. The challenge to the Roman Church was profound, for unacceptable beliefs were spread by unacceptable means. Wandering preachers spread heresy into regions which were either unserved by the existing parish structure, or where landownership was so fragmented that the basic patronal links between Church and laity were hardly in existence. Men such as the Cathar *perfecti* who eschewed all food produced by procreation, and lived lives of exemplary rigorousness and poverty, stood as living critics of the worldliness of contemporary clerics and the inability of the Church to reach out to the faithful in its preaching. Wherever it emerged, heresy stood as testimony to the inadequacies of the orthodox Church. In the east, the insistence on Greek as a liturgical language may have alienated the Slavonic-speaking peoples of the Balkans; in Languedoc opposition was more personally directed at absentee prelates (such as the archbishop of Narbonne, away from his see from 1190 to 1212) and thrived in a region where secular learning flourished but education of the clergy was woefully inadequate. But heresy was also a sign of social change. Heretics, like traders and the new urban leaders, were those who were ready to break with tradition and to question the bases of existing authority. They flourished in areas where political authority was weak: Italy, the lands of Toulouse, where the departure of Count Raymond

IV on the First Crusade had inaugurated a period of conflicting political claims, and, to a lesser extent, the Balkans, where Byzantine political power was never, in reality, quite as firmly entrenched as propagandists in Constantinople liked to believe.

The response of the western Church authorities to heresy was, at first, to mobilize the forces of persuasion. By the 1180s, the authorities of Languedoc were formally condemning heretical groups. Bernard Gaucelin, archbishop of Narbonne, after making an enquiry into Waldensian beliefs, issued an ineffectual condemnation of their practices; William VIII of Montpellier expressed his disapproval and in Aragon, both Alfonso II (1192) and Peter II (1194) issued edicts against them. In Milan, the archbishop destroyed a heretical school flourishing in the city in the 1190s. The papacy itself had finally taken the lead in 1184, when the bull *Ad abolendam* insisted on the jurisdiction of bishops in all matters concerning heresy and ordered that they should institute enquiries in parishes where heresy was reported or suspected. The secular authorities were ordered to assist these measures. Of more lasting significance was the realization that a concerted effort of 're-education' by orthodox clergy was necessary. Cistercian monks, including St Bernard, were active in the south of France in the early twelfth century, but it was not until the Dominican and, to a lesser extent, Franciscan friars began their widespread preaching campaigns at the beginning of the thirteenth century that inroads began to be made into urban-based heresy. Its continued existence, especially in the country districts of Languedoc, was to call for more severe methods—inquisition and military repression—in the years after 1200.

The Expansion of Latin Christianity: Spain—a Frontier Society

Religious differences created tensions within Christian states, but the concept of Holy War—a just war against the enemies of the Faith—was increasingly drawn upon in the eleventh century to justify attacks on unbelievers. The expansion of Christian power into Muslim lands—from Spain to the Holy

Land—is one of the most striking developments of the period and was both a reflection and a catalyst of profound structural changes within both Christian and Muslim society.

In Spain, the movement usually referred to as the *Reconquista* has often been seen in purely political terms, as a period of military expansion of the Christian kings fuelled by crusading fervour which led, inexorably and inevitably, to the conquest of the Muslim states of the south. In reality, both the process and the end results were much more complex. Muslim rule may have been brought to an end in many parts of Spain and Portugal by 1200, but Islamic influences remained all-pervasive in Iberian life and although crusading ideology gained considerable influence amongst the knightly élite of Spanish society, the first impetus towards *Reconquista* came from other causes.

Iberian historical development has been most successfully interpreted in terms of a 'frontier experience' in which the Christian populations overcame geographical constraints to push forward colonization and settlement. A shortage of manpower encouraged a relaxation of social bonds and conventions, the need for able military leadership precipitated men with no claims to high birth to positions of power. It was a period in which heroes, like the famous El Cid (Rodrigo Díaz de Vivar, 1043–99) could be made almost overnight.

The location of Christian power in the tenth and eleventh centuries clearly demonstrates these geographical determinants. Two 'clusters' of Christian states lay to the north-west and the south-east of the *meseta*, the great central plateau of Spain. The court of the kingdom of the Asturias was transferred to the city of León by King Ordoño II in 914 and from the new centre at the junction of the roads to Galicia and the Asturias and those to the Duero and Ebro rivers, the kings of León held back the incursions of the Muslim forces of the south. Castile, under Count Fernán González, had split away from León in the mid-tenth century and constituted an independent kingdom. East of the *meseta*, in the foothills of the Pyrenees, lay the other centre of Christian power. From the counties of the Carolingian marches emerged more consolidated states with powerful

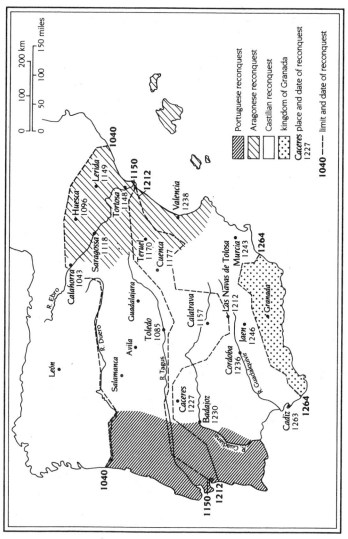

THE CHRISTIAN RECONQUISTA IN SPAIN

Portuguese reconquest
Aragonese reconquest
Castilian reconquest
kingdom of Granada
Caceres place and date of reconquest
1227
1040 —— limit and date of reconquest

200 km
150 miles

León

Calahorra
1043

Huesca
1096

Lerida
1149

Saragossa
1118

Tortosa
1148

Valencia
1238

Teruel
1170

Cuenca
1177

Salamanca

Avila

Guadalajara

Toledo
1085

Calatrava
1157

Las Navas de Tolosa
1212

Murcia
1243

Granada

Jaen
1246

Cordoba
1236

Caceres
1227

Badajoz
1230

Cadiz
1263

R. Ebro

R. Duero

R. Tagus

R. Guadalquivir

R. Guadiana

1040

1150

1212

1264

1264

rulers: Navarre, Aragon (a kingdom by 1035), and, on the Mediterranean coast, the Catalan districts, expanding under the leadership of the counts of Barcelona. The first gains were made as the men of the Asturias and Galicia pushed southwards to the River Duero. By 1085 the Castilians had reached the Tagus and by the beginning of the twelfth century the Aragonese and Catalans were consolidating their power in the Ebro valley.

In this early period, where nothing so definite as a fixed frontier between Christian and Muslim territory can be envisaged, power was based on the taking of strongholds and the exaction of tribute from the fragmented Muslim powers which had succeeded the great caliphate of Cordoba. The *taifa*, or 'party kings' fought amongst themselves in the south and were easy prey for the working of what has aptly been described as a 'protection racket system' run by the neighbouring Christian powers. This involved the payment of *parias*, fixed cash sums in return for military help against their Muslim rivals. The *parias* provided an essential part of the regular income of the Christian rulers; Alfonso VI exacted payments from ʿAbd Allah, ruler of Granada, amounting to 30,000 dinars down and a further 10,000 dinars annually.

The successful working of this system of profitable extortion was dependent on two factors: the inability of the Muslim princelings to form lasting alliances amongst themselves and the consolidation of territorial gains by the Christian forces. The existence of a Christian settler population, which moved into areas freed from the threat of Muslim attack, provided the necessary infrastructure to survive any Muslim counter-attack. The tenth-century northern migration of Mozarabs (Arabized Christians) and the subsequent encouragement of colonists from north of the Pyrenees, provided a settler population which could consolidate the successes of the Christian raiding parties. Their presence in often dangerous regions was encouraged by the Spanish monarchs and this chiefly explains the prevalence of freeholdings in the countryside and the granting of town customs (*fueros* or *cartas pueblas*) which gave their populations a high degree of autonomy. In many areas, small or medium-sized estates predominated. Their owners, far from being restricted in their activities by feudal controls, often chose their own lords. The demand for grazing land in the predominantly pastoral economy of the *meseta* gave a further impetus to territorial expansion and the inhabitants had a vested interest in keeping them safe from attack. The establishment of safe refuges in the towns was also vital. The newly captured cities, such as Salamanca, Guadalajara, and Avila— with its great granite walls and eighty-eight towers—were controlled by their own inhabitants and their *fueros* reflected the importance of organization for both offensive and defensive warfare. They usually contained detailed instructions on the organization of urban militias, on the command structure of the forces of the town, on the duties of service relating to the nobility and on the distribution of booty. In frontier society such as this, fortunes could be made from the profits of raiding, and those of humble origin could easily aspire to join the company of the mounted knights—the *caballeros*—a group which owed its status to military prowess, not birth, or the *hidalgos*—men of often obscure birth enjoying the same esteem as those born into the lower ranks of the nobility.

The resilience of this Christian settler society was put to serious test at the end of the eleventh century. Events after the capture of Toledo in 1085 by the forces of Alfonso VI of Castile (1065–1109) reveal a fundamental change in the attitudes of the victors to the conquered Muslims. At the instigation (it was said) of his queen, the chief mosque of Toledo was converted into a cathedral and the pleas of the Mozarabs for the toleration of the faith of their Muslim fellow townsmen went unheard. Now all land north of the Tagus was in Christian hands but the forces from beyond the Pyrenees which had helped to make the conquests possible brought their own attitudes and prejudices with them. Under Cluniac encouragement, the native Mozarabic liturgy was condemned in favour of the Roman rite and the Spanish kings were encouraged to consider themselves loyal vassals of the pope and thus ready both to eradicate religious practices which were deemed to be improper, and also to do their duty as leaders in wars which were now fought not merely for territory, but for the Faith. It was in this heady spiritual atmosphere that, according to the later Arab chronicler al-Maqqari, Alfonso I 'the Battler' (1104–34), king of Aragon and Navarre 'sent messengers ... summoning all the Christian nations to come and help him' continue the conquest of the cities of the Ebro valley. The projected attack on Saragossa was the subject of a council at Toulouse in 1118, where such influential Provençal lords as Gaston de Béarn, Centulo de Bigorre, and Bernard, viscount of Carcassonne, all of whom had already fought in the Holy Land, discussed the plans for the siege. Pope Gelasius II granted remission of sins to all those who took part and thus laid the basis for the full recognition of Spain as a legitimate area of crusade by Eugenius III's revised crusading Bull, *Divina dispositione* (1148). Thus the twelfth century saw the full panoply of crusading warfare reach the Iberian peninsula. Military Orders, in imitation of the Templars and Hospitallers in the Holy Land were founded: the Order of Calatrava in 1158 and that of Santiago, given papal confirmation in 1175. Spanish knights were encouraged by the papacy to remain at home fighting the infidel, rather than taking up the cross in the east.

There was a similar hardening of spiritual attitudes amongst the Muslims. After the fall of Toledo, al-Muʿ tamid of Seville appealed for help against Alfonso VI from the Almoravid rulers of North Africa. These new armies helped to stem the tide of Christian advance, but they brought with them a more austere and combative Muslim ideology, an active criticism of the cultured but effete *taifa* rulers for their policy of compromise and forceful promotion of the Holy War. The Almoravids and their successors, the Almohades, controlled Muslim Spain for most of the twelfth century and held the Christian armies in check. It was only after the preaching of a crusade in Italy, northern France, Germany, and Provence by Rodrigo Ximénez de Rada, the archbishop of Toledo, that a massive Christian army was able to inflict a decisive defeat upon the Almohades at the battle of Las Navas de Tolosa (1212).

The polarization of religious attitudes did much to harm indigenous Spanish traditions, but the peninsula still provided an important meeting-place for Christian, Muslim, and Jewish culture. An influential school of translation emerged in Toledo under the leadership of the Italian Gerard of Cremona (*c.*1114–87) and attracted scholars from all over Europe. Its main area of interest was scientific and mathematical works, such as those of the Muslim Averroes of Cordoba (1126–98), many of which preserved Greek learning which had been lost to the west. But the distinguished abbot of Cluny, Peter the Venerable, on a visit to Spain in 1141, commissioned a translation into Latin of the Koran and other short Muslim texts from a team which reflected the cosmopolitan nature of Toledan scholarship: an Englishman, Robert, probably from Ketton in Rutland; Hermann from the northern Balkans; a Mozarab, Peter of Toledo, and a Muslim, Muhammad, also from Toledo. They were to provide the first material from which a scholarly refutation of Muslim beliefs could be made which would raise the level of understanding amongst western theologians about Islam from the abyss of legend and uninformed supposition in which it had previously languished. Jewish scholars also made a major contribution. They could move with ease between Latin, Hebrew, and Arabic and often provided a vital link in the chain of translation. But distinguished scholars such as Moses Maimonides (1135–1204), perhaps the greatest commentator on the Torah, made their own specifically Jewish contribution to the cultural achievements of the period. On a less elevated level, Peter Alfonsi (the converted Jew Moses Sephardí) was responsible through his works for the introduction of many oriental tales into the literature of western Europe—both Chaucer and Boccaccio were to draw upon his stories. Many of the musical instruments familiar to medieval men were also of Moorish origin. The conflicts and contacts between Christian, Muslim, and Jew provided a stimulus not only to the ideology and intellect of medieval Europe, but also to its imagination.

Southern Italy: the Politics of Assimilation

In the tenth century the Muslim threat to peace in Italy came from raiding. Liutprand, bishop of Cremona wrote that the situation was particularly dangerous because attacks could be expected both from the Saracens of Fraxinetum (La Garde Freinet) and from the Muslims of North Africa harrying the coasts 'so that no one coming from the west or north to make his prayers at the thresholds of the blessed apostles was able to get into Rome, without being either taken prisoner by these men or only released on payment of a large ransom'. A joint expedition of Lombard, Greek, and papal forces successfully rooted out the Saracen camps from the mouth of the River Garigliano in 915 and the base at Fraxinetum was destroyed in 973. But the Saracen danger in southern Italy and the apparent inability of local forces to dislodge them, provided a pretext for intervention by the German emperors. In 982 Otto II, marching south from Salerno was able to announce that he had come 'to defend the Christian population'. This campaign ended in disaster—the young emperor died in Rome the following year after his army had been defeated at Tarento —but it paved the way for further incursions by northerners.

Legendary history, written after the events, obscures the circumstances of the first coming of Norman mercenaries into southern Italy, but their involvement in the politics of the region was further proof of the inability of the existing powers to provide security. Revolts of Byzantine-held cities such as Bari against the representatives of a distant government (itself distracted by a long campaign in Bulgaria) and the bickering of Lombard princes amidst an ever-present threat of Muslim attack provided a fertile field of activity for groups of knights whose only loyalty lay to their own leaders. Norman knights were reported south of the Garigliano in 1017 and at first were simply 'lances for hire': small groups of men whose families were of little prominence in Normandy, who would fight for whoever promised them a share of the booty. It was not long, however, before the possibility of more permanent rewards presented itself. The Norman knight, Rainulf, became count of Aversa in 1030 and this marked the beginning of their permanent settlement. The most famous adventurers, the de Hauteville brothers, provide a characteristic example of the rewards which military prowess and diplomatic shrewdness could bring in a society which, like that of Spain, was geared for war. Hautevilles were present in the force of three hundred Normans which joined a large Byzantine expedition which unsuccessfully attacked Sicily in 1038. When the riches of the emirates proved for the moment unobtainable, many Normans took service with the emperor in Constantinople, but others, including the Hautevilles, turned against their erstwhile employers and in 1040 inflicted a series of defeats upon them. At this stage, some semblance of loyalty to the local rulers still remained. William de Hauteville, elected Norman count in 1042, accepted the Lombard Prince Gaimar of Salerno as his overlord, and Robert Guiscard (his half-brother) made an advantageous marriage to the formidable Lombard Princess Sichelgaita. But the characteristic Norman skill of benefiting from rival claims to authority soon manifested itself.

At an assembly held at Capua in 1047, in the presence of the Emperor Henry III, the Norman claims to rights and possessions in the south were confirmed. This action, though clearly intended to emphasize imperial rights of disposition in Italy, in reality provided a crucial *de jure* recognition of the territorial presence of the Normans, regardless of the rights of those whose lands they had usurped. The papacy, alarmed at the prospect of a *rapprochement* of these dangerous newcomers with the empire, was also compelled to grant recognition. Pope Leo IX (1049–54) had hoped to take advantage of the confused political situation to reassert long-held papal claims to the territory of Benevento. But his forces were ignominiously defeated by the Normans at the battle of Civitate in 1053 and six years later, at the Synod of Melfi (1059), Pope Nicholas II confirmed Richard of Aversa (Rainulf's nephew) as prince of Capua and Robert Guiscard as the holder of Apulia, Calabria, and Sicily when (as was confidently expected) the island would fall to Christian forces. In fact, it was another thirty years before Sicily was entirely subdued by Robert's brother Roger 'the Great Count', although the great city of Palermo fell in 1072 and the emirate of Taormina in 1079.

Two events mark the final confirmation of Norman power in southern Italy and the formation of important new alliances

NORMAN KINGS OF SICILY

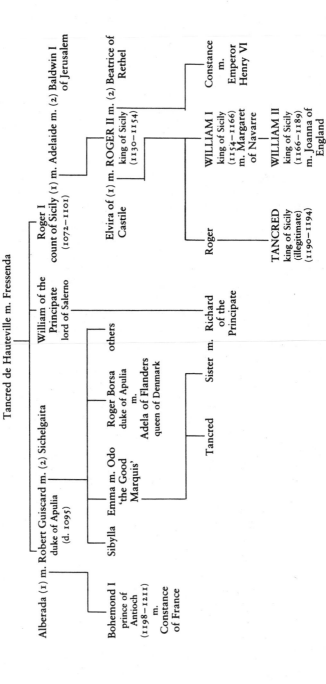

which were to have repercussions throughout the Mediterranean. In 1080 Robert Guiscard swore fealty for his lands not to the Emperor Henry IV, who had offered imperial investiture in return for support against the papacy, but to Pope Gregory VII himself. In 1130 Roger II was crowned 'king of Sicily, the duchy of Apulia, and the principality of Capua'. In political terms papal recognition meant little; the Normans continued to follow the dictates of their own self-interest and in 1085, Gregory VII found himself a virtual prisoner in their hands after a request for aid against imperial forces marching on Rome had simply resulted in a Norman sack of the city. But in ideological terms the papal grant of the lands of southern Italy and Sicily were important steps in the Norman leaders' quest for international recognition. The establishment of a kingdom was the final stage in their progress from virtual obscurity to the heights of acquired aristocracy. The 'irresistible rise' of Norman power in southern Italy cannot merely be explained by the military prowess of their knights, though this was considerable. Only when Sicily, the richest of their prizes, was captured could their future be assured and it was the support of the Church in the achievement of this triumph over the infidel which provided the Normans with the respectability they craved. The campaigns against Byzantine lands in the Balkans led in the 1080s by Robert Guiscard and his son Bohemond of Taranto, confirmed the Normans in the view of many of their contemporaries as champions of the true faith who could be seen to be 'fighting the good fight' against schismatic Greeks. There might be moments of tension in the 'special relationship' between the Italian Normans and the papacy, but their enthusiasm both for the reform of the Church and for the spreading of the faith made them a natural source of recruitment when the First Crusade was preached in 1095. For those, like Bohemond, whose inheritances in Italy were problematic, the possibility of territorial gains in the east coupled with the opportunity to fight for Christendom, once more proved irresistible.

Unlike their counterparts in Spain, the Normans brought no settlers with them. They stood as a ruling élite above peasants, administrators, and clergy—Lombard, Byzantine, and Muslim—who remembered other traditions and other lords. Rather than impose their own ways, the first generations of Norman settlers assimilated the political and cultural heritage of the regions they conquered. Though the Latin Church made steady headway, especially through the endowment of new monastic houses with the possessions of Greek monasteries, other religions were tolerated. The newcomers did not refer to themselves as 'Normans' and their kings were known as the 'king of the Sicilians'. The rulers took upon themselves the mantle of the most powerful Christian ruler of the Mediterranean: the Byzantine emperor. The autocratic powers, stiff ceremonial, and monopolistic management of the state economy were all continued in the Greek tradition. Many of the administrative organs of the state were Byzantine or Islamic in origin and although recognizably Norman officials such as justiciars, chamberlains, and constables made their appearance, they governed on behalf of a monarch whose all-pervading power was something not to be found in contemporary northern Europe.

It was this oriental outlook which was to dominate Sicilian culture in the twelfth century and to make its rulers an object of admiration and, it must be said, more than a tinge of suspicion in the eyes both of northerners and of visitors from the east. The Muslim writer, Ibn Jubayr, who was in Palermo in 1184, commented on the number of Muslims he found in high governmental posts and at court, and the fact that they seemed quite free to follow their own faith. The kings patronized scholars of eastern origin: the great Arab geographer al-Edrisi who wrote his *Book of King Roger* in honour of Roger II; the Greek scholar Eugenios, who translated Ptolemy's *Optics* from Arabic into Latin, and a certain Henry, known as 'Aristippus' after Socrates' Syracusan disciple, who translated Plato's *Meno* and *Phaedo* from Greek into Latin. Both these men worked at the court of King William I (1154–66). Many, such as Peter of Blois, the celebrated twelfth-century Anglo-French churchman, travelled to Apulia to study Greek philosophy, whilst others crowded to the leading medical school of Europe at Salerno. The cosmopolitan nature of the kingdom is also revealed in its monuments: from the palace chapel at Palermo with its Arabic-influenced ceiling to the mausoleum of Bohemond at Canosa di Puglia built like the tomb of a Muslim holy man; from the great Greek Pantokrator in the apse of the cathedral at Cefalù to the Church of St Nicholas of Bari built under the direction of the Italian Abbot Elias of La Cava with distinctly Lombard features.

It has been argued that the logical culmination of Norman expansion would have been the conquest of the Byzantine Empire, but although the Sicilians consistently raided the shores of the Balkans (on one notorious occasion in 1147 they kidnapped the silk craftsmen of the city of Thebes in Greece) and had, of course, incurred the lasting hostility of the Byzantines for their seizure of the southern Italian land of the empire, there is no real evidence to suggest that they planned a full-scale onslaught on the empire. Nor did they take an active part in the crusades against the Muslim powers of the Near East. They preferred to reap the lucrative profits of buoyant luxury trade with the great ports of North Africa and Egypt and thus kept on friendly terms with neighbouring Arab powers. They successfully balanced general support for the papacy with periodic gestures of friendship towards the empire and cultivated relations with other European powers by marriage alliances with Castile, Navarre, and even England. But it was this policy of diplomacy on an international scale which precipitated the fall of the Norman dynasty in Sicily. King William II, having no legitimate male heirs, married his aunt Constance to Henry, son of the Emperor Frederick Barbarossa, a move disliked by many of the old Norman families and which led to a civil war on William's death in 1189. Henry VI marched south to claim his wife's inheritance and, after bitter fighting, was crowned king of Sicily in Palermo in 1194. The kingdom's riches were now used to finance the Hohenstaufen struggle to maintain imperial power and it became a pawn in the international political game being played out between pope and emperor.

Crusader Palestine: the Colonial Experience

Within four years of the preaching of the First Crusade at Clermont in 1095, the city of Jerusalem fell. It was the remarkable speed of the westerners' progress, above all, which ensured the successful conclusion of the expedition. Neither the Byzantines—who were, in any case, generally well disposed to the aims of the crusade, though alarmed by the unruly behaviour of many of those who took part—nor the Muslim powers of Asia Minor and Syria, were able to turn back the thousands who took up the cross and who braved extraordinary privations to reach the Holy Land. The first groups to leave, the so-called Popular Crusades led by the preachers Peter the Hermit and Walter Sans Avoir, having pillaged their way across the Balkans, arrived in Constantinople in the late autumn of 1096. They insisted on being transported across the Bosphorus to Bithynia, where they were promptly massacred by the Turks. More caution prevailed amongst the forces led by the experienced western counts who waited for the full strength of their armies to assemble in the Byzantine capital before crossing to Asia Minor. The Byzantines, too, were eager to put these battle-hardened knights to good use and, whilst the leaders of the crusade wintered in Constantinople in 1096–7, agreements to provide mutual assistance were made with many of the western leaders. Some of the western leaders may have sworn oaths of fealty to the emperor, for the Byzantines were certainly familiar with what they referred to as 'the customary oaths of the Latins'. There is little doubt, however, that Alexius made some form of agreement with Raymond of St Gilles and other Franks by which he undertook to support the crusading armies with his own forces as they crossed Anatolia on the understanding that the crusaders would return all the former Byzantine territory which they recaptured to imperial control.

The turning-point of the First Crusade was reached outside the walls of Antioch. The army besieged the city from 21 October 1097 until 3 June 1098 and then was itself surrounded by Islamic forces which had marched from Iraq. Dreadful privations afflicted those who had only recently survived the long march across Anatolia. Food and water were in desperately short supply and eye-witnesses wrote of barbarism and even cannibalism amongst both the humbler soldiers and those who had once been knights, but who, having lost both their horses and the means to replace them, had forfeited their social status and their money. Raymond of Agiles, the chaplain to Raymond of St Gilles, blamed the loose living in the army for the danger that the expedition seemed to be in and he vividly described the penitential processions and fastings which were ordered by the clergy. In this highly charged emotional atmosphere, came the amazing news of the discovery, on 15 June, of what was believed to be the Holy Lance which had pierced the Saviour's side on the cross. Visions and dreams had led two men, Peter Bartholomew and Stephen of Valence, to the place where the lance had been hidden and similar spiritual experiences began to spread through the army. When the Muslim armies surrounding them were finally defeated at the end of June, many reported seeing saints on white chargers leading the attack. Christ Himself appeared in visions to chide them for their delay in continuing the march to Jerusalem. The exhausted crusaders seemed to have drawn new resolution from such reports and certainly amongst the humbler soldiers there was increasing impatience to continue the march. Matters were delayed, however, by a violent disagreement between Raymond of St Gilles and Bohemond of Taranto about which of them should be granted control over Antioch. In the event, Bohemond gained possession. He did not hand the city over to the representatives of the Byzantine emperor and his reason for doing this was partly that, mistakenly informed that the crusader army was about to be annihilated outside Antioch, the Emperor Alexius had withdrawn his forces and was preparing to return to Constantinople. Bohemond maintained that any alliance was thus rendered null and void; the Byzantines, on realizing that he had no intention of giving up his prize, marked out the Latins in general and Bohemond in particular as potential enemies who could not be trusted to keep their word. This 'treachery' was to sour Latin–Byzantine relations for the immediate future.

It is significant that Raymond of St Gilles led the first contingent to set off southwards again. He may well have decided that there was more to be gained by showing devotion to the ideals of the crusade than delaying any further in a fruitless pursuit of power in Antioch. The armies marched quickly down the seacoast of Palestine, avoiding prolonged sieges and accepting money from local Muslim rulers to leave them, for the moment, in peace. By the beginning of June, the crusader army was encamped outside Jerusalem and after a short siege, the city fell on 15 July 1099 amidst scenes of slaughter of its Jewish and Muslim inhabitants.

Jerusalem was now in Christian hands; but what was to become of the crusaders? Many, including such nobles as Hugh of Vermandois, brother of the king of France, Robert of Normandy, and Robert of Flanders clearly considered their vows had been fulfilled and set off for home taking with them many of the most experienced soldiers who had managed to survive the long march. But for others, settlement in the Holy Land and the enjoyment of a status which had been denied them in the west proved more attractive. But how should the new state be organized? Unlike Spain or southern Italy, where Muslim and Greek expertise in administration could be put to use, there was no question of allowing any Muslim participation in government in the Holy Land. Indeed, all those who were not either Latin Christians or the Syrian and Armenian Christians who were allied to them, were considered as potential enemies. The kingdom of Jerusalem and its associated states of Edessa, Antioch, and Tripoli were, in fact, the precursors of later colonial territories. The customs, values, and outlook of the conquerors were imposed on the indigenous populations. The fact that their new homeland was always referred to in the west as Outremer ('the land overseas') indicates that for many contemporaries, the crusader states in Palestine, though increasingly subject to oriental influences, were still considered to be an extension of western society and the structures created in the east give an interesting perspective on what they considered proper forms of government.

Kingship might have seemed one of the most obvious, but

there were certain difficulties inherent in the designation of a ruler for the new state in Jerusalem. Raymond of Agiles reported that his master, Raymond of St Gilles, though offered the crown by a group of influential nobles, refused it because he would not allow himself to be crowned king in the city where Christ had been crucified as 'King of the Jews' and had worn the Crown of Thorns. Godfrey of Bouillon who (after some intrigue and a form of election which is still unclear) was appointed ruler, took the title of *advocatus Sancti Sepulchri*— 'Protector of the Holy Sepulchre'—though later commentators, such as the great Palestinian-born historian William of Tyre, did consider him as the first king of Jerusalem. The new ruler's relationship with the other crusader principalities was also unclear. On Godfrey's death, his brother Baldwin, who had established a county in Edessa during the course of the crusade, was crowned king, thus transforming Edessa into a fief of the crown, to be granted out by the kings of Jerusalem, but Antioch and the county of Tripoli always remained more independent of the kingdom. It was only when their rulers were captured, too young to rule effectually, or female (and thus unable to lead the armies) that the king of Jerusalem was able to exert his influence. There was no doubt that the king was the feudal superior of the new nobility of the kingdom, for he it was who granted them out their fiefs, either in land, or, increasingly frequently in a country where fertile and safe territory was in short supply, in revenues, and recent research has shown that, until the middle of the twelfth century, the king of Jerusalem enjoyed considerable power. He was the commander-in-chief in time of war, held large amounts of territory in Judea and Samaria, controlled monopolies on dyeing, tanning, fishing, and copper-working, and enjoyed considerable revenues from port dues and various taxes on commercial activity and the passage of pilgrims. But by the mid-twelfth century, problems were beginning to arise. The descendants of those who had stayed after the First Crusade had now had time to consolidate their holdings and to intermarry, thus forming a recognizable noble 'class'. Newcomers from the west found it difficult to establish themselves and the

THE ROYAL HOUSE OF JERUSALEM TO 1187

Ida of Lorraine m. Eustace II of Boulogne

Eustace III of Boulogne

GODFREY (1099–1100)

BALDWIN I (1100–1118) m.
(1) Godvere of Tosni
(2) daughter of T'oros
(3) Adelaide, countess of Sicily

Ida m. Hugh I of Rethel m. Melisende

Baldwin of Le Bourg count of Rethel

BALDWIN II (1118–1131) m. Morphia

Cecilia m. Roger prince of Antioch

Hodierna

MELISENDE m. FULK of Anjou (1131–1143)

Alice m. Bohemond II of Antioch

Hodierna m. Raymond II of Tripoli

Joveta, Abbess of Bethany

BALDWIN III (1143–1163) m. Theodora Comnena

Agnes of Courtenay (1) m. AMALRIC I (1163–1174) m. (2) Maria Comnena

SIBYLLA (1186–1190) m.
William of (1) Montferrat
(2) GUY of Lusignan (1186–1192)

BALDWIN IV (1174–1185)

ISABELLA (1192–1205/6) m.
(1) Humphrey of Toron
(2) Conrad of Montferrat
(3) Henry of Champagne
(4) AMALRIC II of Lusignan, king of Cyprus (1197–1205)

(2) Balian of Ibelin

BALDWIN V (1185–1186)

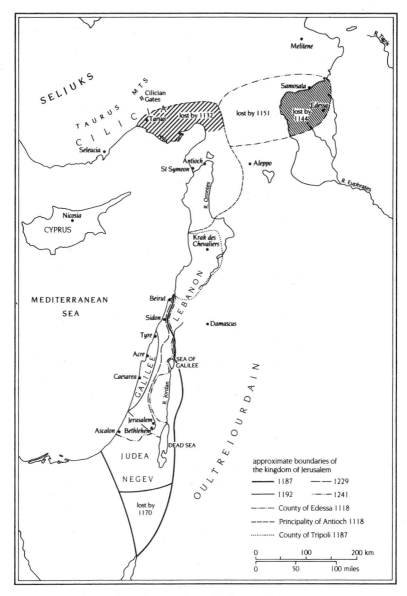

MELITENE

SELJUKS

TAURUS MTS

CILICIA

Cilician
Gates

Tarsus

lost by 1132

lost by 1151

Samosata

Edessa
lost by
1144

Seleucia

R. Tigris

Antioch

St Symeon

Aleppo

R. Orontes

R. Euphrates

Nicosia

CYPRUS

Krak des
Chevaliers

MEDITERRANEAN

SEA

LEBANON

Beirut

Sidon

Damascus

Tyre

Acre

SEA OF
GALILEE

Caesarea

GALILEE

R. Jordan

Jerusalem

Ascalon Bethlehem

DEAD SEA

JUDEA

NEGEV

lost by
1170

OULTREJOURDAIN

approximate boundaries of
the kingdom of Jerusalem

——— 1187   — — — 1229

——— 1192   —·—·— 1241

—·—·— County of Edessa 1118

— — — Principality of Antioch 1118

·········· County of Tripoli 1187

0		100		200 km

0	50	100 miles

LATIN POWER IN THE NEAR EAST

royal lands were depleted in grants made in order to persuade them to stay and help defend the kingdom. Those born in the east showed increasing hostility to western knights who came on later expeditions, such as the Second Crusade of 1147. In the second half of the century, the authority of the crown was further weakened by noble revolts and the increasing tendency of the greater landholders to act independently. It was bitter faction rivalry over the succession which seriously weakened the kingdom in the 1180s at a time of considerable danger from Arab attack.

Just as the position of king resembled that found in the west, so, too, did the other institutions of the kingdom. As in all colonial societies, the conquerors brought their own religious institutions with them. Latin clergy were installed in the cities as they fell to the crusading armies and a Latin patriarch was enthroned in Jerusalem as a matter of urgency in 1099. Greek bishops were not allowed to return—another cause for Byzantine hostility. Monastic orders soon followed. The Syrian Christians were allowed to keep their clergy and, most important of all, their access to the Holy Places, such as the Church of the Holy Sepulchre in Jerusalem, but it was clear that, in Outremer as in southern Italy and Spain, the Latin Church was to be supreme. It was not, however, the post-Reform European Church. The kings of Jerusalem exerted much more influence over the choice of senior clergy than would have been acceptable in the contemporary west. The great distance between Rome and the Holy Land made it almost impossible for papal influence to make itself significantly felt and the need to support the mónarchy that was, after all, charged with the guardianship of the Holy Land and the safety of the shiploads of pilgrims who arrived from the west each Easter made it difficult to protest too strongly about uncanonical practices.

Defending the Holy Land was the major preoccupation of its rulers and in this sphere, too, the practices of the west were imported into the Holy Land. The army was feudal in composition; those who held land or revenues from the crown were bound to answer the king's summons in time of war. There was always a shortage of experienced fighting men: in 1100 there were probably only 300 knights and some 1,200 *serjeants*, and the legislation of the kingdom (*assises*) tried to remedy this by allowing women and any other descendants to inherit land (and thus provide the military service due on it); by forbidding knights who already held one fief to acquire another and by allowing those who had moved in to cultivate the lands of those who had returned to Europe to keep the land if the former owner had not returned within a year and a day. The Holy Land also saw the development of a new kind of knighthood: the brethren of the Military Orders. Whilst the origin of the Knights of St John the Baptist (the Hospitallers) can probably be traced back to those who had taken care of the pilgrims visiting Jerusalem before the crusade, and the Hospitallers of St Lazarus concerned themselves with the care of lepers, the Templars and the later orders, such as the Teutonic Knights and the Knights of Our Lady of Montjoie were fighting brotherhoods, subject to monastic vows and discipline, but devoted to the active defence of the Holy Land. Churchmen as influential as St Bernard saw nothing incongruous in monks taking up arms; it was as 'soldiers of Christ' that they fought. The Military Orders garrisoned the great castles of the Holy Land and their experience of eastern warfare made them an indispensable, if sometimes self-willed, part of the kingdom's defences.

Many of the difficulties of maintaining Latin power in Outremer stemmed from the fact that few Franks lived in the countryside. Their settlement was almost entirely urban—the castle garrisons being one of the few exceptions. To maintain their power entailed continual campaigning, more and more difficult after 1144 when the city of Edessa fell to Arab forces and the Muslim armies united under the great generals, Nur al-Din, Zangi, and Saladin. The kingdom had few ships of its own. It relied on the sea power provided by the Italian communes first to conquer the coastal cities, then to protect trade and the pilgrim traffic from the powerful Egyptian fleet and, as we shall see, had to grant privileges in return. Whilst their naval assistance was, on many occasions indispensable, their profitable trade with Muslim powers meant that there was always a potential clash of religious and economic interest in their conduct of affairs in the east.

The fall of the first kingdom of Jerusalem in 1187, though ostensibly the result of the disastrous Christian defeat at the battle of Hattin was, in a sense, inevitable from the moment the Franks took the city in 1099. For the enthusiasm of the First Crusade was never to be repeated; the kingdom, from the moment of its inception, was forever on the defensive and its very nature as a means of establishing exclusively Christian control over Holy Places just as significant in Islam meant that it was a matter of honour amongst the Muslims for the holy city to be recaptured. But even after the recapture of Jerusalem the 'matter of the Holy Land' remained uppermost in the minds of many of the leaders of western Christendom and whilst the idea of crusade was to undergo significant alteration in the course of the thirteenth century, the old dream of Christian rule in the Holy Land remained just as potent.

The Rise of Long-distance Trade

The establishment of Latin power in the eastern Mediterranean was a major stimulus to international trade, but the expansion of mercantile activity in Italy from locally held markets serving regional needs to international enterprises covering long distances had already begun by the end of the ninth century. The northern cities of the Lombard plain had developed contacts with regions as far away as Anglo-Saxon England. A document dating from the late tenth or early eleventh century, but reflecting earlier circumstances, the *Honorancie civitatis Papie*, provides a mass of detail concerning the organization of trade in the northern city of Pavia. The taxes on various commodities were enumerated, amongst them horses, slaves, wool, linen, tin, and swords, and various groups of merchants were granted safe conducts and rights to trade in the city. No *decima* (tax) was to be paid by Anglo-Saxons, but, in return, they made gifts of silver, greyhounds, shields, lances, and swords to the local official in charge of trade. The Venetians, on the other hand, gave gifts of silk cloth and money to be freed from taxes, but still made tribute payments in the form of spices and money, as did the merchants from the southern cities of Salerno, Gaeta, and Amalfi. It was not merely within the city that the power of the Pavia officials extended, for the document provides a list of ten customs houses on the Alpine passes controlled by the city; only those travelling as bona-fide pilgrims to Rome were to be exempted. Towns on the routes south of the passes such as Vercelli, Asti, Verona, and Cremona also expanded.

By the year 1000, however, the role of chief trading town of Lombardy had been taken over by Milan. Geographical factors played a part, but the main impetus came from political activity such as the granting of trading rights to the 'Church of St Ambrose' by the Emperor Otto I in 952. From such small beginnings, the city soon became the major trading town of northern Italy and the revenues from trade a cause both of the emergence of civic wealth and of political interference from outside political powers.

Towns further to the south gained wealth from seaborne trade. Two of them, Amalfi and Venice, were already trading widely before the year 1000. Much of our evidence for their prosperity comes from the works of Arab travellers and geographers, usually to be relied upon because they shared the Muslim interest in trade and commerce. The writer Ibn Hawqal, in his *Book of the Routes and the Kingdoms*, written *c.*977, commented that Amalfi was 'the most prosperous town in Lombardy [in this case, southern Italy], the most noble, the most illustrious on account of its conditions, the most affluent and splendid'. Amalfi's prosperity was based on its trade with the Muslim world; in 996 it was reported that some two hundred Amalfitan merchants had been attacked in Alexandria after a Muslim fleet, being prepared for an attack on Byzantium, had been burned there. Though the figure may be something of an exaggeration, it reflects a considerable trading presence.

Trade within the Byzantine Empire formed the basis of the prosperity of Venice, though her merchants, too, were also to be found in Alexandria as early as the ninth century and were the subject of a complaint by the Byzantine Emperor John Tzimisces in 971 because of their willingness to export arms to the Muslims. The *Honorancie civitatis Papie* commented that the Venetians were 'a nation that does not plough, sow or gather vintage', and by the end of the ninth century their control of trade had been established in large areas of Lombardy along the Po valley and the Adriatic coastline, where by the tenth century their power extended as far as Ancona. On the opposite shore, Istria and parts of northern Dalmatia became Venetian protectorates in return for help against the attacks of Slav pirates. The maintenance of safe passage in the Adriatic was always of prime importance to Venice, for her trade with the east, as well as other parts of Italy, had to pass along this route. In addition, the Dalmatian coasts and islands provided Venice with grain to feed her population and wood to construct the larger and cheaper vessels produced from the eleventh century onwards. The increasingly privileged position of the Venetian merchants in Constantinople can be traced in a series of Byzantine imperial documents (chrysobulls) issued in the tenth and eleventh centuries. In 992 Basil II agreed that Venetian goods should be admitted to Constantinople at lower tariffs than those levelled on their rivals, Jewish and Lombard traders, and merchants from Bari and Amalfi. About a century later the Venetians were assigned a trading quarter in Constantinople on a prime site on the shores of the Golden Horn and freedom from trade tolls and taxes in the Byzantine ports in the Aegean, though probably not in the Black Sea. The successful maritime expansion of Venice in the eastern Mediterranean has often been attributed to these treaties and it was certainly the case that they became bargaining counters in the political relationship between Byzantium and Venice, to be withdrawn and reinstated at the will of the empire. Much of the tension between Venice and the empire in the twelfth century arose from Byzantium's skilful manipulation of trading rights and their award in turn to Venice's rivals, especially Genoa and Pisa. In 1111 the Pisans were also allotted their own wharf in Constantinople and were guaranteed protection against the Venetians; by the 1160s they had sworn fealty to the emperor. The mutual hostility between the various trading groups erupted into a series of riots in the city in the 1160s and 1170s and led to growing anti-Latin feeling amongst the Byzantines.

Whilst Venetian ambitions were set upon exploitation of the eastern Mediterranean, the merchants of Genoa and Pisa developed lucrative trading links with the Muslim cities of North Africa. Genoese exports to North Africa through ports such as Bougia, mainly consisted of cloth—fustians brought to Genoa from Milan and Pavia by Lombard merchants, linens from Germany and Spain, and unspun cotton—dyestuffs for the weaving and leather industries, and precious stones, perfumes, and spices shipped onwards via Genoa from the east. In return, she imported skins and leather goods, grain and alum—used to fix dyes in cloth. Pisa, too, had *fondachi* (trading posts) in Africa. Both these cities had interests in the Holy Land, and, together with Venice, obtained trading rights and the establishment of communes in the cities reconquered from the Muslims in return for indispensable naval assistance to the crusading armies.

The phenomenon of long-distance trade was not confined to the Christian powers of the Mediterranean. Muslim writers delighted in enumerating the commodities which passed backwards and forwards through the Islamic world and beyond and although the Muslim world may have looked mainly to the east for its most profitable trade, Ibn Hawqal was able to report in the tenth century that Kairouan was the largest town of the Maghrib, active in the export of such commodities as silk, wool, and mulatto slave girls, whilst Sijilmasa, at the end of the caravan route from the Sudan, provided significant returns from tolls.

Muslim and Christian merchants were not often found within each other's territory and, in many respects, the Italian merchants simply fulfilled the function of a border market between continental Europe and the Mediterranean basin. Jewish traders were, however, active throughout the Mediterranean particularly in the slave and fur trades. In the ninth and tenth centuries the wars against the Slavs of eastern Europe provided a lucrative human booty to be traded to merchants in the slave market at Verdun and finally sold in the caliphate.

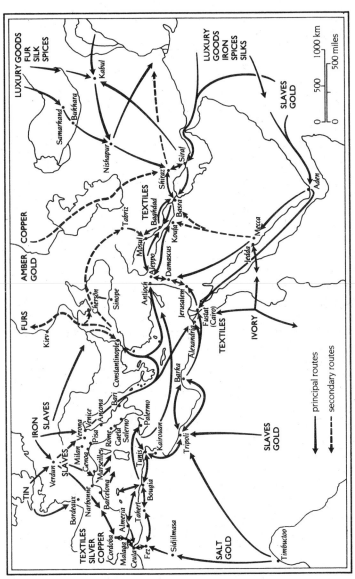

LUXURY GOODS
FUR
SILK
SPICES

Kabul

Bukhara
Samarkand

LUXURY
GOODS
IRON
SPICES
SILKS

SLAVES
GOLD

1000 km
500
500 miles
0
0

Nishapur

Siraf

Aden

AMBER
GOLD

COPPER

Shiraz
Tabriz

TEXTILES

Baghdad
Basra

Mosul
Koufa
Aleppo
Damascus
Mecca

FURS

Cherson
Sinope

Antioch

Jerusalem
Fustat
(Cairo)

Jedda

Kiev

Constantinople

Alexandria

IVORY

TEXTILES

Barka

IRON
SLAVES

Verona
Venice
Milan
Bari
Ancona
Genoa
Pisa
Rome
Gaeta
Salerno

Palermo

Kairouan

Tripoli

SLAVES
GOLD

Verdun

Marseilles

SLAVES

Tunis

TIN

Narbonne
Bordeaux
Barcelona
Almeria
Tahert
Bougia

TEXTILES
SILVER
COPPER
Cordoba
Malaga
Ceuta
Fez

Sidjilmasa

SALT
GOLD

Timbuctoo

— principal routes
--- secondary routes

WESTERN TRADE WITH ISLAM IN THE NINTH TO ELEVENTH CENTURIES

Later on, the Jews can be seen exchanging luxury goods from east to west, just as much at home in Christian as in Muslim lands.

The development of long-distance trade in the Mediterranean regions demanded new approaches to mercantile financing, the organization of expeditions, and the settlements of debts. The sea crossings presented considerable dangers; the high value of many commodities demanded a system of payment which could not rely on barter or the transportation of large amounts of money and the sheer complexity of business relationships—middlemen and agents often intervened between the principals—led to the emergence of highly sophisticated trading mechanisms. The Genoese notarial records reveal two common methods of financing trading expeditions: the *commenda*, where the investor provided all the capital to finance the expedition and gained three-quarters of the profit (his travelling agent receiving one-quarter) and the *societas maris* where the investor who stayed at home provided two-thirds of the capital, the travelling factor one-third, and each took half the profits. By the end of the twelfth century the increasing use of the *commenda*, backed up by loans to investors payable only when their ships returned ('sea loans'), reveals a growing number of small investors who wanted to gain as much from their investments as they could. Whilst there were, of course, powerful merchant élites in the Italian trading cities, such as the della Volta, Burone, and the aptly named Usodimare family, the evidence from Genoa, at least, suggests that a considerable proportion of the population was engaged in overseas trading ventures of one kind or another.

The importance of commerce in the Mediterranean world at this time influenced both the topographical and social structures of the urban societies in which it was based. Towns both Christian and Muslim organized their trading quarters on the bazaar system; the shops and booths of the traders in each commodity were grouped together, to encourage competition and benefit the consumer. The proximity in which merchants and traders found themselves contributed to the sense of group solidarity which had long been evident. But from the tenth century, mercantile and other urban groups began to claim a much greater voice in the political life of the cities. The greatest changes came in Italy, where a lack of strong centralized rule allowed towns as well as rural areas to evolve their own, individual forms of government. In many towns and cities, the eleventh century saw a series of major upheavals; uprisings against the existing forces of authority—such as bishops and counts—and the evolution of a new type of association, the commune.

Urban Freedom and Civic Government

Just as urban life produced its own forms of economic organization, it also brought to the fore political structures based on groups and associations. The commune, originally a sworn association of citizens bound together to keep the peace, developed particularly in Italy. It has often been seen as a new departure, but recent research suggests that it was simply another means medieval men found of articulating the collectivity which lay behind much of what they did. But it is still important to consider why this form of government evolved in many Italian towns and cities during and after the eleventh century. There were many focal points of urban solidarity: a sense of civic identity which in many cases had survived from the Roman period and the continuing existence of notaries and lawyers as repositories of that tradition; the fact that Italian dioceses were often small so that many cities had cathedrals, bishops to provide a lead in society, and patron saints to keep watch over their particular faithful; and the fact that many landowners also lived in towns, so that civic solidarity stretched out beyond the walls into the countryside beyond.

In Milan, for example, there were three main groups: the *capitanei*, important landowners with property not only in the countryside but in the city; the *vavassores*, lesser landowners who often owed services to the *capitanei*; and the *cives*, the merchants and professional men of the town. The power of the *capitanei* improved significantly after 843, when the emperor granted them lands which had once been held by the

Church. But in the course of the eleventh century, the emperors favoured the *vavassores* at the expense of the greater feudatories and, by the *Constitutio de feudis* (1037), made them into free proprietors of their land and reduced their duties to their overlords. Many *vavassores* moved into the city of Milan and made common cause with urban groups such as lawyers and merchants against the greater landowners. It was out of such associations, where groups with common aims joined together, that the communes emerged. The groups within the cities elected their own leaders—the consuls—often members of important families, to protect their interests against the claims of the magnates, or other powers such as the Church.

There was nothing intrinsically new in the association of citizens in common aims and activities but the political circumstances of the eleventh and twelfth centuries meant that their influence increased. In Milan, for instance, the archbishop had always played a leading part in the government of the city and his appointment was a matter of considerable interest both to the pope and to the German emperors who claimed suzerainty over Lombardy. Both wished their nominee to be accepted by the citizens and the clergy, and as the battle for supremacy in Milan continued, the groups who controlled the trade and landed wealth of the city, alternately wooed by the two powers, stood to gain most. In other towns in northern Italy, too, hostility to imperial claims (such as the right to impose taxes and tolls on trade and the *fodrum*, a levy to support imperial armies in Italy) lay at the root of the political demands of the communes. In 1081 the Emperor Henry IV confirmed the customs of Pisa and also agreed that he would not appoint a marquis in Tuscany without the consent of the twelve representatives of the city given in the town assembly. The customs of Genoa indicated the areas in which urban interests demanded change: legal independence and the right to hold courts in which land, inheritance, and commercial claims could be settled; the freedom from dues imposed by outside political powers and the right to control immigration into the city.

By 1150 the leaders of the commune were usually known as

consuls—a clear reference to antique tradition. Their number varied. In Verona in 1140 seven consuls signed a document; in Orvieto there were two consuls in 1157, though in 1170 and 1172 the number had risen to four. Beneath the consuls were councils of the leading men of the towns; in Orvieto in 1200 the council had a hundred members. The consuls in Pisa, like many of their fellows elsewhere, claimed authority from 'the people gathered in assembly', but this should not be taken as an indication of any democratic franchise. The citizens who took the oath to defend the commune were members of important families within the city; artisan groups and the poorer inhabitants of the towns were excluded from direct participation in their government. It was the joint involvement of these potentially competing family groups in the government of the towns that meant that, in many places, struggles were not so much concerned with resistance to outside political control as with internal jockeying for position. In Venice, although the old ruling families, such as the Orsoleo, Candiani, and Morosini, continued to dominate the city, other groups pressed for their share of power. By the end of the twelfth century the *arengo*, the old popular gathering, had disappeared, and a new assembly of 480 members, the *maggior consilio* had evolved. Its members were to be elected by two representatives of each of the *sestieri*, the districts of Venice. In 1185 the system was further modified; the *maggior consilio* was itself to nominate a Council of Forty to carry out legislative activity. None of these arrangements were democratic, nor were they intended to be. By 1200, in most northern and central Italian cities, as in Venice, there was a charmed circle of families and interest groups which kept power within its own hands.

The rise of communal government in northern Italy was both an effect and a cause of a lack of centralized political authority. Whilst remaining hostile to such 'unnatural' forms of government, both pope and emperor had to learn to come to terms with them. The Lombard League, formed by the cities of the region in 1167 to counter the claims of the Emperor Frederick Barbarossa that he had attacked Milan to restore 'justice and right government' was the first of many such associations which countered the strength of the imperial armies with the force and enthusiasm of the civic militias. The treaty of Constance of 1183, by which the emperor recognized the right of the towns to belong to the Lombard League, marked a realization by the imperial power that the freedom of political action of the cities had to be accepted to some degree, though it did not prevent continued imperial interference in their affairs. Similarly, Pope Adrian IV chose to favour the town of Orvieto in 1157 by accepting the oath of fealty proffered by its consuls and whilst thus accepting the existence of the commune, used the city to police its region of the papal states.

By the end of the twelfth century, however, the problems of communal government had become only too clear. The need for decisive leadership on a military campaign, or at a time of danger to the commune had often, in the past, led to the appointment of a consul for one occasion. But as the problems of factionalism increased in the twelfth century, recourse was made to the figure of the *podestà*, sometimes an imperial representative, but often an outsider called in for a limited time. In Viterbo, a similar figure, the rector, appeared in 1170; by 1171 one could be found in Orvieto and by 1174 in Perugia. Whilst these men were often appointed by the forces of the commune to preserve its independence, there were dangers inherent in their position. They could show favour towards particular factions within the city; and more serious was the possibility that the *podestà* would seize power for himself. The seeds of the despotic government common in many Italian cities in the later Middle Ages were already sown by 1200 and reflected the difficulty of reconciling the various group interests present within the governing élites of the cities.

The Fall of the God-guarded City

The role of the Italian cities in the diversion of the Fourth Crusade to an attack on Constantinople rather than the Holy Land has been much debated. Certainly, the lucrative trading they enjoyed in the Byzantine capital encouraged a growth in Italian settlement there in the twelfth century and led to increasing friction amongst the various Italian groups in the city. Sections of Byzantine opinion were irritated by what was perceived to be the acceptance of 'western' customs in court circles. Manuel Comnenus' not altogether successful attempt to introduce jousting is often cited, but far more obnoxious to the Byzantine aristocracy were the increasing numbers of imperial marriages with western princesses which deprived them of a traditional method of gaining influence at court. But the political thinking behind them was clear. The creation of a system of Mediterranean alliances—with Venice, the empire, and the kingdom of Jerusalem—was aimed at the encirclement, and, if possible, the eradication of Norman power in southern Italy. But after Manuel's unsuccessful invasion of Italy in 1150, the political spectrum began to change. Venice had been seriously alarmed by the prospect of Byzantine troops marching as far north along the Adriatic coast as Ancona and when, in 1164, Hungarian possession of Croatia and Dalmatia was accepted by the empire, the old alliance with Byzantium began to crumble.

It was the tacit acceptance of the loss of imperial power in the Balkans which was one of the most obvious signs of weakness in the empire. Old spheres of influence were lost in the rise of new, independent states. Grand gestures might be made, such as the triumphal entry of Manuel Comnenus into Antioch in 1159, at which the king of Jerusalem took a minor role and at which Byzantine lordship over the city was, for a short time, reasserted. But the dynastic struggles in the empire which followed Manuel's death in 1180 reveal the real power vacuum in the empire. The young Alexius II Comnenus ruled for only three years (1180–3) and came increasingly under the control of a distant cousin, Andronicus Comnenus, a battle-scarred veteran of wars in the east with an unsavoury personal reputation which was the talk of the eastern Mediterranean. The coup which brought the Angelus family to power in 1185 and in which a mob tore Andronicus to pieces in the Hippodrome was the culmination of a century of aristocratic resentment at the success of the Comneni in keeping power in the empire in the hands of their own family. But the Angeli were not themselves immune from faction. It was the flight of the young Alexius IV Angelus, to the court of Philip of Swabia, an uncle by marriage, after his father the Emperor Isaac had been dethroned and blinded in 1195, that involved the Germans in the political manœuvres which surrounded the launching of the Fourth Crusade in 1202. The debate about whether Pope Innocent III sent off the expedition in the full knowledge that it would attack Constantinople rather than the Muslim powers is still an active one though there is certainly evidence to suggest that he was unhappy about the way Venetian and German interests dictated the direction the enterprise took. It seems clear, however, that the Venetians looked upon the crusade, for which they had supplied the ships, as a means of increasing their own power in the east. In the event, after a hard-fought siege, Constantinople finally fell to Latin forces on 12 April 1204 amidst scenes of carnage and pillage which shocked even hardened contemporaries.

And so perished the empire of the God-protected Kostyantingrad and the Greek land in the quarrel of Tsars; and the Franks rule it.

The gloom-laden comment of the Novgorod Chronicle summed up the shocked reaction of the Byzantine world to the loss of the city. For many, it was the price to be paid for imperial mismanagement and corruption; for some, God's punishment for consorting with schismatic Latins and seemingly accepting their outrageous views on papal primacy. But although it would be misleading to describe the fall of Constantinople as 'inevitable', it was the culmination of a process already noted by the crusader historian Fulcher of Chartres in 1100. Describing the Frankish settlers in their new homes in the Holy Land he commented that 'we who were occidentals are now orientals'. The reverse was also true and it was the growing interdependence of the Mediterranean world—in trade, in religious observances, and in political attitudes and alliances—that culminated in the temporary eclipse of Byzantine power in 1204. The Mediterranean was now a Frankish Lake.

5

The Mediterranean in the
Age of the Renaissance

1200–1500

PETER DENLEY

The Papacy, its Enemies and its Allies

IN 1202 a learned hermit, Joachim of Fiore, died in his native
Calabria. His writings were to rank amongst the most influential of the later Middle Ages. Joachim envisaged a re-
classification of the 'ages of the world'. To the conventional
two ages of the Father and of the Son he added a third, that
of the Spirit, which would be the equivalent of Paradise on
earth. According to Joachim's calculations man was coming to
the end of the second age. The transition to the third age,
scheduled for the year 1260, would come about through a
monumental struggle between the forces of good and evil, and
would involve the appearance of the Antichrist. Interest in
apocalyptic soon grew with the diffusion of these texts, which
of course were capable of many interpretations, making them
just as influential when 1260 had come and gone.

An early stimulus to the fashion of apocalyptic was the
career of Frederick II (1194–1250), the last great emperor to
clash with the papacy in the struggle known as the Investiture Contest. Startling though the equation of emperor with
Antichrist might seem, there were aspects of Frederick which
appeared to justify it. Half-Sicilian, and brought up in Sicily,
Frederick was heir to much more than German aristocratic
traditions. He made the cosmopolitan culture of Sicily his own,

and his court was rich in scholars of Islam, astrologers, exotic animals, and, it was alleged, strange and cruel experimentation on humans. Although there is nothing to prove accusations of heresy or scepticism, it was Frederick who achieved one of the few technical successes of the crusading movement, not by force of arms but by parleying with the Sultan, and as an excommunicate; and his policy towards Muslim dissidents on the island of Sicily involved their wholesale transplantation to the plains of Lucera and thus the establishment, within 200 miles of Rome, of an infidel colony with full rights to their own customs and worship. Such behaviour was shocking (and perhaps intentionally so) especially in an emperor, whose traditional justification in the conflict with the pope was that he was the temporal champion of Christendom. But it was not without precedent; and in any case much of this image of Frederick is the result of careful, often papally inspired, propaganda. In the eyes of the popes, Frederick was much more than a maverick or evil ruler. Frederick Barbarossa (1152–90) had seen to it that the escalating conflict between pope and emperor was increasingly being conducted in Italy, near the centre of papal power. The marriage between his son the Emperor Henry VI and Constance, heiress to Sicily, threatened not merely further pressure but outright encirclement of Rome. The prospect was so terrifying for the popes that, from the moment of the birth in 1194 of their son Frederick, everything had to be done to prevent the realization of the joint succession. Frederick was thus of immense political significance long before he was responsible for his own actions.

Frederick's youth coincided with the career of one of the ablest and most dynamic men to occupy the papacy, Innocent III (1198–1216). Innocent was tireless in the furtherance of papal authority and influence throughout Christendom, intervening in the grand political rivalries of England and France, obtaining the obeisance of rulers from one end of Europe to the other. Yet the future of the empire was a dominant question which he failed to influence to his satisfaction. After the double election of 1197 Innocent allied first with the Welf candidate, Otto of Brunswick, though he was eventually reconciled with the Staufen Philip of Swabia who emerged as the preferred German candidate. When Philip was killed, Innocent revived his support of Otto in exchange for guarantees of papal independence, and when Otto showed total disregard of these guarantees and began a menacing foray into Italy the pope turned to the only remaining option, Frederick, supporting him through to victory over Otto in Germany. Frederick thus added Germany to Sicily despite the best efforts of the pope. All Innocent had gained was temporary control over Sicily, where Constance had made Frederick his ward, in a period of civil war, and perhaps more significantly promises, first made by Otto and confirmed by Frederick, of the independent territory in central Italy that was to become the papal state.

The new emperor returned to Italy, which became his base, in 1220, and within a few years the papacy's worst fears were realized. Frederick's initial efforts were directed towards bringing order to Sicily (the kingdom consisted of not just the island but also much of the boot of Italy from Naples downwards). Soon, however, he turned to the northern Italian towns, and summoned a diet, at Cremona, for 1226, with the purpose of restoring imperial rights in the area. The challenge galvanized the towns back into the concerted opposition which had developed, in the form of the Lombard League, in resistance to his grandfather Frederick Barbarossa. A majority of them defied Frederick, who backed down. By now he was forced to fulfil his promise to go on crusade, but when he returned he found himself up against not only the towns but also a new pope, Gregory IX, a nephew of Innocent III and an implacable opponent, who had used Frederick's period of absence to weaken his hold over Sicily as well as to consolidate opposition in the north of the peninsula. For the rest of his life Frederick was almost constantly locked in conflict in northern and central Italy. The death of Gregory IX saw Frederick menacing Rome, attempting to influence the choice of his successor. There followed two years without a pope, but the eventual choice, Innocent IV, was if possible even more uncompromising than Gregory. The new pope soon fled to Lyons, claiming that Frederick's pressure on Rome made it unsafe, and summoned a council at which the emperor was deposed. For his part Frederick continued to have limited military fortunes in the north, while the burdens of the war on Sicily, which was paying for it, led to discontent and sedition.

The death of Frederick in 1250 undid all his work almost at a stroke. Of his three surviving sons only the illegitimate Manfred was able to continue Staufen rule of Sicily and the anti-papal cause in the rest of Italy. He was killed at the battle of Benevento in 1266. With the capture and execution of Frederick's grandson, Conradin, after the battle of Tagliacozzo in 1268, Staufen power was at an end. So, largely, was imperial activity in Italy. Nearly half a century elapsed before another emperor, Henry VII, felt strong enough to launch an Italian campaign (1310–13), and although he did so with a massive army, and caused great commotion in Italy, he stood no chance of a lasting increase in authority there. His death on campaign brought it to an abrupt end. One further emperor, Lewis 'the Bavarian', came into bitter conflict with the papacy in the 1320s, but by then Italy was increasingly peripheral to the struggle, and the struggle itself increasingly peripheral to the direction of European politics.

In some respects Frederick's greatest mistake was the choice of northern Italy as theatre of conflict. Tight control over the resources of Sicily gave him the opportunity to be an almost continuous threat in northern Italy, something no emperor, with German resources only, had been able to keep up. Yet his decision to assert imperial rights in the area—while natural enough, indeed almost inevitable for one imbued with the imperial tradition—was anachronistic. It was no simple conflict between major powers; in the Lombard towns Frederick was up against fiercely volatile independent political communities, racked by internal factionalism, unable, even when willing, to offer any continuity of policy or allegiance. It is a measure of the unacceptability of what the emperor was trying to do that so many warring towns came together in alliance against him. What opportunities there were Frederick largely missed— by poor tactics and sense of timing, but especially by total insensitivity to the aspirations and the potential of the towns.

This is seen in his policies in Sicily and Germany as well, and is a sense in which Frederick, in sustaining the traditional imperial role, was deeply conservative. The popes in the end found that much of their work had been done for them. The papacy required of the towns not subordination but alliance, and was thus bound to be a more attractive proposition than this unorthodox but ultimately reactionary emperor.

Papal opposition to Frederick contained several strands. There was the ideological war, the continuation of the dispute over the respective roles of pope and emperor. There was the territorial issue; in northern Italy, where loss of influence would bring imperial control much closer to Rome, and in the central papal states where the pope was attempting to create a buffer zone. Southern Italy figured as well. The papacy's co-operation in the Norman conquest of Sicily had given it particular interests in the kingdom. That Constance had made the infant Frederick a papal ward was typical of the relationship. Frederick's restoration of order in Sicily was more than acceptable to the pope; his exclusion of clerics from government, and his use of Sicilian resources against the pope, emphatically were not. Gregory IX had made influence within Sicily a keystone of his campaign against Frederick. After 1250 control of Sicily became paramount, and the popes, as always dependent on the military resources of others for the execution of their policy, cast about for allies. Fatefully, they settled on the house of Anjou. The French king's brother Charles was invited to southern Italy to oppose Manfred; and with this began three generations of close Franco-papal alliance, hardened and consolidated by war and the strategy for first the south and then also the rest of Italy.

The 'question of Sicily' is of great significance. Indeed, it has been described as 'the beginning of modern political history'. For Sicily itself, the introduction of the Angevins meant not only a continuation of alien rule but also a protracted period of division and warfare. Frederick had restored order, quashed rebellious barons, and introduced control over office-holding which placed them in a more dependent position. He had provided the kingdom with a law code, a university to train its administrative personnel, and a court which acted also as a focus for many cultural activities. These achievements are not negligible, although historians nowadays tend to emphasize more the self-interested nature of all this and, above all, the iron fiscal hand which gripped the kingdom at the expense of economic development. With Charles of Anjou the negative aspects persisted without being accompanied by the benefits. The establishment of a new foreign ruler, with a new foreign ruling class and yet further burdens of taxation for essentially non-Sicilian purposes such as the recovery of Byzantium, aroused deep resentment which in 1282 exploded in the bloody rebellion of the Sicilian Vespers and an invitation to Peter III of Aragon to take the throne. For ninety years a succession of mostly weak monarchs, Angevin in Naples, Aragonese on the island of Sicily, attempted to establish control over their own territory and to gain the upper hand in the conflict between the two. The damage to public order and royal authority was matched only by that to the economy, and much of the impoverishment of land and people of what was once the 'granary of Europe' was determined in this period. If Sicily had once benefited from being a meeting-point of Mediterranean cultures, now, with a succession of rulers interested in using it as, at most, a resource for their policies elsewhere, it was paying the price of that internationalism.

The consequences for Italy as a whole were no less important. The close alliance between the papacy and the Angevins provoked a rise in the fortunes of the pro-papal or Guelph party, and of Guelphism, throughout Italy. The Angevins were to be the rulers of Naples but also champions of the papal cause throughout the peninsula, and for a time it looked as if this alliance had the best chance of bringing some measure of peace and stability to the area's tortured political scene. But it was not to be; and a more ominous consequence of the introduction of first the Angevins and then the Aragonese into the peninsula was that the interest and claims in Italy of one foreign power, the emperor, were replaced by those of two others, altogether more modern in outlook, with whom the future of Europe in a sense lay. At the end of the fifteenth century, when France and then Spain invaded the peninsula and put an end to Italian independence for over three centuries, they were both merely restating claims which had developed gradually out of that initial interest. In this sense the events of the late thirteenth century were both the antecedent and a sort of dress rehearsal for the transformation that was to befall Italy later.

For the papacy, too, the alliance was momentous and fateful. A powerful ally was indispensable if the popes were not to fall completely victim to the pressures of the Roman and central Italian aristocracy; yet papal involvement in the continuous military programme of the alliance involved considerable expense. The papacy became one of the first European powers to experience the sharp rise in the cost of warfare that characterized the thirteenth and fourteenth centuries. The administrative reforms, and the extension of papal control over the Church, initiated by Innocent III, were soon put severely to the test. One solution was the definition of such wars as crusades, which gave them moral standing and propaganda value, and also entailed the right to raise taxes from the clergy. The preaching of crusades against Christians who had opposed the papal will was not new, but the custom developed above all in the context of the papal–Angevin alliance. It laid the popes open to charges of perverting the crusading movement. A more serious consequence of the alliance was that it made the popes increasingly dependent on France, both in the sense of dependence on the French king, the power behind the Angevins in Italy, and in that it brought the French closer to the curia itself. Urban IV, who invited the Angevins into Italy, and who was himself French, created enough French cardinals to ensure that a new factional element was added to the natural instability of papal elections.

All these factors came together in a critical manner in the pontificate of Boniface VIII. Benedict Caetani succeeded the unworldly Celestine V, who had resigned the office, in 1294, the twelfth pope to be elected in forty years. An Angevin candidate, and an old but vigorous, not to say stubborn, politician, Boniface soon demonstrated an attentiveness to personal and dynastic interests which went beyond what the

Angevins had expected. A crusade against the rebellious cardinals of his rivals the Colonna family, and intrigues within the Guelph party culminating in a split, soon alienated or embarrassed his natural allies. But it was in his relations with the French king, Philip the Fair, that Boniface was to meet his match; and it was the matter of taxation which initially sparked off their dispute. The conflict between Philip and Boniface is discussed in the next chapter. Here it must suffice to note that its consequences for the papacy were dramatic, and led directly to the abandonment of Rome for Avignon.

Italy had proved too unstable a home for the papacy. The next seventy years saw attempts by the popes to achieve pacification, and control of the papal states, from a distance, away from the political quagmire that had so vitiated its record in the thirteenth century. Yet it would be wrong to assume that politicking was the only feature of that period. The papacy had placed itself at the helm of the most invigorating revival of the period, with the arrival of the friars. The ideals of St Francis— and in a less charismatic but equally profound way those of St Dominic—were harnessed, with the encouragement of Innocent III and his successors, to provide powerful 'storm troops' of reform and revitalization. An energetic programme to combat heresy was pursued, concentrating, in Italy at any rate, on the towns—another reason why papal control in Italy was seen to be essential. In this sense the distinction between the political and religious activities of the papacy is artificial. The political authority of the papacy was necessary if the authority of the pope in administrative and hence pastoral terms—control over bishops and clergy who administered religion to these urban populations—was to be preserved. Judged in that light, the thirteenth century was by no means as disastrous for the papacy as the dramatic resolution of the conflict of 1302–3 might suggest.

The Italian City-states: Ideals and Reality

That great revolutionary, St Francis, son of a well-to-do merchant of Assisi, underwent his formative experiences in an urban environment. His espousal of poverty was a reaction to the great contrasts between the thrusting mercantile affluence and the abject immigrant poverty thrown up by the rapid rise of the towns. The order he fathered was equally revolutionary in its determination to be active in the world while renouncing worldly possessions. In Italy the friars were above all urban orders, living off chiefly urban charity, acting as a focus for urban piety and addressing urban problems, preaching, teaching, and educating at all levels.

It was no accident that the vigour and success of the mendicants was so closely allied to that of the towns. In speaking of the 'miracle' of the triumph of the city-state the great French historian Fernand Braudel was justly admiring perhaps the most spectacular political, economic, and cultural phenomenon of the Middle Ages. The fact that the late medieval history of northern and central Italy is largely the history of its city-states meant that the region underwent a range of political experience and sophistication, of economic innovation and even hegemony, of technical and scientific expertise and cultural ferment on which the rest of Europe would continue to draw for centuries. And Braudel's emphasis on the *triumph* of these states is also telling. As Machiavelli observed at the beginning of the sixteenth century, political vitality stemmed from the tensions that were inherent in the political systems which the city-states threw up. One can go further. All these achievements stem, in one way or another, from the intense driving forces of conflict and competition within and between the towns, as well as with the rest of society.

The conflict that had led to the rise of these states had initially been that against the city's overlord, be it the bishop, a count, or other representative of the pope or the emperor. The struggle between these two often remote powers was wholly to the advantage of the towns, which were able to play the one off against the other. For a while the growth of the papal or Guelph (from 'Welf') and the imperial or Ghibelline (from 'Waiblingen', the name of a castle, and hence the war-cry, of the Staufen) parties provides some sort of structure to the complex web of internal factions and inter-communal alliances and counter-alliances that characterized urban politics. To a certain extent, even, their respective ideologies were reflected in the alignment of the towns; in many towns of central Italy, and especially in that mainstay of the Guelph alliance, Florence, anti-aristocratic sentiment fitted well with Guelph propaganda, while aristocratic interests, especially in northern Italy, were naturally served by the Ghibelline outlook with its justification of structured aristocratic power derived ultimately from imperial authority. But it would not do to push the argument too far in order to find patterns where none exist. The dominant factions in the towns more often regarded these labels as flags of convenience, to be dropped or bargained for at will.

The next main problem for the emergent communes—indeed the test of whether they could become viable city-states—was the extent to which they could gain control over a sufficient area of the surrounding countryside or *contado* to ensure defence against predatory neighbours, the capacity to feed themselves and to raise adequate taxes, and the capacity to restrain large landowners in or around their territory. Control over powerful rural magnates was often never totally achieved; but subjection to at least manageable proportions was a *sine qua non* of the 'territorial state', which was what these city-states were soon to become. The process of bringing rural nobles into urban affairs had begun in the twelfth century and continued into the thirteenth. Once involved in the cities they tended to organize themselves in large extended families and alliances of them, *consorterie*, and thus became chiefly responsible for what all commentators of the time identified as the chief evil and weakness of the towns, namely factional rivalry which reached very violent and debilitating dimensions. The symbols of the *consorterie*'s status were the defensive towers they built, a prime characteristic of the medieval urban landscape (several remain, particularly at San Gimignano and Bologna), and it was equally symbolic of the rise of communal authority when legislation was passed, and enforced, to raze these, and to limit the height of future buildings to less than that of the town hall. Other more practical measures were taken to stem the unfettered violence which was always associated with the aristocracy. The consuls of the twelfth century were succeeded, by the end of the twelfth and in the early thirteenth centuries, by the *podestà*, a non-citizen official appointed on a short-term contract with extensive executive powers. In opposition to the excesses of these magnates there also grew in many cities a rival pressure group known as the *popolo*. Often, especially in Tuscany, it was aligned with the Guelph faction, and its triumph, by the mid-thirteenth century, is usually seen as the moment at which the aristocratic tradition of violence was brought under some control. The culmination of this control can be seen in reforms such as the Florentine Ordinances of Justice (1293), whereby families named as magnates were barred in perpetuity from civic office.

The 'triumph' of the *popolo* is of great significance in those towns in which it occurred. In its wake developed much of the most sophisticated government and many of the finest monuments to the civic spirit of the time. But certain features must be stressed. It was class-based, a broad coalition particularly of guild members, be it of major guilds such as those of bankers, merchants, and professionals or of minor guilds of artisans and petty traders. And it was easy for the *popolo*, having subdued the magnates, to develop factionalism and violent behaviour of its own; in Florence, where the Guelph party triumphed along with the *popolo*, it soon divided into rival parties of Black and White Guelphs. The debarred magnatial families were soon replaced by others; by merchant families attaining nobility by wealth and by manufactured family trees, by *gente nuova*, new families, much scorned by the old ones. The influence of the aristocracy continued in other ways. In Siena, where many of those debarred were banking dynasties, their real power continued, indispensably, outside the formal political forum. Aristocratic culture—adaptations of troubadour traditions, ideals of nobility, and the whole complex of snobbish attitudes—continued to permeate urban life.

Just as the city-states saw perpetual social and political changes, so too with their institutions. The thirteenth century saw the addition of two new levels of government which effectively superseded them: the General Council, often three hundred people or more, drawn from those families eligible for office, and a higher, executive committee of Priors who held office for two months and who were responsible for proposing legislation to the General Council and for formulating policy. The process of election to the priorate, as to most other offices, was extremely complex, and was indicative of the aspirations of the system. It consisted of a mixture of sortition or lot and selection, sometimes in extremely protracted combinations, to ensure that factions could not easily obtain control of the whole body. Short terms, 'syndication', or checking on the conduct of an official at the end of his term and fining him for shortcomings, restrictions on tenure of offices in combination or when relatives were in office, were all geared to the same purpose, and all were ultimately ineffective. In time the obvious weaknesses of the system—the need to consult widely, the difficulty of making rapid or confidential decisions—led to a further modification, the adoption of *balìe* or special committees with special powers and fewer rules about membership. These soon became the norm of government in those towns which remained republics.

Communal constitutions were all idealistic, and their citizens were forever falling short of those ideals. Compulsive tampering with the constitution and compulsive legislation are often signs that the mechanism is not working. In most towns, though, the system soon collapsed; not so much under the weight of its own bureaucracy or ideals, for much of that survived in altered form, but because for all its electoral niceties and its checks and balances it was no match for the brutally simpler system of 'seigneurial' government. The 'strong man' as palliative or replacement for independent government by committee appears already in the first half of the thirteenth century, when Uberto Pelavicini and Ezzelino da Romano, both protégés of Frederick II, rapidly carved out states for themselves in northern Italy. Their exceptional cruelty marks them as extreme manifestations of the old quarrels of the aristocracy rather than new-style rulers; but they are a foretaste of what was to come.

And yet the idealism of the communal phase makes it worth

noting how much this type of government achieved. The sheer extent of government activity in a commune is impressive. Though untypical, Siena provides a good illustration since during a quite exceptionally stable regime, the Government of the Nine (1287–1355), it took the aspirations and achievements of government to an extreme degree. Siena first of all developed its system of taxation to sophisticated levels. The cost of warfare—it had been in the thick of the Guelph–Ghibelline struggles of Tuscany—ensured this. Taxation implied control of the *contado*, which remained the chief supplier of taxation. Lists of subject territories were kept from 1263, and they were obliged to supply candles on certain feast-days as symbols of their subjection. The *contado* was also regulated in great detail. New towns were set up, well into distant southern territories of the commune, and citizens were encouraged to settle there by tax exemptions. A network of fortifications was built, and irrigation and dam schemes followed. Similar activities took place in the city itself. Town planning was taken to its highest form. The height, distance, and type of building materials allowed were all specified and heavy fines or demolition were the penalties for contravention. The commune's own building programme was monumentally ambitious. A water supply for the town was created; today's visitor notes the famous fountains, but does not see the 25 kilometres of underground aqueducts the commune had tunnelled in order to bring the water from springs outside the town. Money was poured into the construction and embellishment of the town hall, churches, and Siena's great hospital, Santa Maria della Scala. These ambitions reached almost megalomaniac proportions with the designs for a cathedral which would dwarf those of all its rivals. When in the fourteenth century money ran out, Siena was left with only the transept, but a transept the size of most other cathedrals' naves.

The communal passion for legislation may have reached extremes in Siena but it was general enough. In most communes all imaginable aspects of life were regulated; hours of curfew, clothing and expenditure on entertainments ('sumptuary laws'), succession and bequests, wardship, trade, manners, rubbish disposal, hostelries, even brothels. To read the administrative documents of such towns—and the documentation too is of unparalleled wealth—is to discover the sophistication of the whole community. Yet such sophistication is not based simply on introspection or self-awareness. At its root is the wealth that enabled urban society to develop these multifarious requirements. Economic precociousness was the foundation for what was achieved; the heyday of communal government coincides with a period in which Italians were at the forefront of international trade. Florentine, Genoese, and Venetian merchants featured regularly at the late thirteenth-century fairs of Champagne, and as these began to be supplanted by other routes and other towns Genoa and Venice established regular maritime Atlantic convoys to Bruges and other ports of northern Europe. Italy pioneered the rise of the more sedentary merchant, in contact with fixed branches in the great northern European cities, and it also pioneered the new commercial techniques—double-entry bookkeeping, credit systems, marine insurance, bills of exchange—which enabled such networks to function. Italians—Florentines, Genoese, Sienese, Lucchese— were also unrivalled suppliers of credit; both the English and the French monarchs borrowed from Italian bankers (and occasionally defaulted, with disastrous consequences).

Urban industry, surprisingly, occupied a secondary position. Most Italian towns were of course local markets for surrounding areas, and many had specialized industries, the most important, although really rather exceptional, being the Florentine cloth industry. Cloth was indeed exported; but apart from that, much of the international trade being handled was through trade in which merchants above all took advantage of Italy's central position in the Mediterranean. In sequence to the Pisan and Genoese 'empires', established in the earlier period in the western and central Mediterranean, came Venetian and Genoese expansion in the eastern Mediterranean, and with that fresh commercial contacts with the Muslim world and, beyond that, the Mongol Empire. Taking advantage of the innovation of navigation by dead reckoning, which made winter sailing practicable, the Venetians had by the end of the thirteenth century established a network of regular, state-controlled convoys of galleys: to the Black Sea (where both Venice and Genoa established colonies), to Syria, Egypt, the North African coast from Tangier to the Straits of Gibraltar, Marseilles, Aigues-Mortes, Barcelona. They had gained total control of the Adriatic and effective control of much more. Salt and grain were transported in the eastern Mediterranean under Venetian monopoly. Venice was closely rivalled by Genoa, but between them the Italians had a virtual monopoly of traffic with the east, and it was quite natural that exploration further afield should follow. Voyages such as those of the Polos were surprisingly common. It was also quite natural that, with Italy at the hub of international trade, it should also be in the vanguard of technological development. The production of glass in the west reached its height in Venice—for tableware, spectacles, and windows; paper was first manufactured regularly in the west at Fabriano; the mechanical clock was an Italian invention; even 'Arabic' numerals were introduced to Europe through an Italian mathematician.

Throughout this development Italy remained profoundly turbulent. The cities were notorious for their instability while continuing to astonish the world, and successive historians, with their brilliance and inventiveness. The word precocious is apt. They were not 'bourgeois' or revolutionary, though in some of their social conflicts and 'pre-capitalistic' innovations they signpost the future. Civic pride achieved much, yet in many ways remained deeply conservative. Of the many writers who exalt civic ideals and virtues while describing the less exalted behaviour of actual flesh-and-blood citizens, perhaps the one who best sums up this mass of contradictions is the poet Dante Alighieri. Dante's writings are an irrepressible commentary on both the ideals and the shortcomings of the age. A Florentine citizen active in the political turmoil of the turn of the thirteenth and fourteenth centuries before being banished from his native town, Dante had been reared in the Florentine civic tradition, and in the Tuscan language and literary tradition which he did so much to develop. His interests ranged over many theoretical disciplines—philosophy, theology, cosmology—for the study of which Florence was perhaps something of an outpost, as well as over classical studies and love-poetry where Florence partook of the lively activity evident throughout Tuscany. In Dante's greatest work, the *Comedy*, an extraordinary fusion of the religious, the philosophical, the poetic, and the political—product of both the political theorist and the embittered political exile—takes place in the construction of a journey through Hell, Purgatory, and Paradise. With what is ultimately the height of conceit Dante, as well as mapping out the theology of the world to come, places his heroes and his villains in appropriate places and passes judgement on the whole political scene of his time. Wholly eclectic, the *Comedy* represents what is most dynamic and constructive in Italian urban life—its aspirations, its creativity, and its vehemence—and at the same time is profoundly 'medieval' in its outlook. It is above all a religious construct in which are made moral judgements, and in one respect at least—his vision and advocacy of universal empire as the solution to these problems—it was hopelessly out of date. Ultimately, though, if his remedy was impracticable the diagnosis was to prove correct; the precocious Italian city-states, as long as they remained in conflict, were going to be overtaken and indeed overrun by those who were able to build something stronger.

Rome, Byzantium, and the Muslim World

The commercial hegemony attained by Venice could not have been established without the momentous events of 1204. The taking of Constantinople by the forces of the Fourth Crusade, discussed in Chapter 4, was more than an outrage and a great psychological blow. For the first time it gave the crusaders extensive territory in south-eastern Europe and Asia Minor. By the terms of the division of the new 'Latin Empire of Constantinople' Venice obtained three-eighths of this territory, the rest being divided between the new emperor, Baldwin of Flanders, and the 'Frankish' barons. At the same time the

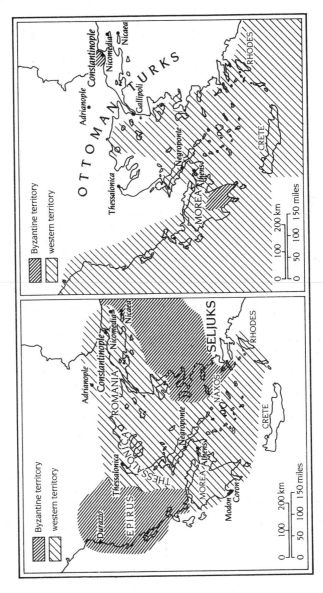

THE BALKANS (*a*) IN 1216 (*b*) IN 1400

schism between the eastern and western churches was notionally healed, the Church of Rome installing itself in Constantinople.

Yet the empire was short-lived. The Byzantines, ousted from Constantinople, regrouped in two main areas, Epirus, on the west coast of Greece, and Nicaea in Asia Minor (a third 'empire', that of Trebizond, had been established before the sack of Constantinople and continued its marginal existence until the late fifteenth century). It soon became clear that the western emperors were out of their depth. Few reinforcements came from the west, and in the long term the Byzantine forces were bound to have the advantage once they could solidify their positions. But equally, there was among the Latins no real conception of how to rule territory with problems such as those of Byzantium. Little attempt was made to forge alliances or to understand the mentality of the conquered, either to exploit their weaknesses or to respect their strengths. Above all the Latins signally failed to appreciate the special role religion played in Byzantine politics. The growing apart of eastern and western territories, accentuated in the eleventh century by religious differences, had always rested on this. Few measures alienated the Latins' eastern subjects more effectively than the imposition of western ecclesiastics, western rites, and the crass reorganization of the Byzantine diocesan structure along 'rational' lines. Religious union had been achieved in name, but by force; it could never work.

In fact little pressure sufficed to dislodge the Latins from a substantial part of their newly acquired territory. Only a year after the conquest an incursion by the Bulgarians—with whom the emperor had refused a proffered alliance—led to a defeat of the western forces in Thrace and the hurried abandonment of territory in Asia Minor; Thessalonica fell to the rulers of Epirus in 1224. That the Latin Empire lasted for over half a century was due to the disunity of the Byzantines, not to an acceptance of the westerners. By the 1240s, though, the Nicaeans, with the superior diplomatic skills and administrative vision of the vigorous John III Vatatzes, came to the fore, and after further delays due to the impact of Mongol incursions pressure on the Latin Empire intensified. The decisive event was the Nicaeans'

THE PALAEOLOGUE RULERS OF BYZANTIUM, 1261–1453

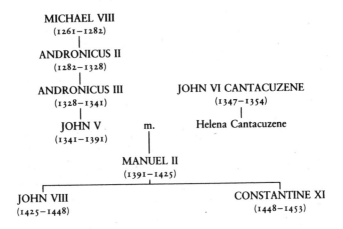

MICHAEL VIII
(1261–1282)

ANDRONICUS II
(1282–1328)

ANDRONICUS III
(1328–1341)

JOHN VI CANTACUZENE
(1347–1354)

JOHN V   m.   Helena Cantacuzene
(1341–1391)

MANUEL II
(1391–1425)

JOHN VIII   CONSTANTINE XI
(1425–1448)   (1448–1453)

defeat in 1259 of the allied forces of Manfred of Staufen, the rulers of Epirus, and the Frankish princes of Achaia at Pelagonia. The retaking of Constantinople of 1261 was then a foregone conclusion.

Return to Constantinople did not mean that the Byzantines had not suffered profoundly from the events of 1204–61. For one thing, however enterprising and efficient the rulers of Nicaea might have been, the pre-conquest territorial unity was never regained. For the next two hundred years western presence—in the Peloponnese, in the islands—was assured. The cause of the Latin Empire was championed by the Angevins who periodically intervened in eastern Mediterranean affairs in the late thirteenth century, and the Emperor Michael VIII Palaeologue's chief concern was the danger of an Angevin expedition. Indeed, a crusade to regain Constantinople in 1282 was only averted by the outbreak of the Sicilian Vespers (in which the Byzantine emperor was suspected of having a hand). But Byzantine resentment of the west, which by now had turned to hatred, caused paradoxically more rather than fewer problems for the empire. The best hope of averting western expeditions—and, later, the best hope of gaining western support against the Turks—was a healing of the schism. Yet each emperor who attempted to reach a compromise with the popes caused deep divisions and usually violent backlash from the religious majority.

In financial and economic matters, too, the emperors found themselves strangely at the mercy of the powers they had ousted. The might of Venice and Genoa in the east now meant that both traded with the empire on terms that can only be called exploitative. Meanwhile, landowners' support had increasingly been bought with privileges and tax exemptions, and this further reduced revenue. Impoverished, with a smaller and smaller territory to call their own and to tax, the emperors cut expenditure on defence and looked increasingly to Venice and Genoa for help with their military enterprises, thus getting dragged into the traditional rivalry between the two which now erupted in a series of wars, most of which were fought in Byzantine waters. Other mercenaries, from west and east, Christian and infidel, all compromised the direction of the empire and increased the need for money. A steady debasement of the coinage followed, and soon Byzantines were preferring the Venetian ducat as a more reliable medium of exchange.

The imperial title, too, had been diminished by exile from Constantinople. Although intrigue, dissent, and nights-of-the-long-knives were endemic to Byzantine rule, these tendencies grew after a period in which the title of emperor-in-exile had been contested. Michael VIII (1261–82), whose accession had been marred by the fact that he. had blinded his co-emperor, the young John Lascaris, was deeply unpopular, especially with the ecclesiastics; his death saw a full-scale return to orthodoxy under Andronicus II. His long reign ended in open civil war over the succession (1321–8), at the end of which he was persuaded to abdicate. A further civil war broke out in the next generation (1341–7) at the death of Andronicus III, when again a factional rift between potential successors was accompanied by a religious controversy. The empire could ill afford these episodes of blood-letting in the face of mounting threats from both east and west. With the coronation as emperor of John VI Cantacuzene, long an adviser to the

Palaeologue emperors but gradually seduced into leading a faction opposing the young Emperor John V, it seemed to many that the imperial office had changed beyond recognition; Cantacuzene had spent the years of the civil war in alliance with both Stefan Dušan, king of the emergent Serbia and another threat to Byzantium, and the Ottoman Turks with whom he even entered into a marriage alliance. Although history has preferred to judge this emperor as an enlightened and high-principled figure, his reign continued to be characterized by struggles between these powers, and Cantacuzene too was eventually forced by public opinion to abdicate, in 1354, the year in which the Ottomans first gained a foothold on European soil by capturing Gallipoli.

From the west's point of view it is traditional to say that there was little to show for the 1204 enterprise. Yet one neglected feature is the ensuing colonization of a new part of the eastern Mediterranean by the west. The carve-up of territory in 1204 involved 'Franks', and Italians, in the Balkans and the eastern Mediterranean islands for more than two centuries. Many of these proved to be small-time rulers of patchwork territory, subject to infinite changes of borders, dynasty, and alliance, and of little significance for the historian. A few of them, though, established sane and tolerably stable rule. One such was the Frankish occupation of the Peloponnese, where despite the Byzantine reoccupation of part of the peninsula some semblance of peace and even some manifestations of Frankish chivalric culture were achieved. Even this was rudely interrupted in the early fourteenth century by the arrival of the Catalan Company, a violent band of mercenaries which found itself at a loose end in southern Italy after the Peace of Caltabellotta of 1302. The Catalans wrought untold destruction on the Greek mainland before seizing Athens and establishing control there. In about 1380 they were ousted by another company, of Navarrese, and they in turn were replaced by a Florentine, Neri Acciaiuoli. The point is that the 1204 'wave' had successors and replacements; individual barons who were minded to carve out for themselves mini-states or at least to get themselves titles, and not too concerned about the evidence that it was rare for the achievements of these adventurers to measure up remotely to their initial aspirations.

Such aspirations to colonialism were of course in many ways a substitute for, or a continuation of, the direction of such activities towards the Holy Land. It is often and correctly said that the exploitation of Byzantium in this way was a major reason for the decline of the crusading movement. Small and pleasant landholding or lordship in the Peloponnese or the Aegean islands could undoubtedly seem more comfortable than enterprises in Outremer. But the decline of crusading in the Holy Land is of course not that simple. For one thing, crusading energies were certainly not diminished after the first three crusades. If anything the movement exhausted itself by an excess and, perhaps, a diffusion of crusading as well as the gradual realization that success was so rare. The Fourth Crusade was merely the first in a long line of expeditions never to reach, and often never even aimed at, the Holy Land. It was soon followed by the Albigensian Crusade, in 1208, fought against the Cathars of southern France, and later by several 'political' crusades of the sort described above. The principle that crusades could be mounted against heretics, or enemies of the Church, as well as against the infidel, was rapidly exercised. Those which were against the infidel tended to be more frequent and less well planned. The Fifth Crusade, led by King Andrew of Hungary, left in 1217 for Acre, and only there decided to attempt to capture Damietta in Egypt. It was successful in this after a long siege, only to lose it again, outmanœuvred in an attempt to march on Cairo. Victims of their own excessive ambition, the crusaders had not heeded the advice of the colonists of Outremer and had rejected a Muslim offer of an exchange of Damietta for Jerusalem. Further crusades, of Frederick II in 1228–9, and of 1239–41, achieved temporary and unorthodox gains more by accident than by design, and the only major crusading figure of the thirteenth century was the French King Louis IX. The loss of Jerusalem in 1244 spurred him to lead an impressive expedition of a more conventional kind—well-organized, well-financed—to Egypt where, however, it ran aground in precisely the same way as had the Fifth Crusade, and through precisely the same tactical mistakes. The king was taken prisoner and released only for a large ransom. Louis's final crusade, in 1270, against Tunis, is really a postscript to the sequence, an attempt to purge his feelings of guilt at the failure of 1248. In the event the French king died at the walls of Tunis and the expedition was aborted.

As crusading to the Holy Land ran out of steam Muslim forces were closing in on the Christian territories there. For the first half of the thirteenth century the crusaders had been fortunate in the comparative disarray of the Muslim world. The Ayyubid dynasty in Cairo, established by Saladin, was experienced in dealing with crusaders, and despite the perennial conflicts was also quite capable of reaching an understanding out of expedience, as had repeatedly been shown. Based in Egypt, it was never a strong centralized state, rather more of a federation. This made for disunity which the Christians were able to use to advantage. The Abbasid caliphate, based at Baghdad, was weaker, while the presence of the volatile extremist sect of the Assassins, bordering the crusader states, was as much a running sore to the Muslims as it was to the Christians. In addition the Muslim world felt the full impact of Mongol invasions. In the 1220s these had destroyed the state of Khwarazm, taking Bukhara and Samarkand; the Near-Eastern states began to look exposed. In 1241 the Mongols swept right into south-eastern Europe, devastating Hungary and reaching the Dalmatian coast, the legend of their ferocity preceding them; then two years later they attacked Asia Minor. In both phases they retreated as suddenly as they had come, and the Christian west, already imbued with the myth of Prester John as eastern prince willing to help the west against the Muslims, began to think hopefully in terms of conversion, or at least alliance with the Mongols to keep Muslim power in check. Good relations were cultivated, but on the matter of using them against the Muslims the idea had only brief value. In 1250, just after Louis IX's crusade had been outmanœuvred in the Nile Delta, an Egyptian army mutinied, the sultan was assassinated, and the Ayyubid dynasty was replaced by the Mamluks. Five years later the Mongols were back, taking Baghdad in 1258 and bringing down the Abbasids, finally taking Damascus in March 1260 with Christian help. In September of that year, though, they were decisively defeated at the battle of Ain Jalut, in Palestine itself, by the Mamluks. The event established their control of Syria and their status in the Muslim world at a stroke.

From now, the Christian states were doomed. The new sultan, the fanatical general Baybars, turned on the towns and fortresses of the crusader states and picked them off one by one. In 1265 he took Caesarea, Haifa, and Arsuf; in 1266 Safad (and with it Galilee); in 1268 Jaffa and Beirut, and in the north, brutally sacked, the town of Antioch, and with it its principality; in 1271 the Hospitaller castles of Krak des Chevaliers and Akkar. He then offered a ten-year truce, which was accepted, and renewed in 1281 by his successor Kalavun; but these were tactical truces only, and when Kalavun felt strong enough he broke it, capturing Tripoli in 1289. Two years later, with the fall of Acre and the evacuation of the remaining strongholds and towns, Christian occupation of Outremer was at an end.

The possessions of Outremer had simply fallen to superior forces. Certainly it had not helped that Frederick II had returned to Italy as soon as he had taken the crown of Jerusalem; or that the military orders, and the omnipresent Venetians and Genoese, were constantly at loggerheads with each other and often in open warfare. Nor can it really be said that the crusaders had built socially cohesive states; they remained distinct from the indigenous population throughout. But the crusader states were not particularly rotten. Without reinforcements from the west no amount of unity would have availed, and that further support, after 1270, was noticeably absent. Potential crusaders were either locked in other conflicts or rightly sceptical of their chances of success. In a sense, since it was perceived that it was moribund, Outremer was allowed to die.

The Muslim revival had been the death-knell for Outremer. But in one area Christians did make decisive and lasting inroads into Muslim territory in the thirteenth century, namely in Spain. A new wave of reconquest, under vigorous monarchs, went most of the way to completing the process begun in the thirteenth century. In 1212 a vast Christian army destroyed the Almohad forces at the battle of Las Navas de Tolosa, a crucial entry point to the Guadalquivir valley. King Ferdinand III of Castile (1217–52) resumed the campaign in the 1230s after the definitive reunification of the crowns of Castile and León (1230), and in 1236 inflicted a great psychological blow by taking Cordoba, the former capital of the caliphate. In 1243 Murcia accepted his overlordship, in 1246 Jaen, and finally in 1248 Seville capitulated under siege. The no less dynamic James I—'the Conqueror'—of Aragon (1213–76) had in 1229 taken Majorca (and subsequently obtained Minorca and Ibiza) in the first step towards the creation of an Aragonese empire in the Mediterranean, and in 1238 he took the town, and by 1245 had the whole region, of Valencia. Parallel to all this the Portuguese were pushing southwards, subjugating the last towns along the south coast in 1249. The reconquest of Iberia was all but complete. Only the southernmost mountainous region of Granada remained under Muslim rule.

The Spanish reconquest is also differentiated from the enterprises in the eastern Mediterranean by the extent and solidity of administrative control achieved, though here Castile and Aragon differed considerably in the methods they adopted. In the territories acquired by Castile, Muslims tended to be stripped of their land and forcibly removed from cities as a security measure; often they fled to Granada. The conquerors followed the usual pattern of rewarding the combatants with land; but the expertise that was needed to continue the economic sophistication, urban and rural, of the Muslims was lacking. Much land was transferred from agrarian to pasture farming, and many landowners, after a few years of desultory farming, returned to the north, selling their property to the military order which soon came to predominate. Southern Castile took on the traditional complexion of a frontier state; a sparsely populated ranching economy with a subject-caste for labour, powerful barons holding large *latifundia*, and little economic progress. It was very much the system that would later be adopted by the same Castile in the New World. The

Aragonese treated their conquests rather differently. In Valencia the Muslim population remained in overwhelming majority; eviction was not a realistic option. Muslims were allowed to continue to live, both in the towns and in the country, under Christian administration, and the economic advantages of their presence were exploited. Cohabitation in close proximity had already been the pattern before the reconquest, so less adjustment was necessary. Above all coexistence was possible because the eastern Spanish seaboard was a natural trading base, giving the races a common interest. Catalan Barcelona, perhaps the only Spanish town in the period to become a major commercial centre to rival the chief Italian towns, became in time also a focus for the whole Aragonese economy.

To varying degrees, and with varying success, both Aragon and Castile saw the coexistence of races. Besides the Muslims, both kingdoms depended heavily on small but important Jewish communities. These tended to be urban-based, and many Jews were involved in the professions, particularly medicine, money-lending (usury was forbidden to Christians), and administration (and especially tax-farming). These last activities often made them natural objects of resentment, although they were in fact fulfilling functions Christians were either forbidden or reluctant to perform. None the less Jews were an important stimulus to the community, and in a sense could play the role of intermediary between Christian and Muslim cultures. Relations between the three communities could be strained, and the years following the reconquest saw many revolts. But on the whole a better job was made of *convivencia* than elsewhere, and for a couple of centuries Spain's role as interface between the three cultures was prolonged. In this Alfonso X—'The Wise'—of Castile, idealistic and even impractical though he may have been, symbolized the challenge of the *Reconquista* when he styled himself 'King of the Three Religions'.

Crises and Transitions

From roughly the end of the thirteenth to roughly the middle of the fifteenth century much of Europe saw a proliferation of difficulties and set-backs which, taken together and feeding off each other as they did, give the appearance of a society in crisis. The fourteenth has rightly been called 'the calamitous century', and the Mediterranean saw its share of the problems as much as northern Europe. It remains a puzzle for historians, a phenomenon that all can observe but for which no single explanation or system of explanations will suffice. In any case, could it be an optical illusion? Do these apparent crises not conceal positive developments, as crises often do? All that the historian can do with any confidence is to describe the problems and, by examining them one by one, observe the changes brought about with their resolution.

If one were looking for a symbol of the phenomenon one would inevitably choose the Black Death. In a sense the culprit for the introduction to Europe of the most devastating disease since late Roman times was the west's very success in developing trading relations with the east, and especially with the Mongols. Bubonic plague has its origins in the Far East, and is transmitted by fleas who in turn live on rats, and it was these, making their way on the ships of Italian merchants, which first brought the plague to Europe. By the autumn of 1347 it had reached Byzantium, Rhodes, Cyprus, and Messina in Sicily, by winter Venice, Genoa, Marseilles, by the spring of 1348 Tuscany and central Italy. The plague raged through the Mediterranean world in 1348–9, at the same time spreading northwards. Victims of the bubonic strain developed swellings at the point of the flea bite and in nearby lymph nodes; purplish blotches—'buboes'—followed and from there the disease attacked the nervous system, resulting in death in over half of all cases. The pneumonic strain, in which the disease also attacked the respiratory system, was almost invariably fatal, and also much more contagious—it could be passed by coughing—and resistant to climatic change. Most deadly of all was the rare septicaemic form, in which the bacilli attacked the bloodstream directly and death followed before any visible symptoms had time to form.

The epidemic was terrifying in its novelty, its symptoms, the speed with which it swept Europe, and the number of victims it claimed. The feeling of helplessness and despair it caused is well instanced by the Sienese chronicler Agnolo di Tura del Grasso:

The plague began in Siena in May, a horrible and cruel event. I do not know where to begin describing its relentless cruelty; almost everyone who witnessed it seemed stupefied by grief. It is not possible for the human tongue to recount such a horrible thing, and those who did not see such horrors can well be called blessed. They died almost immediately; they would swell up under the armpits and in the groin and drop dead while talking. Fathers abandoned their children, wives left their husbands, brothers forsook each other; all fled from each other because it seemed that the disease could be passed on by breath and sight. And so they died, and one could not find people to carry out burials for money or friendship. People brought members of their own household to the ditches as best they could, without priest or holy office or ringing of bells, and in many parts of Siena large deep ditches were dug for the great number of dead; hundreds died day and night, and all were thrown into these pits and covered with layers of earth, so much that the pits were filled, and more were dug.

And I, Agnolo di Tura, known as the Fat, buried five of my children with my own hands. And there were those who had been so poorly covered with earth that dogs dragged them from there and through the city and fed on corpses. Nobody wept for the dead, since each was awaiting death; and so many died that everyone thought that the end of the world had come.

Chroniclers are much less helpful in telling us how many died. As always with large figures, they are prone to exaggeration, and the problem is difficult for historians to assess; but one contemporary estimate which has found favour is that 30 per cent of the population at least was wiped out in Europe, and recent researh suggests a similar proportion in the Near East. The mortality rate was not even, though; the figure is probably higher in urbanized Italy, certainly in the Tuscan towns where much research has been done, although Milan escaped lightly, possibly because of rapid preventative measures; while in Spain there is a contrast between Aragon and Castile, the latter's denser population suffering greater losses.

That plague must have had deep psychological effects is obvious; but historians have not found it easy to describe exactly what those effects were. An immediate reaction, observed in many places, was the suspension of conventional values, a decline in moral restraint, hedonistic abandonment; and to this some have wished to connect, in the longer term, the questioning of authority and of religious truths, sentiments of equality and satisfaction at those brought low, the rebellions that were widespread a few decades later, even a new spirit of enquiry and the development of new medical and intellectual interests. At the same time others have pointed to the development of a new piety, of repentance movements, and of a more sombre style of painting (as has been noted in Tuscany). All these are difficult to attribute to the Black Death, or at least to the initial epidemic of 1347–50. The true impact was more gradual and more subtle. The plague returned with great frequency over the next 130 years. As sucessive generations experienced it and understood it to be an unpredictable but ever-present threat, the feeling of precariousness became more rooted and attitudes changed.

There is equal difficulty in assessing the economic impact of the plague, and historians have retreated substantially from the view which saw the whole of the fourteenth-century depression as its consequence. Among the consequences that are most obviously attributable to plague are those arising from the sudden depopulation of certain areas. In much of Spain and Portugal, southern and central Italy, as in much of the rest of Europe, there was a crisis on the land; labour was scarce, wages rose, the landlords were temporarily disadvantaged, governments tried to prevent these trends by legislation against peasant mobility. In many places the existing tendency to replace agrarian with the less labour-intensive pasture farming was speeded up, and many landlords were quick to recover their position by switching to the short-term renting out of land and other devices to protect themselves against changing conditions. Equally wide-spread was the phenomenon of urban immigration; peasants abandoned the land (in some cases whole villages were deserted) in the fond hope of finding employment, or at least chancing their luck, in the towns. But much of this, and even the decline in population, had begun before the Black Death, and continued long after, and plague is only one of the many factors in the economic developments of the fourteenth century. Likewise the symptoms of economic 'crisis' are not always what they seem to be. True, many ports on the Mediterranean showed a dramatic drop in through trade. But as some towns, industries, and trade routes declined, others sprang up. The Mediterranean saw in the fourteenth century not uniform crisis but rather the beginnings of shifts in emphasis, of which more were to follow in the fifteenth.

One of these shifts was started by another 'plague from the east'. On its eastern flank thirteenth-century Byzantium had had to contend with a number of Turkish tribes. The early fourteenth century saw the rise to prominence of one of these, the Osmanlis or Ottomans, named after their first leader, Osman. The rise of the Ottomans was very rapid. When in 1302 Osman defeated the Byzantines in Bithynia he seemed just one of several tribal leaders. In 1326 his son Orchan captured Bursa, just across the sea of Marmora from Constantinople itself, and in 1329 he defeated the Byzantine forces twice near Nicomedia. In 1331 Nicaea fell, and in 1337 Nicomedia. In a short time the Byzantine Empire had lost all its possessions in Asia Minor, and by the terms of a treaty made with Orchan in 1333 even had to pay him an annual tribute. But that was only a first taste of Ottoman might. By the time they had captured Gallipoli (1354) they were already involved in military enterprises in Europe, often in alliance with Byzantium. Next, all this was rapidly consolidated by Orchan's successor Murad I. Adrianople was taken, and the Turkish court set up there. There was victory over the Serbs at the River Marica in 1371, and in 1387 the second largest Byzantine city, Thessalonica, fell. Murad was killed in battle at Kossovo in 1389, but the Serbs themselves were defeated, and with that the empire was completely encircled. In 1394 Bajezid I turned to Constantinople itself.

From the capture of Gallipoli onwards the prevention of engulfment by the Ottomans had been the Byzantine emperor's dominant concern. The Emperor John V became the first of a series of emperors to humiliate themselves by making journeys to the west to beg for help. He was rewarded with only sporadic reaction. Only the threat to Constantinople itself finally galvanized the west, which sent a huge and splendid expedition with John, son of the duke of Burgundy, at its head. When this ended in fiasco at Nicopolis (1396) the west appeared to lose heart totally. No further forces against the Turks were sent until a similar venture met its end at Varna in 1444. That Constantinople held out until the mid-fifteenth century was due more to the unexpected respite caused by the sudden advance into Asia Minor of the Mongol Timur, who defeated and captured Bajezid in 1402. Already in the late fourteenth century it was left largely to the Serbs to defend Europe and Christendom against the Ottomans. The Byzantines, who had by now become Turkish vassals, were so impotent that they were but waiting for the end. What vigour there was among the Greeks centred on the regained territory of the Peloponnese, based on Mistra, where the late Byzantine cultural revival, a splendid flowering in the face of political adversity, found its main focus.

The Ottomans by contrast were assuming the characteristics of an organized state. The Balkan acquisitions were colonized, the subjected people assimilated, taxed, and drawn on for troops. Some of that territory had been yielded readily. As well as the stick of their terrifying military prowess, the carrot of superior organization and stability and of religious tolerance made them attractive to many by comparison with the divided and ineffective rule of the Byzantines. The real impact of the Ottoman advance came in the next century as the threat spread to include western possessions in the east and even the Italian mainland. But the basis for the Muslim hold on Europe was laid in the fourteenth century, and the Mediterranean was already beginning to feel the consequences.

The appearance of crisis is also present in the development of the Spanish kingdoms in the period. The rapid absorption of so much territory in the reconquest of the early thirteenth century brought its particular problems. At the same time the Spanish kingdoms became increasingly involved in the international political scene, in the Mediterranean and on the northern

THE RULERS OF ARAGON AND CASTILE

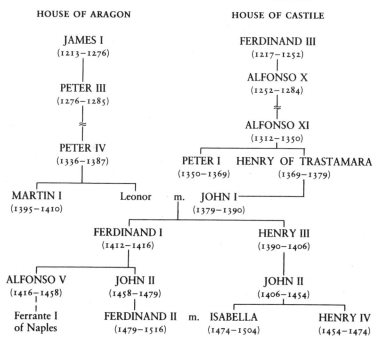

HOUSE OF ARAGON

HOUSE OF CASTILE

JAMES I
(1213–1276)

FERDINAND III
(1217–1252)

ALFONSO X
(1252–1284)

PETER III
(1276–1285)

ALFONSO XI
(1312–1350)

PETER IV
(1336–1387)

PETER I   HENRY OF TRASTAMARA
(1350–1369)   (1369–1379)

MARTIN I   Leonor   m.   JOHN I
(1395–1410)   (1379–1390)

FERDINAND I
(1412–1416)

HENRY III
(1390–1406)

ALFONSO V   JOHN II
(1416–1458)   (1458–1479)

JOHN II
(1406–1454)

Ferrante I   FERDINAND II   m.   ISABELLA   HENRY IV
of Naples   (1479–1516)   (1474–1504)   (1454–1474)

border with France, and they were from then on more prone to being dragged into European issues such as the Hundred Years War. This international dimension is especially characteristic of Aragon, which by the end of the thirteenth century had an extensive empire in the western Mediterranean including Sicily and Sardinia, and interests in southern France. Throughout the late Middle Ages the international policy of the kings of Aragon was often in conflict with internal needs, and excessive emphasis on foreign policy was often followed by a reaction or by unrest at home. In addition many of the Spanish kings of the period were weak, inclined to place personal ambitions and infatuations before the interest of the country, and by the proliferation of illegitimate offspring apt to leave the succession wide open to dynastic squabbles. The most ruinous of these was the long civil war which followed the death of Alfonso XI of Castile in 1349 (he was the only European ruler to die of plague), in which the illegitimate Henry of Trastamara eventually gained the throne over Alfonso's legitimate son Peter the Cruel (in 1369). Civil wars were briefer but more frequent in Aragon, where the nobility took a leading part in the crises of succession. The advanced development of representative institutions, the *cortes*, in Aragon gave them and the other estates an important political role, although it should not be assumed always to work to the disadvantage of the king; many historians have assessed positively this development of a close relationship between crown and subjects in what is known as 'pactism'.

The kingdoms were also fighting amongst each other, for the ruling dynasties were frequently intermarried, and many aspired to annex a neighbouring kingdom or even to unite the whole peninsula. From the mid-fourteenth century a number of conflicts stemmed from the aspirations of the house of Trastamara. They acceded to Castile in 1369; in 1383 attempts at Trastamaran succession to Portugal led to a national revolt there and the establishment of the house of Avis; in 1412 the Trastamarans won the succession to Aragon. All this was eventually vindicated, in that it paved the way for the union of the Castilian and Aragonese crowns later in the fifteenth century, but in the mean time it was a repeated source of disorder.

Political conflicts were closely tied up with economic and social problems, indeed often had their roots in them. The massive breakdown of law and order in the wake of the Black Death was merely a foretaste. In the late fourteenth and early fifteenth centuries Catalonian trade took a dramatic downturn. Barcelona was particularly affected. Along the eastern seaboard banks collapsed, and the country witnessed a flight of gold and silver as exports declined. Both Aragon and Castile saw repeated and ruinous debasement of the coinage as monarchs took the easy way out of their financial predicaments. In the countryside post-plague retrenchment by landlords, whether the nobility or the Church, and their insistence on traditional rights over tenants and serfs, led to unrest among the peasantry which in northern Spain in particular became almost endemic, and which in the late fifteenth century helped to trigger civil war. Long before that unrest had begun to vent itself more ominously against the Jews. In 1391 a wave of pogroms, starting in Seville, swept the whole country within two months. The Jews were a sitting target for discontent, and all, including monarchs, began to exploit the tendency. It was an important milestone in the hardening of attitudes towards the non-Christian population, a change which by the end of the fifteenth century was to culminate in programmes of forced conversions and expulsions.

None the less it would be a mistake to judge the fourteenth century in a wholly negative fashion. Spain remained an area of great promise. If Catalonia bore the brunt of economic decline, Castile on the other hand saw equally dramatic growth of sheep-farming and wool exportation. The Hundred Years War, which had severely hit the English wool trade, was Castile's blessing. Along with the wool trade grew wool-related industries, and there was an important growth in Castile's ports—Santander and Seville—and in shipbuilding, and these in turn led Castilian trade in the Atlantic in other produce. In this as in many other ways Castile can be seen to be preparing itself for a new era.

In Italy, where political conflict had long been endemic, crises might appear difficult to spot. But there are signs, and more substantive ones than the anguish of contemporary commentators about the country's plight. There is evidence of a decline in population before the first outbreak of plague, and also of economic problems, heralded by the spectacular crashes of the Bardi and Peruzzi banks in the 1340s. Italy was dealt if anything more than its due share of waves of plague and famine, often in combination or rapid succession, and for the century or so following the Black Death there are figures pointing to the decline of trade and industry for several towns, notably Florence and Genoa. But the evidence does not all point in the same direction, and the picture of decline could equally be contrasted by the trade of Venice—which adapted rapidly to the Turkish shadow, partly by establishing commercial relations with them and partly by expanding other, Near-Eastern routes through which links with the east could continue; or that of Lombardy, where trade links with northern Europe were improving, and new products such as silk and rice were being developed. Again, the evidence points to qualitative changes and geographical shifts, of which specific crises are perhaps symptoms.

Whether or not the Italian economy was yet in decline, it is clear enough that in the fourteenth century the peninsula threatened to be overwhelmed by its political problems. The Guelph alliance was now coming under great strain. The papacy was out of Italy, though it had to be a priority to make the way safe for a return to Rome, the fount of its authority. In Naples the death of Robert of Anjou plunged the kingdom into over a century of unrelenting instability as barons and outsiders fought to influence a succession of weak kings and queens. The other eminent partner of the alliance, Florence, increasingly bore the burden and resented the cost and instability of the quagmire of the political scene in the papal states. Strangely it was during the period of absence that the papacy took the first serious steps towards the pacification of these states, with the career of the cardinal and general Gil Albornoz. Peace treaties were drawn up and the aspirations of some of the *signori* of the region were recognized by the establishment of vicariates, a useful innovation. Yet the pacification soon came up against the limits of what was possible. The weak point was the northern border of the states, and particularly the strategically placed town of Bologna, over which the Florentines and the popes eventually fell out. The War of the Eight Saints, in which Florence incurred interdict and fought papal forces, was a low point. It culminated in a rebellion of some of Florence's poorly paid industrial workers, the *ciompi*, who briefly seized power in one of Europe's first clear examples of urban social revolution. Things were no better in northern Italy, where a succession of towns were taken over by rulers who attempted to found dynasties, with varying success and, as in the communal phase, in perpetual rivalry. The most significant of these were the Visconti of Milan, who dominated northern Italian politics from the mid-fourteenth century. With the career of Giangaleazzo Visconti at the end of the century Milan's significance became greater still. Military and diplomatic prowess gave this energetic ruler control, within a very short period, of not only virtually all of northern Italy but also of much of Tuscany and some of the towns in the papal states. The isolated Florentines had to address themselves to the very real threat that Italy might finally have found its unifier. In practice, of course, the Milanese hegemony was founded almost entirely on the personal *virtù* of its ruler, and at his death it disintegrated overnight.

All this took place against a backdrop of numerous lesser wars and squabbles, intertwined and interdependent. The situation was made endemic by the way in which the wars were fought. By the fourteenth century most towns had abandoned militia troops in favour of mercenary forces, and the system had developed to the extent that mercenary bands under their leaders or *condottieri* were available for hire as a unit, saving the towns the trouble of having to recruit. The system received an unwelcome boost with the lull in the Hundred Years War which brought many discharged foreigners into the peninsula in search of further employment. French, German, and English *condottieri* dominated the wars of the late fourteenth century, to the point where Giangaleazzo Visconti could present his expansionism as a bid to save Italy from foreigners. Like all such armies they perpetuated the cause of war; as campaigns ended towns found that it was in their interests to retain the soldiers in peacetime to prevent them from turning on their former employers—a veritable protection racket. Things were no better when the foreigners were replaced by Italians; the *condottieri*, a majority of whom originated from the papal states, now sought to acquire their own territory and lordships, and their aspirations prolonged many conflicts, and the general state of turbulence, well into the fifteenth century. As they were also ruinously expensive they managed incidentally to exacerbate the internal affairs of individual city-states as well.

The fourteenth century has traditionally been seen as the

period in which the communal system declined and was replaced by seigneurial or despotic rule. And this is perfectly accurate; by the end of the century only Florence, Siena, and Venice had any success in maintaining republican status. But perhaps also this trend is of less significance than was once thought. Nineteenth-century historians painted a picture of the end-of-century crisis as one of freedom versus tyranny, while others have favoured the opposite interpretation, of the victory of efficiency over factionalism, of despotism as the 'pragmatic criticism of republicanism'. More recently historians have been pointing to the similarities between the two systems; the way in which the surviving communes became more and more oligarchical and the new despots depended on consensus to survive. What may be more important than the style of governments is the reduction in their number and the growth of the territorial state. The result of the fourteenth-century conflicts was the survival of the fittest. This is what eventually made Italian politics more manageable, and even brought the peninsula some years of peace.

Consolidation and Expansion

By the early fifteenth century, indeed, there were five major powers in Italy. Milan had seen steady territorial growth; Giangaleazzo Visconti's career was a flash in the pan. Visconti dukes ruled for the first half of the century. Naples was still sunk in problems which would only be resolved with the Aragonese acquisition of the kingdom. In Florence the reaction to a period of broad-based government (and the revolt of the *ciompi*) had led to an oligarchical government which in 1434 yielded to control by the Medici family, who 'ruled' entirely unofficially, so that Florence could parade its outwardly republican constitution while tacitly acknowledging the importance of its first citizen—a remarkably convenient and effective arrangement. Venice was in a sense the newcomer. It became seriously involved in mainland politics for the first time towards the end of the fourteenth century for several reasons: the need to ensure grain supplies in a period of Ottoman

SAVOY

Turin

MONTFERRAT

GENOA
Genoa

Milan

MILAN

MANTUA

MODENA
Modena

LUCCA
Lucca
Pisa

Padua

Venice

VENICE

to VENICE

Ferrara

FERRARA

Bologna

Ravenna

Florence

FLORENCE

Siena

SIENA

PAPAL

STATES

to VENICE

CORSICA
(Genoa)

Rome

KINGDOM

Naples

O F

NAPLES

SARDINIA
(Kingdom of Naples)

SICILY
(Kingdom of Naples)

| 0 | 100 | 200 km |
| 0 | 50 | 100 | 150 miles |

ITALY AFTER 1454

expansion, Milanese and Paduan aggression which threatened its frontiers. Now it took its place as a mainland power, though not without dislocation for others. Venice's government was unlike any other; a republic with a formal head of state, the doge, who was appointed for life, a political system that presented to the outside world the picture of a model of stability; all this was much admired and 'mythologized'.

The fifth power, the papacy—and it must be viewed, by the fifteenth century, above all as a political power—was surrounded by a mass of special and destabilizing circumstances. It still had the least control over its territory, and unlike most territorial states where one might expect to find control stronger at the centre and weaker at the periphery the papacy had the core of its political weakness at its doorstep. The Rome to which the popes formally returned at the end of the Great Schism was backward, underdeveloped, with no industry to speak of apart from religious tourism; it was still very much in the clutches of rival families of the landed nobility from the surrounding area, including Neapolitan families (and papal and Neapolitan affairs continued to be intertwined). The nature of papal power itself, too, could be a source of weakness. Non-domestic, non-political considerations were always present; above all the system of election, whereby the electors, the cardinals, had all been appointed by previous popes, made for instability. It was important psychologically as much as anything else. Popes had always been prone to feather the nest for their relatives, and the reasonable explanation for this nepotism was that they required advisers and officers whom they could trust. The fifteenth-century papacy shows the trend very clearly; almost each pope was succeeded, two or three elections later, by a member of his family whom he had usually himself promoted to the cardinalate and whose political standing had grown in the intervening years. It meant that the papacy was as open to factionalism as ever, and was likely to be subject to regular changes of diplomatic alignment, as Venetian, Genoese, or Sienese popes succeeded in turn.

War broke out between Florence and Milan in 1423—by now these were traditional enemies—and was to last for twenty-two years. The Florentines involved Venice, which soon gained further territory in an early truce (1427), while Florence paid the price of bringing the unwelcome attentions of the Milanese into Tuscany itself. For many of the central years of the war, though, the main protagonists were really the two *condottieri*, Niccolò Piccinino, who fought for Milan, and Francesco Sforza, who fought unreliably for Florence, going over to the side of Milan no fewer than three times and in the process carving out for himself substantial territory. By the end of the war he had become such a menace that he was attacked by Alfonso of Naples, who had been fighting for the acquisition of the kingdom, drawing papal interests into the conflict, so that by the 1440s all Italy was again embroiled in warfare. With the death of Filippo Maria Visconti in 1447 Sforza, who had married Filippo Maria's daughter, laid claim to Milan, in rivalry to Alfonso, and three years later was successful. In 1454 Milan and Venice finally agreed to a peace, the Peace of Lodi, and this was followed by general pacification and the formation of an Italic League. And surprisingly this time the peace held, by and large, for forty years.

Many reasons can be advanced for the pacification, and for the continuation of peace. The documents of the period show that financial exhaustion from the war was general, and was producing strains on the internal governments of the participants. The years immediately preceding the peace of Lodi also saw the arrival of more reasonable men, who clearly saw the need to end the wars; Alfonso of Aragon and Cosimo de' Medici in particular. The *condottieri* were by now relatively under control, and Francesco Sforza, too, was more amenable now that he had fulfilled his ambition by becoming duke of Milan. For Venice and the papacy there were also arguments of a different nature. The Turks had just taken Constantinople (1453), a long-expected act, of by now little more than symbolic significance, but no less important for that in psychological terms. And fear of outside intervention, be it from the Turks or elsewhere, proved a powerful force in holding the new alliance together.

Less tangible explanations can also be detailed. Diplomatic

skills were developing. Late medieval Italy is the home of modern diplomatic institutions, with their resident embassies, conventions of immunity, and intelligence-gathering. The system was already perhaps sophisticated enough to replace, or at least to supplement, warfare as a prime means of conducting international affairs. The peace was also possible because the major powers, and the lesser ones, were in many ways becoming rather similar. They were all territorial states (even if the papacy's claim to this position looked weak), they were almost all governed by princes (for foreign policy purposes the Medici in Florence assumed this role), all of whom were diverting increasing energy and funds into the splendours of the court and courtly culture, another channel for rivalry. It may be, as has been suggested, that this closed court life increasingly began to isolate the rulers and their entourages from some of the pressures which were beginning to tell on their subjects. By the second half of the fifteenth century Italy's commercial position was weakening and being overtaken. The famous collapse of the Medici bank was not just due to mismanagement; newer and stronger rivals, in Germany and elsewhere, were emerging, new trade routes were being established. Yet the aristocracy continued to pour spectacular amounts of money into 'luxuries': buildings, paintings, the patronage of literature, feasting, and spectacle on an extravagant scale. Funds were increasingly being diverted from the land, and from raised taxation, but were less and less channelled into economically productive use.

The Italic League also worked, most obviously, because a balance of power had been achieved. The five major powers were of roughly equal political or strategic weight, and had indispensable functions to play. But there remained weak points. In Ferrante (1458–94) Naples once more acquired an aggressive monarch, while the papacy saw both threats to stability on its southern flank and renewed unrest among its vassal princes in the papal states. Repeatedly it was this part of the peninsula which destabilized the balance of power, and it was the initiative of the notorious Sixtus IV which caused the first serious threat to the alliance when he caused a rift with Florence which then dragged the other powers into conflict.

That the peace could not last was perhaps inevitable. That it should be shattered, in 1494, with such totality, plunging Italy into decades of the most serious fighting Europe had seen, was largely the responsibility of others. Behind the Italian scene were two foreign powers, France and Spain, both with claims to titles in Italy, both geared up for war, both willing to use Italy as the arena for that war. The Italian forces, at best in uneasy alliance, were no match for the power of these foreigners. The French and Spanish armies in Italy represented states with a new scale of resources. If 'survival of the fittest' had reduced the number of states within Italy, that principle was now about to be taken to its logical conclusion.

The union of the Spanish crowns nearly never happened, or rather, nearly happened in a quite different combination. Isabella of Castile had fought for the succession in that kingdom with Joanna, the betrothed of the king of Portugal, and had she not won there might well have been a union of the crowns of Castile and Portugal. Nor was the union by marriage of the two crowns of Castile and Aragon the same thing as a union of Spain. The terms kept them strictly separate and closely defined the spheres of action of the two monarchs. Ferdinand ruled solely in Aragon, jointly with Isabella in Castile, from which he could not absent himself without her consent. And although for a long time it was the fashion, particularly among Spanish nationalist historians, to regard the two as the founders of modern Spain, more recently historians have tended to emphasize the continuity in the development of the Spanish kingdoms and the ways in which the policies of the 'Catholic kings', as the pair was dubbed by the pope, developed from those of their predecessors.

That said, the time was certainly ripe for such collaboration. Castile and Aragon in many ways complemented each other well. Aragon's interests lay, above all, eastward, in the Mediterranean, and although the economy had suffered, there were still opportunities, used to the full, notably in relations with the now Spanish southern half of the Italian peninsula. In terms of foreign policy and trade Castile's interests by contrast lay in the Atlantic, with northern Europe, and eventually with the Atlantic islands and beyond. There was no obvious clash of interests, and little economic rivalry. In their foreign policy Ferdinand and Isabella could use the duality to excellent effect.

The two rulers had no unifying programme, and initially few policies to be applied in both kingdoms. Due regard for the most pressing problems of each made this inevitable. Thus in Castile the most urgent need was for a restoration of royal authority over the nobility. In the large, still in many parts underpopulated, country the extensive property patterns of the reconquest remained; the nobles had acquired shares in royal taxation, which they helped to collect, and other privileges from the crown. The rulers used both firm measures and gentle incentives. Military force was invoked to check abuses of privileges; there was a revival of the *hermandades* or town-based militias, as an additional check: the monarchs continued the process of replacing the nobility as administrators by *letrados* or university-trained professionals. The aristocracy was to be made into a courtier class, dependent on the favours of the monarchs. At the same time the rulers recognized their immunity from taxation, and indirectly compensated them particularly by granting extensive privileges to the Mesta, the organization of livestock owners which included many of the aristocracy. All this kept Ferdinand in Castile; Aragon saw him for a total of less than seven years in the thirty-seven of his reign. Here, despite his absence, viceroys and the parliaments continued with government and some reforms were effected, especially in Catalonia, where Ferdinand recognized the need to heal the scars of the recent civil war and to encourage economic revival.

Ferdinand and Isabella's achievement, though, lies less in the detail of their administration than in the strong sense of direction achieved during their reign. That classic recipe, of a popular foreign war of aggression to unite opinion, took on special significance in this last phase of *Reconquista*; the time had come to complete the process. War—it was a crusade, and was subsidized by the papacy—for the conquest of Granada began in reaction to provocation by the king of Granada in

1481, and lasted for a decade. The final victory in 1492 owed not a little to dissension among the Muslim leaders, though naturally this was played down by the propagandists. The end of the war also saw the culmination of waves of hostility to Muslims and Jews that had been developing over the previous century. The Jews were finally expelled in 1492, a popular act, presented as an act of Christian faith, and a remunerative one in the short term, since they were given little opportunity of taking their possessions with them. The Muslims of Granada were initially given favourable terms, being allowed by the peace treaty of 1492 to remain and to practise their religion. But the next ten years saw intense manœuvring about this on the part of the ecclesiastical hard-liners, and the result was that in 1499 the Muslims of Granada were given a choice between conversion and departure, and this was extended to the Muslims of Castile in 1502. Those who stayed were further discriminated against, like the Jewish *conversi*, by the extension of the principle of purity of blood (*limpieza de sangre*), which barred them from many public offices and positions of eminence.

All this represents a concerted effort towards a sort of unity; not political unity, which would follow in the next century, but unity of purpose, sentiment, and 'Spanishness'. The ideology of conquest and conversion was accompanied by the development of the one organization which in practice was standardized throughout Aragon and Castile, the Church, which was also an overwhelmingly Spanish institution; the 'Catholic' kings allowed minimal interference by the pope, and the ecclesiastical personnel was controlled by them. The pope was even excluded from a significant role in the Spanish Inquisition. Set up in both Aragon and Castile to investigate the orthodoxy of converts from Judaism, the two branches were united in 1483, the first institution officially to span both kingdoms. The Inquisition was not, nor did it ever become, the secret police of legend, but it is an unsurprising assumption to make; Church and State, religion and politics, were uniquely close in their association.

Ferdinand and Isabella's rule was not 'absolute'. If anything it is interesting to note how they always opted for the popular policies, favouring reconquest and the Mesta, expelling Muslims and Jews. The reconquest above all was extremely popular, and their achievement was the way in which they used this tide of popular concerted action to extend royal power and build the foundations for a united state. The same talent for reconquest stood Castile in excellent stead for the colonization of the New World. Progress was made very rapidly; before Isabella's death in 1504 detailed legislation had already been passed regulating existing and future colonies.

The credit for colonization may go to Spain, but it is for colonization more than for discovery. The story of the exploration of the Atlantic, which culminated in Columbus's voyage to the New World, is a long one, and is mainly a Portuguese achievement. Of the three areas of exploration, the Atlantic islands, the African coast, and then the New World, Portuguese predominate in the first two. The Portuguese programme of exploration is said to have begun with the capture of Ceuta, near the Straits of Gibraltar, from the Moors in 1415, in that that episode whetted the religious and commercial appetite for exploration. The islands of the Atlantic, though, were already known. Sporadic visits to the Canaries had been made in the fourteenth century by both Portugal and Castile, but in the fifteenth century interest in them was revived, and led to rival claims. Eventually Castile's rights were confirmed by the papacy (1479), which pitched the Castilians into long battles to subdue the indigenous Guanche population. Madeira and the Azores were also known in the fourteenth century, and were now colonized by the Portuguese (Madeira from 1424, the Azores from 1439). The Cape Verde Islands were discovered by the Portuguese in 1462. Many of these islands became stopping-off points for further exploration, but their significance at the time was that of colonies, for example for sugarcane plantations, which were an important feature of the Portuguese economy.

The West African coast was not really colonized because of the indigenous population; but the Portuguese saw the opportunities for raiding, especially for slaves, and then for trade. The discovery of Guinea was particularly important in this respect. The attractions of these voyages were the prospect of gold, a real need in Europe, slaves, and the legendary wealth of Africa, so far exploited only through middlemen on the North African coast. Religious motives were also important; the desire to convert pagans, to find out how far Muslim power extended, and perhaps to make contact with the legendary Christian king of the east, Prester John (as late as 1497 Vasco da Gama, on his epoch-making voyage to India round the Cape of Good Hope, took with him a letter to Prester John). There has been endless debate about which of these motives predominated, and the extent to which Prince Henry—'the Navigator'—the alleged intellectual mastermind of the Portuguese expansion, deserves any credit for it. But it seems that it was the amalgam of these motives that won royal support for such enterprises, at least initially; economic and religious arguments make a strong combination. In this the explorations were thoroughly 'medieval'. The element of curiosity grew as the operation developed its own momentum (and became self-financing), culminating in the truly long-distance enterprises. The boldness of Columbus's intentions, to discover a westward route to India, was of an altogether different dimension. Although he had a greatly distorted idea of the size of the globe, and thus quite underestimated what the journey might entail, what he was proposing still entailed a much larger step into the unknown. It was not surprising that the Portuguese turned him down. Their efforts had been based on step-by-step accumulation of knowledge and contacts on the West African coast; they had been unfortunate in the Atlantic (and had only recently lost the Canaries to Spain); and Columbus's expectation that they should pay for the expedition ran contrary to the whole tradition of Portuguese maritime activity. Although Columbus eventually sailed under Castilian patronage, the costs were borne by Genoese financiers.

The real significance of the discoveries was of course apparent only as they progressed, in the sixteenth century. But the explorations had already changed Europe's trade picture. Specifically, they had vital economic and then political consequences for the Mediterranean, as indeed, one could argue, they had been intended to have. This is a real sense in which the opportunities of the old world were being supplanted by those of the new.

New Ideas and New Directions

The theory that Columbus was to put to the test, that it was possible to sail westwards to reach Cathay and the Indies, had been elaborated by the Florentine Paolo Toscanelli, who wrote about it to the confessor of the Portuguese king in 1474. It was the product of an interest in geography and cartography which had a long history in the maritime towns, but which had also developed steadily in the intellectual community since Ptolemy's *Geography* had been made available in Latin through the translation of another Florentine (1409). It was just one of the many areas of intellectual life affected by the movement known as humanism, which began to spread from Italy extensively in the first half of the fifteenth century.

However revolutionary humanist and Renaissance ideas were to become, their origins are firmly rooted in medieval culture, to the extent that it is difficult to pin-point the beginning of the movement. In the thirteenth century several features of western European cultural activity were truly international, and Italy participated in these fully along with the rest of Mediterranean Europe. One was the aristocratic culture of chivalric values, courtly love, heroic epic, and so on, much of which had its original focus in southern France, and which is to be found richly in late medieval Spain, Frankish Greece, and to a large extent also in Italy, both in the towns and in the less urbanized south. Another was the deeply religious nature of culture. Religion imbued the *Reconquista* and the crusading ethos hand in hand with chivalric ideals, and in different forms was prominent in the intellectual ferment of the thirteenth century, the flowering of theology and philosophy with the development of scholasticism, the intellectual stance against heresy, and the organization of preaching. Though Paris was the unquestioned capital of this achievement it was equally an international culture. (St Thomas Aquinas, the great thirteenth-century theologian of Paris, was an Italian.) Religious culture was spread particularly by the friars, whose *studia* covered much of Europe, including the Italian towns, and with whose influence the popularization of religious concepts and religious education gained major impetus which was to continue right to the end of the Middle Ages.

These two strands, the chivalric and the religious, were fundamental, and continued to be of great significance in the Renaissance. The Italian towns, however, added a third element, a secular culture of a different kind. The need for professional expertise—for administrators, lawyers, doctors, and commercial training—led to a growth in secular education, present in Italian towns virtually from their beginnings, but now to expand enormously. Private and communally funded schools grew up alongside cathedral and church schools and were considerably more important than them. Reading and writing schools, 'abacus' schools, and grammar schools all burgeoned, and fed into the universities which, from the early thirteenth century onwards, were set up by towns all over northern and central Italy, teaching in particular medicine and above all law. The need for lawyers was fundamental to the defence of a town's rights and to the administration of justice, and lawyers were a highly esteemed group. Even more fundamental was the need for notaries. Ubiquitous figures in late medieval towns, and for that matter in the countryside, they oiled the wheels of administration and of private and commercial transaction; virtually all legal documents had to be drawn up or at least 'rogated' by them. The education of notaries was also crucial, although we know less about it; but we do know that the thirteenth century saw a great development of the *ars notarie* alongside formal legal training, principally at Bologna.

Finally, the towns needed rhetoricians. These are harder to slot into 'professional' divisions, which are in any case artificial and capable of much overlap. But alongside the *ars notarie* developed the *ars dictaminis* and the *ars rhetorica*, the medieval arts of writing and rhetoric, basic educational building-blocks, and these were widely influential. Rhetorical skills were developed particularly in Tuscany, where a high proportion of writers, lawyers, and notaries had such training, and it could be described as the true mark of most intellectuals of the period. And the study of rhetoric led, in many cases almost instinctively, to an interest in the classics. If by humanist were meant simply someone who was interested in the classics, or for whom there is evidence that he had read classical writers, one would have to use the term right back into the thirteenth century and indeed before. Classical culture had never been totally absent; it was only that interest in it was growing. Historians tend, however, to use the term humanist (from 'studia humanitatis', a term already common in the fifteenth century) to mean people for whom the study of the classics was of overriding importance or an end in itself, and whose activities in whatever field are deeply imbued by that study. The most prominent among these in the fourteenth century was Francesco Petrarca (known to the English-speaking world as Petrarch), who is often called the father of humanism. Another Florentine, although born in exile and destined to spend much of his life near Avignon, Petrarch is an example of a new kind of intellectual in that he depended for his living on writing for and advising a sequence of patrons. We might call him a freelancer.

Petrarch's career drew on many of the traditions described above (although one, scholasticism, he rejected decisively). His interests ranged across many disciplines and literary genres. A trained lawyer and a cleric, he is as famous for his love-poetry and his letters as for his treatises. The most significant feature, though, which he bequeathed to posterity was his love and pursuit of the classical authors, his search for manuscripts, his admiration for Cicero in particular. Petrarch is also important because his personality was what might be called high-profile. He thrived on influential contacts, was fascinated by power, and was extremely adept at self-publicization. He did much to establish a model or ideal of the humanist. The late fourteenth century saw a growth in the number of his emulators, and with this growth came, crucially, an emergent sense of community between them. These men were active in many fields, and between them they turned what had been a growing fashion into the established activity for secular intellectuals.

How can one sum up a movement that was so pervasive and so multifaceted? Perhaps best by starting with what was at its centre, the interest in the classics. This took many forms. In the first place, it involved the literal search for physical remains. Scholars such as Flavio Biondo, with his treatises on Roman and Italian topography and history, and Cyriac of Ancona, with his collection of classical inscriptions, pursued this aim in the first half of the fifteenth century. The search was also on for texts; monastic culture might have preserved these through the dark ages, but had by no means yielded up all its treasures. Another part of the process of recovery was the translation of texts from Greek, for which knowledge of Greek was obviously an indispensable preliminary. The arrival of Manuel Chrysoloras to teach at the University of Florence in 1396 heralded the beginning of this process; it continued throughout the fifteenth century, accelerating with the dispersal or exile of scholars from Byzantium. Translation unlocked for the west the hitherto unknown or imperfectly translated among the works of Aristotle, and later in the fifteenth century Plato, in their turn both profound influences on humanist culture. The digestion of all these texts required philological skills, brought to new heights with the translations, and the 'theory of translation', of Leonardo Bruni, another Florentine chancellor, and then of Lorenzo Valla, who is often called the father of modern philology.

Specific interest was aroused by the rhetorical texts of the ancients. Poggio Bracciolini's rediscovery of Quintilian and of the full text of Cicero's *De oratore* was decisive. In them humanists found the full theoretical basis for classical Latin rhetoric, which led to an understanding of the use of the classical periodic sentence, a powerful tool of analysis as well as of advocacy. The Latin 'purism' that followed has aroused mixed judgements; the humanists have been accused of turning Latin into a dead language by their insistence on high standards and their scorn for anything less. But the importance of classical rhetoric goes far beyond this. At its root are principles of balance, appropriateness (*decorum*) and harmony (*concinnitas*)—the principles of aesthetics, in fact. By applying these so widely across disciplines humanist scholars helped to link them, creating an intellectual and verbal rationale for what was happening in the visual arts, for example, and elsewhere.

From the last part of Cicero's *De oratore*, too, humanists drew the ideal of the orator as responsible citizen using his skills of forensic argument for the good of the state. This is equally important, and brings us back to the fact that humanists continued to have close connections with government, either through employment or through membership of the patrician class. So it is not surprising that an early manifestation of this scholarly activity was the propounding of fresh ideas about the ideal state and ideal civic conduct. Florence in particular saw a growth of 'civic ideology', closely allied to the interests of the ruling oligarchy, in the decades following the political crisis caused by the Visconti threat around 1400. This civicism, drawing on classical sources, was not new; it can be found in the writings of Remigio de' Girolami, Dominican and teacher of Dante, in the late thirteenth century, while in the fourteenth century Marsilius of Padua had elaborated ideas of republican or at least representative government that were surprisingly modern for their time. The novelty was perhaps the extent to which parallels with classical models were invoked, and the extent to which civic ideas were elaborated as a 'programme', including the exaltation of the active over the contemplative life, the definition of the desirable conduct of the private individual, the definition of the historical role of the republic, the idealization of the city. All this was a phase. Classical models could equally be produced to exalt the role of the prince—and were, especially later in the century.

Classical models also had a powerful influence on the writing of history. They transformed it into a more literary, prescriptive discipline but also into one more organized and more penetrating. It is also possible to detect a new sense of perspective on the past. Lorenzo Valla's final proof that the Donation of Constantine—in which the emperor had allegedly given temporal control of his dominions to the pope, a source of much controversy in the Middle Ages—was a forgery, was based on philological principles; that specific words and notions in the text simply could not have been used at the time when it was supposed to have been written. A sense of anachronism was a key to the development of a sense of the past; but that too was developing as scholars studying classical texts, as well as taking models from the past, saw with great clarity that contemporary Italy was not ancient Rome or Greece. Yet this also produced a great sense of self-consciousness among humanists, a sense that by returning to the classics, after a long period of poor transmission of classical values, they were making a break with the immediate past. The pioneers of the Renaissance knew that they were participating in a rebirth. As with Petrarch, their sense of their own importance and their excitement at what they were doing were to some extent a self-fulfilling wish, and if we tend to think of the Renaissance as a break with the 'Middle' Ages this owes something to the way they saw themselves.

Humanist activity spread into many areas. In the universities it gradually began to influence the study of law with its philological principles. In the courts it was adapted to the requirements of the princes; Renaissance literature saw a new development of the chivalric epic, for example, based on classical models (as were the growth of comedy and tragedy). In the long term one of the most important areas of influence was in education. The humanist educational programme had initially been formulated largely as a defence against hostile clerics alarmed at the fashion of the classics and fearful of an outbreak of paganism. It was soon tried out, though, by teachers such as Vittorino da Feltre in Venice and Guarino da Verona at the court of Mantua. These schools were intended chiefly for the élite, and the effects of the humanist programme in actual classrooms of schoolchildren and students were arguably slow and gradual. But education was one of the first aspects of humanism to be exported beyond the Alps, and inasmuch as it ensured the transmission of the basic starting-point of humanist values, the classics, it was vital.

Contemporaneous with this remarkable upsurge in activity among literati were similar and ultimately more celebrated developments in the visual arts, again focused for a time principally, though not exclusively, on Florence. The precise connections between these two aspects of the Renaissance will always remain difficult to pin-point, but there are many parallels. Both go a long way back. If the decisive change in fifteenth-century painting was the invention of perspective, equally important developments had taken place as far back as the early fourteenth century with Giotto's innovations in spatial representation and the mastery of the art of fresco painting. The embellishment of the city, to some extent interrupted after the Black Death, was now taken up by a battery of new artists, Brunelleschi, Donatello, Ghiberti, Masaccio, and the polymath Alberti foremost among the many. To the cathedral Brunelleschi added the majestic cupola, a brilliant technological feat as well as the purest expression of harmony; façades were added to the Dominican Church of Santa Maria Novella and others; new buildings such as the Churches of Santo Spirito and San Lorenzo rose. There were also a host of private patrician patrons—of the building and decoration of chapels, later of individual paintings. Painting saw the achievement of greater realism, wide experimentation with colour, perspective, and proportion, and the vogue of classical iconographical themes; sculpture saw a new sensitivity to movement and proportion, and in-the-round, as opposed to bas-relief, work became the norm.

The excitement all this generated is attested by the speed with which Florence's reputation spread and other patrons tried to woo its chief stars. By the mid-fifteenth century the centre of attention had shifted to Rome, where under several popes, and principally Nicholas V, the next generation of erudite and often temperamental scholars gathered, bringing blatantly secular and often quite *risqué* culture to the heart of the papacy. There followed several popes with impressive performances as Renaissance princes; Pius II, previously the humanist Aeneas Silvius Piccolomini, Paul II, who directed attention to reviving the physical appearance of Rome itself, and Sixtus IV, who in addition to his warlike record also gathered several humanists to his court. But by this time the movement was truly pan-Italian. The Venetians, Milanese, and Neapolitans all had humanists in their pay and artists working under commission, and culture was an area in which lesser powers—the Gonzaga of Mantua, the Este of Ferrara—could easily outshine the greater.

Ultimately, though, Renaissance Italy was the focus for a movement that soon transcended nationality. Indeed, it always had been so; from the period of the Avignonese papacy Italian art had been exported and writers had been in contact with their colleagues north of the Alps. The great church councils helped to accelerate this process; humanists of court and curia alike attended, and indeed it was the Council of Constance which had given Poggio Bracciolini the opportunity to search the nearby monasteries and to make his discoveries. The travels of the Italian Aeneas Silvius Piccolomini, and the many contacts he had made before becoming pope, helped spread an interest in humanist activity, and the development of the Roman court added a fresh focus and a multiplication of international contacts through cardinals and courtiers. Spain received much of the new culture through the Aragonese court at Naples, and also through the growing numbers of Spanish merchants and students throughout the peninsula. The universities also became a focus for German interest, many coming to pursue higher education in Italy, and there soon germinated, there and in some of eastern Europe, that persistent idea that a visit to Italy was an important part of one's cultural formation. It worked both ways, of course; as well as exporting the Renaissance, Italy imported; Flemish painters, and particularly musicians, found a home in Italy just as Italian artists and humanists did in northern Europe. The parallel with the commercial hegemony of Italy in the thirteenth and fourteenth centuries is not entirely fanciful. To remain with the metaphor for a moment, the international wars at the end of the century were no check to this production and exchange. Even as its political independence was being destroyed, and its economy was being undermined, Italy continued for a while to be thought of as the crossroads of European culture.

6

The Civilization of Courts and Cities in the North

1200–1500

MALCOLM VALE

Kings and Princes: Image and Reality

THE relation of the ecclesiastical and secular arms had always been a major theme in medieval European history, but during the later Middle Ages secularization was especially significant. The papacy's attempt to control and consecrate the secular state had failed. By 1500 the secular power exerted a greater degree of control over the Church in northern Europe than its precursor had done in 1200. In Germany, princely and aristocratic influence was dominant; in France, the powers of the monarchy over ecclesiastical appointments and privileges had greatly increased, while in England a 'national' Church had already emerged in which papal influence was severely restricted. Rulers were still obliged to protect and support the Church within their lands; in return, the higher clergy confirmed and sanctified their authority. Both churchmen and laymen attached great importance to the elevation of secular power into something holier and greater than mere rule by brute force or even by consent. But the temporal ruler was no longer perceived as an instrument, even less as a servant, of the Church's will because the Church had to a large extent been absorbed by the state.

The eclipse of ecclesiastical power—and especially papal

power—was accompanied by an expansion and elaboration of secular rule. The image of kingship changed. Later medieval kings were unlike other men: they dressed differently, carried and wore special insignia, and were supposed to possess certain traditional kingly attributes, amongst them law-giving, judging, and maintaining peace and order. The ceremony and ritual associated with kingship, however, became much more complex and elaborate during this period. This was clearly evident at coronations, royal entries into principal towns, royal funerals, and plenary sessions of judicial and representative assemblies (French parlements and Estates, English parliaments, imperial, Polish, and Hungarian diets). Like the saints, kings were identified by the display of certain emblems—above all, the crown, orb, and sceptre.

The significance of the crown in later medieval Europe cannot be underestimated. Although some great nobles claimed the right to wear a crown (such as the dukes of Brittany or the counts of Armagnac in France), that symbol of power became increasingly confined to monarchs. The Holy Roman emperor claimed exclusive use of the closed crown, resembling the papal tiara, but the rulers of Bohemia, Austria, Poland, and Hungary had also assumed the right to wear the closed crown of sovereignty. The English monarchy only adopted an 'imperial' crown in the reign of Henry VIII, and in France that symbol of absolute sovereignty did not emerge until c.1550. The orb signified terrestrial power, and its use had been confined to the emperor until it was adopted by the crown of Aragon in 1204 and the English monarchy in the fourteenth century. The French, however, did not use the orb, preferring two sceptres: the long rod of state, and the shorter *main-de-justice*, which symbolized the role of the king as a giver of justice from the reign of Philip the Fair (1285–1314) onwards. Both the Capetian and Valois kings of France also laid great stress upon their ceremonial sword. This was not so much a symbol of martial prowess and military strength but of royal justice and this sword, called *Joyeuse*, attributed to Charlemagne, was carried before them on state occasions by the constable of France. The combination of the sword of justice and the lilies of mercy provided a potent image for the French monarchy at the end of the Middle Ages.

To emphasize their distinction from other men, kings and emperors wore special vestments: the Eagle Dalmatic (*c.*1300) of the Holy Roman Empire, or the chasuble sewn with fleurs-de-lis of the kings of France. On less solemn and sacred occasions they needed to impress both their own subjects and other rulers (or their envoys) with their power. The richer their attire, the more lavish their display of treasures, the more powerful they were thought to be. This tendency towards conspicuous display was not, however, confined to kings. One of the major problems of later medieval monarchs—the control of their higher nobilities—was exemplified by the extent to which the houses of Burgundy or Anjou in France, Lancaster or York in England, Saxony or the Rhine Palatinate in Germany presented an image of quasi-regal power. Philip the Good, duke of Burgundy (1419–67), for example, was accustomed to display his gold and silver plate to the representatives of foreign powers in order to impress them with his ability to pay the costs of war and to secure alliances. Henry VII of England showed his jewels and illuminated manuscripts to visiting ambassadors with similar intent.

The elaboration of ceremonial was accompanied by important developments in the organization of princely courts and households. The itinerant courts of earlier medieval kings such as Henry II of England, which had dragged themselves over appalling roads in all weathers, full of a motley and somewhat disordered throng of people, gave way to a more formal institution which reached its later medieval peak of development with the court of Valois Burgundy (1384–1477). As an extension or an elaboration of the prince's domestic household the court became a larger, more expensive, and extravagant power-centre. There was an increasing tendency for princely courts to gravitate towards towns. Their financial resources, skilled craftsmen, and entrepreneurs (goldsmiths, tailors, armourers, tapestry-makers, painters, illuminators, and suppliers of luxury goods) made towns such as Paris, Brussels, Lille, Tours, Aix-en-Provence, Innsbruck, Prague, and Vienna the natural centres of court life and court culture. Access to credit supplied by bankers and money-lenders, and the parallel rise of capital cities all contributed to a progressive 'urbanization' of political power during this period. By 1450, Brussels had emerged as the favourite residence of Philip the Good of Burgundy, who made the Coudenberg palace there a centre for his court; Westminster began to dominate over other English royal residences during the reign of Henry III (1216–72); while courtly Prague was enlarged and beautified by the building of the Karlštejn castle and the creation of the New Town (1348) under Charles IV of Bohemia. It was only in France that political conditions rendered Paris—already a capital city by the early thirteenth century—unpopular to Charles VII (1422–61) and Louis XI (1461–83), thereby locating the French court in a series of towns and castles along the Loire (Tours, Loches, Chinon, Amboise). The châteaux of the French Renaissance thus have their origins in the Hundred Years War and the Anglo-Burgundian occupation of Paris (1420–36). Elsewhere, with permanent buildings close to the great Departments of State (Chancery, *Hofgericht*, Exchequer, *Chambre des Comptes, Rekken kammer*) princely administrations now had power-centres within an essentially urban setting.

The consequences of these developments were far-reaching. The nobilities of western European states found that they needed to maintain a presence at court either in person or by proxy. To hold a town house as well as a rural castle was not alien to some nobilities (such as those of Flanders or Holland), but others were obliged to establish urban *hôtels* in order to make their presence felt at court. The town residences of the dukes of Burgundy, Bourbon, or Orléans at Paris in the later fourteenth century, or of great English magnates in London, such as John of Gaunt's Savoy palace, pointed to the fact that seigneurial castles in remote rural settings were no longer a sufficient guarantee of political power. One should not exaggerate the significance of this change, because the elaborate building works of Robert II, count of Artois (d. 1302), Jean, duke of Berry (d. 1416), or Ralph, Lord Cromwell (d. 1455), at their own castles of Hesdin, Mehun-sur-Yèvre, or Tattershall

respectively demonstrated the continuing significance of territorial power. But gravitation towards the rulers' court, especially
at a period of diminishing returns from agricultural rents and
sometimes dramatic decline in the purchasing power of money,
was a marked tendency among many nobilities in the west.
Pensions, court sinecures, and offices (butler, bread-bearer, cup-
bearer, horn-bearer, or carving squire) all played an important
part in bolstering noble incomes (as in France, with a pension
list of about 700 names by 1483) or in the exercise of some
degree of control by princes over their nobles (as in Burgundy
or the German principalities). The court and the courtier were
to be among the most durable legacies of the later Middle Ages
to the so-called 'new monarchies' of the Renaissance.

Old and New Dynasties

Many ruling houses of this period shared a tendency towards
natural extinction in the male line or more violent replacement
by other dynasties. In 1254 the last Hohenstaufen, Conrad
IV, was killed and an interregnum began in the Holy Roman
Empire which was to last until the election of Count Rudolf of
Habsburg as king of the Romans in 1273. Even then, his childless death in 1291, the unprecedented deposition of his successor Adolf of Nassau in 1298, and the murder of Albert I of
Habsburg in 1308 merely increased the dynastic instability of
the German Empire. It was left to the house of Luxemburg
to make the best of the unpropitious situation bequeathed to
them by the Interregnum, and they looked increasingly to their
kingdom of Bohemia for the power and support which their
imperial title failed to give them. Only in 1438, with the
election of Albert II as emperor, did the Austrian house of
Habsburg unite together the Hungarian, Bohemian, and German
crowns. In 1421 Albert had married the heiress of the last
Luxemburg emperor, Sigismund, king of Hungary (1410–37)
and the latter's death without male heirs ensured the reality of
an Austro-Hungarian union. From this dynastic arrangement
was born the empire which was to last until 1806, first welded
together (not without acute set-backs and difficulties) by the

GERMAN EMPERORS: HOUSE OF HABSBURG

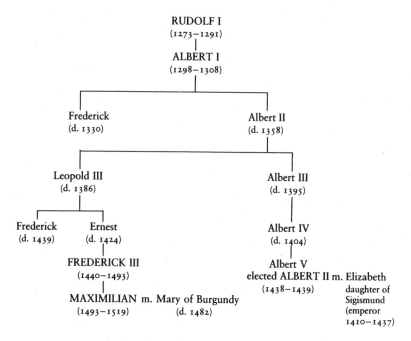

Habsburg Emperors Frederick III (1440–93) and Maximilian I (1493–1519).

Yet among dynasties not subject to election by the seven princes of the empire, whose powers were fixed in the Golden Bull of 1356, a similar pattern of rise and fall can be detected. The old Austrian ruling house of Babenberg died out in 1246 and the last of the Árpád kings of Hungary died without heirs in 1301. In the kingdom of Bohemia, the last of the Přemysl line (d. 1306) left a daughter Elisabeth, whose marriage to John of Luxemburg (the blind ruler who was to die fighting for the French at Crécy in 1346) ensured the Luxemburg succession there. In France, the death without a direct male heir of Charles IV (1328) left the ancient Capetian dynasty which had held the French crown since 987 without a successor. The

GERMAN EMPERORS: HOUSE OF LUXEMBURG

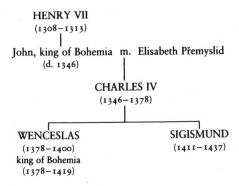

HENRY VII
(1308–1313)

John, king of Bohemia m. Elisabeth Přemyslid
(d. 1346)

CHARLES IV
(1346–1378)

WENCESLAS
(1378–1400)
king of Bohemia
(1378–1419)

SIGISMUND
(1411–1437)

acceptance by the peers of France of Philip, count of Valois, as King Philip VI was a breach in continuity which was soon to be exploited by rivals, above all by Edward III of England. In Poland, the last of the Piasts, Casimir the Great, died leaving no son to succeed him in 1370, and another western dynasty—the house of Anjou—moved into both Hungary and Poland through marriage alliances, thereby creating the temporary union of the two crowns under Louis the Great of Anjou (d. 1382). Yet the joint rulership did not endure, and Hungary and Poland went their separate ways—one to Sigismund, the other to Ladislas, the heathen Lithuanian ruler who, converted to Christianity, preserved the integrity of the Catholic Slav kingdom of Poland against the incursions of the Germans, above all of the Teutonic Order. Lastly, England witnessed the violent deposition of four kings during the period 1327–1485: the Plantagenet crown was usurped by the Lancastrians in 1399, while their successors the Yorkists (1461–85) were replaced by the more durable house of Tudor. To talk of a European crisis in hereditary monarchy would be an exaggeration, but the striking fact remains that most of the ruling houses of the later Middle Ages were of recent origin, whether they were formed by ancient dynasties enlarging their territorial power or by more modest houses, newly elevated to regal status.

The relative insecurity and instability of dynastic politics, based upon the unpredictable consequences of usurpations, marriage alliances, and the procreation of male heirs, led to the emergence of important distinctions between the person of the ruler and the impersonal office or dignity of kingship. Some of the increasingly elaborate ceremony and display which surrounded rulers at this time stemmed from this notion, and the idea of an impersonal 'crown' which survived the vagaries of dynastic fortune and the removal of mortal kings from power gained added emphasis. Possession of the insignia of kingship or princely rule was of the highest importance—hence Edward I of England's capture of the crown of the Welsh princes and the ceremonial stone of Scone from the Scottish kings, or the purchase by Matthias Corvinus (1458–90) of St Stephen's crown, the sacred symbol of Hungarian kingship, from the Emperor Frederick III. Charles the Bold of Burgundy (1467– 77) sought a crown, but had to be content with an archducal hat.

France and Burgundy

The two most significant developments in western European politics at this period were first, the rise of the Capetian house of France to the zenith of its prestige and power under Louis IX (1226–70) and secondly, the emergence of a new political and dynastic force which lay between France and the German Empire—the Valois house of Burgundy (1363–1477). Under Philip Augustus (1180–1223) the Capetian monarchy of France had extended its territorial and jurisdictional boundaries to embrace Normandy (1204), and much of the Languedoc began to be more closely subjected to Capetian influence. The Albigensian Crusades, initiated by Louis IX against the Cathar heretics, led to a political as well as religious dominance of northern Frenchmen over the south. With the extinction of the old Raymondin counts of Toulouse who had governed much of the Languedoc, Louis IX created a great *apanage*, or prin-

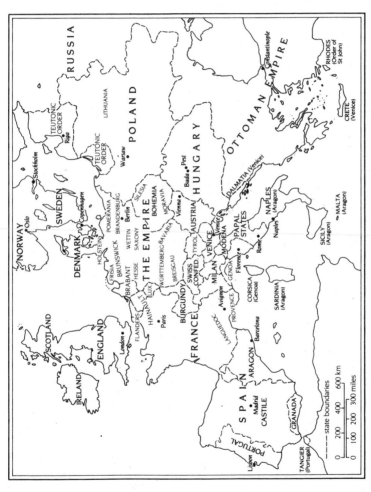

THE STATES OF THE WEST IN THE LATER MIDDLE AGES

cipality, for his brother Alphonse de Poitiers (d. 1271), on whose death the county of Toulouse reverted to the crown. The success of Louis IX was partly attributable to his personal qualities—intense devotional piety, a concern for justice and peace, and his reputation as a crusader and exponent of the sanctity of kingship. One might trace the emergence of what has been called a 'religion of monarchy' to his reign, a theme taken up and inflated by Philip IV (the Fair). But Louis IX had been well served by his own relatives, by a bureaucracy which was increasingly staffed by laymen, and by the French Church. He also profited in large measure from the collapse of Hohenstaufen power. It was to the kings of France, rather than the German emperors, that men increasingly looked for moral leadership, sanctification of secular power, and impartial arbitration of their conflicts.

These themes were expressed at their fullest state of development under Philip the Fair (1285–1314). Louis IX was canonized as a result of French pressure upon Pope Boniface VIII in 1297 and he cast a heavy shadow over Philip's reign. Yet the assertions of Philip and his advisers did not meet with universal acclaim. The relative harmony of Franco-papal relations under St Louis and Philip III (1270–85) was ruptured by the outbreak of a great quarrel (or series of quarrels) with Boniface VIII between 1294 and 1303. The issue was fundamentally one of a secular ruler's right to tax the clergy within his kingdom and was not confined to France. Edward I of England encountered similar problems in the 1290s. However, the Franco-papal conflict was characterized by a virulent intensity that had probably not been seen since the struggles of Pope Gregory VII and the Emperor Henry IV in the late eleventh century. The propaganda which issued from both sides—Boniface VIII's fulminations and resounding statements of papal claims in the bull *Unam Sanctam* (1302) or Philip the Fair's attacks upon the pope's universal sovereignty, doctrinal orthodoxy, and capacity to undertake inquiries into heresy—demonstrated that the role formerly played by the German emperor as champion and leader of the secular powers of Christendom had, at least temporarily, passed to the French

KINGS OF FRANCE: CAPETIAN AND VALOIS

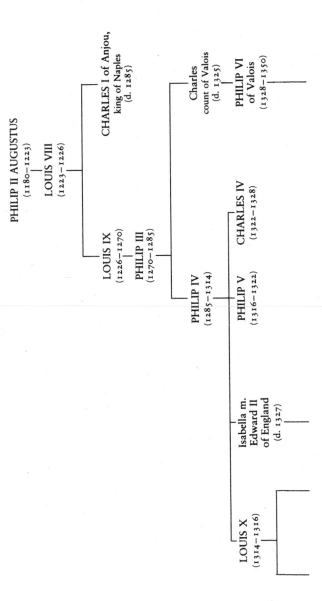

PHILIP II AUGUSTUS
(1180–1223)

LOUIS VIII
(1223–1226)

CHARLES I of Anjou,
king of Naples
(d. 1285)

LOUIS IX
(1226–1270)

PHILIP III
(1270–1285)

Charles
count of Valois
(d. 1325)

PHILIP VI
of Valois
(1328–1350)

PHILIP IV
(1285–1314)

PHILIP V
(1316–1322)

CHARLES IV
(1322–1328)

Isabella m.
Edward II
of England
(d. 1327)

LOUIS X
(1314–1316)

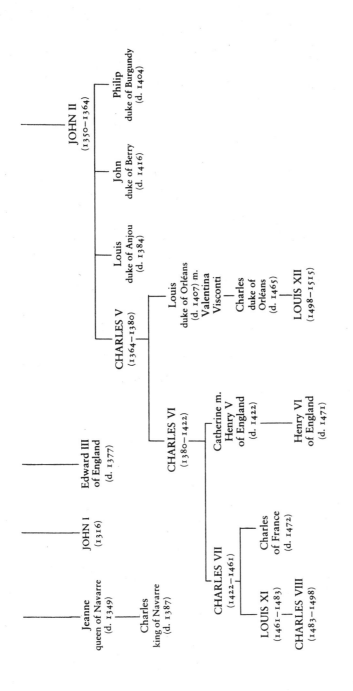

JOHN II
(1350–1364)

Philip
duke of Burgundy
(d. 1404)

John
duke of Berry
(d. 1416)

Louis
duke of Anjou
(d. 1384)

CHARLES V
(1364–1380)

Louis
duke of Orléans
(d. 1407) m.
Valentina
Visconti

Charles
duke of Orléans
(d. 1465)

LOUIS XII
(1498–1515)

Jeanne
queen of Navarre
(d. 1349)

Charles
king of Navarre
(d. 1387)

JOHN I
(1316)

Edward III
of England
(d. 1377)

CHARLES VI
(1380–1422)

Catherine m.
Henry V
of England
(d. 1422)

Henry VI
of England
(d. 1471)

CHARLES VII
(1422–1461)

Charles
of France
(d. 1472)

LOUIS XI
(1461–1483)

CHARLES VIII
(1483–1498)

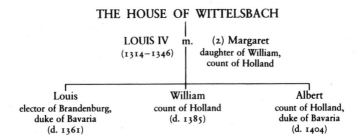

THE HOUSE OF WITTELSBACH

LOUIS IV m. (2) Margaret
(1314–1346) daughter of William,
count of Holland

Louis
elector of Brandenburg,
duke of Bavaria
(d. 1361)

William
count of Holland
(d. 1385)

Albert
count of Holland,
duke of Bavaria
(d. 1404)

crown. Advised and abetted by legal experts who were no longer clerics (such as Pierre Flote, Guillaume de Nogaret, Pierre Dubois, and Guillaume de Plaisians) and who thus owed nothing to the papacy, Philip the Fair was in effect responsible for the demise of Boniface VIII and his subsequent prosecution for alleged heresy. A violent assault on the papal palace at Anagni in 1303 by French and Italian troops under Nogaret and Boniface's enemies among the cardinals—the Colonna— led directly to the pope's death a few weeks later. After a brief interregnum, the election of Clement V (1305–14) opened up a new era in Franco-papal relations, and some of the former harmony was restored. The price was a greater degree of dependence by the popes upon the crown of France, although it is easy to exaggerate this tendency. Yet it cannot be denied that the authority and stature of the medieval papacy had been gravely threatened and compromised by the events of Philip the Fair's reign. In *his* conflict with a secular ruler—the Emperor Louis IV of Wittelsbach (1314–46)—Pope John XXII (1316– 34) found the legacy of Boniface VIII's pontificate difficult to overcome.

The end of the Capetian line in 1328 abruptly terminated a remarkable example of dynastic continuity. Philip VI of Valois (1328–50) was essentially a weak monarch, selected by his princely peers on principles not so very different from those held by the German princes of the empire, and faced rival claimants to his throne. The Anglo-French war of 1337–1453 was brought nearer by the Valois accession to the Capetian throne. Yet the French monarchy also had internal problems in the fourteenth century. Not least of these was the formation of quasi-independent principalities under the rule of great princes. The territorial lordships held by the dukes of Orléans, Bourbon, Brittany, or Anjou, and by the counts of Foix or Armagnac formed princely 'states' profiting from the disputed succession to the French throne and from the crises which befell the Valois monarchy—the disaster at Poitiers (1356) when King John II (the Good) was captured by Edward, the Black Prince, or the madness of Charles VI after 1392. Signs of revival in the monarchy's authority and prestige were clearly evident, however, under Charles V (1364–80) and it is from his reign, as well as Philip the Fair's, that much of the political theory, iconography, and ritual of kingship in later medieval France stems. The elaboration of the coronation ceremony, for instance, as set out in the *Coronation Book of Charles V* (1365), or of the king's entries into his principal towns, stressed the theatrical qualities of monarchy and the significance of public appearances, costume, and insignia which were exclusive to the king alone. Under Charles V, the image of French monarchy certainly underwent changes. The king was presented to his subjects not only as a quasi-sacerdotal figure, directly descended from Charlemagne, and endowed with thaumaturgic power to heal diseases such as scrofula, but as an educated, literate, and astute individual. Christine de Pisan's posthumous *Livre des faits et mœurs* of Charles V, called 'the Wise', exemplified this development. With his much-advertised preference for diplomacy rather than warfare, his exploitation of the sovereign rights of the French crown to hear appeals from all its subjects against the judgements of the princes and their courts, and his patronage of letters and the arts, Charles V has sometimes been seen as a prototype of those 'princes of the Renaissance' who emerged at a later period. But much of his reign was devoted to the construction of an edifice of government, partly inherited from his predecessors, to military and financial reforms, and to diplomatic alliances (with the empire and with Castile) which were to set the monarchy upon a firmer footing.

It is perhaps no coincidence that internal tensions developed within the French kingdom after Charles V's death in 1380 that were to divide the higher nobility and play into the hands of the enemies of the house of Valois. The endowment by John the Good of his youngest son Philip with the duchy of Burgundy in 1363 was to create problems unforeseen by that monarch. From its relatively minor beginnings, as an *apanage* of the French crown, the duchy of Burgundy was to form the kernel of a European power-bloc ultimately hostile to that crown. Once again, marriage alliances, purchases, and conquests combined to create the Burgundian 'state' or, more accurately, the Burgundian lands or dominions. The term 'empire' might be more appropriate for this conglomeration of territories built up between 1363 and 1477. The marriage of Philip of Valois, later called Philip the Bold, duke of Burgundy, to Margaret, daughter of Louis de Mâle, count of Flanders and Artois in 1369 was to change the fortunes of the house decisively. On the death of his father-in-law in 1384 Philip entered upon the Flemish inheritance which held the key to Burgundian aggrandisement in the fifteenth century. He also became count of Burgundy (an imperial fief) thus amalgamating his southern lands. Burgundian history is a classic example of what German historians have aptly called *Hausmachtpolitik* in which the dukes outdid their neighbours and rivals in gathering territories and displaying their wealth. In principle there was nothing peculiar about Burgundian methods of territorial and dynastic expansion. What set the Valois dukes apart from their contemporaries was the immense wealth which their Netherlandish lands brought to them. By the reign of Philip the Good, the ducal lands in the Low Countries accounted for well over 70 per cent of his income, while the old Burgundian duchy provided nobles and lawyers to serve the duke rather than financial resources. The tendency among all principalities towards autonomy at this time could only be furthered by Burgundian access to credit facilities, urban wealth, and tolls on trade and merchandise in the Low Countries. Without the textile industries, maritime commerce, river traffic, and banking houses of the Netherlands the house of Burgundy might never have achieved its dominance in north-west Europe.

THE VALOIS DUKES OF BURGUNDY

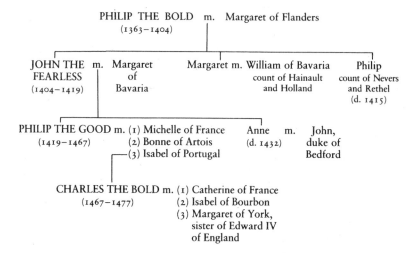

PHILIP THE BOLD   m.   Margaret of Flanders
(1363–1404)

JOHN THE   m.   Margaret   Margaret m. William of Bavaria   Philip
FEARLESS   of   count of Hainault   count of Nevers
(1404–1419)   Bavaria   and Holland   and Rethel
                                                                                    (d. 1415)

PHILIP THE GOOD m. (1) Michelle of France   Anne   m.   John,
(1419–1467)   (2) Bonne of Artois   (d. 1432)   duke of
                        ┌─(3) Isabel of Portugal   Bedford

CHARLES THE BOLD m. (1) Catherine of France
(1467–1477)   (2) Isabel of Bourbon
                        (3) Margaret of York,
                            sister of Edward IV
                            of England

Although the dukes had sprung from the Valois house of France and remained peers of the French kingdom, an increasing detachment from their parent dynasty can be observed. The loosening of the bonds which tied them to Valois France was greatly assisted by the murder of John the Fearless (1404–19) by partisans of the Valois dauphin Charles on the bridge at Montereau during a diplomatic interview. John's son, Philip, was obliged to renounce all loyalty to the dauphin and by the time he succeeded to the French crown in 1422 the house of Burgundy had moved into the camp of his rival, the infant Henry VI of England and his regent John, duke of Bedford. Burgundian alliance with England thus furthered ducal independence of Valois France and, after his reconciliation with the dauphin (now Charles VII) at Arras in 1435, Philip the Good never regained the central position in French politics held by his father. While professing to be a 'good, true, and loyal Frenchman', Philip's political energies were absorbed by the government of turbulent subjects in Flanders, by dynastic

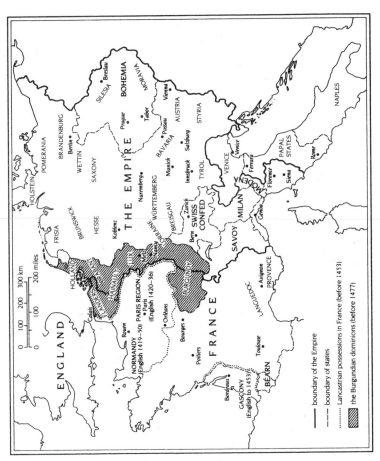

FRANCE AND THE GERMAN EMPIRE, C.1450

boundary of the Empire
boundary of states
Lancastrian possessions in France (before 1453)
the Burgundian dominions (before 1477)

expansion in the Low Countries, and by intervention in the politics of the German Empire. The annexation of the duchy of Brabant and the counties of Hainault, Holland, Namur, and Luxemburg between 1428 and 1443 began a series of Burgundian incursions into areas which lay in the Franco-imperial borderland. Philip's son, Charles the Bold, carried these ventures to their conclusion by invading Alsace-Lorraine (1474–7) and attempting to secure a marriage alliance between his house and that of Habsburg so that he might succeed to the empire or, at the very least, carve out a kingdom for himself between France and imperial territory to the east of the Rhine.

There was a chance of success for Charles's ambitions and grandiose schemes because some German princes were not averse to the concept of a Burgundian kingdom, held by a ruler unlikely to interfere with their autonomous regimes and well able to support himself from his own resources. The contrast with the shabby and penurious Emperor Frederick III could hardly have been more marked. But Charles the Bold possessed little of his father's political tact and diplomatic caution. He succeeded in alienating many of the towns which bolstered his rule, provoked René II of Lorraine into an alliance with the Swiss Confederation which led to Charles's defeat and death at Nancy in 1477, and lost the financial support of the Medici bank at Bruges. The re-creation of a 'middle kingdom' on the pattern of the ancient Carolingian kingdom of Lotharingia proved impossible in fifteenth-century political conditions. There were too many obstacles and entrenched interests opposed to Charles. Not least was the hostility of Louis XI of France (1461–83), of great towns such as Strasbourg, allied to the city of Berne and the Swiss *Eidgenossen*, as well as resistance from Lorraine and its allies in the German Empire. Charles was killed in battle and his lands were divided between the Habsburgs and the kingdom of France. The marriage of his daughter Mary and the future Emperor Maximilian I ensured that the Netherlandish territories (which had attained a certain degree of autonomy by 1477) passed into imperial hands while the southern Burgundian duchy reverted to the French crown in 1482. The political shape and structure of early modern Europe, in which the United Provinces of the Netherlands were to play so significant a role, was therefore largely determined by fifteenth-century dynasticism.

The Hundred Years War

The ever-present nature of warfare in the later Middle Ages was much commented upon by contemporaries. With pardonable exaggeration, the inhabitants of the Welsh March or of certain southern French dioceses, such as Cahors, could complain that they had seen nothing but war in their lifetimes. War was endemic in one form or another. In many parts of Germany the prevalence of private warfare, stemming from feuds between noble families or urban factions, was recognized by the formal institution known as the *Fehde*. This form of regulated private war—which inevitably became uncontrollable—was paralleled in parts of southern France by outbreaks of feuding between private parties, often taking the form of *cavalcate* or mounted raids, conducted by one noble family and their adherents against another. The most notable and protracted of these was the great rivalry and conflict between the south-western houses of Foix and Armagnac, which began in 1290 and ended only in the second half of the fifteenth century. But such feuds were to be found, normally of a less protracted nature, among most northern European nobilities—from the gentry 'gangs' of fourteenth-century England to more serious feuding in areas of extreme political fragmentation such as the Pyrenean frontier of France, or the German province of Westphalia. Some of these conflicts assumed proportions of more general significance. The clashes of the houses of Armagnac-Orléans with that of Burgundy in the 1390s, or the great quarrel between those of York and Lancaster in England, elevated feud into the arena of national politics. Yet even apparently insignificant regional affairs could erupt into more general warfare, such as the breaches of the peace in the south-western French province of the Agenais which led to an Anglo-French war in 1324–5.

Historians have inevitably concentrated on the large-scale 'national' conflicts of this period; above all on the so-called Hundred Years War between England and France (1337–1453). In some senses the conflict was part of a more protracted rivalry between the two kingdoms which began in the Norman and Angevin period as a result of the tenure of continental lands by the kings of England. By 1259 Henry III in effect held only the duchy of Aquitaine within the realm of France and in that year the situation was formalized by the treaty of Paris in which he became a vassal of the French king, to whom liege homage was due. It was an acknowledgement that the Angevin Empire—Normandy, Maine, Anjou, Poitou, and Aquitaine—was now a very truncated version of its twelfth-century precursor and it has been argued that these terms could lead only to war. How could a ruler who was a king in his own right act as the vassal of another king in his continental lands? The problem was not, however, insoluble by peaceful means and more or less successful attempts were made by both sides to prevent the outbreak of war. Despite the short-term conflicts of 1294–8 and 1324–5, Anglo-French relations had developed a *modus vivendi* which depended upon marriage alliances between the ruling dynasties, a readiness to seek judicial and diplomatic means to resolve disputes, and a willingness in the Capetian kings of France to compromise over the precise form of the English king's homage for his southwestern French domains. Some of the Capetians were very accommodating over these questions and even Philip the Fair, who had gone to war with Edward I of England in 1294 over Gascon and maritime issues, agreed in 1303 to a reconciliation between the two powers, sealed by a marriage. War could be ruinously expensive, as both sides discovered to their cost between 1294 and 1303, especially when the theatre of operations widened to include Flanders as well as Aquitaine.

The loss of Normandy by King John in 1204 was perhaps the beginning of a process whereby the claims of the French crown to sovereignty over its kingdom were gradually translated from theory into reality. The Plantagenet dominions on the Continent became more Anglo-centric as the centre of

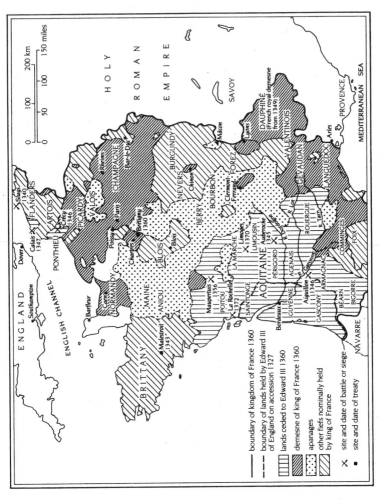

THE HUNDRED YEARS WAR (*a*) IN THE FOURTEENTH CENTURY

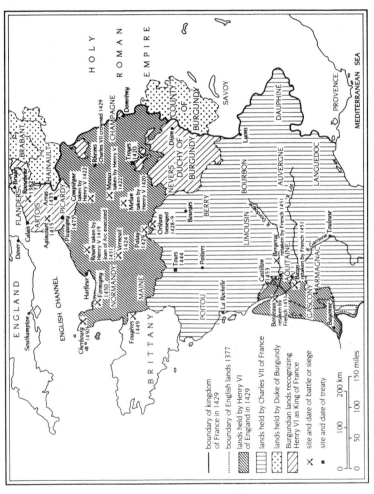

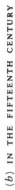

(b) IN THE FIFTEENTH CENTURY

boundary of kingdom
of France in 1429

boundary of English lands 1377

lands held by Henry VI
of England in 1429

lands held by Charles VII of France

lands held by Duke of Burgundy

Burgundian lands recognizing
Henry VI as King of France

X   site and date of battle or siege

■   site and date of treaty

0   50   100   150 miles

0   100   200 km

gravity of their rulers' activity naturally shifted towards their English kingdom. Aquitaine under Edward I was subject to English administrative procedure, such as accountability to the English Exchequer and the hearing of Gascon petitions in parliament, and the great act of administrative reform which the king issued, as duke of Aquitaine, in 1289 formed the basis of the duchy's administration for the rest of the Middle Ages. It would be a distortion of the evidence, however, to see French policy as a consistent and unrelenting desire to expel the Plantagenets from Aquitaine. The degree of control which the Capetians might exercise over English foreign affairs, however slight, was a valuable asset, and it was often in the best interests of the French crown to let an intermediate lord, such as the duke of Aquitaine, attempt to govern an area renowned for its turbulence and intractability. Much the same could be said for the county of Flanders, where the great towns were often in a state of war with the count, who sought external aid from France and England in turn. But the problems which had to some extent been overcome by the Capetians were exacerbated by the accession of Philip VI of Valois in 1328. As a result of his father's marriage to Isabella, daughter of Philip the Fair, Edward III of England possessed a claim to the French throne. None of his Plantagenet pre-decessors had had quite so close a kinship with the ruling house of France. It was the crisis of the Capetian succession which enabled Edward, fiercely supported by his mother, to lay claim to the French crown and, by declaring Philip of Valois a usurper in 1340, to cut the feudal connection between England and France once and for all.

From the time of Edward's own betrothal in 1326 to Philippa, daughter of William III, count of Hainault, rather than a princess of the house of France, English policy abroad had begun to change. Alliances were sought, as Edward I had sought them in 1294–7, with the princes of the Low Countries and north Germany, but these were to be based upon Edward III's claim to the French throne rather than on his position as a wronged vassal of Philip IV. The means of attack were very similar, but the pretext was different. By claiming the French crown, Edward effectively removed one source of Anglo-French tension at a stroke. Appeals from his subjects in Aquitaine to the Paris parlement (the supreme appellate jurisdiction of the French crown) were outlawed, because any such appeal would be to seek justice from a usurper. No longer could ducal authority in Aquitaine be undermined by the solicitation and encouragement of such appeals, as appears to have been the policy of Philip the Fair before the Anglo-French war of 1294–1303. There were willing supporters of Edward's claim both outside France and within its boundaries. The Flemings, especially the men of Ghent, saw his assumption of the title in 1340 as a vindication of their own claim to be free from the authority of their pro-French count, Louis de Nevers, and there were nobles within France (such as Charles 'the Bad', king of Navarre (1349–87) or the Gascon counts of Armagnac) who welcomed the choice of allegiance offered them by the Plantagenet–Valois rivalry for the throne. Local feuds could be prosecuted in the name of one side or another in the greater conflict, and such houses as those of Foix or Armagnac gained much from the lieutenancies which they held from either side.

In many areas of France, as in certain parts of Germany, the fourteenth century was the age of mercenary companies and *Raubritter*. Yet it would be an exaggeration to speak of 'anarchy' or of the total dislocation of French society at this time. Fourteenth- and fifteenth-century armies possessed only limited capacity for destruction and devastation, and much of the damage inflicted on the countryside by the Hundred Years War was very localized, confined to areas close to the main roads along which invading armies passed. More generally damaging were the private wars (as in Germany), or the subjection of an area to ransoming by a garrison of mercenaries or *routiers*, who in effect preyed upon the inhabitants of regions such as the marches of Brittany, Poitou, and Périgord. Peace between the two kingdoms spelt disaster for some areas: the demobilization of troops after the Anglo-French treaty of Brétigny-Calais (1360) unleashed companies of unemployed mercenaries upon the countryside. Some solution to the problem was found in expeditions to Spain or Italy, but the plague of the *routiers*, succeeded in the fifteenth century by that of the *écorcheurs*, was not effectively solved until the creation by Charles VII of a French standing army between 1445 and 1448. Even then, the crown found it difficult to enforce a monopoly over the raising and maintenance of troops in the kingdom, and noble leagues such as the Public Weal (1465) or the 'Guerre Folle' (1488) demonstrated the difficulty of exercising control over the *gens d'armes*. This could defeat even the most resolute of later medieval regimes. Warfare waged abroad, especially the Italian campaigns begun by Charles VIII in 1494, probably contributed most to the process whereby the nobility of France and their military following came to see the crown as the primary focus of their loyalty.

Yet the Valois monarchy emerged victorious from the English war in 1453. In the fifteenth century a war of raids, or *chevauchées*, gave way under Henry V (1413–22) to one of conquest and occupation which the English war effort was unable to support. Edward III's war had been based upon plundering expeditions of relatively short duration. The only strong-point which experienced English occupation (and colonization) on a permanent footing in the fourteenth century was the town and March of Calais (1347). With Henry V's second Norman campaign (1417) the war began a new and far more ambitious phase. To conquer and hold down not only Normandy but all France then subject to 'Charles, who calls himself dauphin', exiled to Bourges after 1418, proved beyond the resources of the Lancastrian crown and its Franco-Burgundian allies. Financial insolvency does much to explain the ultimate Lancastrian defeat, but the defection of Philip the Good of Burgundy in 1435, as well as the moral superiority achieved by the Valois monarchy after the success of Joan of Arc's mission to have Charles VII crowned and anointed as 'true king of France' at Rheims in 1429, must also figure prominently in any analysis. But the recovery was gradual—it was not until twenty-two years after Joan's execution at Rouen in 1431 that the last English possession in France (with the exception of Calais) fell to Valois troops. There was resistance to French sovereignty in Aquitaine and fear of subjection to French taxation—the *aides, taille,* and *gabelle*—which provided the means whereby Charles VII was able to recover Normandy and Aquitaine. But the victory over the English in 1453 undoubtedly bolstered the international standing of the Valois monarchy and Louis XI, despite his early mistakes and over-complex intrigues, was able to build on the foundations laid in his father's reign. Between 1453 and 1500 a number of great principalities reverted to or were annexed by the French crown—Burgundy, Provence, and Brittany were brought into a much closer relationship with the ruling house through marriage and conquest. The kingdom of France had largely achieved the form in which it was to endure under the *ancien régime* by the end of the fifteenth century. The war with England was to some extent the anvil upon which the identity of early modern France was forged.

War, as has been observed, was costly in material as well as human terms. The Anglo-French war of 1294–8 cost the English £360,000 sterling and the French at least 1,730,000 *livres tournois* (£432,500 sterling). Periods of inflation and monetary debasement often coincided with those of most intensive warfare, such as the inflationary spiral of 1180–1220 which afflicted the Angevin monarchy of England, or the acute monetary problems of 1290–1310 which afflicted both England and France. Military costs—of equipment, fortification, horses, armour, and supplies—increased markedly during these periods and it was more costly to put an army in the field or to conduct a siege in the fifteenth century than it had been a century earlier. Technical improvements in armour, castle-building, and the advent of firearms and artillery contributed greatly to this rise of military costs. In 1470 Louis XI of France spent 928,000 *livres* on the army and artillery from a total budget of 1,854,000 *livres,* while his father, it was estimated, had spent only about half that sum. In the German Empire the defence of the eastern frontier against the incursions of the Ottoman Turks (who had defeated a western crusading army at Nicopolis (1396) and successfully taken the city of Constantinople in 1453) absorbed Habsburg revenues, especially under Maximilian I (1493–1519). The Hussite wars brought war and devastation to many parts of central Europe and defence against the fanatical armies raised by the Bohemian heretics was a primary preoccupation of both the Emperor Sigismund and many German princes before the Hussite extremists were crushed by the more moderate nobility at Lipany in 1434. The different regions of northern Europe came to terms with endemic warfare, and societies that were particularly badly affected had developed means to combat its worst effects, such as the *Landfriede* of Germany or the local truces of southern France. War was a terrible affliction to the peasantry but it was the nobility's *raison d'être*. The resilience with which certain regions (Bordelais, Quercy, Lower Normandy), however, emerged from the damaging effects of endemic warfare is striking and the rebuilding of villages, repopulation of the countryside, and immigration of labour must be set against an excessively gloomy picture of fifteenth-century rural society.

Plague and its Effects

We must also consider the devastating effects of epidemics and sudden demographic change. The great age of northern European demographic expansion was coming to an end by the early fourteenth century. There is some evidence for population decline from the 1290s onwards—vacant agricultural holdings, a scarcity of tenants, cessation in new town foundation, and rural depopulation in areas affected by warfare—but the European harvest failures and famine of 1315–17 are normally taken to mark the beginning of a period of economic contraction. There was recovery in some regions and the demographic crisis of the later Middle Ages came only in 1348–9, when bubonic plague struck most of western Europe, carrying off something in the region of a third of its inhabitants. Some areas were extremely badly affected, and towns and religious communities of monks and friars bore a particularly heavy burden, but there were apparently pockets, such as the kingdom of Bohemia, which largely escaped both the Black Death and subsequent epidemics in the 1360s and 1370s. Whatever their local incidence, epidemics as virulent as these inevitably had a profound impact on later medieval society. Precise figures are hard to establish and difficult to interpret, but a general European death-rate of about 35 per cent would lead to substantial depopulation of rural areas, a dearth of labour in both town and countryside, and a redistribution of wealth among those who survived. The gaps in the ranks had to be filled and the period 1350–1400 saw a series of violent reactions to the increased social mobility precipitated by the epidemics. Prospects of material improvement beckoned the artisan, unfree peasant, or urban pauper, and the frustration of these classes at their lot after the enactment of labour laws or the closing of ranks by urban oligarchies was vented in the popular risings of the period. The Jacquerie (1358), the Tuchinat of Southern France (1380s), the English Peasants' Revolt (1381), and the risings in maritime Flanders (1382–4) were not the product of organized collaboration among the excluded classes of northern Europe, but they seem to have had common origins in postplague economic and social conditions. All were suppressed, generally brutally, by the governing classes and only in Flanders did social conflict continue, fuelled by the quasi-independent stance of the three great towns, above all Ghent, towards their new Burgundian rulers.

Other classes of society besides the most unfortunate felt the impact of plague. Human distress took many forms, some extreme—such as the outbreak of self-flagellation which accompanied the penitential processions of the 1350s—others less spectacular, such as the devotional cults of St Sebastian and St Giles who were invoked as protectors from the terrors of the plague. The clergy suffered badly: the abbey of Saint-Martin at Tournai, for example, lost 80 per cent of its monks between 1348 and 1362. New ordinands had to be found to fill vacant benefices and bishops' ordination lists were often long in the second half of the century. But a problem of recruitment affected many areas of human activity, not merely the Church. Governments found soldiers harder to recruit, and their wages consequently rose, while apprentices, masons, and rural labourers appear to have benefited from the scarcity of both skilled and unskilled workers. The evident decrease in the size of armies and the increasing emphasis laid by governments on professionalism and expertise in their ranks, may also have some connection with the aftermath of the epidemics. It is notable that the largest English army (32,000 men) which sailed to France during the Hundred Years War was the force Edward III sent to besiege Calais in 1347, one year before the onset of the plague.

By 1420 the worst visitations of the disease were over and there was a discernible population increase in many European towns, especially in the densely urbanized regions of the Low Countries. By 1470, for example, over 45 per cent of the total estimated population of Holland and 36 per cent of Flanders, were urban dwellers, whereas only 10 per cent of the German emperor's subjects (excluding Hungary and Bohemia) lived in towns. Holland under the Valois dukes of Burgundy thus qualified for Fernand Braudel's appellation 'a modern, capitalist economy', while Flanders just failed to enter that privileged category. The effects of the Black Death must have played an important part in the early development of capitalism, opening up resources which had perhaps previously been more thinly spread to opportunistic and adventurous merchants and financiers such as the Fugger of Augsburg, the Stromer of Nuremberg, the Bladelin and Moreel of Bruges, or the de la Poles of Hull and the Braunches of King's Lynn. The Medici bank—successor to the bankrupted Bardi and Peruzzi—did not possess a monopoly over the provision of credit in northern Europe and indigenous banking houses and financial syndicates, such as the English Wool Staplers at Calais, secured a larger share of the money market. Great wealth could be amassed in the northern world after the crises of the mid-fourteenth century, but it was very unevenly distributed.

Popes, Heretics, and Friars

The later medieval papacy has often been seen as the shadow of a formerly vigorous institution. As papal claims to universal authority came under attack and contemporaries were increasingly struck by the worldliness and wealth of the popes and cardinals, it is tempting to speak of a 'decline of the medieval Church'. But later medieval popes and higher churchmen were no more worldly than some of their eleventh- and twelfth-century predecessors such as Odo of Bayeux or Ranulf Flambard. They were certainly highly educated men, well versed in theology and canon law, admirably fitted for the positions of authority and government which they occupied. It was not the quality or character of the Church's personnel which had changed for the worse, but the nature of the institutional Church itself. Since the aftermath of the Gregorian reforms popes had been obliged to devote an increasing proportion of their time to administrative and judicial tasks. Papal sovereignty was not only expressed in doctrinal statements, but also in the administration of justice, the issuing of judgements and arbitrations. An institution which lacked coercive force, which was highly dependent upon secular rulers to enforce its edicts and which could only establish an effective presence within the kingdoms and principalities of Europe by proxy, had necessarily to be headed by a lawyer-pope. The perils of electing a saintly hermit to the papal office were spelt out in 1294, when a divided conclave elected the recluse Pietro Morrone as Celestine V. His pontificate was a disaster, and he was forced to resign after four months.

Unworldly spirituality was thus no qualification for the supreme pontiff in the later Middle Ages. Popes might be personally ascetic and devout men, but their public lives resembled those of princes. What made their lives more difficult than they might otherwise have been was the rise of a cult of unworldly spirituality among both clergy and laity. As the Church became more temporal an institution, the quest for a purer, more apostolic expression of the Christian life became more intense. The pontificate of Innocent III (1198–1216) represented the summit of papal authoritarianism and the Fourth Lateran Council of 1215 laid down rules for the Church's conduct of its affairs and its relations with secular powers which were to determine much of its later medieval development. Under Innocent IV (1243—54) the fiscal apparatus of the Church was reformed and a larger number of benefices were reserved to the appointees of the pope and the Roman curia. The volume of business handled by the central offices of the Church, such as the *Camera Apostolica*, had increased substantially by the end of the thirteenth century and the hearing of appeals, the conduct of diplomacy, the reviewing of financial accounts, the appointment to benefices (often to kinsmen), and award of arbitrations represented a large part of the popes' and cardinals' activity.

It was thus hardly surprising that a reaction against the institutional Church set in. The way had to some extent been prepared by the establishment of a Cathar Church, organized into dioceses, in southern France in the later twelfth century. Catharism, or Albigensianism, was a dualist heresy of eastern origin, claiming that the Roman Church was a product of the forces of evil and that the 'true' faithful were holy men and women whom they called *perfecti* (*parfaits*) marked off from the rest of the world by their ascetic and holy lives. This was one of the first manifestations of a notion which took poverty as its doctrinal basis and which spread in different forms throughout western Christendom. To be poor was an attribute of true sanctity. Christ's Church, it was argued, should tread the road taken by the apostles, preferably barefooted, and mendicancy became one of the highest Christian virtues. To this was added evangelism. The recognition by Pope Honorius III of the order of Friars Minor, created by St Francis of Assisi (*c.*1181—1226), was an acknowledgement by the Church that the age of monastic withdrawal from the world had passed away and that a body was needed within the Church which would be both mendicant and evangelical. The needs of the laity, especially the urban laity, greatly increased by demographic expansion, were to be met by the new order of Franciscans. Unlike earlier orders of monks such as the Cistercians, the friars lived in houses set up in or very close to towns, addressing themselves to works of charity and preaching the Gospel, often in the open air. It was less easy to be a true mendicant in the streets of Bruges, or York, or Prague than in southern Europe, where climate favoured begging, and soon the Franciscans and their more intellectual brothers the Dominicans, or friars preacher, were comfortably settled in friaries throughout western Christendom. Here the rule of St Francis could not be properly observed and a destructive internal conflict developed within the Order between the 'conventuals' (who advocated the necessity of property) and the 'spirituals' (who urged the rule of absolute, apostolic poverty upon their fellow mendicants). This split within the Franciscans was symptomatic of a more general crisis.

In a society which was developing a profit economy, where the Church itself was a beneficiary, the carrying out of Christ's injunctions to the disciples concerning poverty was more difficult to implement. It was all the more striking to contemporary minds that Francis of Assisi, a rich merchant's son, should abandon all worldly goods and follow Christ. Among the wealthier and most worldly of the urban laity, the cult and patronage of religious poverty was well advanced. Hence the initial success of the friars—the Franciscans were seen to practise apostolic poverty, while the Dominicans preached, taught, lectured, and fought against heresy. St Dominic failed, however, to eradicate the Cathar faith by preaching in the Languedoc, and the first in a series of persecutions of heretics took place under the guise of a crusade between 1220 and 1240. These laid the foundations for the creation of the Dominican Inquisition, or Holy Office, which was to dominate the Church's attempt to control error and disbelief. Although Catharism had been severely damaged by the Albigensian Crusades, it was still deeply rooted in Languedocian society. The support given to its exponents by the nobility and its concentration in rural areas, such as the dioceses of Pamiers, Narbonne, and Carcassonne, marked it off from most other later medieval heresies which tended to be centred upon towns. By 1300, the last traces of Cathar heresy were revitalized for a time in the activities of the *parfait* Pierre Authier and his associates, burnt for heresy by the inquisition of Toulouse in 1310. The inquisitor of that province was the Dominican Bernard Gui, whose *Inquisitor's Manual* (written *c.*1320) provided a source of information, advice, and procedural guidance for his colleagues. In a sense, the Church had itself created the heresies of the later Middle Ages—not only by providing what was viewed as a scandal against which men might react, but by drawing up articles of accusation of a formalized kind and declaring those who subscribed to the beliefs contained in those articles to be heretics. The uniformity of belief and practice which inquisitorial records tend to reveal among the victims of prosecution might suggest that the Church was formulating propositions which gave a spurious consistency and coherence to disordered and inchoate beliefs. When interrogation under duress and the material inducements to inform upon suspected heretics offered to their associates and neighbours are also taken into account, the possibilities for abuse of inquisitorial procedure were obvious. Political, material, and other motives might colour the operations of the Inquisition—Joan of Arc was not the only victim of such distortions of the Holy Office's purpose.

The Papacy, the Hussites, and Lay Piety

A further object of criticism of the Church was its territorial location for most of the fourteenth century. The feuds among the Italian cardinals and their allies among the Roman nobility, with the Orsini and Colonna at their head, led to Pope Clement V (1305–14) seeking refuge at Avignon. Here the papacy hoped to render itself independent of the faction fights which had rent the conclave of cardinals and had led to the impasse from which the hapless Celestine V had emerged. Avignon was geographically remote from Rome, part of a papal fief in the Comtat Venaissin, but it was independent of any secular ruler and was well fitted to act as an entrepôt between Italy and northern Europe. The pope had left the seat of St Peter; he was now a Frenchman and the College of Cardinals was filled with his French kinsmen. Clement V and his two successors have been characterized as essentially subservient to French interests. His part in the affair of the Templars (1307–12) was not entirely creditable, but he did at least ensure that the possessions of the military order, declared heretical under pressure from Philip the Fair, passed to the Hospitallers, not into the hands of the French crown. But Clement V, John XXII (1316–34), and Benedict XII (1334–42) were not northern Frenchmen by origin. They came from the south of France: Clement was a Gascon, John was from Cahors, Benedict from Pamiers—all with connections among the southern French nobility rather than the court circle of northern France. The fact that there was no major Anglo-French conflict between 1303 and 1324 and 1326 and 1337 can partly be attributed to the vigilance of the Avignon popes, who dispatched mediators and legates to areas which they knew and (in Clement's case) loved well to appease feuds and reconcile disputes. It was under Clement VI (1342–52), formerly archbishop of Rouen and counsellor of Philip VI of France, that French interests began to dominate papal policy. Under Urban V (1362–70) very substantial concessions were made, especially in matters of finance, to the French crown at a time when it most needed papal support. By sanctioning the marriage of Philip the Bold and Margaret of Flanders, for example, in 1369 rather than giving a dispensation to one of Edward III's sons to marry her, Urban demonstrated to the English that the papacy was a partisan of Charles V of France. There was little respect for the French papacy, for political reasons, in many parts of Christendom.

The papal return to Rome under Gregory XI in 1378 brought no solution to the Church's problems. A body of cardinals opposed to the move from Avignon elected a rival pope and the western Church entered a period of schism which was to last until 1417. During that time various attempts were made to resolve the problems which had caused it, but it was left to a council of the Church to agree upon the election of Pope Martin V and to depose his rivals. The Conciliar Movement produced an important body of political theory and was to some extent an expression of a more general movement towards representative government in Europe as a whole. Conciliar theory, propounded at Pisa (1409), Constance (1414–17), and Basle (1431–49), was to influence later reform movements within the Roman Church but it was a spent force by 1440. The Church was manifestly not a democracy, it was not suited to government by a representative assembly, and both theological and political divisions among the conciliarists themselves gravely undermined the authority of the council. From this period of aberration in the history of the hierarchical Church emerged the Italian papacy of the Renaissance. This was firmly grounded on a temporal, territorial foundation in the papal state, largely recovered by military force and purchase under Martin V and deeply involved in the politics of the Italian peninsula. Yet the tribulations of the Church during the Avignonese period and the schism had some positive results. Ideas of reform were in the air and in England, France, and Germany reforming circles grew up inside the Church which were not without influence. Improved clerical education was undertaken in England under the aegis of the bishops, diocesan and provincial councils valiantly strove to check abuses in Germany, and the late fifteenth-century humanist reformers at Paris, such as Lefèvre d'Étaples, contributed to the Church's development as a many-faceted institution which comprehended a remarkable diversity of pastoral, intellectual, and devotional styles.

The Church had experienced two great shocks during the schism: the rise of the Wycliffite or Lollard heresy in England and the outburst of Hussitism in Bohemia. Both movements had certain beliefs in common, particularly upon the sacramental role of the clergy and the disendowment of the Church, but the eventual outcome of their activities was very different. Whereas the Wycliffite heresy lost the support of members of the ruling classes (the so-called 'Lollard Knights'), Hussitism was taken up and championed by many of the Bohemian nobility. Before 1414 the English nobility had certainly harboured and patronized Wycliffite clergy, but the association of Lollardy with political sedition by that date meant that members of the knightly class, although they had welcomed proposals for the disendowment of the Church, rejected Lollard beliefs. The rising led by Sir John Oldcastle deprived the movement of the support which was crucial to its survival as anything more than an underground sect, though influential among the middle and lower strata of society. Infiltration of the Church by Lollard priests was stopped and the severe penalties laid down in the statute *De haeretico comburendo* (1401) gave England the equivalent of continental procedures against heresy, although the English Church and secular government, rather than the papacy or the Dominicans, exercised firm control over them. In Bohemia, the beliefs held by Jan Hus, scholar and preacher, were subsumed in a movement of more far-reaching proportions. Bohemian opposition to the papacy had grown since Charles IV's alliance with the popes at Avignon in pursuit of his political schemes and objectives. Bohemia was brought more fully into the western Church through the use of Czech benefices to reward German ecclesiastics. This could only fan the flames of Bohemian national sentiment which, when allied to religious fervour kindled by evangelical preaching at the Bethlehem Chapel of Prague, broke out in extreme form after Hus's condemnation and execution at the Council of Constance (1415). The Hussite revolt was many things—a political protest against the Emperor Sigismund, a doctrinal statement of the laity's right to take communion in both kinds, and a nationalistic assault on German immigrants in both Church and State. It threw central Europe into confusion and created the only alternative Church since the Cathars, out of communion with Rome, which northern Europe was to know before the sixteenth-century Reformation.

The challenge flung by the Hussites in the face of the Roman Church extended beyond the borders of Bohemia. A mass of organized peasant and town levies, officered by Bohemian nobles and gentry such as the knight John Žižka, were unleashed into territories held by the Emperor Sigismund and the German princes. Attacks on Austria and Franconia were launched by the Hussite armies, plundering and pillaging as they went, and the crusading forces of Catholic Christendom under German nobles met defeat at the hands of this common soldiery, armed with hand-guns as well as pikes and crossbows in their war-wagons. Only with the defeat of the Taborite extremists, who had formed themselves into a communistic settlement on Mount Tabor, by the moderate Utraquist nobility in 1434 was the Hussite threat lifted. But the remnants of Hussite armies, ready to be hired by anyone in search of man-power, were scattered over central Europe and hardly con-tributed to its stability. Pope Martin V had viewed the spectacle of Bohemian revolt with considerable anxiety, preaching a crusade against the heretics in 1427, to which other western kingdoms and principalities were invited to contribute both men and money. England was particularly solicited by the papacy, for it had been the root, the pope wrote, of the pernicious heresy first planted by John Wycliffe and which had spread to infect the kingdom of Bohemia. But the monarchies of the west had other preoccupations and calls on their military and financial resources and a proposed English crusading army was diverted to the siege of Orléans in 1428. Popes might preach the crusade but, as was clear after the fall of Constantinople in 1453, the concerns of western rulers lay elsewhere. Dynasticism and the defence or acquisition of territory, rather than crusad-ing expeditions against Bohemian heretics or Turkish infidels, absorbed the diplomatic, military, and financial resources of the national monarchies and princely states of northern Europe.

Besides the more dramatic outbreaks of religious dissent, less spectacular forces were at work within the Church. The search for a more deeply personal relationship with God, mediated through the saints, was a common phenomenon in the later Middle Ages. Heretics, while seeking such a relationship, erred in the eyes of the Church because too often the clergy were eliminated or their significance greatly reduced as sacramental mediators between man and God. It was through the adminis-tration of the sacraments—of baptism, confession, absolution, and the Eucharist or mass—by ordained priests that the in-dividual and sinful layman was brought into a proper relation-ship with Christ's redemptive power. The reconciliation of tensions between the formal offices of the Church, especially the mass, and the desires and promptings of individual con-science and devotional fervour was not an easy task. But be-tween the extremes of dogmatic orthodoxy and heretical error lay more moderate forms of religious sentiment and behaviour. Among these one of the more important was the so-called *devotio moderna*, which had developed from modest beginnings in Holland in the late fourteenth century. Probably influenced initially by Rhineland devotional cults and by some of Meister Eckhardt's (d. 1327) teachings on the sanctity of the everyday and mundane, a Carthusian novice called Gerhard Groote (1340–84), who was ordained a deacon in 1380, established a community of brethren at Deventer. These Brethren and Sisters of the Common Life, as they came to be known, lived a communal existence, receiving lay people into their houses, and provided an excellent example of an attempt to channel lay piety into non-heretical, practical activities. One of the most important functions of the Brethren's houses was the production of books. Their inmates were scribes, bookbinders, and illuminators who formed veritable publishing houses for the production and dissemination of religious books, of which the house at Zwolle in north Holland was among the most noted. But houses were soon established in Westphalia and Württemberg. Lay piety, practical work, and evangelism by means of the written word combined to make the brethren exponents of a devotional life which had a certain realism about it.

The days of heroic monasticism, such as that of St Bernard's early Cistercians, were over and the Brethren of the Common Life demonstrated the extent to which the laity actively sought a place within a clerically dominated Church. Although the houses of the Brethren became increasingly clerical in composition during the later fifteenth century their influence extended far beyond their walls. Among the older religious orders within the Church there were indeed attempted reforms—of the Carmelites and Cistercians in particular—but the order which gained most later medieval support and endowment from laymen were the Carthusian brothers. In England the only new monastic foundations of any significance were Charterhouses—at London (1370), and Mountgrace in North Yorkshire (1396). The Carthusian monk was essentially a hermit, occupying his own cell or small house within the cloister, but meeting for a common meal on certain specified occasions. His major occupation, apart from prayer and meditation, came to be very similar to that of the Brethren of the Common Life: the production and composition of books. The works of Richard Rolle, Nicholas Love, or Denis the Carthusian were popular and widely disseminated in their time and lay predilection for saintly hermits was institutionalized by the Charterhouses. Anchorites and recluses proliferated, often on the lands of the secular nobility, and their absolute renunciation of the world commended itself to the wealthier sections of later medieval society. There was perhaps an element of vicarious asceticism or self-denial by proxy in all this and the penitential literature of the period (some of it composed by laymen) would support such an idea. In his *Livre de Seyntz Medicines* (1351) Henry, duke of Lancaster, wrote of his sins and of the many temptations put by the world in the way of the rich and powerful. Atonement for sin could take many forms—from the performance of personal penance to the endowment of a religious house, hospital, almshouse, or school—and the more practical tone of much later medieval lay piety suggests that the performance of good works was becoming increasingly important. Entry into paradise and remission from the pains of purgatory could be achieved in many ways and it is an indication of the varied and multiform character of lay piety that so many charitable acts were undertaken.

Popes might come and go, councils meet and disband, but the horizons of most inhabitants of northern Europe were bounded by their parish, collegiate, or cathedral church, in which all participated. Baptism was universal and obligatory, binding men and women together as the body of the faithful, not yet riven (outside Bohemia) by the doctrinal schism of the Reformation. But there were disturbing signs at the end of the Middle Ages that the traditional forms and institutions of the Roman Church were, unless reformed or adapted, insufficient to contain and satisfy the demands and aspirations of a more literate and educated laity.

Culture: the Visual Arts

Just as the later medieval Church has been described by historians in terms of decline and decay, so northern European culture in the period from *c*.1300 to *c*.1500 has been seen as an autumnal conclusion to the Middle Ages, over-ripe and beginning to rot after the spring and high summer of the twelfth and thirteenth centuries. Such an interpretation owes much to the great Dutch cultural historian Johan Huizinga, whose *Waning of the Middle Ages* (1919) painted a pessimistic picture of a civilization in decline. The seasonal metaphor—of a cultural spring, summer, and autumn—has not been much pursued by later historians, and rightly so. Unitary interpretations inspired, as Huizinga's was, by the philosophy of Hegel no longer dominate the writing of cultural history. It is to such themes as patronage of the visual arts, lay literacy and book-collecting, and the effects of changes in religious sentiment and sensibility that we must turn to characterize a 'culture' as rich and productive as this. Between 1200 and 1500 artistic and literary patronage by the laity, both noble and non-noble, played a fundamental part in producing the culture that Huizinga described but did not analyse.

A central theme of any study of northern European culture must be the rise and decline of Paris as a source and centre of artistic patronage. Under St Louis the building works undertaken by the king in the city and in the Île-de-France (such as the Sainte-Chapelle) brought masons, sculptors, and painters to work for the French court. In book production Paris came to be perhaps the most important city in northern Europe: its workshops produced great illuminators such as the Parisian Master Honoré, documented in French royal accounts, and his successor Jean Pucelle. St Louis's Bible (*c*.1250) was a characteristic product of this Parisian school of manuscript painting, carried on with a somewhat higher degree of representational realism by later illuminators such as Master Honoré. Paris had a thriving book trade, regulated largely by the university and its demands. As late as 1344, Richard de Bury, bishop of Durham and lover of books, could still describe the city as a 'worldly paradise' (*paradisium mundi*) for the bibliophile. The artists who illuminated these volumes—bibles, psalters, breviaries, Books of Hours, and secular romances—were generally laymen, not monks or clerks, and it is this laicization of book production which in large part determined its character. Books of Hours, for example, in which the canonical hours of the day (Mattins, Lauds, Vespers, and so on) were recorded, accompanied by prayers and liturgical rites according to various 'uses' (of Paris, Rouen, Sarum, or Utrecht, for example), largely escaped the surveillance and control of ecclesiastical authorities. They were composed and illustrated for lay people by lay people. Other liturgical books, of course, might be intended for the use of the clergy and conformed to certain prescribed rules, but there was also a market for highly decorated Bibles and psalters among the chaplains and confessors of the secular nobility. The Luttrell psalter (*c.*1340) is a good example of such a volume, with chivalric depiction of its patron and scenes of rural life at the base of each page. But the primacy of Paris as a great European storehouse of books and other works of religious art, such as altar-pieces or retables, began to wane by the later fourteenth century. There were political reasons for this, as well as causes more closely related to the history of art.

The rifts opened up within the higher French nobility by the Armagnac–Burgundian feud were to have an impact upon artistic patronage. With the death of Jean, duke of Berry, in 1416, the greatest Maecenas of the age was removed from the Parisian scene and the French capital was also adversely affected by the subsequent murder in 1419 of John the Fearless, duke of Burgundy. Philip the Good, unlike his father, very rarely resided in the city and Burgundian patronage of the visual arts turned increasingly towards sources within their Netherlandish dominions. 'French' art became distinct from 'Burgundian'—the Master of John, duke of Bedford, continued to work in Paris, but other towns, such as Rouen in Lancastrian France, and Tours or Bourges in Valois France, began to eclipse the capital as centres of illumination and book production. The Burgundian lands saw the growth of Bruges, Lille, Mons, and Utrecht as producers and exporters of illuminated books. It was from the Burgundian Netherlands and the territories adjoining them—Limburg and Guelders—that some of the most accomplished painters had come in the period before 1416. Artistic influences from the court of Charles IV at Prague also moulded the movement towards greater realism in painting which can be discerned from the 1380s onwards. The early panel portrait of Duke Rudolf of Austria (c.1365) reveals this Czech influence, which had in turn experienced the infiltration of both Italian and French styles under Charles IV. Bohemian painters were found in England under Richard II and the Parler family of Cologne, who built St Vitus's cathedral at Prague with Matthew of Arras, acted as intermediaries between central Europe, the Low Countries, and France. In 1425 one Jan Van Eyck, painter, from Maastricht, appeared in the service of Philip the Good of Burgundy and this was the beginning of ducal patronage of the new, realistic panel-painting which was soon to be taken up by the duke's Netherlandish subjects and his Italian creditors.

Clearly the art of Van Eyck met certain needs and demands. The degree of realism and accuracy which his oil portraits, for example, displayed was unprecedented. From the portrait of the donor in altar-pieces (diptychs, triptychs, or polyptychs) offered to private chapels (or chantries) within parish or cathedral churches stemmed the independent portrait. Commemoration of the individual was now possible, and the donors of panel-paintings could see themselves in the company of the saints, in adoration of the Virgin and Child, on the same scale and within the same spatial setting as the objects of their devotions. This was 'personalized' devotional religion at its most individualistic. Pierre Bladelin, financier of Bruges, or Canon George Van der Paele, prebendary of the Church of St Donatian at Bruges were depicted by Jan Van Eyck and Roger Van der Weyden in close and intimate proximity to the Christ child and his Mother. This was what they wanted as both patrons and believers, and Van Eyck and Van der Weyden ministered to these desires. To speak of 'profanation' in this context, as Huizinga does, is to let subjective value-judgement enter the question. Lay and indeed clerical piety at this time expressed a desire for familiarity with the saints and with the human drama and tragedy of the Christian story that was unprecedented in the Middle Ages. Religious sensibility was now conditioned by the cult of the Virgin, by the collections of saints' lives in the *Golden Legend*, by mystery or miracle plays, and by an art of domestic realism that was both a symptom and a cause of changes in outlook. The highly realistic panel-painting and illumination of these northern artists perfectly expressed the sentiments of their noble and bourgeois patrons. Representational realism and religious symbolism merged, and the theory that naturalism in art betrayed a lack of interest in religion is untenable. Art of this quality reinforced and illustrated doctrinal truths and stimulated devotional practices. We may with some confidence reject Huizinga's idea that familiarity with the sacred led inevitably to its profanation.

In France the exile of the dauphin Charles and his court to Bourges in 1418 meant that the arts were henceforth to be concentrated in the Loire valley. Jean Fouquet was the greatest of a group of painters who were working for the Valois court at the town of Tours by 1450. Fouquet also gave his patrons what they wanted. And for some of them this was clearly something newer and less traditional than that provided by the workshops of Paris or Rouen. The first evidence of Italian, or Italianate, influence upon northern European painting during this period is in the work of Fouquet. His patrons were primarily royal financial officers such as Étienne Chevalier, Simon de Varye, or Laurent Girard, or legal civil servants such as Guillaume Jouvenel des Ursins. Perhaps these relatively 'new' men, recently ennobled for their services to the Valois crown, were expressing their *arriviste* nature by preferring Fouquet's gilded, quasi-Italian products to the more conventional styles of his contemporaries. Whatever the case, Italianate decorative motifs are not found in other northern painting, certainly not in the Burgundian Netherlands, until a much later date. Even in France it was Charles VIII's Italian campaigns after 1494 which introduced the styles of the later Renaissance to French patrons. German painting during the period also owed little to developments across the Alps. At Cologne a vigorous school of painters produced spikier and more attenuated Gothic figures of saints and martyrs than did the Netherlanders, although there was much common ground between them. Portraiture throve in the German lands and by 1500 few German princes and higher ecclesiastics did not have their likenesses taken by artists. But the way towards the art of Albrecht Dürer and Hans Holbein had been prepared in the Low Countries during the fifteenth century.

Secular culture: Literacy and Chivalry

Secular culture during this period was shaped by two major factors: by a more general and widespread lay literacy and by the cult of chivalry in its literary, artistic, and practical manifestations. Although the proportion of literate people among the population of northern Europe was probably lower than that found in Italy by 1500, nevertheless the creation of universities (Prague 1347, Vienna 1365, Caen 1432, Bordeaux 1441, Dôle 1422, Louvain 1425) and the increasing provision of grammar schools clearly increased the demand for books of all sorts. A lay readership was in existence well before Johann Gutenberg began to print with movable type. Manuscript production was a thriving industry, subject to guild regulations in most northern towns and many of the vernacular books from these workshops were paper copies, which were much cheaper to produce and to purchase than parchment. They met a demand for inexpensive, often unbound, books in English, French, Netherlandish, and German among a less affluent clientèle. Taste tended to be dictated by what was available and by the preferences of great nobles of the age. None of the books first chosen by William Caxton for printing would have been out of place on the shelves of a nobleman's library, and it was indeed from such a source—the Burgundian ducal library and that of Louis de Bruges, lord of la Gruthuyse that suitable volumes came. Northern European typefaces also tended to imitate the hands of late fifteenth-century manuscripts—especially the so-called Burgundian 'bastard' script. The new literate laity eagerly accepted the romances, histories, and chronicles of courtly love and chivalry, often in recently re-worked prose versions emanating from the Burgundian court.

There was no reason why this should not have been so. Ideas of chivalry were still dominant among the ruling classes, while urban patricians and merchants imitated the nobility, staging their own chivalric displays. However, the cult of chivalry in the later Middle Ages has often been presented as a hollow sham, the mere husk or shell of what had once been a vigorous and dynamic military and social code. This is to lay too great a stress upon the concept of high medieval idealism (which existed only in theory) in contrast to later medieval decay. Chivalry and the cult of knighthood had certainly received an infusion of religious sentiment and idealism during the twelfth century, but it was in origin an essentially secular ideology. The Church's resistance to the tournament, for example, because it could be an occasion for violence, excess, bloodshed, and eroticism, was only overcome in the fourteenth century when some of its more lethal elements were gradually eliminated. But even in the period from 1350 to 1500, jousts and *tournois* were sometimes very dangerous, with fatal casualties. In the German lands the practice of the *Scharfrennen*, or jousting with sharpened rather than blunted lances, was a popular activity among nobles renowed for their private feuding. The tourna-ment, however elaborate, artificial, and theatrical it was, could act as a safety-valve for noble violence and probably both Charles the Bold of Burgundy and Maximilian I of Habsburg recognized this fact in their patronage of chivalric encounters that could become very rough, where vendetta had its place.

The medieval tournament, in both the collective forms of *tournois* or *mêlée* and the more individualistic joust, had also assumed a theatrical character since the early thirteenth century. Arthurian romance, widely popularized by 1230 through the works of Chrétien de Troyes in France and Gottfried von Strasbourg or the anonymous author of *Moriz von Craun* in Germany, provided themes suitable for dramatized re-enactment at a tournament. Arthurian-based Round Tables were formed by groups or teams of knights and the fiction that a tourna-ment took place under the patronage of Arthur and his knights is found, for instance, in 1278 at the encounters at Le Hem in northern France. There was an honoured place for noble-women on these occasions, and the blend of military prowess and amorous pursuit, which was condemned by the institutional Church, could be a heady mixture for young nobles. By 1316, however, papal disapproval of the tournament was greatly moderated by John XXII, and the Church's recognition of the new secular chivalric orders (the Garter, Star, Crescent, or Golden Fleece) of the fourteenth and fifteenth centuries was an indication of a change in attitude. These orders met and held their 'chapters' in churches—St George's Chapel, Windsor, Notre-Dame at Bruges, or Saint-Maurice at Angers—and a liturgy was devised for these solemn occasions. To claim the services of nobles at a period when loyalty was negotiable, often in monetary terms, princes found chivalric orders to be of political value. Philip the Good of Burgundy was able to enforce a prior claim upon the loyalty of his knights of the Golden Fleece (founded 1430), and the order bound together nobles from the heterogeneous Burgundian lands which lacked a parliamentary peerage on the English pattern. The Habsburgs were also to make use of it after they inherited the Burgundian Netherlands and the culture of Maximilian's court at Innsbruck and Vienna was profoundly influenced by the example of the Valois dukes. The court of Edward IV of England (1461–83) was similarly affected and the extraordinary efflorescence of literature, music, and the visual arts in fifteenth-century Flanders, Brabant, Hainault, and Holland made the Low Countries a source of cultural patterns copied elsewhere—even in Italy.

Yet the court of Burgundy and the art of the Flemish 'primitives', as we have seen, did not emerge from a vacuum. Although there was a flourishing Netherlandish literary court culture in Brabant until the mid-fourteenth century, the dominance of French as a literary language in the Low Countries was already pronounced even in Netherlandish-speaking areas by 1300. French was the language of courtly society and the households of the counts of Artois, Flanders, and Hainault actively promoted secular literature of the pre-

Burgundian period. From Hainault came Jean Froissart, perhaps the most celebrated and influential of the later medieval chroniclers of war and chivalry, followed in the fifteenth century by Georges Chastellain at the court of Burgundy. Froissart was a clerk, rewarded by a canonry in the church of Chimay, but he was among the last of his kind and his writing—both verse and prose—is extremely secular in character. Burgundian taste in the fifteenth century was not only for prose romances and histories, but for didactic treatises which were often stoic in nature, drawing upon ancient (especially Roman) history for edifying or cautionary examples. These were written by courtier-nobles (such as Guillebert de Lannoy) who provided instruction for their peers in the arts of persuasion and influence in the ducal council. The universities of the Burgundian lands (and of Germany) were also receiving a larger number of students described as *nobiles* (noblemen) in their matriculation registers. Princes were now served by a more educated and literate nobility, vying with the clerical and legal counsellors whose eloquence and rhetoric they sought to emulate.

The language which they used, however, was not clerical or legal Latin, but the vernacular. In England, northern France, and the Low Countries an increasing tendency to draw up documents and keep records in a vernacular language developed after c.1250. This was paralleled by the growth of a courtly vernacular literature and by the popularity of fraternities, or *puys*, in which verse competitions took place as they did in the German lands. The *grands rhétoriqueurs* of the Burgundian dominions, such as Chastellain and Molinet, were in part a product of these developments. In England the emergence of Middle English as a literary language, acceptable to the French-speaking (or Anglo-Norman) nobility, began in the fourteenth century. It owed a great deal to French forms and influences, most marked in the verse of Geoffrey Chaucer. By 1500 the language of the English court was no longer French, although acquaintance with that language was considered a necessary accomplishment for a nobleman. There can be little doubt that many princes and nobles of this period were multilingual—René of Anjou was proficient in five languages, while the

Emperor Charles IV decreed in 1356 that the nobles of the German Empire should learn tongues other than that of their native land. But the rise of the vernacular had begun to make inroads into the dominantly francophone courtly culture of the later Middle Ages by 1500. French-inspired themes and cultural forms continued to be admired and adopted, but they were increasingly expressed and absorbed by men and women for whom French was an acquired rather than an indigenous skill.

Later medieval civilization in northern Europe had its own distinctive character, to which criteria derived from earlier or later periods are inapplicable. A 'high and strong culture' (Huizinga) expressing itself in artistic realism, vernacular literature, lay piety, and a chivalric heyday remained dominant. New things were certainly being born but they carried the unmistakable imprint of their medieval antecedents.

EDITOR'S POSTSCRIPT

By 1500, the date at which we have chosen to end this book, the flowering of medieval European civilization which accompanied the great population explosion of the years from 1000 to 1300 was already in the distant past, as far away from the men of that time as the *ancien régime* before the French Revolution is from us. The immediate effect of the period of expansion had been to create a society in western Europe in which the evidence of uniformity and the pursuit of common purposes had been strong. We see this, for example, in the enterprises of the crusades which began in 1094 and extended with varying intensity and success until the late thirteenth century. Crusading armies were drawn from the knightly aristocracy of England, northern France, and Germany. They also involved ships from the Italian commercial cities and soldiers from Sicily and Catalonia. Kings such as St Louis of France and Edward I were still drawn across the Mediterranean by the impulse to free the Holy Land and attack the Muhammadan in the middle of the thirteenth century.

If we look more closely at the internal structure of civilization before 1300 we shall also see widespread evidence of a common culture and a tendency towards common ideals and even centralization, especially in the world of religion. From one point of view the most remarkable creation of the medieval world was the papacy. By the mid-thirteenth century priests throughout Europe to the west of the area dominated by the Greek Orthodox Church had become willing to accept the authority of Rome in matters of doctrine, in the judicial power to settle disputes involving benefices, in the power of veto over appointments of bishops and even in the levying of heavy taxation. The power of the pope was of course very imperfect, limited by the resistance of kings who wanted to control churches in their kingdoms and by the wish of lords to appoint their relations to churches on their estates. It was to some extent a power which depended on the existence of alternative lay authorities because priests found it convenient to turn to the jurisdiction of a spiritual power in Rome as a safeguard against more immediate threats near at hand. Nevertheless, it was a considerable power which enabled Innocent III to carry on a successful diplomatic battle against King John of England and which tempted Boniface VIII, admittedly with disastrous results, to set his authority against that of Philip IV of France. It enabled the popes for a long period to fight wars in Italy with funds collected far away in northern Europe and to intervene successfully in appointments in Scotland and Ireland.

The centralizing power of the papacy was connected with the great religious orders which emerged in the twelfth and thirteenth centuries. The early medieval Benedictine monasteries, which contributed so much to the colonization and education of Europe, had in common their devotion to the rule of St Benedict, one of the most important documents of the Middle Ages, but they were independent foundations not linked in a common organization. The novel monastic enterprises of the twelfth century, such as the Cistercians, had a much stronger sense of belonging to a single administration. The mendicant orders of the thirteenth century, the Franciscans and Dominicans, went still further in their devotion to the papacy, in acceptance of papal privileges which freed them from the control of the local bishop and in attendance at annual general chapters made up of representatives drawn from convents throughout Europe. The mendicant orders were in a sense the fullest expression of the sense of ecclesiastical unity.

This can also be seen in the world of ideas, with which of course the papacy was very much concerned. The university of Paris in the thirteenth century had a prestige and influence in matters of philosophy and theology to which there is no parallel in any educational institution in modern Europe. There were of course other important universities. But Padua and Oxford, for example, belonged to an important extent to the ideological world dominated by Paris. Other thinkers might not agree with the conclusions reached by Albertus Magnus or Thomas Aquinas but they were involved in the same problems posed by the acceptance of Latin translations of Aristotle and the difficulties raised by the urgent need to reconcile biblical revelation with pagan science. And all of them wrote their treatises and conducted their disputations in the dog Latin, distinguished by its precision though rarely by literary grace, which provided a common language for medieval Europe and the understanding of which everywhere divided the literate from the user of the uncultivated vernacular.

The lay world was in some respects separate from the clerical, but here too we find widespread evidence of a common culture. One of the most remarkable creations of the twelfth century was romance poetry. The stories of Arthur, of Charlemagne, and of Tristan were read and heard in every country in Europe in the thirteenth century. The literary dominance of French was facilitated by the use of the language by the knightly aristocracies of England and Sicily. The stories elaborated by French romancers were repeated in other languages as well. The literary dominance of romance was assisted by the prevalence of knighthood and chivalry, also partly French in their origins but spread everywhere in the medieval world. A knight could recognize his social equal anywhere in Europe just as a priest or a bishop could.

The pan-European expansion of forms of culture found its most obvious—and still surviving—expression in Gothic architecture. Any modern tourist can see that the cathedrals of Salisbury or Florence belong in a general way to the same architectural genre as the central masterpieces of Chartres and Notre Dame. The invention of the Gothic style in France in the mid-twelfth century was followed by an extraordinary spread to every part of Europe to replace the more localized Romanesque taste which it had replaced. It would not be misleading to take the basilica of St Francis at Assisi—a Gothic church built in Italy in the mid-thirteenth century in imitation of French models above the tomb of a saint whose order spread throughout the western world under papal patronage—as a visual symbol of the European unity of the high Middle Ages.

In the last centuries of the medieval world between 1300 and 1500, with the decline of crusading activity, the devastation of papal authority during the Great Schism from 1378 to 1415 and the dissipation of the great scholastic enterprise of Paris, that sense of European unity was much weakened. It is difficult to point to precise reasons for such a vast phenomenon but we should certainly attribute some force to the decline of seignorial landowning during the population fall and the relatively increased strength of the commercial cities of Italy and the Low Countries. Late medieval Europe was certainly not a poor society. On the contrary we find evidence everywhere of high levels of income, greater sophistication in domestic comfort and artistic taste, and great vigour in both the economic and aesthetic spheres. Paradoxically it was a Europe reduced in population by the plagues but bursting with energetic life which began the conquest of the non-European world with the explorations of Vasco da Gama and Christopher Columbus.

As we have seen in the chapters contributed by Peter Denley and Malcolm Vale we must now look for the development of civilization to a number of geographically separate areas which, while they were certainly connected, gave birth to contrasting manifestations of culture. We should not press the distinctions between them too far of course. If we look at important local cultural schools such as, for example, the decorated style of architecture produced in the cathedrals of Wells and Norwich in the early fourteenth century out of the common Gothic heritage, at Chaucer's development of chivalric literature in *Troilus and Cresseide* or at the expansion of the ideals of the rhetorician in the Renaissance classicism of Florence—in all these cases we are seeing creations which are both highly novel but also very clearly related to medieval antecedents. Nevertheless, the mark of the later medieval world is the extraordinary richness and diversity of its ways of life which made it a far more complex civilization than any which had preceded it and foreshadowed the inventiveness of modern Europe.

A major factor in the new diversity was the exploitation of a variety of languages in important writings. Latin and French which had dominated the twelfth and thirteenth centuries gave way to Italian, English, Flemish, Catalonian, and Czech. The origins of this movement may be in some ways mysterious but its results are obvious and spectacular. The sudden emergence of English as a great literary language at the end of the fourteenth century in the writings of Chaucer, Langland, and Wycliffe was accompanied by the increasing use of English in letters written by ordinary people. Italian had emerged out of obscurity into brilliance around 1300 propelled forward by Dante who was followed by Boccaccio in a society in which it was already the normal vehicle of commercial correspondence. The reformation in Bohemia, inspired by Hus in the early fifteenth century, owed its great success in part to the attractiveness of translations of the Bible, hymns, and religious treatises in Czech which could be understood by ordinary people. The development of the vernaculars was promoted by religious reformers, by merchants, and by poets, all of whom escaped with relief from the dominance of Latin. The Renaissance Latin which was evolved by Petrarch and the later Italian humanists of the fifteenth century was in effect a new language, no doubt an unfortunate scholarly diversion from the greater subtlety offered by the vernacular tongue but still a language capable of a new kind of literary charm.

As we have seen in preceding chapters, the civilization of the fifteenth century contained a variety of local cultures vying for influence in different languages and of social forms ranging from the largely rural society of the English gentry to the highly developed city capitalism of Venice and Genoa. As we have also seen, it involved a complex interpenetration of the world of the court, the still-active chivalry and the tournament, the cathedral chapter and the monastery with the life of the city, the merchant and the industrial proletariat. The English parliament which emerged in the fourteenth century, containing representatives of the nobility, the prelates, the gentry, and the burgesses, was a microcosm of the late medieval world. Nevertheless, if we look for the most brilliant achievements of that world, it is in the cities in the two areas in which they were most highly developed—northern Italy and north-west Europe—that we shall find them.

The richest society of late medieval Europe was probably to be found in the cities scattered over the land to the north-west of Paris and Strasbourg: Bruges, Antwerp, Cologne, and many others. It is there that we shall find the outstanding industrial developments of printing, tapestry-making, and machinery such as the crane. Among the technical innovations which gave an added sophistication to temporal life we should include the painting of the Van Eycks and Memling which achieved quite new standards in the precise representation of the human face and the natural landscape. The Flemings and Brabanters of the fifteenth century are plainly the precursors of the commercial civilization of Holland in the age of Rembrandt.

Early Renaissance Italy was less inventive industrially but its astonishing artistic movement, which had given birth before 1500 to Leonardo and Michelangelo as well as the exquisite classicism of Botticelli, was related to highly original innovations in the world of ideas. The humanism of the cities created a new kind of political thought to justify republican liberalism and despotic efficiency. If Machiavelli had not yet written *The Prince* he must already have developed some of his ideas before 1500. At the same time Lorenzo Valla's investigation of the text of the New Testament and Marsiglio Ficino's translation of Plato gave birth to a variety of speculations which were to disturb the spiritual life of Europe for centuries to come.

As we approach 1500 we find ourselves in a world which is quite fundamentally different from the one with which we began a thousand years earlier. We have moved out of the period of the great world empires and seen the creation of a civilization of a different kind. It was distinguished by its wealth, based on highly successful agriculture and industry. But it could not have taken the form it had or presented the springboard for future expansion without the diversity of a hundred centres of political and cultural aspiration competing for success. That untidy fragmentation was the ground for the extraordinary fertility of our cultural forebears.

FURTHER READING

1. The Transformation of the Roman Mediterranean

GENERAL

R. S. Lopez, *The Birth of Europe* (London, 1967), a lively if idiosyncratic survey of the Middle Ages from a mainly Mediterranean perspective.

L. Musset, *The Germanic Invasions. The Making of Europe, A.D. 400–600* (London, 1975), an admirably lucid and penetrating discussion.

D. Talbot Rice (ed.), *The Dark Ages. The Making of European Civilization* (London, 1965), profusely illustrated, with some chapters much more stimulating than others.

J. M. Wallace-Hadrill, *The Barbarian West* (3rd edn. London, 1967), the best short work on the early Middle Ages, to be used with caution on the Mediterranean because of an underplaying of Byzantine influence.

ROMANS AND BARBARIANS UP TO 565

P. Brown, *The World of Late Antiquity* (London, 1971), the most stimulating short account of the Late Roman Empire.

R. Browning, *Justinian and Theodora* (London, 1971) sensible, thorough, and well illustrated.

J. B. Bury, *A History of the Later Roman Empire from the Death of Theodosius to the Death of Justinian* (2 vols., repr. New York, 1958), still the most reliable narrative account in English.

W. A. Goffart, *Barbarians and Romans, A.D. 418–584* (Princeton, NJ, 1980), a provocative work of revisionism.

A. H. M. Jones, *The Later Roman Empire* (3 vols., Oxford, 1964), a magisterial survey of all aspects of the subject; his *The Decline of the Ancient World* (London, 1966) is a dull condensed version.

BYZANTIUM AND THE BALKANS

R. Browning, *Byzantium and Bulgaria* (London, 1975), a concise, scholarly study.

J. V. A. Fine, *The Early Medieval Balkans* (Ann Arbor, Mich., 1983), a good synthesis of recent research.

C. Foss, *Byzantine and Turkish Sardis* (Cambridge, Mass., 1976), like his *Ephesus after Antiquity* (Cambridge, Mass., 1979), traces the evolution of a Byzantine city, but his views have met with some criticism.

R. J. H. Jenkins, *Byzantium, the Imperial Centuries, A.D. 610–1071* (London, 1966), sound but unimaginative.

C. Mango, *Byzantium. The Empire of New Rome* (London, 1980), the most stimulating of many surveys of Byzantine civilization; concentrates on the early period.

D. Obolensky, *The Byzantine Commonwealth* (London, 1971), a masterly account of Byzantium's relations with her Balkan neighbours.

G. Ostrogorsky, *History of the Byzantine State* (2nd edn. Oxford, 1968), the best political handbook, although some of his conclusions are now questioned.

THE CHURCH IN EAST AND WEST

A. A. M. Bryer and J. Herrin (eds.), *Iconoclasm* (Birmingham, 1977), an invaluable collection of papers from a symposium.

P. Brown, *Augustine of Hippo* (London, 1967), a masterly biography, full of insights into the life of the fifth-century Church.

J. Hussey, *The Orthodox Church in the Byzantine Empire* (Oxford, 1986), a thorough and scholarly survey.

C. H. Lawrence, *Medieval Monasticism* (London, 1984), one of the few treatments of a surprisingly neglected subject, rather cursory on the early Middle Ages.

J. M. Richards, *Consul of God* (London, 1980), a clear but limited biography of Pope Gregory the Great.

—— *The Popes and the Papacy in the Early Middle Ages, 476–752* (London, 1979), a straightforward account which eschews some wider theoretical issues.

AFRICA

C. Courtois, *Les Vandales et l'Afrique* (Paris, 1955), the best survey of the Vandal kingdom.

D. Pringle, *The Defence of Byzantine Africa from Justinian to the Arab Conquest* (Oxford, 1981), discusses politics and administration as well as military and archaeological developments.

ITALY

T. S. Brown, *Gentlemen and Officers. Imperial Administration and Aristocratic Power in Byzantine Italy, 554–800 A.D.* (London, 1984), an examination of the society of Byzantine Italy.

T. S. Burns, *A History of the Ostrogoths* (Bloomington, Ind., 1984), useful but conventional.

R. Krautheimer, *Rome. Profile of a City, 312–1308* (Princeton, NJ, 1980), a balanced and well-illustrated survey.

P. Llewellyn, *Rome in the Dark Ages* (London, 1971), offers a guide to Rome's complex political history.

T. F. X. Noble, *The Republic of Saint Peter* (Philadelphia, 1984), an original analysis of the rise of the papacy to political independence.

C. Wickham, *Early Medieval Italy* (London, 1981), excellent on society and economy, weak on culture and the Church.

SPAIN

R. Collins, *Early Medieval Spain* (London, 1983), thorough and especially good on the Church.

P. D. King, *Law and Society in the Visigothic Kingdom* (Cambridge, 1972), a dry but valuable study.

E. A. Thompson, *The Goths in Spain* (London, 1969), emphasizes the Germanic exclusiveness of the regime.

SOUTHERN GAUL

J. Dunbabin, *France in the Making, 843–1180* (Oxford, 1985), a guide through the morass of southern French history in the ninth century.

A. R. Lewis, *The Development of Southern French and Catalan Society, 718–1058* (Austin, Tex., 1965), a controversial view of a dynamic society.

THE ISLAMIC WORLD

F. Gabrieli, *Muhammad and the Conquests of Islam* (London, 1968), clear and concise.

H. Kennedy, *The Prophet and the Age of the Caliphates* (London, 1986), judicious and up to date.

M. Lombard, *The Golden Age of Islam* (Amsterdam and Oxford, 1975), views Islamic civilization in an economic light.

M. A. Shaban, *Islamic History. A New Interpretation* (2 vols., Cambridge, 1976), offers challenging insights.

W. Montgomery Watt, *Muhammad, Prophet and Statesman* (London, 1961), one of the author's many illuminating studies of the Prophet.
—— and P. Cachia, *A History of Islamic Spain* (Edinburgh, 1965), clear and to the point.

ART

J. Beckwith, *Early Christian and Byzantine Art* (2nd edn., Harmondsworth, 1979), a good general guide.
O. Grabar, *The Formation of Islamic Art* (New Haven, Conn., 1973), extremely stimulating.
J. Hubert, J. Porcher, and W. F. Volbach, *Europe in the Dark Ages* (London, 1969), full of lavish illustrations.
E. Kitzinger, *Byzantine Art in the Making* (Cambridge, Mass., 1977), the stimulating views of a master.
C. Mango, *Byzantine Architecture* (New York, 1976), a thorough and original survey.

LITERATURE AND LEARNING

Byzantine Books and Bookmen. A Dumbarton Oaks Colloquium (Washington, DC, 1975), contains important contributions on literary life in early Byzantium.
M. L. W. Laistner, *Thought and Letters in Western Europe A.D. 500 to 900* (2nd edn., London, 1957); a wide-ranging but dull survey.
P. Riché, *Education and Culture in the Barbarian West, Sixth through Eighth Centuries* (Columbia, SC, 1976), a thorough and imaginative study.

EAST—WEST RELATIONS AND ECONOMIC LIFE

M. F. Hendy, *Studies in the Byzantine Monetary Economy* (Cambridge, 1985), a vast study, often penetrating but frequently eccentric.
R. Hodges and D. Whitehouse, *Mohammed, Charlemagne and the Origins of Europe* (London, 1983), a brave attempt to re-examine the economic history of early medieval Europe in the light of archaeology.
A. R. Lewis, *Naval Power and Trade in the Mediterranean, A.D. 500—1100* (Princeton, NJ, 1951) a wealth of factual information but has to be read with caution.
G. Luzzatto, *An Economic History of Italy from the Fall of the Roman Empire to the Beginning of the Sixteenth Century* (London, 1961), a useful short account.

H. Pirenne, *Mohammed and Charlemagne* (London, 1968), dated but
still interesting if read together with modern critiques such as
Hodges and Whitehouse (see above) or A. Havighurst (ed.), *The
Pirenne Thesis* (rev. edn. Boston, Mass., 1969).

2. The Northern World in the Dark Ages

GENERAL

D. M. Wilson (ed.), *The Northern World* (London, 1980), a
beautifully illustrated guide, neglects the Roman background.

J. Campbell (ed.), *The Anglo-Saxons* (London, 1982).

A. P. Smyth, *Warlords and Holy Men: Scotland AD80–1000*
(London, 1984).

W. Davies, *Wales in the Early Middle Ages* (Leicester, 1982).

E. James, *The Origins of France: from Clovis to the Capetians 500–
1000* (London, 1982).

Z. Vana, *The World of the Ancient Slavs* (London, 1983).

THE MIGRATIONS

L. Musset, *The Germanic Invasions: The Making of Europe AD
400–600* (London, 1975), the best general guide to the subject.

S. Johnson, *Later Roman Britain* (London, 1980).

J. N. L. Myres, *The English Settlements* (Oxford, 1986).

THE CONVERSION

J. N. Hillgarth, *The Conversion of Western Europe, 350–750* (2nd
edn. Philadelphia, 1986), an excellent collection of translated texts.

R. Van Dam, *Leadership and Authority in Late Antique Gaul*
(Berkeley, 1985), provides a subtle analysis of the development of
Christianity in Gaul through the period of invasions.

J. M. Wallace-Hadrill, *The Frankish Church* (Oxford, 1983).

Bede: The History of the English Church and People, trans. L. Sherley-
Price and R. Latham (Harmondsworth, 1968), a major text.

H. Mayr-Harting, *The Coming of Christianity to Anglo-Saxon
England* (London, 1972), the best commentary on Bede.

K. Hughes, *The Church in Early Irish Society* (London, 1966),
discusses the conversion of Ireland.

L. Bieler, *Ireland: Harbinger of the Middle Ages* (Oxford, 1963), treats
also of the missions of the Irish abroad.

BARBARIAN SOCIETY AND KINGSHIP

J. M. Wallace-Hadrill, *Early Germanic Kingship in England and the Continent* (Oxford, 1971) and *The Long-Haired Kings and other studies in Frankish history* (London, 1962), essential studies of German kingship.

P. H. Sawyer and I. N. Wood (eds.), *Early Medieval Kingship* (Leeds, 1977).

History of the Franks by Gregory of Tours, trans. L. Thorpe (Harmondsworth, 1974).

Gregory of Tours, *Life of the Fathers*, trans. E. James (Liverpool, 1985).

Beowulf in various translations, most conveniently together with nearly all other surviving poems in Old English in S. A. J. Bradley, *Anglo-Saxon Poetry* (London, 1982).

K. MacNiocaill, *Ireland before the Vikings* (Dublin, 1972).

D. O. Corrain, *Ireland before the Normans* (Dublin, 1972).

F. J. Byrne, *Irish Kings and High-Kings* (London, 1973).

CAROLINGIAN EUROPE

R. McKitterick, *The Frankish Kingdoms under the Carolingians, 751– 987* (London, 1983), a thorough guide.

H. Fichtenau, *The Carolingian Empire* (Oxford, 1968), a stimulating introduction.

D. Bullough, *The Age of Charlemagne* (London, 1965).

R. Folz, *The Coronation of Charlemagne: 25 December 800* (London, 1974).

Translation of Einhard in *Two Lives of Charlemagne* trans. L. Thorpe (Harmondsworth, 1969).

P. Riché, *Daily Life in the World of Charlemagne* (Liverpool, 1978), shows that studies of 'daily life' are almost but not quite impossible for the Dark Ages.

THE NORTH

P. H. Sawyer, *The Age of the Vikings* (London, 1962) a controversial and stimulating introduction, now slightly modified by his *Kings and Vikings* (London, 1982).

G. Jones, *A History of the Vikings* (Oxford, 1968), more detailed and conventional.

P. D. Foote and D. M. Wilson (eds.), *The Viking Achievement* (London, 1970).

R. Hodges, *Dark Age Economics* (London, 1982) contains much useful information about recent archaeological discoveries.

3. Northern Europe in the High Middle Ages

GENERAL

C. N. L. Brooke, *Europe in the Central Middle Ages 962–1154* (London, 1964), a good textbook introduction.

A. Murray, *Reason and Society in the Middle Ages* (Oxford, 1978), wide-ranging with many new ideas.

R. W. Southern, *The Making of the Middle Ages* (London, 1953), illuminates the period with matchless sympathy and insight.

THE LINEAMENTS OF POWER

W. Anderson, *Castles of Europe* (London, 1970), superbly illustrated.

M. Bloch, *Feudal Society* (London, 1961), a classic, broadly conceived and rich with example.

P. Contamine, *War in the Middle Ages* (Oxford, 1984).

G. Duby, *The Knight, the Lady, and the Priest* (London, 1984), turns a dry eye on noble marriages.

M. Keen, *Chivalry* (London, 1984), valuable on the knightly ethos.

S. Reynolds, *Kingdoms and Communities in Western Europe 900–1300* (Oxford, 1984), concentrates on bonds of association rather than those of dependence.

T. A. Reuter (ed.), *The Medieval Nobility* (Amsterdam and Oxford, 1978), helpfully includes some important German contributions.

A REVIVING ECONOMY

The Fontana Economic History of Europe, vol. i, The Middle Ages, ed. C. M. Cipolla (London, 1972), provides a helpful introductory account.

G. Duby, *Rural Economy and Country Life in the Medieval West* (London, 1968), strongest on France and England.

E. Ennen, *The Medieval Town* (Amsterdam and Oxford, 1979).

N. J. G. Pounds, *An Economic History of Medieval Europe* (London, 1974).

LORDS AT PRAYER

R. and C. N. L. Brooke, *Popular Religion in the Middle Ages* (London, 1984).

G. Constable, *Cluniac Studies* (London, 1980).

H. E. J. Cowdrey, *The Cluniacs and the Gregorian Reform* (Oxford, 1970), rests upon definitions of the Cluniacs and of the Reform which not all will accept.

G. Duby, *The Three Orders* (Chicago, 1980), links the development of this theory with disorder in tenth-century France.

C. Erdmann, *The Origin of the Idea of The Crusade* (Princeton, 1977), a classic since its publication in 1935.

P. J. Geary, *Furta Sacra* (Princeton, 1978), discusses the theft of relics.

N. Hunt, *Cluny under St Hugh* (London, 1967), a reliable account, but somewhat insulated.

C. H. Lawrence, *Medieval Monasticism* (London, 1984), a helpful general account.

H. Leyser, *Hermits and the New Monasticism* (London, 1984), one of those rare books which can be called too short.

K. F. Morrison, *Tradition and Authority in the Western Church* (Princeton, 1969), effectively disentangles the issues in the Investiture Contest.

J. Riley-Smith, *The First Crusade and the Idea of Crusading* (London, 1986), complements Erdmann's account, with more stress on developments during the crusade itself.

I. S. Robinson, *Authority and Resistance in the Investiture Contest* (Manchester and New York, 1978), discusses the pamphlet war.

R. W. Southern, *Western Society and the Church in the Middle Ages* (*The Pelican History of the Church*, vol. ii) (Harmondsworth, 1970), selective, but rich with insight.

G. Tellenbach, *Church State and Christian Society* (Oxford, 1959), an important contribution to the history of the Investiture Contest.

B. Ward, *Miracles and the Medieval Mind* (London, 1982).

THE TWELFTH-CENTURY RENAISSANCE

R. L. Benson and G. Constable (eds.), *Renaissance and Renewal in the Twelfth Century* (Oxford, 1982), an excellent and comprehensive collection of recent work.

J. Bony, *French Gothic Architecture of the Twelfth and Thirteenth Centuries* (Berkeley, 1983).

C. N. L. Brooke, *The Twelfth Century Renaissance* (London, 1969), a helpful introductory account.

S. Ferruolo, *The Origin of the University: The Schools of Paris and their critics 1100–1215* (Stanford, 1985).

D. E. Luscombe, *The School of Peter Abelard* (Cambridge, 1969), examines Abelard's influence.

B. Smalley, *Historians in the Middle Ages* (London, 1974).

R. W. Southern, *Medieval Humanism and other Studies* (Oxford, 1970).

G. Zarnecki, *Art of the Medieval World* (New York, 1975), a very well-illustrated introduction.

The Letters of Abelard and Heloise (Harmondsworth, 1974), includes Abelard's autobiography; despite scepticism the letters are now thought to be genuine.

GERMANY AND ITS NEIGHBOURS

G. Barraclough, *The Origins of Modern Germany* (2nd edn. Oxford, 1947), provides a helpful general account, but needs revision at many points.

B. Arnold, *German Knighthood 1050–1300* (Oxford, 1985), looks at relations between knights and lords and considers the wider implications.

J. Fleckenstein, *Early Medieval Germany* (Amsterdam and Oxford, 1978), covers the earlier part of this period.

H. Fuhrmann, *Germany in the High Middle Ages c.1050–1250* (Cambridge, 1986), an excellent account by one of Germany's leading historians.

K. J. Leyser, *Medieval Germany and its Neighbours 900–1250* (London, 1983), a collection of essays rather than a unified treatment but still a most valuable contribution. His *Rule and Conflict in an Early Medieval Society: Ottonian Saxony* (London, 1979), is of seminal importance, but is not for the beginner.

P. Munz, *Frederick Barbarossa* (London, 1969), the fullest account in English, but its judgements are very questionable.

K. Jordan, *Henry the Lion*, trans P. S. Falla (Oxford, 1986).

THE KINGDOM OF FRANCE

J. Dunbabin, *France in the Making 843–1180* (Oxford, 1985), looks at France as a whole and has many fresh points to make.

R. Fawtier, *The Capetian Kings of France* (London, 1960), now seems a rather dewy-eyed view of the monarchy.

E. M. Hallam, *Capetian France 987–1328* (London, 1980), a good general account.

A. W. Lewis, *Royal Succession in Capetian France* (Cambridge Mass. and London, 1981), looks closely and profitably at Capetian family policy.

J. le Patourel, *The Norman Empire* (Oxford, 1976), discusses the Anglo-Norman lands.

J. Gillingham, *The Angevin Empire* (London, 1984), perhaps overestimates its strength.

EASTERN EUROPE AND SCANDINAVIA

N. Davies, *God's Playground, a History of Poland*, vol. i (Oxford, 1981).

T. K. Derry, *A History of Scandinavia* (London, 1979), a fuller account in English of post-Viking Scandinavia would be very welcome.

F. Dvornik, *The Making of Central and Eastern Europe* (London, 1949), perhaps gives excessive importance to the role of Bohemia.

C. A. MacCartney, *Hungary, a Short History* (Edinburgh, 1962), contains some helpful pages.

A. P. Vlasto, *The Entry of the Slavs into Christendom* (Cambridge, 1970), concentrates on the Christianization of these peoples, but has much to say on other aspects too.

A. Gieystor provides some excellent pages on medieval Poland in the collaborative *History of Poland* (Warsaw, 1968).

4. Northern Europe invades the Mediterranean

BYZANTIUM

M. Angold, *The Byzantine Empire: 1025–1204* (London, 1984), the best narrative history of the period.

C. M. Brand, *Byzantium Confronts the West* (Cambridge, Mass., 1968), particularly good on the tensions of the twelfth century.

H. Haussig, *Byzantine Civilisation* (London, 1971), beautifully illustrated survey of Byzantine society and culture.

J. M. Hussey, *The Orthodox Church in the Byzantine Empire* (Oxford, 1986), a general but admirably lucid and perceptive survey.

D. Obolensky, *The Byzantine Commonwealth* (London, 1971), deals with relations with the Slavs.

S. Vryonis, Jr., *The Decline of Medieval Hellenism in Asia Minor* (Los Angeles and London, 1971), idiosyncratic but fascinating account of the 'Turkification' of Asia Minor.

340 *Further Reading*

MUSLIM WORLD

P. M. Holt, *The Age of the Crusades* (London, 1986).

H. Kennedy, *The Prophet and the Age of the Caliphates* (London, 1986); two recent introductions to Islamic history.

ITALY AND THE EMPIRE

D. J. Herlihy, *Cities and Society in Medieval Italy* (London, 1980); *The Social History of Italy and Western Europe* (London, 1978). The dearth of material on Italian social and economic history in English is partly compensated for by these two volumes of lively studies.

J. K. Hyde, *Society and Politics in Medieval Italy* (London, 1973), concentrates on the evolution of urban society.

P. Munz, *Frederick Barbarossa* (London, 1969), a controversial work, but containing a useful account of imperial struggles with the communes.

S. Reynolds, *Kingdoms and Communities in Western Europe, 900–1300* (Oxford, 1984), thought-provoking chapter on the communes.

C. J. Wickham, *Early Medieval Italy* (London, 1981), excellent on law and society.

PAPACY

H. E. J. Cowdrey, *The Age of Abbot Desiderius* (Oxford, 1983), one of the best accounts of the post-Gregorian papacy, disguised as a biography of the most able eleventh-century abbot of Monte Cassino.

P. Partner, *The Lands of St Peter* (London, 1972).

W. Ullmann, *A Short History of the Papacy in the Middle Ages* (London, 1974), a work of fundamental importance on the evolution of papal ideology.

MONASTICISM

B. Bolton, *The Medieval Reformation* (London, 1983).

C. H. Lawrence, *Medieval Monasticism* (London, 1984), both outline the major developments in the spiritual life.

H. Leyser, *Hermits and the New Monasticism* (London, 1984).

H. E. J. Cowdrey, *Popes, Monks and Crusaders* (London, 1984), collected studies, covering Cluniac history, heresy (especially in Milan), and crusading.

HERESY

B. Hamilton, *The Medieval Inquisition* (London, 1981).
M. D. Lambert, *Medieval Heresy* (London, 1977), wide-ranging and perceptive study of the evolution of heretical ideas.
R. I. Moore, *The Origins of European Dissent* (London, 1977).
—— *The Birth of Popular Heresy* (London, 1975), excellent collection of documents in translation.
D. Obolensky, *The Bogomils* (repr. London, 1978).

SPAIN AND SOUTHERN FRANCE

E. M. Hallam, *Capetian France: 987–1328* (London, 1980), some treatment of the south.
A. R. Lewis, *The Development of Southern French and Catalan Society* (Austin, Tex., 1965).
G. Jackson, *The Making of Medieval Spain* (London, 1972), well-illustrated introduction.
A. Mackay, *Spain in the Middle Ages* (London, 1977), an important reassessment, written with great panache.

NORMANS IN SOURTHERN ITALY

R. H. C. Davis, *The Normans and their Myth* (London, 1976), a shrewd 'de-bunking' of Norman propaganda.
D. C. Douglas, *The Norman Achievement* (London, 1969).
—— *The Norman Fate* (London, 1976); both deal with cultural and artistic matters as well as providing a reliable narrative which places the Normans in their European context.

CRUSADES

C. Erdmann, *The Origin of the Idea of Crusade*, trans. M. W. Baldwin and W. Goffart (Princeton, 1977), a classic.
J. Godfrey, *1204: The Unholy Crusade* (Oxford, 1980).
B. Z. Kedar, *Crusade and Mission: European Approaches Towards the Muslim* (Princeton, 1984), particularly good on the background to the crusades.
H. E. Mayer, *The Crusades* (London, 1972), the best survey.
J. Prawer, *Crusader Institutions* (Oxford, 1980), collected studies.
—— *The Latin Kingdom of Jerusalem* (London, 1972).
D. E. Queller, *The Fourth Crusade* (Philadelphia, 1977).
J. Riley-Smith, *What were the Crusades?* (London, 1977), short but invaluable.

J. and L. Riley-Smith, *The Crusades: Idea and Reality* (London, 1981), collection of documents in translation.

E. Siberry, *Criticism of Crusading 1095–1274* (Oxford, 1985).

TRADE AND COMMERCE

R. S. Lopez. *The Commercial Revolution of the Middle Ages: 950–1350* (Englewood Cliffs, NJ, 1971).

—— and I. W. Raymond *Medieval Trade in the Mediterranean World* (3rd imp, New York, 1968), a gold-mine of translated documents with useful short introductions, covering all aspects of trade and commercial organization.

N. J. G. Pounds, *Economic History of Medieval Europe* (3rd imp, London, 1980), a superior textbook incorporating the fruits of very wide research.

ARTISTIC AND CULTURAL DEVELOPMENTS

C. N. L. Brooke, *The Twelfth Century Renaissance* (London, 1969).

R. Cormack, *Writing in Gold: Byzantine Society and its Icons* (London, 1985), a major reassessment.

O. Demus, *Romanesque Wall Painting* (London, 1970), superb illustrations.

K. M. Setton (gen. ed.), *History of the Crusades*, vol. iv contains a survey of the arts in the Holy Land.

SOURCES

Anna Comnena, *The Alexiad*, trans. E. R. A. Sewter (Harmondsworth, 1969), Byzantium through the eyes of an eleventh-century princess.

Geoffrey de Villehardouin, *The Conquest of Constantinople* in *Chronicles of the Crusades*, trans. M. R. B. Shaw (Harmondsworth, 1963), a Frankish account of the Fourth Crusade.

Liutprand of Cremona, *Works*, trans. F. A. Wright (London, 1930), Pride and Prejudice at the tenth-century Byzantine court.

The Poem of the Cid, ed. and trans. I. Michael *et al.* (Manchester, 1975), a classic epic poem.

5. The Mediterranean in the Age of the Renaissance

THE PAPACY, ITS ENEMIES AND ITS ALLIES

M. Reeves, *Joachim of Fiore and the Prophetic Future* (London, 1976), a general introduction to this important thinker.

T. C. Van Cleve, *The Emperor Frederick II of Hohenstaufen* (Oxford, 1972), a full and detailed biography.

D. P. Waley, *The Papal State in the Thirteenth Century* (London, 1961).

S. Runciman, *The Sicilian Vespers* (Cambridge, 1958), contains much information on Mediterranean politics in the thirteenth century.

N. Housley, *The Italian Crusades* (Oxford, 1982), an important work on the papal-Angevin alliance and the use of crusading in this context.

T. S. R. Boase, *Boniface VIII* (London, 1933), a readable biography of this crucial figure.

R. B. Brooke, *The Coming of the Friars* (London, 1975), a good short introduction.

L. K. Little, *Religious Poverty and the Profit Economy in Medieval Europe* (London, 1979), emphasizes the social context of the growth of the mendicant orders.

THE ITALIAN CITY STATES: IDEALS AND REALITY

D. P. Waley, *The Italian City-Republics* (2nd edn., London, 1978), a basic thematic introduction.

J. K. Hyde, *Society and Politics in Medieval Italy* (London, 1973), a chronologically based overview.

J. Larner, *Italy in the Age of Dante and Petrarch, 1216–1380* (London, 1980), a valuable and rounded study full of new approaches.

J. K. Hyde, *Padua in the Age of Dante* (Manchester, 1966), an informative all-round case-study.

J. Hook, *Siena. A City and its History* (London, 1979), a useful general introduction.

F. C. Lane, *Venice. A Maritime Republic* (Baltimore, 1973), a solid introduction to the history of Venice through the ages.

A. Sapori, *The Italian Merchant in the Middle Ages* (trans. New York, 1970), general introduction.

I. Origo, *The Merchant of Prato* (London, 1957), an outstandingly vivid portrait of the world of a fourteenth-century merchant.

ROME, BYZANTIUM, AND THE MUSLIM WORLD

J. Godfrey, *1204. The Unholy Crusade* (Oxford, 1980), a well-written account of the whole crusade.

D. M. Nichol, *The End of the Byzantine Empire* (London, 1979), a clear introduction.

D. M. Nichol, *The Last Centuries of Byzantium, 1261–1453* (London, 1972), a full narrative account.

N. Cheetham, *Medieval Greece* (New Haven and London, 1981), a detailed account, particularly of the 'Latin' colonization of Greece in the late Middle Ages.

K. M. Setton (gen. ed.), *A History of the Crusades*, esp. vol. ii, *The Later Crusades, 1189–1311* (Madison, 1969), vol. iii, *The Fourteenth and Fifteenth Centuries* (Madison, 1975), and vol. v, *The Impact of the Crusades on the Near East* (Madison, 1985), chapters by leading historians on a wide range of topics relating to the crusading movement and eastern Mediterranean history generally.

G. Jackson, *The Making of Medieval Spain* (London, 1972), a lively introduction with special emphasis on the multi-cultural history of Spain.

L. W. Lomax, *The Reconquista of Spain* (London, 1978).

R. I. Burns, *Medieval Colonialism* (Princeton, 1975), on the administration of Valencia after the reconquest.

J. F. O'Callaghan, *A History of Medieval Spain* (Ithaca, 1975), a basic history of the Iberian peninsula.

A. MacKay, *Spain in the Middle Ages. From Frontier to Empire, 1000–1500* (London, 1977), a powerful synthesis.

CRISES AND TRANSITIONS

P. Ziegler, *The Black Death* (London, 1969), a thorough introduction.

M. Meiss, *Painting in Florence and Siena after the Black Death* (New York, 1964), an important study of the change in sentiment as expressed in painting after the plague.

H. Inalcik, *The Ottoman Empire: the Classical Age, 1300–1600* (London, 1973), a thorough introduction.

J. N. Hillgarth, *The Spanish Kingdom 1250–1516* (2 vols., Oxford, 1976–8), particularly useful summary of recent research in the field.

J. E. Law, *The Lords of Renaissance Italy* (London, 1981: Historical Association pamphlet), a valuable introduction.

D. G. Bueno de Mesquita, *Giangaleazzo Visconti, Duke of Milan* (Cambridge, 1944), both an account of his career and a valuable case-study of despotic rule.

M. Mallett, *Mercenaries and their Masters* (London, 1974).

CONSOLIDATION AND EXPANSION

J. R. Hale, *Florence and the Medici: the Pattern of Control* (London, 1977), a useful synthesis of this active area of research.

A. J. Ryder, *The Kingdom of Naples under Alfonso the Magnanimous. The Making of a Modern State* (Oxford, 1976).

M. Mallett, *The Borgias* (London, 1969), with opening chapters useful also for general background on the fifteenth-century papacy.

J. A. F. Thomson, *Popes and Princes, 1417–1517* (London, 1980), an overview of papal history of the fifteenth century from several angles.

W. L. Gundersheimer, *Ferrara. The Style of a Renaissance Despotism* (Princeton, 1973), a good 'case-study'.

D. Herlihy and C. Klapisch, *The Tuscans and their Families* (New Haven and London, 1985), an important social study of Florence and its territory based mainly on the tax assessment made in 1427, one of the great social documents of the late Middle Ages.

F. Fernandez-Armesto, *Ferdinand and Isabella* (London, 1975), a good and readable biography.

H. V. Livermore, *A New History of Portugal* (Cambridge, 1976), a basic introduction.

P. Chaunu, *European Expansion from the Thirteenth to the Fifteenth Centuries* (trans. Amsterdam, 1978), fundamental for orientation among the sources and historiography of the explorations.

J. H. Parry, *The Age of Reconnaissance* (London, 1963).

G. V. Scammell, *The World Encompassed. The First European Maritime Empires c.800–1650* (London, 1981), a useful comparative study over a long period; includes discussions of Genoa, Venice, Spain, and Portugal.

NEW IDEAS AND NEW DIRECTIONS

D. Hay, *The Italian Renaissance in its Historical Background* (Cambridge, 1960), a good introduction to the context of the Renaissance.

P. O. Kristeller, *Renaissance Thought* (2 vols, New York, 1955, 1965), now classic essays, full of insights and valuable as an introduction.

P. Burke, *Tradition and Innovation in Renaissance Italy* (London, 1972), a bold and provocative inquiry into the Renaissance and its origins.

E. Garin, *Italian Humanism* (trans. Oxford, 1965), an introduction to some of the themes that occupied the humanists.

G. A. Holmes, *The Florentine Enlightenment, 1400–50* (London, 1969), a full portrait of the Renaissance in its first main home.

P. Burke, *The Renaissance Sense of the Past* (London, 1969), texts and commentary introducing ways in which humanism influenced the writing and perception of history.

M. Baxandall, *Giotto and the Orators* (Oxford, 1971), a clear illustration of ways in which rhetorical concepts and aesthetic principles interacted in humanist writings on art.

D. Chambers (ed.), *Patrons and Artists in the Italian Renaissance* (London, 1970), documents, with commentary; a useful 'reader' in the relationship of artists and their patrons.

R. Weiss, *The Spread of Italian Humanism* (London, 1964).

6. The Civilization of Courts and Cities in the North

GENERAL

D. Waley, *Later Medieval Europe* (London, 1964).

D. Hay, *Europe in the Fourteenth and Fifteenth Centuries* (London, 1966).

G. A. Holmes, *Europe: Hierarchy and Revolt, 1320–1450* (London, 1975).

B. Guenée, *States and Rulers in Later Medieval Europe*, trans. J. Vale (Oxford, 1985), political ideas, government, and the emergence of the state excellently treated, with an up-to-date bibliography of 1,400 titles.

J. R. Hale, J. R. L. Highfield, and B. Smalley (eds.), *Europe in the Late Middle Ages* (London, 1965), a valuable collection of essays on various subjects.

FRANCE

P. S. Lewis, *Later Medieval France. The Polity* (London, 1968), provides a stimulating and analytical account.

K. Fowler, *The Age of Plantagenet and Valois* (London, 1967), a more narrative treatment.

E. Perroy, *The Hundred Years War*, trans. W. B. Wells (2nd edn. London, 1965), older but still readable.

P. S. Lewis (ed.), *The Recovery of France in the Fifteenth Century* (London, 1971), essays offering useful material.

M. W. Labarge, *St Louis: the Life of Louis IX of France* (London, 1968).

J. R. Strayer, *The Reign of Philip the Fair* (Princeton, 1980).

R. Cazelles, *La Société politique et la crise de la royauté sous Philippe de Valois* (Paris, 1958) and his *Société politique, noblesse et couronne sous Jean le Bon et Charles V* (Geneva and Paris, 1982).

F. Autrand, *Charles VI* (Paris, 1986).

M. G. A. Vale, *Charles VII* (London, 1974).

For Burgundy, the four volumes by Richard Vaughan: *Philip the Bold* (London, 1962), *John the Fearless* (1966), *Philip the Good* (1970), and *Charles the Bold* (1973) are good political narratives, and his *Valois Burgundy* (1975) gives a concise summary of the Valois dukes and their reigns.

C. A. J. Armstrong, *England, France and Burgundy in the Fifteenth Century* (London, 1983), a valuable series of essays.

GERMANY

F. R. H. Du Boulay, *Germany in the Later Middle Ages* (London, 1983), the most recent study of later medieval Germany in English.

Bohemia has received more attention from English-speaking scholars than other parts of the German Empire, especially from R. R. Betts, *Studies in Czech History* (London, 1969).

H. Kaminsky, *A History of the Hussite Revolution* (Berkeley, 1967), an excellent survey.

F. Heymann, *George of Bohemia, King of Heretics* (Princeton, 1965).

H. J. Cohn, *The Government of the Rhine Palatinate in the Fifteenth Century* (Oxford, 1965).

M. Burleigh, *Prussian Society and the German Order* (Cambridge, 1984); two more specialized studies of important aspects of German history.

THE CHURCH

R. W. Southern, *Western Society and the Church in the Middle Ages* (Harmondsworth, 1970), particularly valuable.

Y. Renouard, *The Avignon Papacy 1305–1403*, trans. D. Bethell (London, 1970).

C. M. D. Crowder, *Unity, Heresy and Reform, 1378–1460* (London, 1977); both books cover the Avignonese and Conciliar periods.

E. F. Jacob, *Essays in the Conciliar Epoch* (Oxford, 1953).

G. Leff, *Heresy in the Later Middle Ages* (2 vols., Manchester, 1967), for religious movements and ideas.

E. Le Roy Ladurie, *Montaillou*, trans. B. Bray (London, 1978).

B. Hamilton, *The Medieval Inquisition* (London, 1981).

L. K. Little, *Religious Poverty and the Profit Economy in Medieval Europe* (London, 1978).

M. Aston, *The Fifteenth Century: The Prospect of Europe* (London, 1968).

A. Hyma, *The Christian Renaissance: A History of the Devotio Moderna* (2nd edn. Hamden, Conn., 1965).

ECONOMY AND SOCIETY

The Fontana Economic History of Europe, ed. C. M. Cipolla, vol. i: *The Middle Ages* (London, 1972); *The Cambridge Economic History of Europe*: vol. i, *The Agrarian Life of the Middle Ages* (Cambridge, 1966), vol. ii, *Trade and Industry in the Middle Ages* (1952), vol. iii, *Economic Organization and Policies in the Middle Ages* (1963); general works through which economic and social questions can be approached.

R. de Roover, *Money, Banking and Credit in Medieval Bruges* (Cambridge, Mass., 1948), an excellent study of the economic and commercial organization of one northern city.

VISUAL ARTS

E. Panofsky, *Early Netherlandish Painting* (2 vols., Cambridge, Mass., 1964).

G. Henderson, *Gothic* (Harmondsworth, 1967).

A. Martindale, *Gothic Art* (London, 1967).

G. Ring, *A Century of French Painting, 1400–1500* (London, 1949).

V. Dvoráková *et al.*, *Gothic Rural Painting in Bohemia and Moravia, 1300–78* (Oxford, 1964).

A. Châvelet, *Early Dutch Painting*, trans. C. Brown and A. Turner (New York, 1981).

E. Dhanens, *Hubert and Jan Van Eyck* (New York, n.d.).

K. B. McFarlane, *Hans Memling* (Oxford, 1971).

L. Campbell, *Van der Weyden* (New York, 1980); contain excellent studies of individual artists.

CHIVALRY AND LITERACY

J. Huizinga, F. Hopman, *The Waning of the Middle Ages*, trans. (London, 1924, many subsequent edns.), a classic study of northern culture.

M. Vale, *War and Chivalry: Aristocratic Culture in England, France and Burgundy at the End of the Middle Ages* (London, 1981).

M. Keen, *Chivalry* (New Haven and London, 1984); two recent studies of aristocratic values and behaviour.

F. Simone, *The French Renaissance*, trans. H. G. Hall (London, 1969).

J. Fox, *A Literary History of France*, vol. i: *The Middle Ages* (London, 1974); discuss northern literature.

C. Bühler, *The Fifteenth-century Book* (Philadelphia, 1960).

L. M. J. Delaissé, *A Century of Dutch Manuscript Illumination* (Berkeley and Los Angeles, 1968).

N. F. Blake, *Caxton and his World* (London, 1969); describe book production and printing.

CHRONOLOGY

511	Frankish kingdom divided into four on death of King Clovis
524	Composition of *Consolation of Philosophy* by Boethius while awaiting execution
c.525	Foundation of Monte Cassino monastery by St Benedict and composition of his rule
c.527–65	Gradual penetration of Balkans by Slav tribes
529	Promulgation by Justinian of first edition of new Roman law code (*Codex Iustinianus*); closing of the Academy of Athens
532	Serious uprising against Justinian in Constantinople (Nika riot)
533	Byzantine reconquest of Vandal Africa by general Belisarius
534	Frankish conquest of Burgundian kingdom; Byzantine occupation of Sicily
535	Byzantine invasion of Italian mainland
540	Byzantine occupation of Ravenna; Persian invasion of Syria and sacking of Antioch
542	Serious outbreak of bubonic plague throughout Europe
c.551	Occupation of Cartagena and south-eastern Spain by Byzantines
554	End of major Ostrogothic resistance in Italy
568	Lombard invasion of Italy
572–91	Renewed war between Byzantium and Persia
582	Fall of Sirmium, leading to invasion of Balkans by Avars and their Slav allies
585	Sueve kingdom in north-west Spain taken over by Visigothic King Leovigild
587	Conversion of Visigothic King Reccared to Catholicism
590	Arrival of Columbanus and companions in Gaul
597	Augustine of Canterbury begins conversion of Kent
603	Beginning of series of devastating Persian raids into Anatolia
	Truce between Byzantines and Lombards in Italy
613	Foundation of monastery of Bobbio by Irish missionary St Columbanus
622	Migration (*hijra*) of Muhammad from Mecca to Medina: start of Muslim era
626	Repulse of Avaro-Slav siege of Constantinople
627	Defeat of Persians by Byzantine Emperor Heraclius

	near Nineveh; Edwin of Northumbria baptized by St Paulinus
627?	Death of Rædwald of the East Angles and burial at Sutton Hoo
c.633	Completion of *Etymologies* of Isidore of Seville
635	Arrival of St Aidan at Lindisfarne
637	Defeat of Persian Empire by Arabs
638	Fall of Jerusalem to Arabs; death of Dagobert of the Franks
642	Fall of Alexandria to Arabs
643	Issue of Lombard law code by King Rothari
c.649	Creation of effective Arab fleet by Mu'awiya
654	Issue of extensive law code by Visigothic King Recceswinth
661	Establishment of Ummayad caliphate based on Damascus
663	Invasion of southern Italy by Byzantine Emperor Constans II
664	Synod of Whitby settled dispute within the Northumbrian Church between Irish and 'Romanists'
c.670	Establishment of first Bulgar Khanate in Balkans
672	Acceptance of Catholicism by Lombards under King Perctarit
674–8	Arab naval blockade of Constantinople
c.680	Treaty made by Byzantine Empire recognizing Lombard kingdom
685	Northumbrian army led by Ecgfrith defeated by Picts at Nechtansmere
687	Battle of Tertry marks beginning of Carolingian supremacy in northern Gaul
698	Final Arab capture of Carthage
711	Beginning of Islamic conquest of Spain
713–35	Legislative programme of Lombard King Liutprand
717–18	Repulse of Arab land and sea siege of Constantinople by Emperor Leo III
c.718	Establishment of Christian kingdom in the Asturias
726	Issue of *Ecloga* code by Leo III; probable issue of first iconoclast decrees
727	Revolts in Byzantine Italy; election of first independent doge of Venice

727–43	Attacks by Lombard King Liutprand on Byzantine territories in Italy
732	Defeat of Arab expeditionary force by Frankish leader Charles Martel near Poitiers
735	Death of the Venerable Bede
740	Major victory of Byzantines over Arabs at Akroinon
750	Overthrow of Ummayad caliphate by Abbasid dynasty
751	Pippin III deposes last Merovingian king and becomes first Carolingian king of the Franks; fall of Ravenna to Lombard King Aistulf
754	Martyrdom of St Boniface in Frisia; meeting of Pope Stephen II and Frankish King Pippin III resulting in alliance
754–75	Period of hard-line iconoclasm under Emperor Constantine V
756	Establishment of independent emirate in Spain by Ummayad prince ʿAbd al-Rahmān
c.760	Composition of forged 'Donation of Constantine' purporting to record massive grant of lands and rights to the papacy
762	Foundation of Baghdad as capital of Abbasid caliphate
c.768	Final Frankish conquest of Aquitaine
772	First of Charlemagne's campaigns against the Saxons
774	Take-over of Lombard kingdom by Frankish King Charlemagne
778	Defeat of Charlemagne's army by the Basques at Roncevaux
783	Beginning of Byzantine reconquest of the Peloponnese
787	Seventh Ecumenical Council at Nicaea; temporary end of iconoclasm
793	Lindisfarne sacked by Vikings
799	Establishment of scholarly centre at monastery of Studion in Constantinople by Abbot Theodore
800	Coronation of Charlemagne as emperor in Rome
800–909	Rule of Aghlabids as independent dynasty in North Africa
801	Beginning of Frankish 'Spanish March' in north-east Spain
811	Defeat of Byzantine Emperor Nicephorus I by Bulgars
812	Byzantine recognition of imperial title of Charlemagne
c.813–c.915	Period of serious Arab naval raids on shores of

Tyrrhenian and Adriatic seas

814	Louis the Pious succeeds Charlemagne as emperor
814–21	Monastic reform movement of St Benedict of Aniane
815–43	Second wave of iconoclasm in Byzantium
c.823	Capture of Crete by Muslim pirates from Spain
824	Establishment of independent kingdom of Pamplona
827	Arab invasion of Sicily
838	Major Arab invasion of Anatolia leading to sack of city of Amorium
840	Vikings found settlement at Dublin
843	Carolingian Empire split up by treaty of Verdun; end of iconoclasm in Byzantine Empire
846	Sack of the Vatican by Arab pirates
849	Splitting up of Lombard principality of Benevento
c.850	Dissemination of forged 'Isidorian Decretals' (canon law decrees), greatly increasing authority of the papacy
860	First attack on Constantinople by Kiev Vikings (Rus)
863	Mission of Cyril and Methodius to the Slavs
863–79	Period of schism between eastern and western Churches
864	Conversion to orthodoxy of Bulgar Khan Boris
865	The Viking 'Great Army' moves from France to England
867	Beginning of Macedonian dynasty in Byzantium
c.870	Viking discovery of Iceland
875	Political fragmentation of kingdom of Italy following death of Louis II
876	Beginning of Byzantine reconquest of southern Italy
878	Failure of Viking assault on Wessex; Arab capture of Syracuse, Byzantine capital of Sicily
c.886–c.1025	Macedonian Renaissance in Byzantium
888	Odo, count of Paris becomes king of West Francia
888–90	Emergence of independent kings in Burgundy and Provence
894	Invasion of Byzantine territory by Tsar Symeon of Bulgaria
899	Hungarian raids in Italy
c.900	Resurgence of Byzantine power in Balkans and Anatolia
906	Magyars destroy the kingdom of Moravia and begin almost annual raids into western Europe

909	Cluny founded by Duke William the Pious of Aquitaine Charles the Simple grants the area surrounding Rouen to the Viking leader Rollo: beginnings of the duchy of Normandy
915	Arab raiders ousted from mouth of River Garigliano in Italy
922	Robert of Neustria rebels against Charles the Simple and wins the French crown
923	On Robert's death Duke Raoul of Burgundy becomes king; Charles the Simple is imprisoned by Herbert II of Vermandois and dies in captivity in 929
933	Henry I of Germany defeats the Magyars at Riade
939–42	Robert of Neustria's son, Hugh the Great, and son-in-law, Herbert II of Vermandois, rebel against Louis IV of France
948	Otto I of Germany founds missionary bishoprics at Brandenburg, Havelburg, Ribe, Aarhus, and Schleswig
953–4	Revolt of Liudolf and other dukes against Otto I
955	Otto I defeats the Magyars at the battle of the Lechfeld and ends their raids
961	Byzantines recapture Crete
962	Otto I crowned emperor by Pope John XII
963	Foundation of the Great Lavra monastery on Mount Athos by St Athanasius; Otto I defeats Mieszko I of Poland and obliges him to pay tribute
965	Byzantines recapture Cyprus; King Harold Bluetooth of Denmark is baptized
966	Mieszko adopts Christianity
968	Otto I founds the archbishopric of Magdeburg; the first Polish bishopric is established at Poznan
978	Lothar V of France and Otto II of Germany lead campaigns against each other
982	Otto II defeated in southern Italy by Muslims
982–3	The Slavs revolt against German rule and recover most of their territories to the east of the Elbe
987	Death of Louis V, last Carolingian king of France, and accession of King Robert's grandson, Hugh Capet
988	Charles of Lorraine contests Hugh's succession and seizes Laon, then Rheims; in 991 he is betrayed and dies in captivity the next year
989	Truce of God first proclaimed, at Charroux

997	Martyrdom of St Adalbert in Pomerania
999–1003	Pope Sylvester II (Gerbert of Aurillac)
1000	King Olaf introduces Christianity to Sweden
1002–18	War between Henry II of Germany and Boleslav Chobry of Poland
1007	Henry founds the see of Bamberg
1009	Martyrdom of St Bruno of Querfurt
1016	Cnut of Denmark becomes king of England, in 1019 of Denmark too, and from 1029 to his death in 1035 also of Norway; first Normans in southern Italy
1016–17	Turkish raiders first reported in Armenia
1024	Boleslav Chobry becomes king of Poland
1032–3	Conrad II of Germany secures the kingdom of Burgundy after the death without heir of King Rudolf III
c.1036	Foundation of monastery at Vallombrosa
1037	*Constitutio de feudis*
1049	Pope Leo IX condemns simony at the Councils of Rheims and Mainz
1046–56	Minority of Henry IV of Germany; considerable loss of crown lands
1054	Patriarch of Constantinople anathematizes Roman Church: the key date in the Schism between Orthodox and Catholic Churches
1055	Seljuks capture Baghdad
c.1056–75	Patarene heretics in Milan
1059–61	Pope Nicholas II
1059	Election Decree on appointment of pope; Robert Guiscard becomes duke of Apulia and Calabria
1061	Roger I the 'Great Count' invades Sicily
1066	Harald Hardrada of Norway invades England and is defeated and killed at Stamford Bridge; Duke William of Normandy defeats King Harold of England at Hastings and gains the English crown
1071	First Saxon revolt against Henry IV; battle of Mantzikert: Byzantines defeated by Turks; Bari falls to Normans
1073–85	Pope Gregory VII
1075	Henry defeats the rebels at the battle of the Unstrut
1076	Henry and the German bishops withdraw their recognition from Pope Gregory VII at the Diet of

	Worms; Gregory excommunicates Henry and urges his subjects to rebel
1077	Under threat of deposition Henry makes peace with Gregory but the rebels elect Rudolf of Rheinfelden as king in his place; civil war ensues
1080	Henry again withdraws his obedience from Gregory; he is again excommunicated
1081	Imperial confirmation of the customs of Pisa
1082	Alexius I Comnenus grants trading concessions to Venice
1085	Christians capture Toledo and reach River Tagus; Gregory VII dies at Salerno, having been driven from Rome by Henry IV
1088	Work starts on the third and largest church at Cluny
1088–99	Pope Urban II
1092	Alexius I Comnenus reforms Byzantine coinage
1093	Revolt of Henry VI's son Conrad
1095	Pope Urban II proclaims the First Crusade at Clermont
1097	First Crusade reaches Constantinople
1098	Siege of Antioch; Magnus of Norway seizes the Orkneys, Shetlands, and Isle of Man; Robert of Molesme founds Cîteaux
1099	Fall of Jerusalem to crusaders; Baldwin of Lorraine elected ruler
1106	Succession to Germany of Henry V after the forced abdication and death of his father; Henry I of England defeats his brother Robert at Tinchebrai and so gains the duchy of Normandy
1107	Henry I agrees not to invest bishops, save with the lands of their sees, but insists upon their homage and his continuing influence in elections
1111	Henry V is crowned emperor and forcibly extracts a concession of his right to invest bishops from Pope Paschal II; trading rights in Constantinople given to Pisans
1112	The inhabitants of Laon proclaim a commune and murder their bishop
1113	Peter Abelard opens his school in Paris
1118	Council of Toulouse plans Christian attack on Saragossa
1121	Abelard condemned at the council of Soissons

1122	Henry V and Pope Calixtus II agree in the Concordat of Worms that Henry may invest German bishops with the lands of their sees, receive their homage, and be present at their elections; in return he renounces his right to invest
1124	Henry V invades France in support of his father-in-law, Henry I of England, but retires when a majority of French magnates rally to Louis VI
1125–30	Flying buttresses used to reinforce nave at Cluny
1127–8	Succession dispute in Flanders following the murder of Count Charles; Henry I and Louis VI both intervene but neither prevails, the Flemings eventually accepting Thierry of Alsace
1127	Conrad of Staufen is elected anti-king against Lothar III of Germany. In revolt until 1135
1128	Henry I's daughter Matilda marries Geoffrey of Anjou
1130	Roger II crowned king of Sicily
1137	Louis VII of France marries Eleanor, heiress of Aquitaine; Abbot Suger begins to build Saint-Denis in the Gothic style
1140	Abelard again condemned at the council of Sens; about this time Gratian compiles his collection of canon law
1144	Geoffrey of Anjou secures Normandy in the civil war which follows Henry I's death in 1135; fall of city of Edessa to Muslims
1145	Preaching of heretic Henry the Monk in southern France
1146	St Bernard preaches the Second Crusade; Louis VII and Conrad III of Germany are among the participants
1147–8	Second Crusade
1148	Bull *Divina dispositione* encourages crusades to Spain
*c.*1150	Promulgation of *Usatches* (Customs) of Catalonia
1150	Byzantine forces attempt to recapture Italy
1152	Louis VII is divorced from Eleanor of Aquitaine who almost immediately marries Geoffrey of Anjou's heir Henry
1154	Henry becomes king of England as well
1155	Frederick Barbarossa crowned emperor; period of almost incessant civil war begins in Norway and Sweden, lasting to about 1230

1156	Frederick Barbarossa restores Bavaria to Henry the Lion, who is already duke of Saxony; the former duke of Bavaria, Henry Jasomirgott, is compensated with Austria
1158	Roncaglia Decrees
1159	John of Salisbury produces his *Policraticus*, a work of political observation drawing heavily upon classical authors
1160	Work begins on the construction of the first Gothic cathedral, Laon; Notre Dame is begun in 1163
1166	Revolt of Serbians under Stephan Nemanja
1167	Formation of the Lombard League
1168	Henry the Lion marries Matilda, daughter of Henry II of England
1169	In the peace of Montmirail Louis VII insists that Henry II must divide his lands between his sons
1171	Downfall of Fatimid caliphate in Cairo
1173	Revolt of Henry, son of Henry II, supported by Louis VII
1176	Byzantine defeat at Myriocephalon
1180	Henry the Lion deprived of his duchies; he is forced into exile the following year
1181	Henry II's sons again rebel
1182	Massacre of Latins in Constantinople
1185	By the treaty of Boves Philip Augustus substantially increases the French crown lands at the expense of Count Philip of Flanders; Revolt of Bulgarians under Peter and Asen; Thessalonica sacked by Normans
1187	Battle of Hattin; Saladin captures Jerusalem
1188	Another rebellion by Henry II's sons, aided by Philip Augustus
1189–91	During the absence of Frederick Barbarossa on crusade Henry the Lion attempts to recover Saxony but is defeated
1192–4	Philip Augustus returns early from crusade and takes advantage of Richard I of England's absence and captivity to secure border fortresses in Normandy; Edicts against Cathars by rulers of Montpellier and Aragon
1194	Chartres cathedral largely destroyed by fire; work begins on its Gothic rebuilding; Henry VI of

Germany conquers Sicily

1196	At the Diet of Würzburg the German princes refuse to make the monarchy hereditary
1197	Richard I completes the construction of a major new fortress, Chateau Gaillard, to defend Rouen against Philip Augustus' attacks
1198	Following Henry VI's death groups of German princes elect his brother, Philip of Swabia, and Otto of Brunswick, son of Henry the Lion, as king; civil war ensues
1204	Crusaders capture Constantinople and establish Latin Empire; Philip Augustus conquers Normandy and other Plantagenet lands in France
1210	St Francis meets Pope Innocent III and is given verbal approval for his movement
1210–29	Albigensian Crusades in southern France against Cather heretics
1212	Christian victory over Moors at Las Navas de Tolosa in Spain
1212–50	Frederick II rules the German Empire and the kingdom of Sicily
1214	Philip Augustus defeats the allied forces of the Plantagenets and the German Empire at Bouvines
1215	Fourth Lateran Council held at Rome by Innocent III; Paris University receives its first statutes
1216	Papal approval of Order of Preachers (Dominicans)
1217–21	Fifth Crusade captures and then loses Damietta in Egypt
1220–2	First Mongol incursions. Bukhara and Samarkand taken, 1220
1222	Foundation of the University of Padua
1226	Emperor Frederick II summons Diet of Cremona; Lombard League of towns revives; 1226–83 Teutonic Knights conquer Prussia
1228–9	Crusade of Frederick II; truce with Sultan, Frederick gains crown of Jerusalem
1230	Final unification of kingdoms of León and Castile
1231	*Liber Augustalis*, law code for Sicily, promulgated by Frederick II
1236	Castilians capture Cordoba, former capital of Muslim caliphate

1239–41	Crusade of Theobald of Champagne and Richard of Cornwall
1241	Mongol invasion reaches Hungary and the Adriatic Sea
1244	Jerusalem falls to Muslims
1245	Frederick II deposed by Council of Lyons
1248	Seville yields to Ferdinand III of Gastile
1248–50	Louis IX of France leads crusade and is captured in Egypt
1250	Abbasid dynasty in Egypt overthrown and replaced by Mamluk
1252	First coining of the Florentine florin reintroduces gold coinage to Europe
1254	Death of Conrad IV, last Hohenstaufen king of Germany
1258	Mongols take Baghdad, the spiritual centre of the Muslim world
1259	Treaty of Paris between Louis IX of France and Henry III of England establishes a feudal relationship in which Henry becomes Louis's vassal; western Christian forces defeated by Byzantines of Nicaea at Pelagonia
1260	Mongols take Damascus but are decisively defeated by the Mamluks at Ain Jalut
1260	Guelphs in Tuscany defeated by Ghibellines at battle of Montaperti
1261	Byzantines regain Constantinople from Latins
1266	Charles of Anjou crowned king of Sicily by Pope Clement IV; defeats Manfred at Benevento
1268	Conradin, last surviving son of Frederick II, defeated at Tagliacozzo
1268	Christian-held Jaffa, Beirut, and Antioch fall to Mamluks
1270	Louis IX of France dies on crusade against Tunis
1273	Election of Rudolf of Habsburg as king of the Romans: end of the interregnum in the empire
1277	Genoese begin annual convoys to Bruges and other Channel ports
1282	'Sicilian Vespers': Charles of Anjou expelled from Sicily, Peter III of Aragon becomes king of the island
1284	Defeat of Pisans by Genoese in naval battle of Meloria
1285–1314	Philip IV (the Fair) king of France

1291	Fall of Acre to Muslims: end of western Christian rule of Outremer
1293	'Ordinances of Justice' passed in Florence, excluding magnate families from participation in government
1294	Outbreak of war between England and France over Gascony; beginnings of Philip the Fair's conflict with Pope Boniface VIII
1297	'Serrata' of Venice's Great Council, limiting membership to established families with hereditary rights
1302	Boniface VIII defines papal power at its most extreme in the bull *Unam Sanctam*; French defeat at the hands of the Flemings at Courtrai; treaty of Caltabellotta brings truce between Sicily and Naples
1306	Death of Wenceslas III, last Přemysl king of Bohemia
1307–12	Philip the Fair's attack on the Templars leads to their destruction by Clement V
1309–77	Papacy at Avignon
1310–13	Expedition of Emperor Henry VII of Italy, last major military intervention of emperors in the peninsula
1311	Catalan Company establishes control over Athens
1312	Council of Vienne
1315–17	European harvest failures and famine
1321	Death in Ravenna of the Florentine poet Dante Alighieri
1321–8	Civil war in Byzantium
1323–8	Risings against the king of France and count of Flanders by the Flemings, ending with their defeat at Cassel (1328)
1324	Marsilius of Padua completes *Defensor pacis*, radical treatise on government fiercely critical of the papacy
1324–6	Anglo-French war of St Sardos breaks out over a boundary dispute in Gascony
1326	Ottomans capture Byzantine town of Bursa
1327–9	Emperor Louis on campaign in Italy
1328	Death of Charles IV, last Capetian king of France; accession of Philip VI, first Valois king
1331	Nicaea falls to Ottomans
1333	Byzantines pay tribute to Ottomans
1337	Outbreak of the Hundred Years War between England and France

1338	Declaration of Rhense abolishes papal approval of the seven Electors' choice of emperor
1340	Edward III of England formally assumes the title of king of France
1341–7	Second civil war in Byzantium
1342	Walter of Brienne, duke of Athens, lord of Florence
1342–6	Peruzzi, Bardi, and other smaller Tuscan banks crash
1343	Kingdom of Majorca definitively united with Aragon
1346	English defeat the French at Crécy
1347	Siege and capture of Calais by Edward III of England
1347–50	First wave of the Black Death sweeps Europe killing over a third of the population
1348	Foundation of Prague University by the Emperor Charles IV, king of Bohemia
1354	Turks take Gallipoli, their first European conquest
1355	Death of Stefan Dušan, ruler of Serbia, a defender of Europe against the Turks
1356	French defeated by Anglo-Gascon force at Maupertuis, near Poitiers; Golden Bull defines powers of the imperial princes
1358	Peasant rising (Jacquerie) in France
1360	Treaty of Brétigny-Calais: Edward III renounces his claim to the crown of France in return for a greatly expanded duchy of Aquitaine; terms never fulfilled
1361	Second wave of plague begins
1365	Vienna University founded by Rudolf, duke of Austria
1369	Hundred Years War reopens after appeal against the Black Prince, governor of Aquitaine, by Gascon lords; Henry of Trastamara gains the Castilian throne
1370	Death of Casimir the Great, last Piast king of Poland; accession of Louis I of Anjou, king of Hungary to the kingdom of Poland
1371	Serbs defeated by Ottomans at the River Marica
1372	English defeat at sea off La Rochelle by a Franco-Castilian fleet
1374	Death of Francesco Petrarca, forerunner of the humanist movement
1376–8	War of the Eight Saints between the papacy and Florence
1377	Pope Gregory XI returns to Rome from Avignon

1378	Great Schism of the western church begins; revolt of the Ciompi in Florence: workers in the wool industry seize power for six weeks
1379–83	Revolts in Flanders against Count Louis de Male and the crown of France led by Philip van Artevelde
1382	John Wycliffe's writings condemned and he is expelled from Oxford
1384	Philip the Bold, duke of Burgundy, succeeds to the counties of Flanders and Artois
1386	Union of the kingdom of Poland and the duchy of Lithuania under Ladislas II Jagellon
1387	Thessalonica, second largest city of the Byzantine empire, falls to Ottomans
1389	Serbs defeated by Turks at Kossovo, though the sultan, Murad I, also killed there
1392–4	First onset of Charles VI of France's bouts of madness: rivalry for power within France between the houses of Orléans and Burgundy
1396	Truce made at Leulinghen between England and France suspends hostilities until 1403; massive western crusade ends in fiasco at Nicopolis; Manuel Chrysoloras hired to teach Greek at the University of Florence
1397	Norway, Sweden, and Denmark united by the Union of Kalmar
1398	Withdrawal of obedience by the French Church from the schismatic papacy
1401	Ghiberti wins competition for the second bronze Baptistery doors in Florence, the beginning of Renaissance sculpture
1402	Death of Giangaleazzo Visconti, duke of Milan, who had briefly united most of northern and much of central Italy under his personal rule
1403	German masters of Prague University condemn Wycliffe's writings, Czech masters oppose this decision
1404	Death of Philip the Bold of Burgundy; Burgundian influence at Paris increases under his son John the Fearless
1407	Assassination of Louis, duke of Orléans at Paris by the Burgundian faction

1409	Council of Pisa deposes both rival popes and elects a third (Alexander V)
1410	Death of Alexander V and election by the council of John XXIII
1412	Compromise of Ceuta: the Trastamarans succeed to Aragon
1414–17	Council of Constance
1415	English defeat the French at Agincourt; Jan Hus is burnt as a heretic by the Council of Constance after further condemnation of Wycliffe's doctrines; deposition of John XXIII by the council and abdication of Gregory XII; Portuguese capture Ceuta on North African coast: the beginning of Portuguese expansion
1416	Jerome of Prague burnt as a heretic at Constance; Emperor Sigismund visits France and England in an attempt to make peace between them
1417	Second invasion of Normandy by Henry V; Council of Constance deposes Benedict XIII and elects Martin V: end of the Great Schism
1418	Dissolution of Council of Constance
1419	Assassination of John the Fearless, duke of Burgundy, by partisans of Charles, dauphin of France, later Charles VII
1419–36	Hussite wars in Bohemia
1420	Treaty of Troyes formalizes Anglo-Burgundian alliance against the dauphinists; crusade preached against the Hussites by Martin V
1422	Deaths of Henry V and Charles VI; Henry VI of England recognized as king of France by the Anglo-Burgundian party, Charles VII proclaimed by the dauphinists
1423	Outbreak of war between Milan and Florence, to last for over thirty years
1424	Madeira colonized by Portuguese; battle of Verneuil completes English conquest of Normandy
1427	Hussite armies threaten Germany
1428–9	Joan of Arc appears; siege of Orléans raised by dauphinist forces; Charles VII crowned at Rheims
1431–49	Council of Basle
1431	Joan of Arc burnt at Rouen after trial by members of

	the French clergy supporting the Anglo-Burgundian regime; Henry VI crowned king of France at Paris
1433	Reconciliation between moderate Hussites and the Council of Basle
1434	Defeat of the Taborite extremists by Catholics and moderate Hussites at Lipany; Cape Bojador, on West African coast, rounded by Portuguese; Cosimo de' Medici comes to unofficial power in Florence
1435	Treaty of Arras: reconciliation of Charles VII and Philip the Good, duke of Burgundy; Anglo-Burgundian alliance collapses
1436	Charles VII's forces enter Paris
1437	Pope Eugenius IV dissolves Council of Basle but the fathers of the council suspend him (1438)
1438	Pragmatic Sanction of Bourges establishes French neutrality between pope and council and confers considerable powers over the French Church on the king
1439	Council of Basle deposes Eugenius IV and elects Amadeus VIII, duke of Savoy as Felix V: schism between pope and council renewed; Council of Florence ends schism between eastern and western Christendom
1440	Conspiracy against Charles VII by French nobility known as the *Praguerie* in which the duke of Burgundy is implicated
1442	French expedition to Gascony recovers some territory from the English
1442–3	Alfonso 'the Magnanimous' of Aragon gains control of kingdom of Naples and begins to rule combined territories from there
1444	Crusade ends in failure at Varna on the Black Sea; Truce of Tours between England and France
1447	Milan declares itself the Ambrosian Republic: three years later the experiment ends with the invitation to Francesco Sforza to rule the city; French recognize the newly elected Nicholas V as pope and work for abdication of Felix V
1448	Renewal of Anglo-French truce until April 1450; remnants of Council of Basle move to Lausanne
1449	Council at Lausanne dissolves itself and Felix V

abdicates, ending conciliar period; Anglo-French truce broken by English raid on border fortress of Fougères

1449–50   French recover Normandy from the English

1451   First French recovery of Gascony

1451–3   War between duke of Burgundy and the city of Ghent

1453   Constantinople falls to the Ottomans and becomes their capital; second (and final) French recovery of Gascony: only Calais remains in English hands

1454–5   Pacification of Italy with the Peace of Lodi and the Italic League

1458   George Podiebrady, a moderate Hussite noble, succeeds to the throne of Bohemia

1460   Turks complete their occupation of the Peloponnese

1461   Death of Charles VII of France; accession of Louis XI

1462   Cape Verde islands discovered and colonized by Portuguese

1465   War of the Public Weal in France in which many great nobles, including the future Charles the Bold, duke of Burgundy, rise against Louis XI

1467   Death of Philip the Good, duke of Burgundy and accession of Charles the Bold

1468   Destruction of the town of Liège by Charles the Bold after its rebellion; marriage between Charles and Edward IV of England's sister, Margaret of York; Anglo-Burgundian alliance against France formally renewed

1469   Marriage of Ferdinand of Aragon and Isabella of Castile paves the way for the union of their two crowns

1470   Turks capture Venetian garrison of Negropont in the Aegean Sea

1470–1   Edward IV of England, exiled to Burgundian dominions after temporary restoration of Henry VI, recovers the throne with Burgundian aid; unsuccessful Burgundian invasion of France

1475   English invasion of northern France in alliance with Burgundy bought off by Louis XI

1475–7   Campaigns of Charles the Bold of Burgundy in Alsace-Lorraine

1477   Defeat and death of Charles the Bold at Nancy ends

	Valois Burgundy; marriage of Charles's daughter Mary to Maximilian of Austria
1478	The Pazzi conspiracy: papal attack on the Medici in Florence
1479	Union of the crowns of Aragon and Castile
1480	Turks capture Otranto, on Italian mainland, and hold it for a year
1481	Beginning of Spanish war against Granada
1482	Death of Mary of Burgundy: treaty of Arras divides the Burgundian lands between France and the empire
1483	Death of Louis XI of France; Charles VIII succeeds him; the Spanish Inquisition formally established by a union of the Inquisitions of Aragon and Castile
1484	Peace of Bagnolo ends conflict in Italy
1487	Bartholomew Diaz rounds the Cape of Good Hope
1490	Death of Matthias Corvinus, king of Hungary; accession of Ladislas II, king of Bohemia, to the Hungarian throne
1492	Fall of Granada to Christians; expulsion of the Jews from Spanish kingdoms; voyage of Christopher Columbus results in discovery of the New World; death of Lorenzo de' Medici of Florence
1494	French invasion of Italy under Charles VIII: beginning of the Italian Wars
1495	Reichstag of Worms attempts imperial reforms at the instigation of Maximilian I
1497	Vasco da Gama reaches India having rounded Africa
1498	Burning of Girolamo Savonarola, a Dominican who had gained a powerful hold over Florence since the fall of the Medici in 1494
1499	Granadan Muslims given choice of conversion or expulsion

INDEX

Persons of the same name are arranged alphabetically, not hierarchically, ignoring descriptions in parentheses. Dates (normally of birth and death) are sometimes conjectural and are given for the purpose of identification only.

Expand your collection of
VERY SHORT INTRODUCTIONS

Available now

1. Classics
2. Music
3. Buddhism
4. Literary Theory
5. Hinduism
6. Psychology
7. Islam
8. Politics
9. Theology
10. Archaeology
11. Judaism
12. Sociology
13. The Koran
14. The Bible
15. Social and
    Cultural Anthropology
16. History
17. Roman Britain
18. The Anglo-Saxon Age
19. Medieval Britain
20. The Tudors
21. Stuart Britain
22. Eighteenth-Century Britain
23. Nineteenth-Century Britain
24. Twentieth-Century Britain
25. Heidegger
26. Ancient Philosophy
27. Socrates
28. Marx
29. Logic
30. Descartes
31. Machiavelli
32. Aristotle
33. Hume
34. Nietzsche
35. Darwin
36. The European Union
37. Gandhi
38. Augustine
39. Intelligence
40. Jung
41. Buddha
42. Paul
43. Continental Philosophy
44. Galileo
45. Freud
46. Wittgenstein
47. Indian Philosophy

Available soon

Ancient Egypt
Animal Rights
Art Theory
The Brain
Chaos
Cosmology
Design
Drugs
Economics
Emotion
Ethics
Evolution
Evolutionary Psychology
Fascism
The Fall of the Soviet Union
The First World War
Free Will
International Relations
Mathematics
Modern Ireland
Molecules
Northern Ireland
Opera
Philosophy
Philosophy of Religion
The Russian Revolution
Terrorism
World Music

Visit the
VERY SHORT
INTRODUCTIONS
Web site

www.oup.co.uk/vsi

➤ **Information** about all published titles

➤ News of **forthcoming books**

➤ **Extracts** from the books, including titles
not yet published

➤ **Reviews** and views

➤ **Links** to other **web sites** and main
OUP web page

➤ Information about **VSIs in translation**

➤ **Contact** the editors

➤ **Order** other **VSIs** on-line

HISTORY
A Very Short Introduction
John H. Arnold

History: A Very Short Introduction is a stimulating essay about how we understand the past. The book explores various questions provoked by our understanding of history, and examines how these questions have been answered in the past. Using examples of how historians work, the book shares the sense of excitement at discovering not only the past, but also ourselves.

> 'A stimulating and provocative introduction to one of collective humanity's most important quests – understanding the past and its relation to the present. A vivid mix of telling examples and clear cut analysis.'
>
> **David Lowenthal, University College London**

> 'This is an extremely engaging book, lively, enthusiastic and highly readable, which presents some of the fundamental problems of historical writing in a lucid and accessible manner. As an invitation to the study of history it should be difficult to resist.'
>
> **Peter Burke, Emmanuel College, Cambridge**

www.oup.co.uk/vsi/history

THE BIBLE

A Very Short Introduction

John Riches

It is sometimes said that the Bible is one of the most
unread books in the world, yet it has been a major force
in the development of Western culture and continues to
exert an enormous influence over many people's lives.
This Very Short Introduction looks at the importance
accorded to the Bible by different communities and
cultures and attempts to explain why it has generated
such a rich variety of uses and interpretations. It explores
how the Bible was written, the development of the
canon, the role of Biblical criticism, the appropriation
of the Bible in high and popular culture, and its use for
political ends.

'John Riches' clear and lively Very Short Introduction
offers a distinctive approach to the Bible … a distinguished addition to the series.'

Christopher Rowland, University of Oxford

'Short in length, but not in substance, nor in interest. A
fascinating introduction both to the way in which the
Bible came to be what it is, and to what it means and
has meant for believers.'

Joel Marcus, Boston University

www.oup.co.uk/vsi/bible